SOCIAL AND PSYCHOLOGICAL PROBLEMS OF WOMEN

THE SERIES IN CLINICAL AND COMMUNITY PSYCHOLOGY

CONSULTING EDITORS

Charles D. Spielberger and Irwin G. Sarason

SOCIAL AND PSYCHOLOGICAL PROBLEMS OF WOMEN
Prevention and Crisis Intervention

Edited by

Annette U. Rickel
Wayne State University

Meg Gerrard
University of Kansas

Ira Iscoe
The University of Texas at Austin

● HEMISPHERE PUBLISHING CORPORATION
Washington   New York   London

DISTRIBUTION OUTSIDE THE UNITED STATES
McGRAW-HILL INTERNATIONAL BOOK COMPANY
Auckland   Bogotá   Guatemala   Hamburg   Johannesburg
Lisbon   London   Madrid   Mexico   Montreal
New Delhi   Panama   Paris   San Juan   São Paulo
Singapore   Sydney   Tokyo   Toronto

To

John, my husband, my enduring support system

Rick, whose encouragement is deeply appreciated

Louise, my wife of 33 years, who knows about these matters

The quotations on page 284 are taken from *The Best of Dear Abby.* Copyright, 1981, The Universal Press Syndicate. Reprinted with permission. All Rights Reserved.

SOCIAL AND PSYCHOLOGICAL PROBLEMS OF WOMEN:
Prevention and Crisis Intervention

Copyright © 1984 by Hemisphere Publishing Corporation. All rights reserved. Printed in the United States of America. Except as permitted under the United States Copyright Act of 1976, no part of this publication may be reproduced or distributed in any form or by any means, or stored in a data base or retrieval system, without the prior written permission of the publisher.

2 3 4 5 6 7 8 9 0   E B E B   8 9 8 7 6 5 4

Library of Congress Cataloging in Publication Data

Main entry under title:

Social and psychological problems of women.

(The Series in clinical and community psychology)
Bibliography: p.
Includes index.
1. Women—Psychology—Addresses, essays, lectures.
2. Women—United States—Social conditions—Addresses, essays, lectures. 3. Social change—Addresses, essays, lectures. 4. Social problems—Addresses, essays, lectures. 5. Psychology, Applied—Addresses, essays, lectures. I. Rickel, Annette U., date. II. Gerrard, Meg. III. Iscoe, Ira. IV. Series. [DNLM: 1. Women—Psychology. 2. Social problems. 3. Mental disorders. HQ 1206 S678]
HQ1206.S664 1984   305.4'2'0973   83-18423
ISBN 0-89116-330-1
ISSN 0146-0846

Contents

II
SOCIAL PROBLEMS OF WOMEN

III

PSYCHOLOGICAL PROBLEMS AND WOMEN

Contributors

JUDITH E. ALBINO, State University of New York, Buffalo, New York

LaRUE ALLEN, University of Maryland, College Park, Maryland

A. KATHLEEN ATKINSON, Wayne State University, Detroit, Michigan

BERNARD L. BLOOM, University of Colorado, Boulder, Colorado

MEG A. BOND, Illinois Institute of Developmental Disabilities, Chicago, Illinois

DAVID W. BRITT, New York Institute of Technology, Old Westbury, New York

KATHLEEN G. BROUGHAN, Child and Adult Clinical Associates, Knoxville, Tennessee

BRENNA H. BRY, Rutgers University, Piscataway, New Jersey

ROBERT A. CALDWELL, Michigan State University, East Lansing, Michigan

BARBARA SNELL DOHRENWEND (deceased), formerly, Columbia University, School of Public Health, New York, New York

DARWIN DORR, Highland Hospital, Asheville, North Carolina

LINDA K. FORSBERG, Wayne State University, Detroit, Michigan

LISA FRIEDENBERG, University of North Carolina, Asheville, North Carolina

MAX FUENTES, University of Southern California, Los Angeles, California

MARGARET GATZ, University of Southern California, Los Angeles, California

MEG GERRARD, University of Kansas, Lawrence, Kansas

BILL D. GEIS, University of Kansas, Lawrence, Kansas

LUCIA A. GILBERT, University of Texas, Austin, Texas

MARGARET T. GORDON, Northwestern University, Evanston, Illinois

WILLIAM F. HODGES, University of Colorado, Boulder, Colorado

IRA ISCOE, University of Texas, Austin, Texas

JAMES G. KELLY, University of Illinois, Chicago, Illinois

ADELINE LEVINE, State University of New York, Buffalo, New York

MURRAY LEVINE, State University of New York, Buffalo, New York

RAYMOND P. LORION, University of Tennessee, Knoxville, Tennessee

LISA McCANN, Capital Regional Mental Health Center, Hartford, Connecticut

ANNE MULVEY, University of Lowell, Lowell, Massachusetts

CYNTHIA PEARSON, University of Southern California, Los Angeles, California

SHULAMIT REINHARZ, Brandeis University, Waltham, Massachusetts

ANNETTE U. RICKEL, Wayne State University, Detroit, Michigan

STEPHANIE RIGER, Lake Forest College, Lake Forest, Illinois

MYRNA B. SHURE, Hahnemann University, Philadelphia, Pennsylvania

LISA A. TEDESCO, State University of New York, Buffalo, New York

Foreword

This book in its diversity of topics reflects the re-emergence of concern with women's issues in the last decade and the vigor and pioneering quality of scholarship in the area. Such extensive, albeit uneven, development says something about the state of our society as well, for organized scholarship is a form of problem solving, part of the process of working through issues that come to the attention of observers of and commentators on the social world. But we can go further. By recognizing that the contemporary women's movement is not new, but is in keeping with a stream of feminism at least 150 years old, we can encourage the current rekindling of interest and consciousness to reflect contemporary events as well.

Not only do women comprise almost half the total labor force of the late twentieth century, but they participate in a way that is different from previous times. No longer is the average female worker a young woman putting in her time until she marries, never to return to work until the children are grown. More adult women are in the labor force, and the average working woman is married and the mother of young children. Because they are working in vastly increased numbers and are entering or increasing their participation in the highest level professional positions, skilled crafts, and political and military service, their needs as *workers* who are women are being recognized both by themselves and by various segments of society. At the societal level, for example, there are legal protections—on the books at least—in measures such as Title VII and Title IX, with their proscriptions against bias in hiring, promotion, and other job-related and education-related matters.

At a different level the presence of women in supervisory and leadership roles has created interest in female assertiveness and has caused men to increasingly accept female authority. At the same time the presence of women in former "male-only" jobs and women's heightened feelings of self-worth have led to recognition that sexual harrassment is not an amusing matter to be quietly accepted as one of the natural conditions of the work place, for either men or women. The stress of work and problems associated with alcohol, drug use, and smoking may be placing an increased number of women at higher risk for some diseases.

In addition to work-related changes, scientific and technological advances have contributed to major changes in the patterns of people's lives. Reproduction is increasingly under control and more people live longer. However, while male life expectancies have increased along with women's, they have not done so to the same degree. In the middle years and beyond, there are fewer men than women, and a significant number of women cannot expect to remain married to one man until close to the end of their lives. There are, for example, nearly five widows for every widower at older age levels.

Improved health care has made it possible for women to attain a desired family size with fewer pregnancies. Thus the child-bearing and -rearing years occupy a sharply reduced portion of the adult life span. With today's longevity a woman who devotes herself to being a homemaker must face the fact that when her last child leaves home, she may have 30 years to live in another role for which she may have no preparation. Reproductive control has made real the possibility of a new sexual freedom and also specific plans for the place child bearing will have in one's life.

Male–female relationships are changing rapidly. Although women earn less than men, the fact that women do work and earn money means they have independence. Power relationships in many families have changed, requiring new adjustments by both males and females. Working women assert a stronger claim to share in the control of family money, and there is greater involvement of their male partners in housework and child care.

The possibility of financial independence may well be related to the increasing divorce rate. Divorced people remarry at a high rate, and remarriage has resulted in highly complex family forms with stepparents, half siblings, and ill-defined relationships within unfamiliar extended families. Most women retain custody of children after divorce, or have sole responsibility for raising out-of-wedlock children. The female-headed household is now common, and it is often an economically deprived unit, its poverty adding to the stress of caring for children without a partner. Some men are challenging women's prerogatives of custody, and some women refuse to accept custody of their children after divorce.

Not only have reproductive control and independence led to changes in more traditional relations, but also to the development of new life-styles. The phenomenon of men and women sharing living quarters is so ubiquitous that it has entered the Census as the POSSLQ. A portion of the older generation views the various new relationships as challenges to cherished values and life-styles they were socialized to accept as right and proper. Members of the middle, transitional generation, struggling to integrate older values with contemporary life-styles, are coping with their own children. The children of people who became parents in the 1950s and 1960s may be maturing sexually at an earlier age, are often sexually active younger, and may experiment with drugs at an early age. Some who had economic and social advantages take risks, move away from home, enter esoteric occupations, or are unable to find themselves in an uncertain economic world, causing anxiety for their parents. Some children move back into their parents' homes because of economic circumstances, creating new issues of relationship and authority.

It would be surprising if we did not experience conflict in a time of change. There would, after all, be no social stability if social structures had no built-in resistances to change. Social structures are maintained through culture, the ways we think, believe, feel, expect, and act. The words we use to describe what we value may be incongruent with what we actually do. Eventually the process of creating congruence leads to changes in our ideas about our world. Acts we once believed dangerous may come to be seen as desirable. Acts denigrated as immoral may come to be tolerated or even seen as part of a preferable way of life. Relationships formerly considered uncomfortable, or wrong, may come to be perceived and experienced more comfortably and naturally as they become common and as new social forms emerge. Self-help groups, political action, professional caucuses, support groups, therapists, books, magazines, films, and advertisements help us to articulate what is right and proper in a socially shared form and help us to adapt to changes.

Laws also change. New concepts of property and duties of support emerge. What was once presented as protective legislation is experienced as a barrier in a new world. The culture, in short, is slowly restructured in the vast web of custom and norms, in informal acts, and in formal statements of reciprocal rights and duties, enforceable through the courts. Social scientists participate in the cultural working through, in the process of social learning, by articulating new ideas and communicating new perceptions reflecting our accommodation to the contemporary world.

Social and Psychological Problems of Women, then, is a reflection of ongoing social change, and it represents an attempt at disciplined and organized efforts to learn, to understand, and to come to terms with what has been happening to all of us. This volume is a result of the efforts of people with intimate knowledge of women's issues who sense the need for better concepts and who explore unknown territory. Society will benefit from this new thrust of scholarship that, in the process of finding its own way, is leading all of us to a deeper and broader understanding. The editors of this volume have done us a service by pulling together scholarship that shows where we have been and where we may be headed.

Adeline and Murray Levine
State University of New York at Buffalo

Preface

Until recently, applied psychology has paid little attention to the growing literature on the psychology of women, and researchers and theorists concerned with the study of women have devoted minimal energy to intervention in or prevention of women's difficulties. Over the past few years, however, the two fields have begun to recognize and develop their areas of common interest. A number of leading applied psychologists have turned their attention to the prevention of women's problems, and the field of psychology of women has seen increasing interest in the treatment of the psychopathology of women.

This increased attention and interest has two advantages. First, it carries the promise of new and productive ways to examine the prevention, development, and treatment of psychological distress in women. Second, it will serve to underline the need to view women as a special population, at risk for developing unique problems, and worthy of study. Nevertheless, at present no single source draws together these advances in uniting the two disciplines. While there are numerous books on the psychology of women, and several on women's problems, none has specifically addressed the contribution social science has made to resolving these problems. In fact, the approximately 15 textbooks on the psychology of women tend to deal predominantly with theoretical rather than applied issues. The goal of this book is to provide a representative collection of research and programs presenting an applied psychology approach to resolving the problems of women in our society, and to stimulate further research and program development. This book examines theoretical, historical, and legal issues concerning the role of women; delineates the social problems faced by specific groups of women (e.g., minority women, divorced women) and by women in general; and presents intervention programs designed to alleviate or prevent problems women face in our society. The contributions were selected with an emphasis on evaluative research, although some theoretical and review papers have been included.

This volume is intended as a textbook for undergraduate and graduate courses in the psychology of women and women's studies that examine women in the psychological panorama of the social environment. Graduate courses in psychotherapeutic techniques may use the book as a supplemental text. The volume will also be useful to both professionals in the mental health field and lay persons as a resource for intervention approaches with women.

Virtually each chapter in its own way indicates the need for further knowledge. Clearly research and evaluation are called for. As a result of being in the work force, will women begin to manifest the same proportion of stress-related disorders as men? Since women outlive men, what is their economic as well as their social-psychological future? What are the concerns of ethnic minority women? While we have developed some knowledge about black women, especially educated black women, we know much less about Hispanic women. How about the safety of women in a violent society? Can the threat of violence to women be reduced in a world of crime that is predominantly male? How can women fulfill their role as mothers and still function in the work force? Although the role of the single parent is, for the most part, one of stress and poverty, we presently need additional information concerning single parents: how they cope and what is needed to make them more effective parents, as well as how they can meet some of their own needs in society.

Finally, we are only beginning to adopt an ecological perspective on women in society. Research on the networks and support systems of women of all ages and at all levels of society is necessary. What are their main barriers to success? What are their strengths? How do they cope in their daily lives? Who helps them and who hinders them? Who respects them as human beings and who demeans them and what can be done about it? As in all psychological research most of the papers contained in this volume are limited in generalizability. We know very little about the semiskilled and unskilled female in our society. Yet it is at this level where there is the most social pathology (for men as well as women), the fewest coping skills, the greatest amount of marital disruption, crime, violence, and social disorganization, and the least attention paid to problems that are of particular concern to females. These problems include health care, employment, education, single parenting, divorce, desertion, child support, and job training.

While there is much to be encouraged about, there is danger of being lulled into a false sense of accomplishment. There are enormous changes to come in the late 1980s and early 1990s. This volume details some of the salient issues. New ones will arise as we carry on research at various levels. Not all this research need be generated at the university level. Immense possibilities exist in industrial and community contexts. It would be a great service to our society at large if we could gather knowledge not only of how many women are working or educated at certain levels but of how they cope with the numerous problems, threats, and issues particular to the world of women. The problems will no doubt change or will appear in different contexts. Nevertheless, women should be a priority for study by the behavioral sciences as well as for those who are in a position to determine social policy.

We hope that the next 10 years will focus attention on the problems presented in this volume as well as other problems and issues of importance to women and society at large. It is understandable that because of the short period of the increased consciousness about the needs of women, comparatively little empirical data exists aimed at preventing or ameliorating women's psychological and social problems. This is in keeping with the emergence of any category of scientific endeavor: First there are observations (many of them inaccurate), then some primitive measurements leading to more refined observations, a reduction of rhetoric, and an increase in precision. Finally a body of valid knowledge emerges that has to be updated and cross-checked. From the material in this book are hopeful signs that we are reaching the "refinement" stage, moving from advocacy to social action. The path is still long. Future progress will depend on behavioral sciences' willingness to shoulder responsibilities in this area.

We are indebted to a number of people who have supported and assisted us in this endeavor. Charles Spielberger candidly critiqued our ideas and encouraged us to move forward with the book. Barbara Snell Dohrenwend and Carolyn Wood

Sherif's untimely deaths during the course of this project made us appreciate anew their help and importance as role models and mentors. We are grateful to the contributors to this volume for their cooperativeness, diligence in meeting deadlines, and helpful suggestions throughout the project. A number of graduate students were of invaluable assistance in the preparation of the volume: we would like to thank Wendy Benn, Linda Forsberg, Christine Homer, Diane Keyser-Wentworth, and Patricia Roehling. Further, the secretarial support of Jean Carlson and Fran Calabro of Wayne State University is greatly appreciated.

Annette U. Rickel
Meg Gerrard
Ira Iscoe

SOCIAL AND PSYCHOLOGICAL PROBLEMS OF WOMEN

I

THEORETICAL ISSUES

Society—the context in which women live their lives—is perhaps the most visible influence on the quality of those lives. An examination of some of the problems women encounter would necessarily deal with social issues. Yet, the inner lives of women, the less visible workings of the mind, are certainly profound influences on those very lives as well. In truth, the boundaries between social and psychological problems are blurred. It would seem more accurate to speak of the interface or interweaving between social and psychological etiologies of women's issues. Likewise, prevention and intervention of problems are probably most successfully viewed as both social *and* psychological. One of the major purposes of this book is to explore some leading problem areas for women in society and to examine what psychology, and psychological research, has contributed to the understanding of these areas.

The first four chapters of this volume deal with theoretical issues. The relationship of women to society cannot be understood without the broader perspective of the past and present roles women fill. The purpose of this section is to provide that broader perspective, by assessing the primary roles women play—achievers, community builders, and mothers—with attention given to the role of minority women in our society.

Chapter 1, by Gilbert, deals with the topic of women's achievement outside the home and the development of their professional lives. As she documents, the woman's climb up the ladder of career achievement is a long, arduous journey requiring females to take two or more steps to every one step by males. The author's two-factor model of internal psychological factors and external structural factors illustrates the complexity of hindrances to achievement and the interaction of these effects. While affirmative action programs to assure hiring, training, promoting, and compensating women executives may be institutionalized as company policy in some large corporations, the road to achievement for women is by no means assured.

The obstacles women encounter in their objective of climbing for high career goals may be internal or psychological, such as: a lack of achievement orientation due to the perceived inconsistency of being feminine and being competent; an

1

underestimation of one's abilities resulting in a lowered expectancy for success; and a lack of goal setting in terms of specific lifelong career pursuits, beyond the traditional socialized goals of marriage and children. Other key factors are termed external to the individual or structural. Social policy dictates these, which include sex discrimination in educational and occupational settings, as an example.

What becomes clear from Gilbert's chapter is the importance of the interaction of internal and external factors for intervention and prevention of women's lack of achievement. Several models for change are proposed.

After documenting the hard struggle women must engage in to achieve personal career goals outside the home, we turn in Chapter 2 to the "other side of the coin," the side of women as problem solvers. It is within the community, often beginning at the grass-roots, neighborhood level, that women exhibit leadership and organizing capacity.

Unlike Gilbert's documentation of women's unreached achievement goals within the professional world, Reinharz portrays a world where women do achieve—the community. This chapter challenges the image of women as incompetent, ambivalent, victimized participants in society by detailing the role of women as community makers. In contrast to Chapter 1, where factors related to *individual* success were delineated, we have here women's activity interpreted in *collective* terms.

Community-building activities are defined by Reinharz as those actions engaged in by a group of people in an effort to enhance the life of a community with which the group identifies. This chapter uses a historical perspective and presents cases of women's collective community-building competence in seven domains: (1) union activism, (2) neighborhood activism, (3) political participation, (4) black women's activism, (5) social service voluntarism, (6) self-help group involvement, and (7) peace movements.

Women's participation in union activism has a long, though little-known, history. Dating back to the 1820s, women had encounters with unions that were fraught with frustration, since their demands were rarely met. Although considered unorganized by male labor, women, early in labor history, formed unions, organized strikes, and negotiated their demands. Women's attempts to reach leadership positions within unions have been largely unsuccessful, with women having been viewed as competitors for scarce jobs or good pay. Reinharz' chapter affords us a detailed view of the historical legacy of male-dominated labor; the patriarchal order is long standing. This chapter helps us understand some of the reasons why even government action or legal mandate to *equalize* economic opportunities for females is so difficult to realize in terms of actual operational realities.

In contrast to the arena of union activity where women have been active for a long time but have not held leadership positions, is the "home turf"—neighborhood organizations—where women do hold the majority of leadership roles. Various activist involvements with a focus on the activity of strengthening and protecting neighborhoods are related.

Another domain of women's community building is political participation. Noting that the traditional gap between male and female voting rates is now gone, the issue of women as a serious political power has become salient. This chapter also points out the trend of increasing office holding by women. Although the number of women elected to office is meager compared to men, the increasing number of women in the work force is a contributing factor to political participation of women, not only as voters, but also as political officeholders.

Reference is made to the special barriers to black women's political participation. In contrast, black women's collective action on behalf of their communities is documented. Reinharz explores three additional domains of women as community builders: social service voluntarism, self-help group involvement, and peace movements.

The author concludes her review of women as community builders, i.e., women's group assertiveness in solving or preventing problems, with suggestions for interventions designed for empowerment. She dispels many of the myths about women, such as "superwoman," which are counterproductive to individual and collective female achievement, and offers suggestions for future research.

One aspect of social policy that has an extremely powerful effect on woman's achievement is child care. As Gilbert pointed out, women have historically assumed the responsibility for child care, and even though there is a trend toward shared parenting, social policy has largely ignored the need for high quality, low-cost, community-based facilities. Clearly, the impact is greater on the achievement of professional women than on professional men.

Chapter 3 deals with women's oldest role—mother. The theoretical perspective taken by Dorr and Friedenburg is forged from an earlier tradition that idealized the role of mother and placed the entire responsibility for early childhood development in the hands of mother. Though many of the authors' premises are psychoanalytic and may be questioned by some readers, the final interpretations go far beyond traditional analyses to contemporary women's rejection of a patriarchal stance. The chapter documents the developmental stages of emotional tasks faced by mother and child during the child's first three years of life. Using *object relations theory* as a conceptual framework, the authors analyze these tasks and, thus, the various influences on the emotional development of both mother and child. Object relations theory is based on the concept of the internalized representations of self and other, the "objects." This theory, while primarily a psychoanalytic conceptualization, reflects the work of developmental and humanistic psychologists as well.

Unlike traditional psychoanalysts, Dorr and Friedenburg do not view motherhood as a unidirectional process whereby mothers are totally responsible or blamed for a child's development. Instead, we are presented with the notion of "mutual cuing," a circular or reciprocal process of interaction established early in the relationship between mother and child. It is this dynamic, dyadic system which is examined.

While the authors draw from the psychoanalytic tradition of mother as primary caretaker in presenting the development of early childhood emotional growth, they reject this solitary maternal stance as epitomized by the writings of Fraiberg and Spitz. The concept of "good-enough" mothering is examined in the context of today's woman and the external demands placed on her as she attempts to fulfill the role of mother. Such possible stresses as single parenthood and teenage motherhood are discussed.

With an increasing number of mothers entering or remaining in the work force, child care has become a social issue, requiring community intervention. Several new, innovative community resources are presented by Dorr and Friedenburg in their chapter. One such program to allow parents more quality time with their children is flex-time scheduling.

The chapter "Black Women in American Society: A Resource Development

Perspective" by Allen and Britt provides a lucid demonstration that we must include all women in our thinking of social and psychological problems. As the authors point out, discrimination and equality for black women may not be eradicated by virtue of the Women's Movement alone, nor by the Black Movement. This special group of women are in a position of "triple jeopardy" (i.e., they are subject to discrimination on three counts: race, class, and sex). Because of this, their role in our society is significantly different from other women's roles.

Allen and Britt proceed to describe three types of resources—economic, social, and personal—which may be used to prevent stress and disorder from reaching crisis proportions. According to the theoretical model proposed by the authors, these three resources can be viewed distinctly on a continuum of vulnerability to disruption. Therefore, an individual's susceptibility or high risk to stress or serious breakdown is dependent on the amount of each resource possessed, as well as on the interrelationship of the resources. The authors hypothesize that of the three types of resources: economic, social, and personal, black women as a group are most vulnerable to a lack of economic resource; black women are unemployed more often than both black men and white women.

Allen and Britt continue to develop their theoretical resource model of susceptibility to stress in this chapter. They conclude that in spite of their relatively weak economic resources, black females seem to have strong personal and social resources, and suggest areas for intervention and prevention of stress which is characteristic of many black women's lives. Specifically, the economic resource needs bolstering. The authors propose social policy changes such as the development of more on-the-job training opportunities to increase career options for black women.

1

Female Development and Achievement

Lucia Albino Gilbert
University of Texas at Austin

"Achievement—its nature, level, and experience—is one of the most significant visible facets of the lives of people" (Mednick, Tangri, & Hoffman, 1975, p. xi). But the development and expression of achievement are crucially influenced by the historical setting and social context in which people live. Because contemporary women live in a largely patriarchal society, understanding the broader social psychological and cultural context of their lives is essential in evaluating their achievements outside the home and the development of their professional lives.

Despite many similarities in the adult development of women and men, a number of factors differentially affect the development and orientation of their achievement and the professional pathways they follow. This chapter addresses the nature and influence of those factors that particularly affect the achievement-related behaviors of women. Key internal, or *sociopsychological factors*, are identified and their influences on women discussed. These personal variables are then viewed within the context of existing *structural factors*, external to the individual and imbedded in the social structure. Finally, constructive ways in which to counter the potentially negative effects of these factors—both at the individual and societal levels, are discussed.

PSYCHOLOGICAL FACTORS

How people think about their circumstances and act upon them is influenced by social ideology, social norms, and social organization. It is well documented that sex-role socialization influences the personality development of women and men, as well as the observed sex-related differences in various achievement areas (Block, 1979, 1982). Recent writings by Chodorow (1978) and Gilligan (1982) also describe how childhood social contexts can account for the development of many psychological sex differences, particularly those reflecting the greater imbeddedness of women in social contexts in contrast to the more individualistic, mastery-directed activities of men. These early influences form an important background against which to consider the personality variables often investigated in relationship to female achievement and professional development. Keeping in mind that women in contemporary society cannot be meaningfully understood if stripped and isolated from the larger social context, let us consider several variables that are closely related to achievement and the professional development of women.

A much briefer and earlier version of this chapter appears in *The Counseling Psychologist*, 1982, *9*, 83–84.

The first of these is *achievement orientation.* A number of writers (e.g., Fitz-gerald & Crites, 1980; Stein & Bailey, 1973) note that women's achievement be-havior is inhibited and circumscribed by the effects of sex-role socialization. A key question in the socialization of women is raised by Sherman (1976), "Shall we socialize females to be competent or to be feminine?" She further points out that "the goals of femininity and competence are not necessarily the same" (p. 181). A woman, for example, need not be intellectually competent to be considered feminine in the stereotypic sense of the word. However, if she is considered intel-lectually competent, her femininity will be doubted and if she is considered femi-nine, her intellectual competence will be doubted. Moreover, many women in-ternalize the belief that competence and achievement are incompatible with their femininity or with their being desired as a woman. That is, if I am female and successfully act on my achievement orientation, I will be less attractive to men than women who do not because men prefer women who want to share a man's professional life and to raise his children.

Instances of this potential double bind for women are numerous. In *The Managerial Woman* by Hennig and Jardim (1977), for example, the women inter-viewed were all single when they climbed the corporate ladder. However, many of those interviewed actively sought out relationships with men in their late thirties—what the authors called "a flight into femininity." One is left wondering whether these women would have been able to achieve their goals had they been "feminine" and in an affiliative relationship earlier in their careers. Similar themes appear in the literature on role conflict in career women (e.g., Holahan & Gilbert, 1979). Achievement oriented women often feel they must choose *between* a career and a family.

Thus many women, although no less achievement oriented than their male peers, are more sensitive to the negative consequences of educational and pro-fessional success for women. The rewards of such successes for them are still far less certain than for their male peers, and the possible costs—in the form of affilia-tive loss—far more certain. As a result, many women may satisfy achievement needs, and reduce some of the conflict with cultural sex-role demands, by choosing a "feminine" occupation and/or by remaining in a low status position in their occupation (Stein & Bailey, 1973). And even today, women still tend to be found in female-dominated occupations and few advance to managerial-level positions (Riger & Galligan, 1980; Scott, 1982).

A related factor here is the *expectancy of success*, the expectation of what one can attempt and successfully accomplish. Across various areas of achievement, females tend to hold lower expectations of what they can and do accomplish. Two aspects of this expectancy are prevalent: Women either (a) believe that they cannot be as successful or as competent as men in certain areas or (b) feel that they are performing less well than their male peers, even when they are, in fact, performing as well, if not better. Cole (1981), in trying to understand why so few women are entering the sciences, identifies the potentially negative effect of societal beliefs on women's achievement orientation and behavior: "The belief that women are less competent than men at science, whatever the validity of this belief, contributes to women's ambivalence toward work and reduced motivation and commitment to scientific careers." (p. 386)

Regarding the underestimation of one's abilities, Widom and Burke (1978) report on a case in point. When junior faculty at two major universities were asked about their number of publications, males saw themselves as above average in comparison to their colleagues, and showed a fairly accurate appraisal of their relative standing. Women, on the other hand, not only saw themselves as having significantly fewer publications than the males, but also showed an inaccurate appraisal of their relative standing; that is, women saw themselves as ranking much lower on the publication dimension then they actually did. Deaux (1979) reports similar findings from a sample of individuals in first-level management positions. Males evaluated their performance more favorably than women and also rated themselves as having more ability and greater intelligence. Men also saw ability as more responsible for their success than did women. These findings are, of course, consistent with sex differences in causal attributions for success and failure. Even when a woman's achievement is acknowledged, her success is more likely to be attributed to luck than to her ability, in comparison to a man in the same situation (Frieze et al., 1982).

Another important area to consider is women's *self-confidence* in achievement settings. Lenney (1977) believes that women vary their opinions of their own abilities and confidence in response to specific achievement situations. Thus, rather than viewing women generally lower in self-confidence than males (that is, across all situations), she proposes that women are discriminative in making their self-evaluations of confidence and competence, and that these self-evaluations are largely situationally determined. Important characteristics of the situation are gender-related and include sex-appropriateness of the task (O'Leary, 1977), sex composition of the group (Megargee, 1969), and the nature of the achievement domain (Travis et al., 1982).

A variable very much related to self-confidence and feelings of competence, yet not typically included in discussions of female achievement behavior, is *goal setting*. Sherman (1976) underscores the importance of people having some place to go and both wanting and knowing how to get there. Women are socialized to want the same global goal—marriage and children (Bernard, 1975). They typically give little concrete thought to what they will do with their lives, to how and along what lines they will develop their abilities, and to how they eventually will use these abilities in the context of meaningful on-going work. Conclusions from a recent review on goal setting and task performance are pertinent here: "Specific and challenging goals lead to better performance than easy goals, do your best goals or no goals; goals affect performance by directing attention, mobilizing effort, increasing persistence, and motivating the development of strategies" (Locke et al., 1981, p. 125). The authors go on to identify the conditions under which goal setting is likely to improve performance. Several of these seem uncannily related to the present discussion of women and achievement—specific and challenging goals, relevant feedback, a supportive milieu, appropriate rewards for goal attainment, and personally acceptable goals. With these points in mind let us now turn to several external or structural factors influencing female achievement and career development.

STRUCTURAL FACTORS

The key external or structural factors related to female achievement fall into four overlapping spheres. These are sex discrimination in educational and occupational settings; availability of role models, mentors, and associational ties with colleagues; attitudes about women's abilities and roles; and the influences of social policy on achievement potential.

Sex Discrimination in Educational and Occupational Settings

When we talk of sex discrimination in hiring and promotion, we often hear the question, But where are the qualified women? The Committee on the Education and Employment of Women in Science and Engineering of the National Research Council found them—mostly at the bottom. In the Committee's report published in 1979, statistics on women doctorates and their male counterparts in selected disciplines of the natural sciences, social sciences, and engineering confirm in academic settings what we know to be the case regarding the status of women in general: Academic women are predominately found in the lower and untenured ranks (postdoctoral fellows, lecturers, or assistant professors), and they receive lower salaries at all levels of attainment than men of comparable status. Moreover, fewer women are employed at first-rate universities. A crucial point made clear by the results of the survey is that women earn their doctoral degrees in the same study time and at similar institutions as men—and usually exhibit better academic records than men. Also, they aspire to careers in teaching and research in equal proportions to men (Skinner, 1980).

These findings reflect the structure of a labor force that shows marked discrimination on the basis of sex (Scott, 1982). Male-dominated occupations typically are not open to women. And those few women who are admitted receive fewer promotions than men with similar credentials and are directed into career paths that are lower in status, power, and pay. In fact, starting with their academic and vocational training programs, women are encouraged, if not forced, to become "homogenized" into a narrow range of fields which offer little chance for advancement or prestige. The National Research Council's report also makes clear that, *even today*, after the many successes of the feminist movement, women at all educational levels continue to earn considerably less than men and are greatly underrepresented in nearly all professional areas. Thus women's acceptance and promotion in careers, unlike that of men, may be based on factors more related to their gender than to their ability.

Role Models, Mentors, and Associational Ties with Colleagues

Same-sex role models are important to women's professional development. Tidball (1973) and Goldstein (1979), for example, both document the relationship between female students' achievement behavior after graduation and their reports of having female professors as role models. Gilbert et al. (1983) report similar findings from a sample of female students studied prior to their graduation from various doctoral programs.

Gilbert and Evans (1983) provide some insight into why same-sex role models are important for women. When asked which qualities they sought in their role models, female students placed greater importance on personal attributes and lifestyle characteristics than males; they also considered the relationship with a role model as more important to their professional development than did males. (Females and males placed equal importance on the model's professional achievement.) Also striking is that the vast majority of the students—both female and male—reported having a same-sex role model, and females did so under circumstances where female role models were far less available than male models. That these women identified female role models when many more male models were available again speaks to the special importance they attribute to a relationship with a same-sex role model and to what women may view as essential to an effective role model relationship.

Women are looking for models who successfully combine professional and personal roles and who, as Douvan (1976) says, integrate professional and feminine qualities. They also seek out role models who are likely to affirm them as professionals and to encourage and support their professional goals. Such affirmation is more likely to come from females than from males (Tidball, 1976), and is perhaps most likely to come from females who are selected on the basis of their life-styles and attitudes about work and parental roles. Moreover, female role models, so selected, would be more able than others in the work or educational environment to show sensitivity to female-related issues such as claims of discriminatory practices against women and sexual harassment (Tidball, 1976). Finally sexual attraction, or fear of sexual attraction, may influence the nature of the interaction of men with female students and employees (Pope et al., 1979). The fact that sexual relations between students and faculty, and employers and employees, occur to the degree that they do—and apparently are an accepted occurrence within academic departments and the corporate world—makes this possible factor all the more salient. Taken together these factors make female students and professionals feel less comfortable, and both seek and receive less professional support and intellectual challenge from men than from women.

An interesting issue emerges here, one that illustrates how internal and external factors interact to influence females' career paths. The psychological burden of disapproval, indifference, and discomfort that women experience in their graduate training and professional settings may undermine their commitment to professional careers, dampen their spirits and energy, and contribute to self-fulfilling prophecies about not being able to make it in a "man's world" (Epstein, 1978). Further confounding this situation is the external reality, provided by our societal norms, that women can "drop out" with few, if any, negative social sanctions. In fact, this "out" provided by society may contribute significantly to conflicts women experience within their student or work roles, potentially resulting in their prematurely putting their career goals aside or lowering their sights because they think they cannot succeed. Data reported by Hirshberger and Itkin (1978) are consistent with this hypothesis: Male graduate students were more likely to complete their graduate degrees than were female students, even though the ability difference between them for the most part favored women.

The problem or structural barrier, here, of course, is that females constitute less than 10 percent of the faculty at major academic institutions where the vast majority of women received their professional training. Thus few same-sex role models are available to women during those crucial years of pre-professional training. A similar situation exists in the work world. How can same-sex role models be made more available to women? One strategy is to increase the number of women in teaching and research positions beyond the primary school level, as well as the number of courses containing content related to women and women's lives. A second strategy is to make these relationships more effective with the role models who are currently available. Williams (1982), for example, has developed teaching methods to enhance the effectiveness of the role model process in educational and work settings.

The difficulties women have in locating and establishing relationships with role models are compounded when it comes to *mentors*. Indeed, the mentor process is largely unavailable to women. In view of the key role mentors have in the professional development of men (Levinson, 1978), this lack of access for women places them at a distinct disadvantage. [Kanter (1977a), in fact, argues that if mentors are important for men in organizations, "they are absolutely essential for women."] According to Levinson, mentors act as teachers to enhance the young man's skills and intellectual development. As sponsors, they use their influence to promote the young man's entry and advancement. Basically, however, mentors help the mentee believe in himself so that his "Dream" can be realized. Kanter (1977a) also emphasizes the power aspects of mentoring. Mentors are essential because they generate power. Mentors can speak up for their mentees and they can short-circuit established procedures and policies.

Three reasons are often cited to explain why mentoring is a predominantly male phenomenon (Harren & Randers, 1980): Males are in higher positions, male proteges are more assertive in initiating mentoring relationships, and cross-sex relationships are likely to become sexual. Essentially these three "reasons" are rationales for maintaining the status quo. Males in power select other males, rather than females, as proteges because the women are too unassertive, too sexy, or both—a clear example of a person-blame interpretation of a social problem (Caplan & Nelson, 1973). The focus (or blame) gets put on characteristics that reside within the individual (here, women as a group), and relevant situational or structural factors external to the individual are ignored. Another way to keep a woman in "her place," in addition to highlighting her feminine unassertive nature, is to make her "sex object" characteristics salient in interactions with her. Quite likely, should women act as assertive as men in establishing mentoring relationships, their intentions would be viewed by the male as having sexual implications.

Women, in fact, learn early in their careers that the quickest way to be "de-skilled" by a male is through eroticism. She talks seriously about work-related tasks, and the employer or colleague comments on her lovely smile. Women quickly develop strategies to deflect or side-step male attempts to make the interaction sexual—with the hope that eventually they will be taken seriously as professional women. It's rare indeed for a young professional male to have to spend time and energy counteracting potential sexual overtures from his colleagues! Yet such behavior on the part of males towards female colleagues is often considered *as part of the social order*, rather than as a harmful structural defect. Here again, then, we see an important difference in the factors influencing the career development of men and women.

A structural barrier related to mentoring in its dynamics and effects is the *social organization of collegial ties*. With whom do females and males interact in their work environments? And how open is the male buddy or old boy system to female peers? Women are often isolated from informal collegial contacts (e.g., Kaufman, 1978) and such isolation, whether by choice or exclusion leaves them at a professional disadvantage. Isolation of this kind may be a form of what Bernard (1976b) calls the "stag effect." This effect, which "is the result of a complex of exclusionary customs, practices, attitudes, conventions, and other social forms, essentially protects the male turf from the intrusion of women" (p. 23). As a result, female professionals may receive less encouragement for their achievements or simply be avoided by their male colleagues. Males also may be ambivalent about interacting with female colleagues because they feel it may threaten role expectations of male dominance (Bernard, 1976b). Finally, Kanter (1977a) states that when few women are present in particular positions, they become "tokens" and, as such, may be evaluated more critically and experience greater pressure to conform to sex-role stereotypes.

The number of women in organizational or educational settings and the nature and extent of networking and support systems among women in these settings are important factors in ameliorating the possible negative effects of isolation from colleagues and of limits placed on participation in organizational and professional activities. Networking among professional women is gaining in popularity, with a number of organizations being formed expressly for this purpose (Beutler, 1980). In addition, once the proportion of females in work groups and professional settings increases sufficiently, the gender-related responses of its members changes (Ruble & Higgins, 1976) and power shifts away from the male members (Kanter, 1977a).

Attitudes about Women's Abilities and Roles

One of the greatest structural barriers to women's achievement involves attitudes about women's abilities and women's roles (Cole, 1981). Related to these attitudes is the differential evaluation of individuals on the basis of gender (the sex-as-status phenomenon). Men are rated higher than "equivalent" women in performing certain tasks (Deaux & Emswiller, 1974), speaking effectiveness (Gruber & Gaebelein, 1979), job qualifications (Etaugh & Kasley, 1981), and other areas. Similarly, women receive lower recognition and economic rewards for their work than men, and lower prestige, knowledge, and expertise are attributed to them as well (Bayer & Astin, 1975). Widely accepted stereotypes depict men, but not women, as having the requisite skills and characteristics for managerial and leadership positions (Lockheed, 1977; O'Leary, 1974; Rosen & Jerdee, 1978). These stereotypes persist even though sex differences are *not* found in leadership ability and job performance (Brown, 1979).

The differential evaluation of men and women not only influences decisions about ability and achievement but also tends to devalue female-related activities and topics (Gilbert et al., 1981; Gruber & Gaebelein, 1979). Many psychologists, for example, view issues such as sex-fairness in counseling and psychotherapy, rape, and battered women as "women's issues" rather than as legitimate topics for teaching, research, and professional practice.

Personal belief systems about women's role as mothers also have a profound effect on women's achievement (Bernard, 1975). In dual-working families the female spouse continues to assume most of the home and parental role responsibilities. Even in marriages among the more educated and liberal professionals, egalitarian role relations in the workplace *and* the home are uncommon (Gilbert, 1980). Thus, the demands of parenting continue to have a far greater impact on the achievements and career paths of women than of men. Men assume they will combine a career and a family without undue difficulty; women assume that combining a career and a family is nearly impossible and a feat only to be achieved by "superwomen." A not so surprising result of these strongly held assumptions is the lower marriage rate among professional women in comparison to their male peers; a secondary result is the increasing prevalence of childlessness among professional couples (Blake, 1979).

Prevailing attitudes about women's abilities and roles are reflected in and buttressed by social policy, the last factor to be considered here.

Social Policy

Social policy is like an umbrella overarching the several structural factors already discussed. It is determined by the norms, values, and beliefs of the dominate group, and in this case, they remain the norms and values of a largely male-dominated, patriarchal group (Laws & Tangri, 1979). The defeat of the ERA; the proposed legislation by Senator Paul Laxalt "focused on restoring a part of the historical family, education, religious and moral training of our young" (Bernard, 1981); and the proposal of Senator Orrin Hatch (S. 1361) to limit Title IX, a law that prohibits sex discrimination in educational institutions receiving federal aid, are all testimony to the continuing strength of traditional attitudes to influence social policy that directly affects women.

Though at times social policy seems far removed from the concerns of individual women, its direct and indirect effects can be considerable. Thus, discriminatory practices in hiring, differential status between the genders, and unequal pay for equal work all reflect social policy. As mentioned earlier, one aspect of social policy that has an extremely powerful effect on women's achievement is child care.

Since women have historically assumed the responsibility for child care, the availability of affordable, good child care facilities is probably the most important prerequisite enabling women to enter and remain in the work force with relatively little guilt and conflict. Moreover, the trend toward shared parenting is still relatively marginal, ascribed to more in theory than in practice. Without doubt, a social policy that ignores the need for high-quality, low-cost, community-based facilities for child care will have greater detrimental effects on the achievement of women than on that of men. Lott (1973), who is concerned with the rejection of child-rearing in dual-working couples, states, "As long as child care is viewed as a woman's duty or destiny, it will also be viewed as requiring few or no facilitating social supports. We need to develop more community-organized and community-operated centers where parents can joyfully and guiltlessly leave their children" (p. 581).

RECOMMENDATIONS

As Riger and Galligan (1980) so aptly point out, "Women today are bombarded with advice on how to succeed" (p. 902). The comprehensive model for change proposed by Parsons et al. (1976), and further elaborated on by Sherman (1976), helps organize the types of advice women are receiving. This model incorporates both personal and societal components and focuses on changing the development and expression of sex-role related behavior. Figure 1 depicts the model. The top cluster of variables (A and D) represents factors operating at the societal level, and the bottom cluster of variables (B, C, and E) represents sociopsychological factors

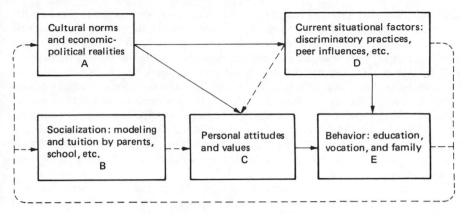

Figure 1 Development and expression of sex-role related behavior in college women (Parsons et al., 1976).

at the individual level. Through a process of socialization (B), women acquire a set of attitudes and beliefs (C) and choices and behaviors (E). Cultural norms (A) provide the background against which choices are evaluated, and these norms in turn affect situational factors (D). (Considerable detail about the model is available in Parsons et al., 1976 and Sherman, 1976.)

Let us turn now to the three general types of strategies for success typically proposed. The first type of strategy requires women to take charge of their lives by developing new skills, becoming more assertive, networking with other women, and so on. (Many self-help books of this type are on the market.) Thus, this type of strategy emphasizes personal growth—what a woman can do to make her life better. The focus is on the sociopsychological cluster of variables, B, C, and E, of the model, and, in particular, variable set C. Often times this type of strategy is proposed and used without much attention being paid to the variable sets A and D—societal factors influencing a woman's behavior and options. As is made clear by the model, however, if the focus remains on personal ways to improve the status of women, the long-term effectiveness of any strategy would be greatly limited.

A second and somewhat related type of strategy makes use of all five sets of variables in the model, with a greater emphasis being given to the cluster of sociopsychological variables (B, C, and E) than to the societal ones (A and D). This type of strategy requires women to recognize and differentiate between the internal (sociopsychological sets of variables) and external aspects (societal sets of variables) of their professional experience. Relevant cultural norms and socioeconomic-political realities include employers' perceptions and attitudes about women, job flexibility should they be members of dual-worker families, the quality of child care should they be parents, and discrimination on the basis of sex. Relevant sociopsychological factors include self-confidence, attitudes about life roles, and degree of career commitment.

This second approach also focuses on *the relationship between sociological and psychological factors*. That is, women need to learn to differentiate between what they have been taught and have accepted as socially appropriate for themselves from what might actually be appropriate. Suppose, for example, you receive feedback that your research is too narrow or that your work is too focused on the concerns of women. Or that you must be feeling insecure in your professional role because you are working so hard and producing so much. Or that you are too involved in your work and are not smiling enough around the office. Or suppose that no one in your department or office ever asks you about what you are doing professionally. One very appropriate reaction in such situations is anger and disappointment. At the same time, the internal factors need to be sorted from the external: What aspects of the feedback or situation reflect inadequate responses and skills or poor judgment on your part and what aspects stem from sources in the environment, such as people feeling threatened by your ability, people wanting you to conform to the societal stereotype for women, or colleagues simply not being interested in your professional work?

The third type of strategy focuses more directly on the top cluster of societal variables (A and D). These strategies aim to change policy, with the ultimate goal of changing the structure of existing institutions. As Bernard (1975) so clearly explains:

> *The feminist critique of the socialization paradigm does not deny that children are socialized for different roles, but it argues that even if socialization no longer emphasized the differences between the pink-clad and blue-clad infants, the infants would still grow up in a world that retains an institutional set of biases ... so long as the institutional structures of our society favor men, the feminist critics say, the question arises as to can women, no matter how well prepared psychologically and intellectually, expect to be dealt with on the basis of their merits rather than on the basis of their sex? Emphasis on socialization merely offers an easy out, it does not open doors. (pp. 17–18)*

Strategies directed toward social policy take numerous forms and range from changes instituted at local levels to changes instituted through broad federal legislation. Many examples come to mind—formal or informal groups who work to remove sex bias in textbooks, to convince their professions that sexual relations between therapists and clients or students and faculty are not ethical, to develop programs that provide new occupational vistas to school girls and reentry women and parenting skills for boys and expectant fathers.

A particularly good example of this third type of strategy is articulated by Rosabeth Moss Kanter (1977) in her book *Work and Family in the United States: A Critical Review and Agenda for Research and Policy*. Kanter argues that there is a fit between the interests of modern American organizations and the myth of separate worlds (family and work), and that social scientists have served to perpetuate this myth. Recent trends in labor force participation by wives and mothers, however, are forcing a recognition of the obvious intersection between work and family roles.

Kanter considers work and intimacy as functions of the individual, rather than as characteristics of occupational and family roles, respectively. That is, work and intimacy are viewed as processes or modes of organizing experience rather than as separate structures or activities. As she so aptly notes, "The family does not own intimacy any more than the occupational-organizational world owns work" (p. 72). This perspective more accurately reflects our current reality. More importantly, however, it also provides a *new organizing framework*, one which replaces the Parsonian theoretical analysis based on the incompatibility of occupational and family systems.

Social policy experiments consistent with her views are also highly consistent with the ideas and findings presented in this chapter. Notable among these are flextime, bringing children (and spouses) to work, on-work-site counseling, community supports for employed women, leaves and sabbaticals, and "family responsibility statements" by organizations.

SUMMARY

The complexity and number of key factors operating as barriers to the development of women's achievement well illustrate the need for *multiple approaches* to the analysis of achievement problems and their solutions. Developing a program for decreasing girls' math anxiety, for example, will be limited in its effectiveness by teachers who continue to view boys as better at math than girls, by girls who continue to see themselves as unsuited for the sciences, and so forth. Thus many avenues must be pursued simultaneously, with the understanding that no one intervention or approach can provide the desired outcome.

In addition, the factors identified here as having a pervasive negative effect on women are *not* limited to the area of achievement. Clearly expectancy of success, goal setting, availability of role models, and social policy operate to varying degrees as influences on women's lives and on the social and psychological problems women experience. Moreover, regardless of the particular problem being considered, the relevant personal variables need to be viewed within the context of existing structural factors, external to the individual and imbedded in the social structure.

REFERENCES

Bayer, A. E. & Astin, H. S. Sex differentials in the academic reward system. *Science*, 1975, *188*, 796–802.

Bernard, J. *Women, wives, and mothers.* Chicago: Aldine, 1975.

Bernard, J. Change and stability in sex-role norms and behavior. *Journal of Social Issues*, 1976, *32*, 207–224. (a)

Bernard, J. Where are we now? Some thoughts on the current scene. *Psychology of Women Quarterly*, 1976, *1*, 21–37. (b)

Bernard, J. Societal values and parenting. *The Counseling Psychologist*, 1981, *9*, 5–12.

Beutler, M. E. *Networking, sponsorship, and peer support: A collection of readings.* Austin, TX: Southwest Educational Development Laboratory, 1980.

Blake, J. Is zero preferred? American attitudes toward childlessness in the 1970s. *Journal of Marriage and the Family*, 1979, *41*, 245–257.

Block, J. H. Concepts of sex role: Some cross-cultural and longitudinal perspectives. *American Psychologist*, 1973, *28*, 512–526.

Block, J. H. *Socialization influences in personality development in males and females.* Master lecture presented at the annual meeting of the American Psychological Association, New York City, September 1979.

Block, J. H. Psychological development of female children and adolescents. In P. W. Berman & E. R. Ramey (eds.), *Women: A developmental perspective.* Washington, D.C.: NIH Publication No. 82-2298, 1982.

Brown, L. K. Women and business management. *Signs: Journal of Women in Culture and Society*, 1979, *5*, 266–288.

Caplan, N. & Nelson, D. S. On being useful. The nature and consequences of psychological research on social problems. *American Psychologist*, 1973, *28*, 199–211.

Chodorow, N. *The reproduction of mothering: Psychoanalysis and the sociology of gender.* Berkeley, CA: University of California Press, 1978.

Cole, J. R. Women in science. *American Scientist*, 1981, *69*, 385–391.

Deaux, K. Self-evaluations of male and female managers. *Sex Roles*, 1979, *5*, 571–580.

Deaux, K. & Emswiller, T. Explanations of successful performance on sex-linked tasks: What is skill for the male is luck for the female. *Journal of Personality and Social Psychology*, 1974, *29*, 80–85.

Douvan, E. The role of models in women's professional development. *Psychology of Women Quarterly*, 1976, *1*, 5–20.

Epstein, C. F. *Ambiguity as social control: The salience of sex-status in professional settings.* Paper presented at the Western Psychological Association, San Francisco, April 1978.

Etaugh, C. & Kasley, H. C. Evaluating competence: Effects of sex, marital status, and parental status. *Psychology of Women Quarterly*, 1981, *6*, 196–203.

Fitzgerald, L. F. & Crites, J. O. Toward a career psychology of women: What do we know? What do we need to know? *Journal of Counseling Psychology*, 1980, *27*, 44–62.

Frieze, I. H., Whitley, B. E., Hanusa, B. H., & McHugh, M. C. Assessing the theoretical models for sex differences in causal attributions for success and failure. *Sex Roles*, 1982, *8*, 333–343.

Gilbert, L. A. *The men in dual-career families—Do the benefits outweigh the costs.* Paper presented at the annual meeting of the American Psychological Association, Montreal, Canada, August 1980.

Gilbert, L. A. & Evans, S. Dimensions of same gender student-faculty role model relationships. *Sex Roles*, in press.

Gilbert, L. A., Gallessich, J., & Evans, S. Sex of faculty role model and students' self-perceptions of competency. *Sex Roles*, 1983, *9*, 597–608.

Gilbert, L. A., Lee, R. N., & Chiddix, S. Influence of instructor's gender on student evaluations during training in sex-fair counseling. *Journal of Counseling Psychology*, 1981, *28*, 258–264.

Gilligan, C. *In a different voice.* Cambridge, MA: Harvard University Press, 1982.

Goldstein, E. Effect of same-sex and cross-sex role models on the subsequent academic productivity of scholars. *American Psychologist*, 1979, *34*, 407–410.

Gruber, K. J. & Gaebelein, J. Sex differences in learning comprehension. *Sex Roles*, 1979, *5*, 299–310.

Harren, V. A. & Randers, S. B. *Applications of adult development theory to careers of counseling psychologists.* Paper presented at the meeting of the American Psychological Association, Montreal, Canada, August 1980.

Hennig, M. & Jardim, A. *The managerial woman.* New York: Anchor-Doubleday, 1977.

Hirshberger, N. & Itkins, S. Graduate student success in psychology. *American Psychologist*, 1978, *33*, 1083–1093.

Holahan, C. K. & Gilbert, L. A. Conflict between major life roles: Women and men in dual-career couples. *Human Relations*, 1979, *32*, 451–467.

Kanter, R. M. *Men and women of the corporation.* New York: Basic Books, 1977. (a)

Kanter, R. M. *Work and family in the United States: A critical review and agenda for research and policy.* New York: Russell Sage Foundation, 1977. (b)

Kaufman, D. R. Associational ties in academe: Some male and female differences. *Sex Roles*, 1978, *4*, 9–21.

Laws, L. J. & Tangri, S. S. *Institutional sexism, or why there is no conspiracy.* Paper presented at the meeting of the American Psychological Association, New York City, August 1979.

Lenney, E. Women's self-confidence in achievement settings. *Psychological Bulletin*, 1977, *84*, 1–13.

Levinson, D. *The seasons of a man's life.* New York: Knopf, 1978.

Locke, E. A., Shaw, K. A., Saari, L. M., & Latham. G. P. Goal setting and task performance: 1969–1980. *Psychological Bulletin*, 1981, *90*, 125–152.

Lockheed, M. E. Cognitive style effects on sex status in student work groups. *Journal of Educational Psychology*, 1977, *69*, 158–165.

Lott, B. Who will raise the children? *American Psychologist*, 1973, *28*, 573–582.

Mednick, M., Tangri, S., & Hoffman, L. *Women and achievement.* Washington, D.C.: Hemisphere, 1975.

Megargee, E. I. Influence of sex roles on the manifestation of leadership. *Journal of Applied Psychology*, 1969, *53*, 377–382.

National Research Council, Committee on the Education and Employment of Women in Science and Engineering. *Climbing the academic ladder: Doctoral women scientists in academe.* New York: National Academy of Sciences, 1979.

O'Leary, V. E. Some attitudinal barriers to occupational aspirations in women. *Psychological Bulletin*, 1974, *81*, 809–816.

O'Leary, V. E. *Toward understanding women.* Monterey, CA: Brooks/Cole, 1977.

Parsons, J. E., Frieze, I. H., & Ruble, D. W. Introduction. *Journal of Social Issues*, 1976, *32*(3).

Pope, K. S., Levenson, H., & Schover, L. R. Sexual intimacy in psychology training: Results and implications of a national survey. *American Psychologist*, 1979, *34*, 682–689.

Riger, S. & Galligan, P. Women in management: An exploration of competing paradigms. *American Psychologist*, 1980, *35*, 902–910.

Rosen, B. & Jerdee, T. H. Perceived sex differences in managerially relevant characteristics. *Sex Roles*, 1978, *4*, 837–843.

Ruble, D. N. & Higgins, E. T. Effects of group sex composition on self-presentation and sex-typing. *Journal of Social Issues*, 1976, *32*, 111–124.

Scott, J. W. The mechanization of women's work. *Scientific American*, 1982, *247*, 167–185.

Sherman, J. A. Social values, femininity, and the development of female competence. *Journal of Social Issues*, 1976, *32*, 181–195.

Skinner, H. C. W. Review of climbing the academic ladder: Doctoral women in academe. *American Scientist*, 1980, Jan–Feb, 101.

Stein, H. H. & Bailey, M. M. The socialization of achievement orientation in females. *Psychological Bulletin*, 1973, *80*, 345–366.

Tidball, M. E. Perspective on academic women and affirmative action. *Educational Record*, 1973, *54*, 130–135.

Tidball, M. E. Of men and research: The dominant themes in American higher education include neither teaching nor women. *Journal of Higher Education*, 1976, *47*, 373–389.

Travis, C. B., Burnett-Doering, J. B., & Reid, P. T. The impact of sex, achievement domain, and conceptual orientation on causal attributions. *Sex Roles*, 1982, *8*, 443–454.

Widom, C. S. & Burke, B. W. Performance, attitudes, and professional socialization of women in academia. *Sex Roles*, 1978, *4*, 549–563.

Williams, M. *Educational strategies for learning to learn from role models.* Paper presented at the annual meeting of the American Psychological Association, Washington, D.C., August 1982.

2

Women as Competent Community Builders

The Other Side of the Coin

Shulamit Reinharz
Brandeis University

The women's movement was revived in America in the late 1960s after a 40-year hiatus (Freeman, 1979; Sochen, 1971) and sprang from two immediate sources. First was the fact that in 1961 President Kennedy created a President's Commission on the Status of Women which led to the establishment of 50 similar state commissions. The men and women who were involved in these commissions formed a network which later became the foundation of NOW, established by Betty Friedan and others in 1966 (Friedan, 1976). In the mid-1960s, the second source emerged. It was a grass roots movement characterized by women coming together in small groups to share their personal experiences, particularly their frustration, anger and unhappiness. Some of these women had participated in the Civil Rights movement and later the anti-war movement and were stunned to find that, despite the rhetoric of equality, they were confined to second-class status in those movements.

A vast research literature has developed to explain the problems discussed by both the commissions and the small groups. The place of women in contemporary American society, in the rest of the world, and throughout most of history has become an arena of study, and most investigations conclude that women have always had and continue to have limited rights and circumscribed opportunities. This universal oppression of women is supported by depreciating beliefs about women, particularly the notion that women are passive.

Research on minority groups (i.e., groups underrepresented in power) such as women has focused primarily on their deviance, i.e., their "otherness." Research on women—young and old, black and white, rural and urban—focuses on their problems (Markson and Hess, 1980). There is an emphasis on women's pathology, suffering and incompetence, just as there is a similar interest in explaining "defects" when research is done on racial or ethnic minorities.

While it is important to understand the dynamics of the oppression of women, there is a danger that extensive documentation of women's oppression is demoralizing (Ehrlich, 1976). The continuous reference to women in social scientific literature as vulnerable, troubled, weak, dependent or malevolent and the continuous discussion of oppression repeat and help form cultural stereotypes about

I am grateful to the following people for helping me locate material for this chapter: Marti Bombyk, Chuck Kieffer, Stephanie Riger, Rhoda Linton, Beth Reed, and Linda Kaboolian. The members of the Feminist Research Methodology group at the University of Michigan gave the first draft of this chapter a very helpful critical review and Mary Roth Walsh made suggestions for the final one. In addition, Carol Lee Sanchez led me to scholarship by women of color.

women. What is called for to balance the stereotypes is not an overcompensating reaction which would describe women in inflated terms. Instead it is important for social scientists to develop a demystified concept of women as human beings with both strengths and difficulties. Simply put, women do not only *have* problems, they also *solve* them. Similarly, an analysis of the relation between women and community must be balanced between views of women as *providers* of services and women as *consumers* of services.

The negativistic skewing of writing on women prompts the attempt in this chapter to document the "other side of the coin," the contributions rather than the victimization, fears or incompetencies of women. This chapter focuses on women not as people to whom things are done, nor as vicarious hangers-on (Lipmen-Blumen, 1973), but rather as doers in their own right. It offers a view of women as subjects or generators of action, rather than as objects of other people's action (Freire, 1970). Documenting the "other side of the coin" thus extends the taxonomy of the images of women (Warner, 1981).

One way to overcome the negative stereotypes about women (Broverman et al., 1972) is to study their actual behavior in everyday life. Only on the foundation of data about women's actual experiences can a new psychology of women as actors be formulated. This is as important for community psychologists planning social interventions as it is for clinical psychologists planning individual therapy.

This chapter examines women's competence in one specific arena—community building. Factors related to the success of women in management, science, sports, art, or other fields have been examined elsewhere (Barnett and Baruch, 1978; Epstein, 1981; Ruddick and Daniels, 1977; Sicherman and Green, 1980). In addition, only women's activity which is *collective* will be considered, i.e., the group effort of women to enhance the life of a geographic or issue-oriented community.

For the purposes of this chapter, *community-building activities are defined as those actions engaged in by a group of people on their own initiative in order to increase social cohesiveness of unrelated persons or to enhance the opportunities or redress the injustices of persons with whom the group identifies beyond their own family*. This definition encompasses activities labelled either as social change efforts or social service efforts. Such activities are intrinsically neither progressive nor reactionary. They represent an attempt by a group to gain control over their life chances by changing the political environment or directly helping others with whom they identify.

Documentation of women's collective community-building activities answers two of the forementioned critiques. It challenges the stereotype of women as passive, dependent and anxiety-ridden and can serve to inspire rather than demoralize women. In addition, women's collective action should be studied since such action is the only sure way to protect women from inequality and oppression.

When women recognize that they have little control over their lives, they may engage in individual or collective acts to gain control. The decision to marry or to divorce, to return to school or pursue a career, to open a bank account or learn to drive are individual assertive acts in the service of personal autonomy and integrity. *Group* assertiveness, on the other hand, depends on locating others with whom one can share concerns and who will offer support for action (Kieffer, 1981). To the extent that women are isolated from one another and have few support networks, group assertiveness will be minimal. However, when a network develops, women have been known to strike, to create new settings and services, and to protect and make demands on powerful institutions.

This chapter presents cases of women's collective community-building competence in seven domains: (1) union activism, (2) neighborhood activism, (3) political activism, (4) racially based activism, (5) social service voluntarism, (6) self-help group involvement, and (7) peace movement activism. Further documentation is needed to expand this set of categories. The material presented here reflects a deliberate effort to root the discussion of women's collective competence within the full spectrum of social classes, races, ages, and the rural-urban dimension.

UNION ACTIVISM

An important place to begin the documentation of women's collective competence is union participation and union organizing, a phenomenon with a long, but little-known history. Several points in this history are particularly significant: (1) although considered unorganizable by male labor, women have formed unions, organized strikes, and negotiated their demands frequently without the support of men's unions (Feldberg, 1980); (2) the economy and unions have been and continue to be dominated by men who see women as competitors for scarce jobs or good pay; (3) as women increasingly enter the labor force, issues of labor organization will become increasingly salient for them; (4) thus far, women are more likely to develop leadership in predominantly female unions and to be underrepresented in the leadership of mixed-sex unions.

By 1973, 21 percent of the members of all unions were women and 4.7 percent of all union office-holders were women, although there is almost no representation by women in the highest union offices such as the executive board of the AFL-CIO. Women do have leadership roles in the United Farm Workers and the California Homemakers Association, a union of household and attendant care workers.

In order to gain more support for working women, a new organization, the Coalition of Labor Union Women (CLUW), held a founding conference in 1974 which drew 3500 female labor union leaders, far exceeding the organizers' expectations of 800. The organizers of CLUW established four major goals for women in relation to labor. They believed that even though more women than ever are wage earners (40 percent of the labor force are women; 5.5 million women are part of labor unions or employee organizations, Wertheimer, 1979, p. 354), there are new areas in which continued activism is needed: (1) Women's access to jobs through affirmative action and their integration into unions and leadership positions must increase. (2) Legislation must be obtained to improve work conditions and pensions in line with women's needs. (3) Women must be encouraged to participate in the political process so as to better affect legislation. (4) Unorganized working women must be helped to organize so that individual workers will not be at the mercy of employers (Wertheimer, 1979, p. 354).

Because the CLUW founding conference excluded nonunion women who make up almost 90 percent of all working women (Terrano et al., 1976; see Wertheimer, 1980, for a full discussion of CLUW), another organization which permits membership by union and non-union women was formed. Named Union WAGE (Women's Alliance to Gain Equality), its purpose is to fight discrimination on the job, in unions themselves and in society generally.

Contemporary strikes among women include the 21-month strike (1970–1972) in Texas of 200 primarily Chicana workers against Farah clothing factory. "In Northern California, 4000 registered nurses struck 40 hospitals, demanding better patient care" (Terrano et al., 1976, p. 11; see Terrano et al., 1976, pp. 25-26 for other strikes by women including cannery workers, publishing employees, domestics, garment workers, clericals, iron foundry workers, technicians, knitters, miners' wives and women farm workers).

Women dominate the clerical labor force and among those workers, male and female, only 8.2 percent were unionized as of 1977 (Feldberg, 1980, p. 53). Nevertheless, a recent strike by clerical workers at the University of Rhode Island is an example of current activism among women which receives little attention. Their strike resulted in a predominantly female union which successfully negotiated a contract with the university (Sansbury, 1980). The factors used to account for the women's success in this instance were the fact that the employees of this small state knew each other personally, their work allowed them to communicate easily with one another, and they became aware that workers in the parent union were paid so much better than they. The issues which the women struck for were "higher salaries, reclassification according to actual job descriptions, rules concerning 'non-university' work, a daycare center on campus, and recognition of sexism in personnel policy at the university" (Sansbury, 1980, p. 7). This strike challenged the prevalent idea in the parent union and university that women are temporary workers, that they work for "pin money," that they cannot be organized or cannot be union leaders, and that they identify more with their men than with their class.

Workplaces with a predominantly female staff do not automatically satisfy the needs of women workers. At PRETERM, for instance, a Boston clinic which provides gynecological services and counselling in addition to abortion, a lengthy strike of workers in 1976-1977 concerned work speed-ups and the poor service workers claimed they were forced to provide ("We walk the line . . .", 1979). Cases such as this strike demonstrate that women can organize in accordance with their values even at great personal cost and even with the danger of jeopardizing critical services for women.

NEIGHBORHOOD ACTIVISM

The arena of union activity demonstrates that women have been active but have been held back from leadership positions. On the home turf, however, in neighborhood organizations, women hold the majority of leadership roles. This section will focus on the neighborhood as an arena of collective community-building efforts, using examples from the white working-class.

The white working-class consists of people whose income exceeds the poverty level, who perform blue-collar or lower level white-collar work, and who do not have a college education. According to Rubin, the working class consists of approximately "40 million workers—just under half the total work force" (1976, p. 4). They generally earn hourly wages and are very vulnerable to fluctuations in the economy. The working class lives with the insecurity of lapsing into poverty (Rubin, 1976, p. 8, p. 12).

More than half of working-class women work outside the home. Their jobs are clerical, factory, sales and service (see Feree, 1976, p. 434 for specific jobs). Some working-class women choose not to work outside the home, and some have husbands who "won't let them work" so as to avoid being thought of as poor providers. Such women are occupied in full-time housework. Feree (1976) found that working-class women with paid jobs are much more satisfied than those who are full-time homemakers; that part-time workers are more satisfied than full-time workers; and that working-class women stay married in part because their low wages would make it impossible for them to support a family on their own. One of the behavioral consequences of the working-class woman's role as homemaker, poorly paid worker, and upholder of traditional values is her physical confinement to activities around the household and its extensions (school, neighborhood, and church).

There are not many studies of white working-class women (see Howell, 1973; Komarovsky, 1962, Schoenberg, 1980/81; Sennett and Cobb, 1973) from which to glean information about their neighborhood activism. Rubin's is one of the few intensive examinations of both the men and women of the working class and uses in-depth interviews and detailed observation of 50 families. She found that the women tended not to belong to church organizations but to overwhelmingly join the PTA if they had school-aged children. Nevertheless, "only a small minority of them are actively engaged in the organization or even go to a meeting" (Rubin, 1976, p. 201). For both the husbands in unions, and the wives in the PTA, there is a wide gap between belonging and involvement. Rubin found the level of community participation to be latent most of the time but intense sporadically:

here and there a woman is a Camp Fire Girl leader ... belongs to a sewing club ... a proposal to institute a busing plan involves some couples in an anti-busing campaign for a few months; an election very occasionally claims the attention of a man or a women. Active participation in the community and its organizations is rare—almost non-existent—unless, as in the case of the struggle around busing in the schools, an issue arises that is perceived as a threat to the family, its way of life and its values. (1976, p. 202)

Other researchers have discovered that working-class women *are* active in protecting their neighborhoods. A new image of woman—the she-lion fiercely protecting her cubs and turf—emerges from these studies. Siefer studied the relationship of working-class women to the Women's Movement (1973) and to community activism (1976) because in her view the social science literature is out-of-date and biased in its portrayal of working-class women as "passive, dependent and uninvolved in the outside world" (Siefer, 1976, p. 25). Current social changes, she argues, are enabling working-class women to emerge "from traditional roles to bring about change in their communities" (p. 25). In other words, changing times bring out different aspects of women's potential. Siefer claims that the ten American working-class women activists in her study (1976) reflect thousands of such women.

These women had been "fairly traditional housewives" and had become activists, although they did not use that term to label themselves. In fact, one theme of these women's lives is the disjunction between their objective accomplishments and their subjective experience which minimizes accomplishments. Many insisted that they "had absolutely nothing of interest to say ... they seemed to feel that their lives had relatively little significance to anyone but themselves, their families and perhaps a few close friends" (Siefer, 1976, pp. 32-33). Though active, these women had internalized a deprecating self-assessment (Bardwick, 1979), and as working-class people they had internalized a sense of inadequacy vis-a-vis those with education. For example, one Jewish woman in Siefer's study tried to save her ethnically mixed neighborhood from physical devastation when her neighbors panicked because of racial demographic changes and sold their homes. When her group failed, she brought the institutions responsible for the panic to court and then wrote a book about her experiences. Despite her achievements, this type of woman resists attention and thinks what she has done "is natural," a phrase women have learned to use when describing their competence.

The women in Siefer's study (1976) are ethnically diverse married mothers. Their concerns range from Chicano politics, coal-mining politics, sexism in the workplace, union organizing, civil rights, to the women's movement (p. 26). Siefer found that

> *working class women were much more likely to change in response to a problem that affected them directly; in their neighborhood, in their family, and in the workplace. They reacted less to abstract ideas about equality than to concrete problems related to their daily existence. [They were] more likely to become activists on behalf of others facing similar problems than feminists seeking their own personal fulfillment in life. (p. 30)*

Siefer claims that working-class women's activism is rooted in buttressing the neighborhood, whereas middle-class activism is oriented toward abstract ideals or self-fulfillment.

Each of the activists in Siefer's study responded to a different catalyzing event which activated her to form an action group: a "child's illness, [the potential loss of one's] life savings invested in a neighborhood, discrimination on the job, [or] the decision about getting a divorce and starting a new life" (Siefer, 1976, p. 37). In each case this personal motivation broadened into a desire to help others in the same plight. Because these women felt rooted in their locale and had a long history of relations with community members, they became activists on behalf of their community when it was faced with a problem.

In response to the growing emergence of working-class neighborhood activism, a national organization has been formed. Called the "National Congress of Neighborhood Women," this Washington, D.C. based organization is a resource and action center to provide training programs for grass-roots organizers and to examine national priorities and public policies as they affect working-class women. In other cases the effectiveness of a particular neighborhood struggle leads to the establishment of a national organization. Thus after Lois Gibbs helped to create the Love Canal Homeowners Association she went on to set up the (national) Citizens Clearinghouse for Hazardous Wastes, Inc. (Gibbs, 1982).

Another scholar who debunks the myth of working-class women's passivity is McCourt (1977). She believes their portrayal as socially isolated and intrinsically apolitical might have been true in the 1950s when women were more homebound, but is not true now. McCourt sees important changes taking place in the degree to which working-class women act on matters of concern to them as women, family members and neighborhood residents. Although not likely to be self-proclaimed feminists, these women are affected by the general impact of feminism on women's roles. She calls this the transition from the "traditional" working-class to the "modern" working-class. McCourt found that although these women's *behavior* is changing, they continue to *think of themselves* as traditional and to repudiate such symbols of change as child care centers, mental health clinics, drug abuse clinics, and sex education in the schools (p. 35). On the other hand, they do support "assertive community organizations." These neighborhood-based organizations arise to make collective demands on "irresponsible businessmen, unhelpful bureaucrats and self-serving elected officials."

Women are frequently the leaders as well as the "most active and most numerous rank-and-file members" in the "assertive community organizations" of Chicago's Catholic ethnic southwest side (McCourt, 1977, p. 17). They are not only the bodies available for demonstrations but the brains who "make decisions, speak publicly and assume more responsible positions in the organizations" (p. 17). They are "involved, articulate, and visible" (p. 4). These women respond energetically to their sense of eroded control over their neighborhoods, particularly with respect to the quality of their children's schooling and the devaluation of their property. Although their actions are frequently defined by others as racist, they define their actions as neighborhood protection. When community organizing groups promote neighborhood activism, they frequently broaden their initial anti-busing orientation and embrace progressive goals over time.

McCourt's study examines empirically the difference between politically active and politically inactive working-class women in this locale. This research model which makes within-group rather than between-sex comparisons is particularly suitable for the study of women's activities. Both active and inactive women participate in church and school groups. But only those who are active in "assertive community organizations" also belong to local civic organizations, Boy Scouts, the Little League, YWCA, or self-help groups (p. 68). Those who are active are less likely to have a paying job or young children and are more likely to think of themselves as informed and efficacious. Their husbands are likely to support their political analysis and political activity. Most interestingly, women who become active are likely to have received a personal invitation to become involved in the organization which made them feel needed. McCourt asked both the active and inactive women about women's roles as leaders. Almost 90 percent of both groups believe that "women can resolve the problems in the community" (p. 135) and therefore must assume the burdens of doing so. As long as domestic responsibilities remain socially defined as women's responsibility, however, women will be prevented from extensive involvements that take them away from their homes and will be more likely to take up local issues. Thus, it is not surprising to find that women today are active in tenants' groups and single issue neighborhood campaigns, such as reducing dangers to children from inadequate traffic signs (Wilson, 1977). Women are socialized to have more interest in local than in state or national issues (Almond and Verba, 1963). This interest is reinforced by the fact that women know their neighborhoods better than men do because they spend more time there than do men (Markusen, 1980).

Another study of working-class women and their organizations analyzes Tupperware parties (Rapping, 1980) as an institution which builds and reinforces these women's new image of themselves as active and competent. A Tupperware party consists of 15–20 women of a neighborhood network coming together to socialize and to sell plastic food containers. The enormous popularity of these parties is related to the success of "assertive community organizations." Both vehicles break down women's isolation in the home and provide new sources of support. Both are neighborhood-based and extend women's family roles while changing their self-image. Both provide career ladders of increasing responsibility and recognition.

Studies of working-class women's activism conclude that this activism is neighborhood-based and likely to mushroom. A similar conclusion has been reached by people who have formed organizations to support neighborhood activism. For example, the National Training and Information Center (NTIC), a non-profit resource center of the grass-roots neighborhood movement, works to protect the interests of neighborhoods as defined by their residents. A representative of NTIC reports that "probably $\frac{1}{2}$ to $\frac{3}{4}$ of leadership in community organizations are women—from being president to running meetings, negotiating with officials, to raising money and doing the administrative and day to day activities of the organization" (Nielsen, 1981). NTIC was founded in 1972 by Gale Cincotta who is also chairperson of National People's Action, "a national network of community groups composed of approximately 80 percent women" (Camp, 1980, p. 6). The neighborhood issues with which they deal range from getting a fire hydrant fixed, on the one hand, to using the courts to challenge utility rates, insurance policies, unemployment, interest rates, and HUD policies on abandoned houses, on the other.

Cincotta believes women are active in the neighborhood movement because their financial resources are small, while their sense of responsibility for their family's welfare in the community is great. She also sees the neighborhood movement as an avenue for women's potential for leadership. If an organization has a female leader, it is likely that other women will identify with her and be encouraged to act on their own behalf. Journalistic reports on such women can be found in the local media. For example, "The Cleveland Press" recently described a typical local leader, Mrs. Marlane Sedlacek, a nurse, who is battling to have her neighborhood's rights defended. Her group has stopped the showing of x-rated films and compelled an insurance company to write homeowners policies in the area. Her group uses the tactics of having a large number of people appear at a business, office, or home and demand immediate action (Schlesinger, 1981).

The most fundamental objective of neighborhood activism is to protect the welfare of the family-in-the-home-in-the-neighborhood. This basic organizing purpose can be seen in Neighborhood Watches, citizen self-help surveillance networks to prevent crime. These are organized by predominantly female groups with the assistance of the local police. Members agree to be alert for suspicious people and cars in the neighborhood and to watch each other's homes to prevent burglaries. Neighbors meet and choose captains who receive observations from residents and report them directly to the police. The police, in turn, teach residents how to identify their property, lock doors and spot suspicious activity. In addition, warning signs are posted in the neighborhood to deter criminals (Child, 1982, p. C-1). Neighborhood Watches formalize the mutual protection function of neighboring. The outcomes are an increased sense of being cared for and a reduced sense of vulnerability and isolation.

Although neighborhood activism has been discussed in terms of working-class women, the concern for protecting one's neighborhood and improving local services is, of course, not confined to women of any one class. Poor women's activism is epitomized in the welfare rights organization; middle-class women's in the struggle for the ERA and equal pay; and working-class women's in "assertive community organizations" to preserve community life. Nor is women's community-building competence confined to a specific age group.

For example, older women in ethnic urban environments are depended on "to maintain the social networks that sustain community action" (Schoenberg, 1980/81,

p. 259). In one instance older women were "mobilized by the associate pastor of the major church to fight the encroachment on the neighborhood character. Pictures of women in black shawls picketing a pool hall and speaking on television against a drive-in movie were effective deterrents in the local area to changes to which the church objects" (Schoenberg, 1980/81, p. 259). Older black women in St. Louis created organizations to reconstruct the historic meaning of their neighborhood in an effort to save it (Schoenberg, 1980/81, p. 260). Agitators and service volunteers working on behalf of the elderly (e.g., the Grey Panthers) are forming alliances with younger service workers in a new community focused on intergenerational interests.

Women's neighborhood activism frequently combines the felt necessity of confronting a shared problem with the desire to enhance the sense of community through increased social interaction. One example of the ability of friends to mobilize resources to address a specific community need is the remarkable case of the development of a large Health Maintenance Organization. The people who initiated this HMO were four housewives who in 1971 "sat around an Evanston, Illinois kitchen table and engaged in a heated complaint session about their health care situation . . . [Although] none had any experience or training in the health field . . . [all] four had worked together in a variety of self-help projects: neighborhood recreation program development, a neighborhood food cooperative, and a seven-year-old alternative religious community" (Brugliera, 1976, p. 397). In their case, attachment to the community over a considerable period of time allowed them to accumulate skills which could be applied to increasingly complex issues.

In summary, neighborhood activism is a manifestation of the women of all classes and ethnic groups. The focus of this activity is the strengthening and protection of neighborhoods. The organizations developed for these purposes add members by tapping into friendship networks. Sometimes they work with and sometimes against local institutional services. Many of them breed female leaders who are further supported by national organizations. To examine more closely women's community-building competence, this discussion will now broaden the range of settings from neighborhood improvement or defense organizations to political parties.

POLITICAL PARTICIPATION

Political participation is one expression of women's ability to act effectively for the welfare of the community. Women did not have suffrage until 1920 and thus were legally excluded from political life for the first 150 years of this nation's history. Even though Black women were formally enfranchised in 1920, they began to vote in "substantial numbers" (Stucker, 1975, p. 108) only with the passage of the 1965 Voting Rights Act. The voting behavior of Black women continues to change. Prestage (1975) cites Lansing's study of the 1972 elections: although Black women feel less politically efficacious than do Black men or white men and women, their likelihood of voting is increasing at a greater rate than these other groups.

In 1920, 43 percent of eligible women voted; in 1924 only 35 percent did so. There is evidence that men outvoted women by a 2:1 ratio in the initial decade of women's suffrage. By 1968 the ratio had shifted and women outnumbered men at the polls. By 1976 the same proportion of men and women voted, so that 53 percent of the votes were cast by women (Zellman, 1978, p. 339). Changes in women's participation in politics reflect changes in "labor force participation rates, the number of women completing college and a trend toward urbanization" (Bokemeier & Tait, 1980, p. 239).

Anderson (1975) studied women's and men's current campaign participation in terms of an index based on activities such as trying to influence someone else's vote or working for a political party. She found that whereas men have consistently been more politically active than women, by 1972 men's level of campaign participation fell between employed women's which was higher and housewives' which was lower. Anderson calls this change "the political liberation of women" (1975, p. 446), a process that has spread over time from professional and white-collar women to blue-collar women and housewives between the early 1950s to the early 1970s. McCourt's (1977) contention that working-class women are increasing their involvement in politicized organizations is supported by analyses of these changes in women's voting behavior and their participation in other political activities (see Zellman, 1978). The feminism of the middle-class is trickling down so that changes in the working-class' definition of women's rights are also now taking place (see Hartmann, 1982, pp. 387-388; Rubin, 1976).

Although women have been increasingly willing to use the vote, they remain severely underrepresented as elected officials, particularly at the national level. In all professional political roles (party leadership, elected office, appointed office, or policy-making in the federal and state civil service) there are very few women. Since World War II, only 3 percent of persons elected to federal and state legislatures have been women (Krause, 1974; cited in Stucker, 1975). There is some recent evidence of increasing office holding by women, but the rate of change has been labelled "glacial" (Murphy, 1974; cited in Stucker, 1975). Although the absolute number of female office holders is still tiny, especially at the highest level, there is an increase in the percentage of women candidates and elected office-holders at most levels. Women are also entering office at a younger age and are likely to stay in power longer (Zellman, 1978). Zellman cites studies showing a jump in the number of female mayors of the 250 largest U.S. cities from 3 in 1973 to 14 in 1976; and a 78 percent increase in the percentage of women state senators and representatives (1978, pp. 341-342). So too the number of women entering the law profession is increasing, a traditional feeder of candidates for political office (Zellman, 1978, p. 347). The availability of more women candidates, plus the increased reported willingness of women to vote for women candidates for high office, make it likely that in the future women will hold political office in greater numbers than they do now.

In a different vein, women's lack of office-holding does not mean lack of political interest. Rather it has been attributed by some researchers to her voluntarism or community activism which can be alternatives to party politics. In other words, women who want to improve social services or accomplish some form of social change may become directly involved in those services or problems rather than rely on an elective process which they perceive as ineffective or corrupt. One community activist put it this way: "Politicians have a role to play and I have a role to play. If I become a politician, I'll either have to become like the rest of them or stand alone and be isolated" (Schlesinger, 1981, p. B9).

From her work as an educator at a women's community college in Brooklyn, Brightman sees the upsurge in women's neighborhood activism not as the *cause* of the disinterest in party politics but as the *result* of the breakdown of the indigenous political machines. Because of the perceived impotence of the intervening electoral structures (Brightman, 1978, p. 52), some of these women choose to leap-frog from their community organizations directly to the national lobbying level rather than run for political office.

Black women who traditionally have little political power as office holders also resort to "nontraditional avenues" of political participation. Notable among these have been voter leagues and protest activities of nonviolent varieties (Prestage, 1975, p. 84).

The Joint Center of Political Studies publishes a National Roster of Black Elected Officials. It finds that Black men and women comprise less than one-half of one percent of elected officials in the U.S. However, its August 1973 report (Bryce & Warrick, 1973) states that although Black women held only 337 of more than 520,000 elected offices throughout the U.S. in 1973, this figure represents an increase of 160 percent since 1969. Black women are approximately 12 percent of all elected Black officials although there are 1.9 million more Black women than Black men of voting age. About 40 percent of Black female elected officials serve on school boards, whereas only 27 percent of Black male elected officials do so. Black women are more likely to be elected to municipal office than to county, state or federal office. Analysts of white and black women's office-holding concur that their lack of political mobility once in office is related to their lack of tenure and their high rate of turnover. In other words, a real increase in the power of women would require not only an increase in the number of elected officials but in their number of years in office and the level of office to which they are elected.

As women enter the labor market in even greater numbers, they confront problems on the job, such as discrimination in hiring, unequal pay, speed-ups, stretch-outs, dead-ends, and lack of child care and maternity benefits. These issues become sources of political activism through unions, party politics, or lobbying. The combination of increased work outside the home, contact with other people, and confrontation with inequity is predicted to enhance white and black women's political interest and involvement (Anderson, 1975).

Another factor which must be taken into consideration when analyzing women's traditionally meager but currently increasing showing as elected officials is that politics and economics are intertwined. When women acquire "an economic identity separate from but equal to that of their husbands" they will compete vigorously to protect that power through political office (Stucker, 1975, p. 112). In addition, since people need personal funds and access to political coffers in order to launch political campaigns, women will gain access to office when they gain access to wealth (Zellman, 1978, p. 345).

In rural areas women participate less in political affairs than they do in urban areas (Bokemeier & Tait, 1980). Explanations of rural women's traditionally lower level of participation are varied. In rural areas, women have traditional constraints which make it difficult for them to be formal politicians: the lack of child-care, the relative resistance to change, and the lower levels of education in rural as compared to urban areas. One feminist sociologist believes that this picture is distorted because male social scientists have overlooked rural women's actual political activity which does not fit into male-defined concepts of political participation (Lofland, 1975). Instead, with limited access to formal power, rural women increasingly tend to fill the role of informal "power actor." In addition, the trend of increasing political activity among women is characteristic of rural areas just as it is of urban areas because traditional barriers are receding. More than half the rural residents queried in one study believe that the changes in rural women's political involvement stem from the women's movement's impact on attitudes and roles (Bokemeier & Tait, 1980, p. 250).

A recent community study has developed the concept of "power actor," i.e., a person perceived by others as having social power and being able to influence community issues, control resources and legitimize final decisions. This study discovered two types of rural women "power actors." The first is the "good-companion" woman (especially housewives and retired individuals) who assumes leadership in expressive domains (e.g., conservation, human rights, child care, welfare). The second is a "resource woman" who combines the roles of wife and career person and has access to a wide range of resources. Persons who fit this model are younger, more highly educated and more affluent than the "good companion" rural power actors (Bokemeier & Tait, 1980, p. 250).

Another study offers twelve in-depth portraits of rural women (Thomas, 1981) which include an example of collective rural activism. Rural women's activism like that of their urban counterparts, springs from the feeling that one's inviolable space was being encroached upon. For example:

> In 1976, the local power company decided to build the world's highest-voltage power lines across Minnesota, carrying power from the coal fields of North Dakota. The power line follows a curious path, zig-zagging to avoid a major corporate farm area and crossing dozens of family farms instead. Alice and John Tripp became involved with their neighbors in a struggle to stop the power line, and eventually Alice ran for governor of Minnesota in 1978. She ran as a protest candidate and pulled a respectable percentage of the Democratic vote in a heavily Democratic state. (Thomas, 1981, p. 165)

Whereas the League of Women Voters was formed at the time of women's enfranchisement to urge women to use the vote in an informed way, the National Women's Political Caucus (NWPC) was founded approximately 50 years later (1971) to urge women to participate even more fully in politics, especially to run for office. The methods used by the NWPC are to interest and support potential women candidates in campaign techniques and political roles (Zellman, 1978). This grassroots approach broadens the pool of women who could see themselves not only as active supporters of someone else's campaign but suitable candidates in their own right. Women's political competence must be understood thus both as an increasing involvement in traditional electoral politics and the establishment of alternative local strategies for creating change.

BLACK WOMEN'S ACTIVISM

In the preceding section, reference was made to the special barriers to black women's political participation. In contrast, black women's collective action on behalf of their communities is expressed in voluntary associations. Black women's activism on behalf of their own communities is difficult to analyze because, like the social history of women in general and black women in particular, it is not well documented (see Gregory & Browns, 1980; Lerner, 1973; and the bibliography, "Other Reading Sources," 1979). Between the first arrival of Blacks in 1619 and their liberation from slavery nearly 250 years later, there were few opportunities for Blacks to form formal organizations other than churches. These churches had a messianic rather than an activist orientation (Dumas, 1982). Later in the Civil Rights Movement the churches became the nucleus of a social network readily mobilized for protests (Piven & Cloward, 1977/79, p. 20).

In the early 1950s middle-class black women in Montgomery, Alabama formed the Women's Political Council when the League of Women Voters in that city refused to admit blacks. On December 1, 1955, Rosa Parks, a department store seamstress and secretary of the Alabama NAACP, refused to give up her seat on a bus and move to the section of the bus reserved for blacks. Her arrest for violating local segregation ordinances triggered a city-wide bus boycott among blacks that the Women's Political Council had been planning. This collective 381-day action became an important foundation of the Civil Rights Movement. Women played behind-the-scenes roles in civil rights organizations, such as the Southern Christian Leadership Conference, a church-based organization established by Martin Luther King, Jr. in 1957.

Black women were among the students who began sit-ins in various public places in the South from 1960 on. This nonviolent direct action strategy became the guiding philosophy of SNCC (Student Nonviolent Coordinating Committee). They participated in the Freedom Rides by which black and white young people challenged segregated states to accept interstate desegregation rulings. In 1961 Black women united in an organization called "Woman Power Unlimited" which helped white and black Freedom Riders who were in southern jails. Black women and men led the voter registration drives, whose massive effort in "Mississippi Summer" (1964) led to the formation of The Mississippi Freedom Democratic Party which challenged the Democratic Party, sent delegates (who were refused recognition) to the Democratic Party National Convention, and then elected the first black state legislator in a southern state. When the philosophy of nonviolent direct action gave way to the more militant Black Power movement, black women continued to participate.

Within the poor black community, women are heavily involved in informal community activities to support their families on minimal resources. The pattern of women's mutual aid, crucial for the survival of their families and communities (see Gottlieb & Todd, 1979), is largely undocumented. However, Stack's (1974) anthropological study of a poor black section of an American city provides one vivid description and analysis. She uncovers the adaptive responses of women in "mutual aid domestic networks," a system of "claims" and "gifts" within networks of kin, friends, and neighbors which disperses goods and income from AFDC payments and poor paying, unstable jobs. Women manage most of these exchanges. Their competence in doing so determines the level of their families' existence.

The policies of the Welfare Department are a major determinant of the quality of life in poor communities. One adaptive response of women who receive AFDC is to form welfare rights groups. Piven and Cloward (1977/1979), social scientists who actively assisted in the formation of the Welfare Rights movement, characterize the movement as "a rebellion by the poor against circumstances that deprived them of both jobs and income" (p. 265). In their view relief insurgency is the "most authentic expression of the black movement in the post-war period" (p. 265) because it involved such large numbers of people (hundreds of thousands) and the very poorest of the poor (black women). Nevertheless, it has received very little attention in the literature (Piven & Cloward, 1977/1979 have a brief bibliography; see also West, 1981).

The root of the problem leading to the formation of the welfare rights movement was the difficulty poor people had in obtaining welfare payments to which
they were legally entitled. Numerous "disqualifications," the humiliating treatment
by welfare workers, and the cost of visiting the welfare office all stood in the way.
The strategy used to rectify these problems was to enroll every eligible family
(in 1965 this would have doubled the rolls) and to have each family enroll for all
the benefits to which it was entitled. This strategy was intended both to reduce
poverty immediately and to trigger a national fiscal and political crisis which would
lead to the establishment of a guaranteed national income (Piven & Cloward,
1977/1969, p. 276).

Women's local welfare groups began forming in the mid-1960s to obtain special
grants to which they were entitled. In August 1967 the National Welfare Rights
Organization office opened in Washington, D.C. Member groups engaged in demonstrations, marches, and pickets. In addition, welfare rights groups brought formal
grievances, received and offered training in welfare regulations, represented one
another at hearings, and staged group actions "demanding that all grievances be
settled before the group left, with the threat that a sit-in would follow if the
demands were not met" (Piven & Cloward, 1977/1979, p. 297). Group actions
were generally successful. Composed primarily of black women, these groups
were frequently organized by VISTA and other antipoverty workers (Piven &
Cloward, 1977/1979, p. 293). In some cases "friendly caseworkers . . . would come
to group meetings and teach members about their legal rights and entitlements"
(Linton, undated, p. 3). By 1972 NWRO leadership was active in the Democratic
National Convention where it pressed that a national guaranteed income be included in the party platform. Although the dollar amount suggested at the convention was not adopted in the platform, McGovern did campaign on a platform that
included a guaranteed income. By the mid-1970s the movement was in a period of
decline, crushed by its own unwieldy bureaucracy and rapid membership turnover.

Today black women are active in the church and in black mixed-sex organizations. Women comprise 62.5 percent of black church membership (Dumas, 1982)
but are poorly represented in church leadership. For awhile, the Black Panthers
had some strong female leadership and participation and later with the rise of the
feminist movement, some black feminist organizations have formed. Generally,
however, black women have not been very involved in the feminist movement
(Jackson, 1972; King, 1975; Solomon, 1980, p. 333).

In the past decade there have been a few instances in which black women alone,
or black women joining with other women, have designed and implemented new
strategies to build supportive communities as women. For example, when in early
1979 one white and 12 black women were killed in Boston, there seemed to be
surprisingly little "official concern by city agencies [and only] cursory press
coverage" (Combahee River Collective, 1979, p. 41). Many community actions
were undertaken in the affected black area but some of the women felt that the
remedy proposed by black males—that they protect their women—was paternalistic
and inadequate. A black feminist organization, the Combahee River Collective,
formed and wrote a pamphlet which analyzed the situation and proposed solutions.
The widely distributed pamphlet focused on self-help, identifying resources, and
creating new conditions which would free women of fear. In addition, their efforts
led to the formation of the "Coalition for Women's Safety—a coalition of Black,
Hispanic, and white groups working to develop a program for community safety"
(Combahee River Collective, 1979, p. 42).

Another example of black women as community builders is a long-lasting service organization for women with special needs in a poor black community. In the early 1970s a group of women in the Cass Corridor, an area of Detroit populated by minorities and characterized by a high rate of crime, unemployment, deteriorated housing and prostitution, came together to confront problems faced by women and children in their community. The organization they formed—Women's Organization Moving against Alcoholism, Inc. (WOMAN, Inc.)—was to serve substance abusers and their dependents. Three years after its founding opiate-addicted women and volunteers created a nonresidential collective structure in the community and received funding from NIDA. This all-female organization uses a sociopolitical analysis of women's oppression as part of the philosophy of treatment. For example, the client-members choose their treatment plan so that they will feel a greater sense of responsibility for themselves. Emotional support, crisis intervention, advocacy, referral, educational services, medical assistance, health education, and legal aid (see Marsh & Neely, undated) are available as well as child care for staff and client-members. The evaluation report of this program concluded that its success rested largely on the fact that the addicted women wanted to be in a treatment setting where they would be assertive, not dependent (for an evaluation of a similar setting see Gottlieb, 1980, pp. 131–151).

In sum, the activity of black women has been most apparent in terms of direct protest on behalf of their race (e.g., the Civil Rights movement), their locale (e.g., churches, service organizations), or their families (e.g., mutual exchange networks) and less frequently for women as women although activism specifically on behalf of black women is now being mobilized as part of the larger women's movement. There are tensions between identifying with one's age, neighborhood, race, class or gender.

SOCIAL SERVICE VOLUNTARISM

The history of women's achievements in America is in large part a history of their voluntary efforts. Sheila Rothman (1978) surveyed the changing history of the middle- and upper-class white American women ideal from the Civil War to the late 1970s. She found that "to a surprising degree, women's conceptions of their domestic responsibilities have often led them out of the household and into the community" (p. 4). She concluded that women have always felt responsible for more than their families. Thus, the voluntary effort of women in groups is a continuous shaper of American history; only its form has changed in different historical periods.

In 1971 Gold estimated that there were 13 million women volunteers in America and cited an economist who estimated the value of volunteer work in 1965 as 14.2 billion dollars (p. 534). Studies of the rate of participation in voluntary activities find that women belong to somewhat fewer voluntary organizations than do men but spend more hours in those organizations (Deaux, 1976, pp. 109–110). Women's willingness to volunteer has not been shown to correlate with age, marital status, or even with state of health (see below for a discussion of relation of voluntarism and class). Demographic factors are related, however, to the type of organization in which a woman will volunteer. The only group which is under-represented in formal voluntarism is women with pre-school children. Women tend to be particularly involved in groups with recreational, charitable and religious purposes. They are as likely to belong to civil and political organizations as are men (Baker et al., 1980, pp. 143–145). The voluntary organizations to which women currently contribute span the gamut of self-help groups, church/synagogue sisterhoods, political parties, PTA's, ladies' auxiliaries, crisis centers and more.

Federal agencies have been responsive to the grassroots efforts of groups willing to assume responsibility on the local level. For example, the Women's Bureau of the Department of Labor supplies information to women's groups on policies which can be used to mobilize women. By contrast, when issues are identified which affect the lives of women, women are likely to organize on the local level to make their needs known at a higher level. For instance, a new organization, Concerned Wives of Laid Off Workers, recently discussed with the Vice President federal initiatives to restore greater employment ("Concerned Wives . . . ," 1982). Mothers Against Drunk Driving lobby for better laws and heightened parental involvement in their children's behavior.

Working-class women tend to limit their involvement to ethnic voluntary associations, church, school, recreational groups, and neighborhood associations. Broader aimed voluntarism is particularly prevalent among middle- and upper-class women who are well-educated. McCourt (1977) believes voluntarism is available to the middle class because they can afford household help, babysitters, and second cars for transportation to the site. In addition, these women have the self-confidence to function in organizations that comes from education. Schoenberg (1980/81) reports a study of middle-class women and voluntarism which found that these women seek service- and family-oriented organizations in which to volunteer in order to enhance the functioning of their own family. Surprisingly, with increased work outside the home, their voluntarism and their neighboring increase.

Affluent women were the predecessors of the social service professions, such as nursing and social work, "but the development of government agencies and professional social workers has altered the nature of volunteer work, forcing affluent women into different activities, largely cultural" (Bolger, 1975, p. 72). Today's upper-class women and their activities are rarely studied, perhaps because they are inaccessible or invisible to middle-class researchers. One study of upper-class women, based on in-depth interviews of 38 women (Ostrander, 1980) reveals the specific nature of their voluntarism and the relation between their voluntary activities and other aspects of their lives. Ostrander shows that the purpose of their volunteer work is to maintain the class structure (and their position in it), prevent social change, further their husbands' careers and ensure the transmission of their values to their children. These women eschew paid work and devote their energies toward maintaining their families' "place." Their motivation in community work is class interest and control, verbalized in terms of "noblesse oblige." The hard-working members of boards of universities, museums, hospitals, orchestras and banks in Ostrander's sample use their money to raise more money and to keep people of other social classes out of positions of organizational decision-making.

Private upper-class volunteerism thus functions to maintain the elite control over matters of public concern. This elite control is defined by upper-class women themselves as an effective holding action against socialism, as an ideological support to American capitalism . . . A woman, from a nationally prominent business and industrial family, when asked how she saw her responsibility to the community as a board member replied: "It's important to keep things from going too far to the left politically. That's our job." (Ostrander, 1980, p. 33)

Currently there is an increasing interest in the subject of women's voluntarism (see Daniels, forthcoming; Gold, 1971, 1981; and Smith & Macauley, 1980) because of the contradictions inherent in it for women. Although it is a commonplace that women have been and are active as volunteers, this effort is often denigrated as trivial do-goodism, as the band-aid that actually harms because it leaves the root of the problem untouched. Thus: ". . . voluntarism is being used as a placebo or crash program to combat current fiascos of poverty, welfare, crime and health" (Gold, 1971, p. 537). Women's voluntarism is also interpreted as a sign of their weakness rather than their strength: it is an avoidance of the "hedonistic" pleasures of real work (p. 540), a sign of their being "lonely and empty" (p. 541), pseudowork, a sign of psychological weakness (p. 542), an unconscious desire to appear innocuous and uncontentious (p. 542), an avoidance of competition with men, a way of being more interesting to their husbands (p. 544), a form of "occupational therapy" (p. 545), extraneous (p. 547). The crux of the controversy is whether voluntarism should be interpreted as evidence of women's competence or as evidence of women's fears and exploitation.

The boundaries between voluntarism as social service and as social change are indistinct. For example, in 1966, the National Organization for Women (NOW) was formed as a voluntary organization to draw the nation's attention to the inequality between the sexes and to motivate women who were isolated in their homes to broaden their concerns and become active on their own behalf. NOW members engage in political activism but have also established an array of service settings such as shelters for battered women. NOW and other feminist organizations have helped to create a new definition of womanhood, a definition upheld even indirectly by women with anti-feminist views who in their attack against the ERA or abortion rights are nevertheless politically active as women.

NOW task forces have been particularly useful in guiding the voluntary efforts of women into arenas where action is needed to improve the quality of women's lives. For example, task forces have been established on older women and on displaced homemakers, which have spurred local groups to conduct their own investigations as a prelude to action.

The newly emerging definition of womanhood, according to Rothman, is "active, energetic, fully competent, and capable of self-definition as a person in sexual and in social terms" (1978, p. 242). This new definition competes with the widely accepted stereotype of women as dependent, subjective, passive, noncompetitive, unadventurous, self-doubting, and unambitious (Deaux, 1976, p. 13).

The stereotype of women as apolitical, powerless and passive is increasingly misleading as documentation becomes available about services created by women for women. For example, the major concerns of the women's movement have been defined as equal pay, readily available abortion and contraception, equality of education and job opportunity, child care facilities, legal and financial independence, and an end to discrimination against lesbians (Wilson, 1977). Each of these demands has necessitated the creation of sustained political activity and the development of new service settings (see Mayo, 1977). To cite one case, interest in making abortion and contraception accessible led a Chicago group to form an organization named JANE in 1969. JANE was first a phone number and then a physical center where women could obtain counselling and referrals. Eventually members of JANE performed 12,000 abortions (Parsons, 1979).

Educational efforts on behalf of empowering women with regard to their bodies were carried out by the collective that produced the bestselling *Our Bodies, Ourselves* (Boston Women's Health Book Collective, 1971, 1973, 1976). An entirely new women's health movement has formed which encourages women to examine themselves systematically, to demand humane, woman-centered health services, and to be well informed. From this set of values have emerged new settings—women's health centers, the self-help health movement, and retraining programs for health-related professionals (Gottlieb, 1980). In the health care area, the emerging values of women's alternative services include: easy access, consumer participation, egalitarianism, interdisciplinary team approach, attention to ethnic minority concerns, and enhancing community awareness of women's health issues.

Women are active in setting up local child care facilities (from cooperative day care to parent support hotlines) because changing family conditions—increase in the number of dual-career families, increase in the number of single-parent families—have created new demands on women. Women today head 15 percent of all American households. In New York City more than 35 percent of all families are single women or headed by women.

Women identifying with the needs of other women have fought against the problem of violence against women by the creation of Rape Crisis Centers and Shelters for Battered Wives (see Masi, 1981, for other organizations created by women).

Gottlieb's (1980) compilation of new services for women indicates that notwithstanding the recession and government cutbacks, a wide array of women are initiating programs throughout the country. Women are defining new service needs, new target groups and new service strategies. These service organizations founded by women usually combine advocacy, education, skill development, and social support supplemented at times by conventional professional therapeutic approaches. Evaluation studies have underscored the effectiveness of "all-women treatment groups and women staff in [terms of the] percentage of women who complete treatment programs" (Gottlieb, 1980, p. 165).

The effectiveness of these feminist-oriented services is all the more remarkable given the fact that they are such recent creations, had little financial backing, encountered much community resistance, and did not have professional staff. For example, the first shelter for abused women in the U.S., Rainbow Retreat, was established in Phoenix, Arizona, as late as November 1973. Since then these retreats have mushroomed all over the country, started by "small groups of dedicated women, often women who themselves had once been victims of abuse" (Gottlieb, 1980, p. 206).

New feminist community competence extends beyond the social service arena into cultural activities, the

> *new urban phenomenon . . . of women's spaces—women's buildings, coffee shops, bookstores, bars, restaurants—which represent an attempt by the women's community to provide an alternative but protected public environment for women . . . This is exemplified by the Los Angeles Woman's Building which has grown from a small group of feminist artists meeting together to a public center for women's culture serving the whole metropolitan area. Just as coffee shops and pubs were important as gathering places and sources of information to men in the eighteenth century, today women's spaces and services are vital in providing opportunities for the geographically scattered women's community to meet, socialize, exchange new ideas, and to move out of the restricted space of the home. (Wekerle, 1980, p. S196)*

A related "spatial" activity of women—squatting—is a collective response to their housing problem. Throughout the world, "groups of women squat in unused property" and thereby "expose the inequities of the housing system and try to initiate new forms of collective living" (Wilson, 1977, p. 2). Architectural constraints may frustrate women's desires to live collectively. Women were successful in a community organizing effort to overturn these ordinances in the Soho section of New York (Markusen, 1980). Ettore (1978) describes lesbian ghettos in Britain, created as a result of women squatting and setting up collectivized households.

Feminist activism has challenged the legality of barring girls from sports leagues and the inequitable opportunities for women in athletics. Beginning with support groups and evolving into new settings, they have modified publishing policies with regard to sexist language and imagery in books. They have established their own conferences, publishing houses, magazines, journals, newsletters and information exchanges in order to make an impact on women's self-image. New challenges, barely begun, are to provide services to lesbian mothers, post-institutionalized women, child-free women, prostitutes, and other groups of women. At the same time, older achievements, like Medicare funding for abortions, require continued political activation, since competing groups are attempting to overturn former judicial decisions. These activities reflect women's self definition as competent actors.

SELF–HELP GROUP INVOLVEMENT

Self-help and support groups are groups in which people agree to meet regularly to share their common problems and to help each other solve those problems, usually without the involvement of professionals. These groups are effective because emotional support, information, and relationships are provided at low cost, there is not much stigma for participating, and the mutual assistance is offered in language everyone understands. Self-help groups in contrast with support groups are usually more formally organized, do not draw their membership only from friendship networks, and are affiliated with national or state networks.

The support or self-help movement is another arena of cooperative ventures engaged in by women which demonstrates their collective community-building competence. There are so many types of self-help groups that one can safely state that there is probably a self-help group for every imaginable social, psychological or medical problem. Tracy and Gussow (1976) suggest that there is an evolutionary development within self-help groups, a tendency to evolve from an organization primarily concerned with supporting its own members to an organization primarily concerned with legislative change.

In his study of self-help groups, Levy (1976) observed that generally membership is predominantly or exclusively female, except in certain groups such as Alcoholics Anonymous. He attributes the reluctance of men to participate in self-help groups to their culturally induced inability "to publicly admit their need for help" coupled with their possible belief that self-help groups are less likely to be effective in meeting their needs (Levy, 1976, p. 315).

Women are not only more likely to participate in self-help groups open to both sexes (e.g., Parents Without Partners), they have also been active in forming and sustaining self-help groups for the various phases of most women's lives (e.g., La Leche League for breastfeeding women, Silverman & Murrow, 1976; or the widow-to-widow program, see Silverman, 1969).

These groups reflect women's ability to form successful organizations, to be active in solving their problems, and to have wider social impact. These groups both provide assistance to their members and affect professional practice, organizations, and policy. As a case in point, the State of Michigan Department of Mental Health's Women's Task Force formally recommends that women be diverted from mental health services to self-help or support groups because "such groups have been found to be especially helpful to women experiencing stressful life events (i.e., aging, raising of a handicapped or chronically ill child, pregnancy, divorce, etc.) . . . Evidence has accumulated that for many [women, self-help groups] are at least as effective as traditional one-on-one interventions" (Michigan Department of Mental Health, 1982, pp. 2–3; see also Borman, 1982). This Task Force applauds the achievements of the following exemplary groups: Stress Management for AFDC Women (to improve their sense of competence), a group for incest victims, a widow-to-widow group, a divorce adjustment program, a women in transition program, and incest family treatment, among others. In the context of this chapter it should be noted that these groups represent not only *effective help for* the members but competent *helping by* the members.

PEACE MOVEMENTS: BUILDING THE WORLD COMMUNITY

Just as women's voluntarism in their local community can be interpreted as an extension of nurturing the family, women's efforts on behalf of peace can be seen as yet a further extension. In 1915, hundreds of women representing national women's associations assembled in Washington, D.C. for a peace conference and formed the Women's Peace Party with Jane Addams, the founder of Hull House, as president. The organization was dedicated to the abolition of war and argued that women "as the mother half of humanity . . . be given a share in deciding between war and peace in all the courts of high debate . . ." (Sochen, 1971, p. 62). After the vote was acquired in 1920, many suffragists chose to work for peace.

"Arguing that war-making was a male pursuit, many women joined the Women's International League for Peace and Freedom. WILPF was instrumental in getting national governments to organize and attend disarmament and peace conferences after World War I" (Baker et al., 1980, p. 21). In 1946, Emily Greene Balch, founder of WILPF, won the Nobel Peace Prize (Altbach, 1974, p. 185).

In the 1950s, women's peace groups took up the issue of the danger of nuclear testing and the desirability of nuclear disarmament. The Women's Strike for Peace appeared on November 1, 1961 when 50,000 housewives and mothers held a wide variety of demonstrations in 60 American communities to warn against nuclear war. This showing is all the more impressive since there was no organization calling its members to action. Rather, a small group of women simply called their acquaintances who called others, and a far-reaching network was mobilized. From these beginnings, WSP became an international network and participated in an 18-nation disarmament conference in 1962 (Decter, 1963, in Sochen, 1971). WSP is still a network with no dues or formal membership. They have organized a milk boycott, protested nuclear testing in Nevada, organized an annual exchange with the Soviet Women's Committee, met clandestinely in Djakarta in 1965 with Vietnamese women thus opening "communications between American POW's and their families" (Williams, 1981/82, p. 19), initiated draft counseling, and consistently protested the Vietnam War by renting billboards which listed body counts.

Another Mother for Peace was a women's anti-war movement during the Vietnam War era.

Women's collective peace related efforts include the organizing of survivors of the Hiroshima and Nagasaki A-bomb attacks. Ironically, male survivors of the bombings formed groups to deal with their medical, emotional, social and economic problems, but excluded women. In 1967, the women began their own organization to locate survivors, offer personal counseling, disseminate information about medical and other benefits, carry out a memoir writing project, collect data on victims, and participate in the international struggle for peace (Bruin & Salaff, 1981). The 1981 Women's Pentagon Action which involved 3500 women, illustrates the power of unusual methods women use when struggling for peace together (Linton & Whitham, 1982). The nuclear freeze movement is becoming widely recognized as successfully drawing on women's organizing activities (see *Women's Studies International Quarterly*, 1981; *Off Our Backs*, 1982).

IMPLICATIONS FOR RESEARCH AND ACTION

This review of women's group assertiveness in solving or preventing community problems has drawn on historic and contemporary materials about diverse women in order to give a sense of the ubiquity of women's activism. The purpose has been to challenge the stereotype of female passivity and to counter-balance the research focus on women's oppression. The task of locating materials proved arduous because women's community-building accomplishments have not been a subject for sustained research. New materials are being developed, however, through various school and community-based participatory projects in which women document their own activism or that of others (see Cantarow, 1980; Jenkins, 1978).

The women's movement has drawn attention to the need to enhance women's sense of competence. Although there are socially structured barriers to women's acknowledgement of their competence, interventions can be designed that do not require massive social change. One strategy is to provide technical assistance. For example, a new federal agency AWED, American Women's Economic Development Corporation, is an organization to assist businesswomen trying to succeed on their own (Masi, 1981, p. 72). Consciousness-raising small group discussions enhance personal clarification and the willingness to take risks. Support groups around particular issues or life changes enable women to convert their previously perceived "problem" into a new avenue of competence. Career-planning, assertiveness training, and other forms of training support women's desire to be active. In addition, the purpose of feminist therapy is to help women feel they can be effective (Barrett, 1981).

Applied psychologists can assist women's recognition of their collective competence by disseminating models of such competence, offering organizational consultation (Grady, 1981), research consultation (e.g. collecting baseline data and evaluating action plans), helping to create interorganizational linkages, and generating funds.

In addition to action research, basic research is needed to understand women's group competence. For example, McCourt's (1977) comparative analysis of activist and non-activist working-class women clarifies the conditions under which particular women will feel capable of accepting leadership in assertive community organizations. Leghorn and Parker's (1981) cross-cultural study found that the degree of women's activity covaries with societal values and structures. Most significantly, they found that the degree of women's safety, freedom and power in a given society depends on women's opportunity to form networks.

When women are isolated from one another psychologically (Friedan, 1976) or economically (Stack, 1974), they are vulnerable and their energies are sapped by trying to remain unharmed and deal with the demands of others to be nurtured. By bringing such women together, networking organizations (such as Displaced Homemakers Network, Inc.) teach them new skills, improve their self-image, and lobby to change the root of their problems.

Women's efforts to build responsive community settings rely heavily on networking. PTA's (Parent Teacher Associations), auxiliary groups, and church groups are *networks for community cohesion.* Women's employment agencies (e.g., Denver-based Better Jobs for Women and Washington, D.C.'s Wider Opportunities for Women), shelters for battered women, rape crisis centers, and other refuges from violence are *networks for confronting the status quo* and nurturing members. Networks as well as formal organizations are women's vehicle for action and protection.

We have seen that women create networks as women, mothers, neighborhood residents, and even world citizens. Every role that women occupy has been a grounds for activity, activism, and competence. There is thus a discrepancy between the image of women as passive and the evidence of their activity. This discrepancy is an unfortunate barrier to women's self-understanding and continued development.

REFERENCES

Almond, G. & Verba, S. *The civic culture.* Princeton: Princeton University Press, 1963.

Altbach, E. H. *Women in America.* Lexington, Mass.: D.C. Heath and Co., 1974.

Anderson, K. Working women and political participation, 1952–1972. *American Journal of Political Science,* 1975, *19*(3), 439–453.

Baker, M., Berheide, C., Greckel, F., Gugin, L., Lipetz, M., & Segal, M. *Women today.* Monterey, CA: Brooks/Cole, 1980.

Barnett, R. C. & Baruch, G. K. *The competent woman.* NY: Irvington, 1978.

Barrett, S. *Making empowerment useful.* Paper presented at the Eighth Annual Meeting of the Association of Women in Psychology, Boston, Massachusetts, March 1981.

Bokemeier, J. & Tait, J. Women as power actors: A comparative study of rural communities. *Rural Sociology,* 1980, *45*(2), 238–355.

Bolger, E. Take it out of my salary: Volunteers on the prestige circuit. *Ms.,* February 1975, 70–74.

Borman, L. Introduction to special issue . . . : Self-help as a service delivery strategy. *Prevention in the Human Services,* 1982, *1*, 3–15.

Boston Women's Health Book Collective. *Our Bodies, Ourselves.* New York: Simon & Schuster, 1971, 1973, 1976.

Broverman, I. K., Broverman, D. M., Clarkson, F. E., & Rosenkrantz, P. S. Sex-role stereotypes: A current appraisal. *Journal of Social Issues,* 1972, *28*(2), 59–78.

Brugliera, M. The self-help roots of Northcare. *Journal of Applied Behavioral Science,* 1976, *12*(3), 397–403.

Bruin, J. & Salaff, S. Never again: The organization of women atomic bomb victims in Osaka. *Feminist Studies,* Spring 1981, *7*(1), 5–18.

Bryce, H. J. & Warrick, A. E. Black women in electoral politics. *Focus,* August 1973.

Camp, M. B. Women in NPA: The neighborhood movement. *What she wants.* Cleveland, Ohio: The Cleveland Press, December 1980, pp. 6–9.

Cantarow, S. *Moving the mountain.* Old Westbury, NY: The Feminist Press, 1980.

Child C. They keep eyes on suspicious cars and people to stop crime. *The Ann Arbor News,* Sunday, February 14, 1982, C-1.

Combahee River Collective. Why did they die? A document of Black feminism. *Radical America*, November/December 1979, *13*(6), 41–50.

Concerned wives of laid off workers. *The Ann Arbor News*, Thursday, February 25, 1982.

Daniels, A. K. *Invisible careers: Women's work in the volunteer world*. In press.

Deaux, K. *The behavior of men and women*. Belmont, CA: Brooks/Cole, 1976.

Decter, M. The peace ladies. *Minneapolis Star and Tribune*, 1963. Reprinted in J. Sochen (ed.), *The new feminism in twentieth-century America*. Lexington, Mass.: D.C. Heath, 1971, pp. 120–132.

Dumas, R. Dilemmas of black women leaders. Lecture delivered at the University of Michigan, February 20, 1982.

Ehrlich, C. *The conditions of feminist research*. Baltimore, MD: Research Group One, Report No. 21, February 1976, 1–19.

Epstein, C. F. *Women in law*. NY: Basic Books, 1981.

Ettore, E. M. Women, urban social movements, and the lesbian ghetto. *International Journal of Urban and Regional Research*, October 1978, *2*(3), 499–520.

Feldberg, R. L. "Union fever": Organizing among clerical workers, 1900–1930. *Radical America*, May-June 1980, *14*(3), 52–67.

Ferree, M. Working class jobs: Housework and paid work as sources of satisfaction. *Social Problems*, April 1976, *23*(4), 431–441.

Freeman, J. The women's liberation movement: Its origins, organizations, activities and ideas. In J. Freeman (ed.), *Women: A feminist perspective*. Palo Alto, CA: Mayfield, 1975, 2nd ed., 1979, 557–574.

Freire, P. *Pedagogy of the oppressed*. NY: Seabury, 1970.

Friedan, B. *It changed my life: Writings on the women's movement*. NY: Random House, 1976.

Gibbs, L. *Love Canal: My story*. Albany, NY: SUNY Press, 1982.

Gold, D. Women and voluntarism. In V. Gornick and B. Moran (eds.), *Women in sexist society*. NY: Basic Books, 1971, pp. 533–554.

Gold, D. *Opposition to volunteerism: An annotated bibliography*. Chicago, IL: CPL Bibliographies, 1313 E. 60th Street, 60637, 1981.

Gottlieb, B. H. & Todd, D. M. Characterizing and promoting social support in natural settings. In R. Munoz, L. Snowden, and J. Kelly (eds.), *Social and psychological research in community settings*. San Francisco, CA: Jossey-Bass, 1979.

Gottlieb, N. (ed.) *Alternative social services for women*. NY: Columbia University Press, 1980.

Grady, K. *Working as a feminist community psychologist*. Paper presented at the Eighth Annual Meeting of the Association of Women in Psychology, Boston, Massachusetts, March 1981.

Gregory, C. E. & Browne, V. Black activists. *Heresies*, 1980, *3*(1.9), 14–17.

Hartmann, H. The family as locus of gender, class and political struggle: The example of housework. *Signs: Journal of Women in Culture and Society*, 1982, *6*(3), 366–394.

Howell, J. T. *Hard living on Clay Street*. Garden City, NY: Anchor Books, 1973.

Jackson, J. Black women in racist society. In C. Willie, B. Kramer, and B. Brown (eds.), *Racism and mental health*. Pittsburgh, PA: University of Pittsburgh Press, 1972.

Jenkins, S. *Past present: Recording life stories of older people*. Washington, D.C.: National Council on Aging, 1978.

Kieffer, C. *The emergence of empowerment: The development of participatory competence among individuals in citizen organizations*. Unpublished doctoral dissertation, University of Michigan, 1981.

King, M. Oppression and power: The unique status of the black woman in the American political system. *Social Science Quarterly*, 1975, *56*, 116–128.

Komarovsky, M. *Blue-collar marriage*. NY: Vintage, 1962.

Krause, W. Political implications of gender roles: A review of the literature. *American Political Science Review*, December 1974, *68*, 1706–1723.

Leghorn, L. & Parker, K. *Woman's worth: Sexual economics and the world of women*. Boston: Routledge & Keagan Paul, 1981.

Lerner, G. *Black women in white America*. NY: Random House, 1973.

Levy, L. Self-help groups: Types and psychological processes. *Journal of Applied Behavioral Science*, 1976, *12*(3), 310–322.

Linton, R. *Brooklyn Welfare Action Council: Council model*. Unpublished manuscript, undated. (Available from author.)

Linton, R. & Whitham, M. The 1981 women's Pentagon action: One woman's experience, one woman's response. *Socialist Review*, June 1982.

Lipmen-Blumen, J. The vicarious achievement ethic and nontraditional roles for women. Unpublished manuscript, 1973. (Cited in L. K. Epstein (ed.), *Women in the professions.* Lexington, Mass.: Lexington Books, 1975.)

Lofland, L. The "thereness" of women: A selective review of urban sociology. *Sociological Inquiry*, August 1975, *45*, 2–3. (In M. Millman & R. M. Kanter (eds.), *Another voice: Feminist perspectives on social life and social science.* NY: Doubleday, 1975, pp. 144–170.)

Markson, E. & Hess, B. Older women in the city. In C. Stimpson, E. Dixler, M. Nelson, & K. Yatrakis (eds.), *Women and the American city.* Chicago: University of Chicago Press, 1980/1981.

Markusen, A. City spatial structure, women's household work, and national urban policy. *Signs: Journal of Women in Culture and Society*, 1980, *5*(4), S23–S44.

Marsh, J. & Neely, B. *Women helping women: The W.O.M.A.N. Center evaluation report, year three.* University of Michigan, undated.

Masi, D. *Organizing for women: Issues, strategies and services.* Lexington, Mass.: Lexington Books, 1981.

Mayo, M. (ed.) *Women in the community.* London: Routledge & Kegan Paul, 1977.

McCourt, K. *Working-class women and grass-roots politics.* Bloomington, Indiana: Indiana University Press, 1977.

Michigan Department of Mental Health, Women's Task Force. *For better or for worse? Women and the mental health system.* 1982.

Murphy, I. L. *Public policy and the status of women.* Boston: Lexington/Heath, 1974.

Nielsen, K. National Training and Information Center. Personal communication, December 14, 1981.

Off Our Backs, special issue, 1982, *12*(7).

Ostrander, S. A. Upper class women: The feminine side of privilege. *Qualitative Sociology*, 1980, *3*(1), 23–44.

Other reading sources. *Heresies*, 1979, *4*(2), 124–125.

Parsons, K. P. Moral revolution, In J. Sherman and E. Beck (eds.), *The prism of sex.* Madison, WI: University of Wisconsin Press, 1979, pp. 189–227.

Piven, F. F. & Cloward, R. A. *Poor people's movements.* NY: Vintage, 1977/1979.

Prestage, J. Black women officeholders: The case of state legislators. In L. K. Epstein (ed.), *Women in the professions.* Lexington, Mass.: Lexington Books, 1975.

Rapping, E. Tupperware and women. *Radical America*, November/December 1980, *14*(6), 39–49.

Rothman, S. M. *Woman's proper place: A history of changing ideals and practices, 1870 to the present.* NY: Basic Books, 1978.

Rubin, L. *Worlds of pain: Life in the working-class family.* NY: Basic Books, 1976.

Ruddick, S. & Daniels, P. (eds.) *Working it out: 23 women writers, artists, scientists, and scholars talk about their lives and work.* NY: Pantheon, 1977.

Sansbury, G. G. Now, what's the matter with you girls? Clerical workers organize. *Radical America*, November/December 1980, *14*(6), 67–75.

Schlesinger, R. 2-fisted ladies. Cleveland Press, 1981, *4(22)* sec. B, 1.

Schoenberg, S. P. Some trends in community participation of women in their neighborhoods. In C. Stimpson, E. Dixler, M. Nelson, & K. Yatrakis (eds.), *Women and the American city.* Chicago: University of Chicago Press, 1980/1981, pp. 258–265.

Sennett, R. & Cobb, J. *The hidden injuries of class.* NY: Vintage Books, 1973.

Sicherman, B. & Green, C. H. *Notable American women.* Cambridge, Mass.: Belknap Press of Harvard, 1980.

Siefer, N. *Absent from the majority.* NY: American Jewish Committee, 1973.

Siefer, N. *Nobody speaks for me: Self-portraits of American working class women.* NY: Simon & Schuster, 1976.

Silverman, P. R. The widow-to-widow program. *Mental Hygiene*, 1969, *53*, 333–337.

Silverman, P. R. & Murrow, H. G. Mutual help during critical role transitions. *Journal of Applied Behavioral Science*, 1976, *12*(3), 410–418.

Smith, D. H., Macaulay, J., & Associates. *Participation in social and political activities.* San Francisco, CA: Jossey-Bass, 1980.

Sochen, J. (ed.) *The new feminism in twentieth-century America.* Lexington, Mass.: D.C. Heath and Co., 1971.

Solomon, B. Alternative social services and the black woman. In N. Gottlieb (ed.), *Alternative social services for women.* NY: Columbia University Press, 1980, pp. 333–340.

Stack, C. *All our kin: Strategies of survival in a black community.* NY: Harper & Row, 1974.

Stucker, J. J. Women as voters: Their maturation as political persons in American society. In L. K. Epstein (ed.), *Women in the professions.* Lexington, Mass.: Lexington Books, 1975, pp. 97–113.

Terrano, A., Dignan, M., & Holmes, M. *Working women for freedom.* Women's Liberation News and Letters Committees, 1976, 2832 East Grand Blvd., No. 316, Detroit, MI 48211.

Thomas, S. *We didn't have much, but we sure had plenty: Stories of rural women.* Garden City, NY: Anchor, 1981.

Tracy, G. S. & Gussow, Z. Self-help groups: A grass-roots response to a need for services. *Journal of Applied Behavioral Science*, 1976, *12*(3), 381–396.

We walk the line: The struggle at Preterm. *Radical America*, 1979, *13*(2), 9–24.

Warner, M. *Joan of Arc: The image of female heroism.* NY: Vintage, 1981.

Wekerle, G. Women in the urban environment. In C. Stimpson, E. Dixler, M. Nelson, and K. Yatrakis (eds.), *Women and the American city.* Chicago: University of Chicago Press, 1980/1981, pp. 185–211.

Wertheimer, B. M. "Union is power": Sketches from women's labor history. In J. Freeman (ed.), *Women: A feminist perspective.* Palo Alto, CA: Mayfield, 1979.

West, G. *The NWRO movement: The social protest of poor women.* NY: Praeger, 1981.

Williams, S. The women's crusade. *In These Times*, December 23, 1981–January 12, 1982, p. 19.

Wilson, E. Women in the community. In M. Mayo (ed.), *Women in the community.* London: Routledge & Kegan Paul, 1977.

Women's Studies International Quarterly, special issue, 1981, *4*(1).

Zellman, G. Prejudice and discrimination. In I. H. Frieze, J. E. Parsons, P. B. Johnson, D. N. Ruble, and G. L. Zellman (eds.), *Women and sex roles: A social psychological perspective.* NY: W. W. Norton & Co., 1978, pp. 279–300.

3

Mothering and the Young Child

Darwin Dorr
Highland Hospital

Lisa Friedenberg
University of North Carolina at Asheville

The aim of this chapter is to sensitize the reader to the specific emotional-developmental challenges faced by mother and child during the child's first three years of life. These tasks, which revolve around the attachment between mother and child, lay the foundation for the child's emerging sense of self and the mother's emerging sense of "motherhood." We chose to focus on this phenomenon because the process of mother-child bonding and separating are such powerful influences on the emotional development of both persons. We selected modern *object relations theory* as a conceptual framework within which to analyze these tasks. In view of the social and preventive orientation of this volume, our choice of a psychodynamic model may strike some readers as unusual. However, even if one has a strong social perspective, a thorough assessment of the challenge of mothering must consider issues of intrapersonal cognitive and emotional development. An understanding of intrapsychic structure and function may augment our understanding of the development of interpersonal relatedness and, thus, may direct our social interventions. We will, therefore, integrate issues of intra-individual development with the role of environmental factors in our assessment of the challenge of mothering the young child.

Because many readers of this volume may not be familiar with object relations theory, we will first briefly summarize its basic elements. We will then attempt to describe the emotional and psychological challenges posed to mother and child in a social context. We will conclude with a brief discussion of some of the implications of this analysis of mothering for prevention and social interventions.

OBJECT RELATIONS THEORY

Although modern object relations theory is a direct linear descendant of classical psychoanalysis, it clearly reflects the "brighter" touch of the neoanalysts and ego-analysts such as Hartmann (1939, 1952). Object relations theory is inherently social in nature. Finally, object relations theory reflects the work of developmental psychiatrists and psychologists, including Mahler et al. (1963, 1965, 1968, 1975), Spitz (1965), Bowlby (1969, 1973, 1980), Goldfarb (1945), and Piaget (1952, 1960). In this chapter, we do not seek to advocate object relations theory as the only heuristic device for understanding mothering. However, because of its rich empirical-theoretical heritage, it provides a very useful theoretical framework for understanding this highly complex process.

The core element of object relations theory is the concept of the internalized representations of self and other, the "objects." An internalized representation of an object is an emotionally laden image of all or part of a psychologically significant person, such as mother, father, self. Healthy persons have relatively accurate internalized representations of self and others, including both good and bad elements. Poorly adjusted persons usually have very distorted or convoluted representations of self and others. The image of self may be fragmented. Good and bad elements of the self may be split apart, and much emotional energy may be devoted to maintaining the split or to attempting to artificially meld disparate elements of the self.

These internalized representations may be understood to be images, or perhaps more accurately as intrapsychic structures, much like Piaget's concept of schemas. However, object relations theory is a psychodynamic theory. Thus, these internalized images or representational structures are said to be invested with emotional energy. For example, a child's internalized representation of mother may be interpreted to be invested with good "libidinal" or bad "aggressive" energy. These accurate or inaccurate emotionally laden cognitive structures determine the way in which the meaning of the world is revealed to the developing child, and thus provide a filter or a basis for determining the meaning of self, others, and interpersonal relationships.

Internalized object representations become important in the study of mothering. First, the mother's own internalized object representations affect her views of herself and others, including her child. This in turn will affect the ways in which she interacts with her child, and thus affect the child's developing representations, which will later influence his or her self-view and interpersonal relationships. One can easily imagine, then, a cycle of "healthy mothering," in which a mother with accurate representations of self and others rears a child with similarly healthy representations. Conversely, one may observe a cycle of "dysfunctional mothering," in which a mother with distorted representations of self and others sets the stage for similar distortions in her child.

In order to better understand how object relations theory contributes to our understanding of motherhood and mothering, we must chart the course of development of these internalized representations. As object relations theory is a psychodynamic theory, it is also a stage theory. There are several conceptualizations regarding the way in which object representations develop in the young child. Notable examples are those by Mahler (1968), Kernberg (1972), and Fairbairn (1954). These conceptualizations are largely similar, differing mainly on emphasis and the times of transition from one stage to another. We will use the work of Mahler (1968) as our guide, although we will also, from time to time, call on the work of Kernberg. Readers interested in a detailed discussion of Kernberg's theory may wish to consult his original works (1967, 1968, 1970, 1972, 1975, 1981).

Mahler's (1963, 1965, 1968, 1971, 1975) sensitive and thorough formulation is a stage theory. The stage sequence is invariant but the ages at which the child passes through each level vary widely as a function of the individual child's temperament and other constitutional factors, the mother's personality, and the interaction between child and mother.

According to Mahler, the newborn infant to about three months is ego diffuse and attachment to the mother is nonexistent or symbiotic. Internalized object representations are vague and undifferentiated. During this period the mother performs all psychological functions for the child, extending and surrounding the infant with her own personality. One mother of a young child said, "It was as though I wrapped my whole self around the baby." Mahler refers to this phase as the stage of *normal autism*. To the child, self and mother are a single system or identity.

The second stage, about three to eight months, has been identified as the *differentiation* stage. During this stage, the child begins to differentiate the mother's body image from its own. Yet, the differentiation is not exactly "real." Mother continues to be more or less an extension of the child and vice versa. The infant's perception of mother's behavior flows through several channels, including touch, smell, proprioceptive, and intraceptive sensations. Kernberg points out that during this period early cognitive-affective constellations become fixated as all good memories encompassing self, mother, and good feelings. This all good self-other internalized (object representation) image is paralleled by the development of an all bad self-other image.

In Mahler's conceptualization, the time from about 8 to 15 months is a *practicing* stage. The child may practice separation from the mother, but has not yet begun to recognize her total separateness. There is little distress in the separation. There is a clearer differentiation of self and other, particularly within the "good" portion of the self-other object representation.

The next stage, spanning from approximately 15 to 22 months, is entitled the *rapprochement* phase. Cognitive and locomotor development facilitate growth during this period. Now the child works intensively on the separation-individuation process. It is during this time that "object constancy" is developing, i.e., fixed images of the good and bad elements of the self or other. The more firmly established the toddler's internal representation of the mother may be, the more confident the toddler will be in making a genuine healthy separation from the mother. The separation must take place in order for the good and bad self representations to become integrated (*individuation*). During this period of time, the emerging toddler, who has previously been relatively oblivious to the presence of the mother, turns again to her with new powerful demands for her responsiveness to his attempts to separate and individuate. Depending on how successfully this phase is negotiated, the toddler eventually moves on toward object constancy.

This brief review of object relations theory is incomplete. Readers interested in further study of this field may wish to consult Bowlby (1969, 1973, 1980), Fraiberg (1959, 1980), Kernberg (1967, 1968, 1970, 1972, 1975, 1981), Mahler (1963, 1965, 1968, 1971, 1975), Masterson (1972, 1976), Spitz (1965), and Winnicott (1957, 1965).

THE CHALLENGE OF GOOD-ENOUGH MOTHERING

Winnicott (1965), a psychoanalyst who has made major contributions to object relations theory, has coined the term "good-enough mothering." To us, the concept of good-enough mothering, which has face validity, would seem to be a healthy standard or goal for the mother of the young child. According to Winnicott, the good-enough mother faces the omnipotence of her infant and, to some extent, understands it, even makes sense of it. She responds to the infant's cuing with reasonable efficiency and sensitivity.

At the core of the concept of good-enough mothering is the sense of a good-enough self. It would seem to be crucial that the mother in order to give freely and openly to the emerging child needs to have a relatively clear sense of who she is, her ego boundaries, a sense of self-esteem, a sense of personal identity.

Yet, as one mother of four children said, "Mothering is a great place to lose yourself."

Mahler's conceptualization of the mother-child interactive process emphasizes the concept of *libidinal availability*.[1] This somewhat cumbersome term, which may be recast as "lovingly available," is central to an understanding of this view of mothering and child development. Mahler (1968) writes:

> *My theory places special emphasis, however, on the interaction of both these factors with the circular processes between mother and infant, in which the mother serves as a beacon of orientation and a living buffer for the infant, in reference to both external reality and his internal milieu. (p. 229)*

Mahler states that when the mother consciously or unconsciously fails to accept the infant, the child may experience a deficit in self-esteem and become very emotionally vulnerable. She stresses the concept of "mutual cuing" between infant and mother, emphasizing its great importance for the healthy mothering process. Mutual cuing is a circular process of interaction established early in the relationship between mother and infant. In this process, mother and child "empathically" perceive and attend to each other's signals and signs and react accordingly.

At issue is the availability of the mother's love when the child is in the process of separating from the mother. If that love continues to be shown to the infant or toddler, even when the infant rejects her, the child may have a greater sense of emotional security and can thus continue to traverse the growth process we call integration.

THE RECIPROCAL NATURE
OF MOTHER–CHILD RELATIONS

Few psychologists would argue with the belief that the way in which the mother and child negotiate the first several years of the youngster's life are crucial for the child's emotional development. However, in our view, many early writers tended to view this process as unidimensional. Indeed, a less than thorough reading of this literature might lead to "mother blaming," a phenomenon that has, until recently, been epidemic in psychology and psychiatry. Obviously, it would be foolhardy to argue that an infant or even a young child has all of the responsibility to raise itself. However, as Bandura (1978) pointed out recently, it may be unnecessary to dichotomize the concept of self from the concept of environment. Spitz (1965) has emphasized the interactive nature of the mother-child relationship. He points out that the infant's individual personality impinges on the relationship in a circular process, influencing the plethora of affects of the mother by its behavior. Spitz stresses that the two do not live in a vacuum but in a socioeconomic milieu which includes members of the immediate family, ethnic groups, culture, technology,

---

[1] The term libido has a very specific meaning in psychodynamic theory. Yet, in our view, it often is an insufficient way to describe the magic of love, particularly in the case of motherly love. A review of the Old and New Testaments clearly indicates that there are several meanings for the word love in both Greek and Hebrew. Perhaps the Hebrew word *raḥum* most clearly describes what is being described by Mahler. *Raḥum* is the love of the womb—the desire to care for, to protect from harm, to give of one's own self and body to the development of another human being.

political-national forces, and historical-cultural traditions. Recent studies by Chess and others (Thomas et al., 1964; Chess & Birch, 1969) clearly indicate that children are born with widely varying temperaments. By extrapolating from clinical observations one may conclude that the temperament of the child may strongly influence the way in which the mother is inclined to interact with the infant.

Kernberg and Mahler both emphasize the importance of constitutional factors in the development or failure of development of healthy object relationships. In discussing deficiencies in development, Mahler (1968) acknowledges the role of innate defects in the child's capacity to neutralize drives. Kernberg (1972) writes that a constitutional overload of aggressiveness makes it difficult for some children to retain the image of the loving, supportive mother. Additionally, this overload of hostility makes it difficult for the youngster to integrate the bad with the good portions of the self. Indeed, the classic borderline patient (Dorr et al., in press; Kernberg, 1975; Masterson, 1976) tends to split the good and the bad apart because the bad is so laden with aggressive energy (because of constitutional overload) there is risk of it destroying the good self representation.

To summarize, if we adopt a systemic view of the mother-child interaction, we may then remove unnecessary value judgements from our assessment of the mothering process. Thus, the interaction can then be viewed in a broader social perspective. The social interactive aspect of the cradle of the development of object relations is clearly ecological or interactive. Though mother and child are unequal partners in a social field of constantly shifting forces, the relationship may also be viewed as complementary.

MOTHERING[2] AND OBJECT RELATIONS

Our understanding of how mothering affects infant development has changed much in the past 40–50 years. With the arrival of Freudian theory, research focussed on the relationship of physical care practices to personality in an attempt to verify Freud's assertions. Caldwell (1964) presents a detailed summary of these 1930s–50s studies, concluding that the evidence does not support the proposal that personality characteristics are the direct result of infant-care practices. Subsequent research has strengthened this conclusion. Clearly, the key to understanding the role of mothering must include an examination of more than mere physical care practices.

During the 1950s–1960s, attention focussed on parental attitudes as well as physical care practices. Again, the data fell short of our expectations. Reports were obtained from mothers on feeding, weaning, toilet training, and also how they handled dependency, aggression, discipline, etc. In several cases (e.g., Schaefer, 1959; Sears et al., 1957), promising relationships emerged. The greatest upset in children resulting from severe toilet training, for example, was found when it was combined with a cold, undemonstrative attitude on the part of the mother. However, the results were frequently unreplicated (e.g., Yarrow et al., 1968).

Research on two more variables in the 1960–70s has put us closer to understanding the effects of mothering: infant temperament, and the continuity of experience.

---

[2] As this volume focusses on women, we devoted little attention to the role of father. We feel that the father is a crucial force in early childhood development. Our light treatment of this subject is motivated by our need to limit the scope of this manuscript.

Thomas et al. (1964) have demonstrated that infants develop stable patterns of behavior and responsiveness to the environment by two months of age. Parents who are able to accept these patterns and approach interactions with understanding and patience enable the infant to grow into a relaxed, cheerful child. Parents who demand from the infant that which is temperamentally unsuitable, may feel and express less warmth to the infant, and produce the kinds of frustrating experiences which, combined with their attitudes, exacerbate the problem.

However, we must still consider the continuity issue. Whether or not infant experiences produce stable personality characteristics also depends on the continuity of experience. Dennis (1973) reported that children moved from a poor quality, restrictive orphanage to a more stimulating institution increased in average IQ, while those remaining in restrictive institutions actually dropped in IQ. Thus, although early experiences are clearly important, the potential for change is determined at least in part by the degree to which the environment changes.

The effects of mothering on object relations development is a complex process, involving (a) her physical care practices, and whether they are satisfying or frustrating, (b) her attitudes about herself and her infant, and her expression of those attitudes, (c) her infant's temperament, which may affect her attitudes and their expression through her behavior, and (d) the degree of continuity or discontinuity in the infant's experiences throughout his or her childhood. Now we are better equipped to understand how mothering affects developing object relations.

The infant's total dependence on mother is instrumental in nature, dependence on her to satisfy all needs. Early social events such as being held, cuddled, or talked to may have little or no meaning for the child at this stage. The infant lacks even rudimentary differentiation between the self and other, analogous to the total egocentrism Piaget (1952, 1960) proposes. The bond between mother and child at this point is not, then, what developmental psychologists refer to as an "attachment." Attachment prerequires an ability to differentiate between self and others, involving an evaluation of others as "good" and "rewarding" and a consequent desire to be close to them.

Nonetheless, there are behavioral demonstrations of this early bond. Condon (1975) examined the rhythm of infant movements made while adults spoke to them. As early as the first day of life, the various body parts—head, eyes, fingers, mouth, etc.—moved in synchrony to the rhythm of that speech. This synchroneity is uniquely interpersonal; infants do not show these patterns to other types of auditory stimuli.

During this phase, the healthy mother interacts with the infant in a stimulating, mutual experience that encourages the infant into new and involving experiences and responses (Masterson, 1976). Problems in the mother-infant relationship during these first two months focus on several issues. Lacking self-other differentiation, infants are unaware of their dependence on mothers, and make no effort to reward those who devote so much time to satisfying their needs. A frequent theme in the child abuse literature is the problem faced by mothers with high dependency needs, who look to their infants for tangible evidence of their love and tangible rewards for their mothering efforts. In the absence of these, they are likely to feel rejected by their infants, and consequently reject them in turn through abuse or neglect.

Recall also the importance of infant temperament and constitutional factors which may result in one type of mothering behavior being incompatible with infant traits, and therefore through an interaction inhibit the development of a healthy sense of self and other. For example, it has been proposed that some people are "stimulus-reducers" and others "stimulus-augmenters" (Petrie, 1967), subjectively experiencing the identical stimulus as less stimulating (reducers) or more stimulating (augmenters). Mothers of augmenters have a more difficult job simply because of the infant's own characteristics.

During the differentiation stage of object relations development, three to about eight months, infants begin to differentiate between "good" and "bad" although they are still unable to differentiate between self and other. This differentiation is a natural consequence of cognitive development. The presence of memory trace ability enables infants to associate actions with outcomes, particularly affective outcomes such as pleasant and unpleasant physical sensations. It is at this point that social events such as being held, cuddled, or fed begin to acquire positive or negative meaning. In addition, neuromuscular maturation enables infants to coo and gurgle to indicate pleasure, and to smile in response to external as well as internal stimuli. Thus the infant can convey both delight and distress.

As early as the eighth week of life, the infant begins to respond differentially to his or her mother, and this unique response to the mother, the maternal attachment, becomes clear by six to eight months of age, the end of this second stage (Ainsworth, 1964, 1969).

Mothers again face many challenges in their mothering roles. Premature infants, slow-to-develop infants, and infants with difficult temperaments may spend more time crying at this age than their peers, and may not show as many "delight" responses. In order for infants to develop balanced representations of the world as good and bad, they require experiences of both a rewarding and frustrating nature. Feisty infants may make it more difficult for mothers to maintain such a balance in their interactions with their infants. Mothers whose interactions decrease or become strained may foster the development of representations of the world as more painful and frustrating than pleasant and rewarding. In fact, infants even demonstrate a subtle awareness of this. The amount of time infants spend crying during the second year of life is dependent on how promptly, consistently, and effectively mothers are able to respond to their distress signals during the first half year of life (Ainsworth & Bell, 1969).

The fact that infants can now indicate behaviorally their pleasure or displeasure provides an important source of feedback for mothers regarding their mothering behavior. It is at this stage, then, that infant behavior begins to have a discernable effect on a mother's sense of herself as a "good-enough mother."

During the practicing stage of object relations development (8-15 months), infants begin to differentiate between "good" self and "good" other. This ability to differentiate between self and other is at the basis of the attachment infants form. Most researchers place the onset of attachment at 6-8 months (e.g., Ainsworth, 1964, 1969), consistent with the beginning of self/other differentiation proposed by object relations theory. Mothers take on a new meaning for their infants; they become powerful fear reducers, and the object of their infants' attention as can be seen by the "proximity-seeking" behaviors (smiling, crying, following, reaching out) that infants direct towards them. Investigations of mother-child interaction have consistently emphasized that the mother's warmth, reinforcement, and nurturance of the child enhances the formation of both this attachment and later social relationships.

Ainsworth (1979) discusses the etiology of two unusual types of attachments which may be viewed as demonstrations of problems in early object relations development. Infants with insecure-avoidant attachments are intensely distressed by separation from their mothers, but are somewhat ambivalent about contact with their mothers on reunion. It is as though these infants do not believe their mothers to be accessible and responsive, and although they form attachments, they lack the rudiments of a sense of security and trust in others, what we might refer to as a sense of "good" other. Mothers of these infants may have either disregarded their signals, or responded belatedly or inappropriately to their signals. However, we must consider the situation from the mother's point of view. How distinctive are the signals which their infants produce? How good are their infants at conveying their needs? Perhaps the problem is as characteristic of "good" mothers whose infants are difficult to interpret as it is of mothers who are simply neglectful or disinterested.

Conversely, infants with insecure-avoidant attachments rarely cry in separation episodes, and in reunion avoid their mothers, sometimes ignoring them altogether. There is a tendency here (Connell, 1976) for insecure-avoidant infants to be also of difficult temperament, implying that the attachment quality is likely to be produced by an interaction of infant characteristics and mothering behavior. Mothers of insecure-avoidant infants were more restricted in expressions of emotion and avoided close physical contact with their infants. However, it is quite possible that these mothering behaviors arose in response to their infant's temperaments. Difficult infants express emotions intensely; perhaps the restriction of affect on the part of the mothers is an attempt at some level to model more appropriate behavior. Difficult infants often resist physical contact; perhaps the mothers' avoidance of physical contact is a response to infant preferences.

The self/other differentiation that begins during this stage is greatly influenced by exploration of the environment. Piaget (1952) describes the infant's progression through secondary circular reactions (4-8 months) and coordination of secondary circular reactions (8-12 months) as an attempt to discover the properties of objects and events and the role of the self in their actions. Letting go of a block and seeing that it falls may at first be experienced by the child as an example of his power to make the block drop. Eventually, however, the child learns that the block has a force of its own (gravity) that is separate from the child. How mothers deal with their infants' needs to explore the world at this stage is related to characteristics in preschool children such as intellectual and social competence. White (1975) reports that, compared to mothers of less competent children, mothers of competent children provide richer language stimulation, more contingent stimulation, more affection and warmth, and more freedom to explore and encouragement of exploration. Thus, it is not necessary that mothers be constantly present, constantly attentive, and constantly orchestrating infant activities to promote competence in children.

Kernberg (1972) points out that during the practicing stage, the concept of object permanence (Piaget's term) or object constancy (the psychoanalytic concept of the lingering image in the absence of the actual stimulus) has not yet been well developed. Continued experience with objects and events during the second year of life solidifies this concept. Evidence of the emerging object concept is found sometime after the first birthday, when infants express distress at separation from their mothers and demonstrate an ability to search for a hidden object after seeing it hidden.

During the rapprochement stage of object relations (15–22 months), good and bad self representations coalesce into a more integrated self-concept. Infant abilities have matured to the point that they can more clearly express their wants, desires, and feelings. Between the first and second birthdays, language emerges and rapidly develops to the point of rudimentary sentences (Brown, 1973). Exploration of the environment expands due to improved locomotor and eye-hand coordination, and infants engage in what Piaget (1952) calls tertiary circular reactions or trial and error experiments about the nature of the world. Experiments such as these are also important in the development of object permanence, an understanding that objects not perceptually evident continue to exist.

Self-concept is continuing to develop and is influenced by how significant people react to the infant's current activities. The increased activity of these toddlers presents additional challenges to mothers to protect them and at the same time ensure that they have adequate freedom to explore their environments. Mothers must also cope with the negativism commonly accompanying developing autonomy, understanding that it is not an indication of rejection but rather a natural out-growth of the painful but necessary separation-individuation process. Toddlers who develop healthy self-concepts are likely to come from homes in which mothers are warm and supportive, and set clear, consistent, and reasonable limits on be-havior. Neither laxness nor arbitrariness in limit-setting facilitates a healthy self-concept (Baumrind, 1967). And, of course, the dimensions of warmth-hostility and consistency-inconsistency continue to be important.

FAILURES IN GOOD–ENOUGH MOTHERING

This chapter focusses on the process of normal, healthy mothering. However, in order to highlight the phenomenon of healthy mothering, it may be helpful to sketch out a background of the various things that can and do go wrong during the early developmental period that may result in serious psychopathology.

Failures in libidinal availability may result in a failure in object constancy. When object constancy is well-developed, the child retains images of the parent as a steady, nurturing, supportive individual even when frustrated. The healthy child does not feel the massive emotional void associated with the removal of the in-ternalized representation of the parent as a result of, for example, being punished. However, constitutional factors (e.g., the child's excessive irritability or inability to develop healthy positive internal images), excessive frustration, and unavail-ability of the mother's love may arrest the development of object constancy. Thus, whenever frustrated by significant others, their positive image disappears entirely, and the child is left feeling empty and alone. Feelings of abandonment (rage, guilt, depression, helplessness, passivity, void, and emptiness) (Masterson, 1976) may wash over the child having far-reaching consequences for subsequent adjust-ment. Additionally, as the mother-child dyad is reciprocal, the effects of an un-healthy relationship may exacerbate the mother's difficulties as well.

One consequence of the pervasive sense of abandonment can be the development of an "as-if" personality (Deutsch, 1942). The as-if personality tends to mimic the personalities of those around them. They have little substance of their own. They cannot engage in healthy identification processes in which the elements of the other may be metabolized and made a part of the stuff of the person. Instead, parts of the other are incorporated indiscriminantly and forced into a personality without true integration. According to Christopher Lasch (1979), many persons in American society are characterized by this kind of as-if, substanceless personality.

Kernberg (1972) argues that fixation at the earliest level of separation-individuation may provide a seedbed for the development of a host of pathologies, including psychoses. Developmental arrest at the middle stages of this hierarchy fosters the development of severe character disorders, such as inadequate personality, narcissistic personality, hysterical personality, borderline personality, and psychopathic personality.

While an exclusive focus on the potential dangers of failing to negotiate the development through the first several years of life has been overdone by some theorists, it is clear that the way in which these years are managed may be crucial for a child's development and the way in which he or she understands and deals with the social-emotional world for the rest of his or her life.

SPECIAL ISSUES IN MOTHERHOOD

The role of motherhood during the early years may be complicated by a number of factors including divorce or death of a spouse, entering the work force, delaying childbearing until later years, or, having children in the teenage years. Each of these presents additional challenges to the mother's role and to the developing child.

Perhaps no event is as stressful for the mother of a young child as finding herself a single mother through death or estrangement of the husband. The divorce rate has doubled in the last decade, and it is now estimated that 40 to 50 percent of children born during the 1970s will spend some time in a single parent home. These mothers are likely to suffer from "task overload," handling responsibilities usually shared by two people. In addition, they often experience financial duress. In 1974, 51.5 percent of children under 18 in female-headed families were in families with incomes below the poverty level (Bane, 1976). Third, single mothers are often socially isolated and lacking in social and emotional support. It might be thought that the presence of children would attenuate this sense of loneliness; however, recent studies (Hetherington et al., 1978) suggest that the presence of children may actually make mothers feel more unhappy, frustrated, helpless, anxious, and incompetent. The children of single mothers differ in important ways from children with two parents. Young boys show more antisocial or aggressive behavior, and score lower on achievement/aptitude tests, often demonstrating higher verbal scores than math scores. Young girls also show lower test scores, but without the patterns of antisocial, aggressive behavior. Single mothers often report increased use of coercion to discipline their children and problems communicating with them and responding to their needs.

Demographic trends suggest that more women are delaying child-bearing until their late twenties and early thirties (David & Baldwin, 1979). More years spent in a child-free life-style may make the transition to motherhood seem greater, particularly if the woman has made a significant investment in a career, what has been termed by Jurgens (1978) "baby shock." However, in the presence of increased financial stability, a more mature husband-wife relationship and the desire to begin a family at this later point, child-bearing in later years need not necessarily pose a threat to their healthy role as mother or the development of the child.

The proportion of births to adolescents is increasing. Births to women under 20 rose from 14 percent of total births in 1960 to 17 percent in 1977 (David & Baldwin, 1979). When good prenatal care is provided, the baby born to an adolescent mother may do well on early assessments, but is still likely to show some decrements on subsequent assessment of intelligence, school achievement, and adjustment. However, it is estimated that over 50 percent of pregnant adolescents do not receive adequate prenatal care, and that these women are most at risk for having a low birth weight baby and for experiencing complications of labor and delivery.

However, even in the presence of good physical care, adolescents who bear children are likely to experience psychosocial problems. The majority do not complete their educations, and their family incomes are usually close to the national poverty level. In addition, adolescent mothers are not well prepared for the total dependence of the newborn infant, and have difficulty entering into the normal symbiosis of early mother-child relationships. Child neglect is a common problem, as are physical illnesses in the young child and developmental delays.

Although entering the work force can increase the stresses on mothers of young children it may also positively affect their self-concepts and their children's development. The most important predictor of how entering the work force affects mother and child is mother's attitude about working. Mothers who have a sense of satisfaction and competence in their work roles have positive relationships with their children, relationships as healthy as those between satisfied nonworking mothers and their children, and actually more healthy than those between dissatisfied nonworking mothers and their children (Hartley, 1966). Their children tend to hold more egalitarian views of sex roles (Hoffman, 1974, 1977), and become more self-sufficient and independent at an earlier age (Hock, 1978). These trends in turn are associated with high achievement motivation and a strong sense of competence in later years (Woods, 1972). A related issue is day-care of young children, extensively examined by Kagan et al. (1977). In general, experiences in high quality day-care are associated with social skill development and good achievement motivation. Poor quality day-care, with high child-adult ratios and unstimulating environments, is associated with effects similar to those associated with unstimulating institutional environments.

However, mothers who feel guilty about leaving their children to work are more likely to begin seeing themselves as poorer mothers, and to develop strained relationships with their children, especially evident in communications breakdowns and more arbitrary and inconsistent discipline (Hoffman, 1974, 1977). In addition, the lack of quality supervision of children of working mothers is associated with difficulties in later school years in both the academic and social spheres. Rather than being more self-reliant, such children are less so and experience a decreased sense of personal freedom (Woods, 1972).

MOTHERING AND MOTHERHOOD

There has been far less research on how mothering affects mothers than on how mothering affects infants, an interesting statement regarding psychologists' priorities. In general, there appear to be five characteristics which mediate how the experience of mothering affects the personal development of a woman (Ferguson, 1977): the timing of children, the marital relationship, the woman's view of her relationship with her own mother, the availability of practical and emotional support, and the characteristics of her infant.

Mothers are most likely to gain satisfaction from their roles as mothers if childbearing occurs at a point in their lives when they are emotionally and financially prepared. Becoming a mother is a major transition in a woman's life. Parenthood involves much greater changes than marriage itself, and is often viewed as the critical sign of achieving adult status (Hill & Aldous, 1969). This subtle social pressure to bear children and enter the adult world may lead a woman to enter the mother role before she is emotionally and/or financially prepared, and thus undermine from the start her developing a healthy sense of herself as a mother. There are, of course, no "instant formulas" for determining when a woman is ready for this complex role—it is a sense of oneself as competent, capable, and ready to give to others that is unique to each individual.

The characteristics of the marital relationship also mediate the experience of mothering. A fulfilling marital relationship provides experience with sharing and meeting the needs of others that can facilitate healthy mother-infant relationships. Being able to count on one's spouse for practical and emotional support in child-rearing is likely to increase a woman's sense of security in taking on the responsibility of the mother role. In contrast, if the parents' earlier experiences and current marital relationship have fostered feelings of competition, a sense of one's needs not being met by others, then the experience of having children is likely to rearouse and intensify those feelings.

Most individuals parent their children in ways similar to those in which they were raised. Thus, a woman's relationship with her own mother, beginning in her own infancy, has great impact on her experience of the mother role. If the relationship has been difficult and stressful, she is likely to have within her a negative internalized "mother image." Many women report that, with the advent of child-birth, memories of their own relationships with their mothers resurface, and if those memories are distressful, the mother role may be viewed more with apprehension than anticipation. This may produce a tendency for strained relationships with their infants, that merely begins anew the internalization of a negative mother image. However, in the presence of a supportive marital relationship, adequate resources, and emotional maturity, along with greater social and cultural recognition of the difficulty of the mothering role, even women who experienced stressful childhoods can achieve satisfaction from the mother role. And, happily, most women facing childbirth report positive feelings about their own mothers, often finally being able to forgive for early missteps, and approach mothering with confidence and pride.

The importance of practical and emotional support for mothers cannot be overstated, especially in the early stages of mothering which are the focus of this chapter. Help from one's husband, one's immediate and extended family, one's friends and neighbors, can be crucial in minimizing the sense of isolation or depression that many new mothers experience. Even as the baby matures and requires less demanding care, help and support can greatly reduce her feeling trapped in a "baby-centered world." In addition, such support can be an important source of reinforcement for her efforts at mothering, and a factor in her sense of success as a mother.

Finally, the characteristics of her infant and her ability to adapt to his or her needs will affect her sense of herself as a competent mother. The infant with physical problems, the infant of difficult temperament, the premature or slow-to-develop infant, place great demands on the mother in terms of time, and in approach to caring for the infant. Mothers who successfully adapt to these infants' special needs may experience great satisfaction in their roles, and an increase in feelings of competence and self-esteem. Here, the presence of emotional and financial preparedness, a healthy marital relationship, and the availability of practical and emotional support become even more important for the development of a satisfactory sense of oneself as a mother.

IMPLICATIONS FOR COMMUNITY INTERVENTION: AN EXAMPLE

It was not our goal to outline extensive social interventive programs that would speak to the issues raised. It was, instead, our aim to sensitize the reader to the psychosocial significance of the mother-child interaction. However, our analysis suggests that it would be desirable to develop social programs to maximize the capacity of the mother to be lovingly available to the young child during its formative years. This would require necessary economic and social support networks aimed particularly at those mothers who are inclined to be the most vulnerable to stress. This is a task that exceeds the competency of psychologists and will require interventions by social planners, economists, educators, politicians, community leaders, religious leaders, and many others whose expertise speak to the social forces that may contribute to diminishing or augmenting the mother's emotional energy that is free for her child. We will give one circumscribed example of how certain social-economic interventions may contribute significantly to the time and energy that the mothers of young children may have available for the mothering process.

Winett et al. (1982) examined the impact of flex time on families with young children. Their major dependent measure was a 15-item survey that examined time activity. The authors found that the workers in the sample who were parents of young children chose to begin and quit work earlier when given this option through the flex time system. Even though the amount of modification permissible was only about one hour under this system, this schedule change permitted persons to increase their late afternoon and evening time with their children, and this in turn resulted in less reported difficulty in engaging in familial recreation, educational, and chore related activities. While there was a reduction in the amount of morning time available to the children, the families tended to rate evening time as much more important. These ratings suggested to the authors that flex time helped increase "quality time" and was not merely a reapportioning.

This study stands as a good example of the use of sophisticated methodology in a naturalistic observational setting to determine the psychological impact of a potentially highly significant socio-economic intervention. Even small changes in work schedules resulted in changes in family and in environmental systems.

Other preventive social interventions might be coordinated through departments of obstetrics. Through proper consulting from clinical psychologists and psychiatrists, obstetricians and other obstetrical workers could be sensitized to signs that indicate vulnerability to stress and decompensation in the intensive mothering setting (e.g., such factors as masked depression, borderline personality organization), and those persons found to be at high risk might be referred to social networks that may provide necessary emotional support for these mothers as they are in the position of having to respond to the emotional demands of their infants.

A third major target for intervention may be in the area of day-care. The working mother has become a social reality. Routinized facilities for care of our young children in this country are not a social reality. Instead, it is a patchwork quilt of disparate programs and individuals, some of whom are highly qualified and others of whom are not. There is clearly much room for improvement in the development of private and social agencies that can provide this kind of emotional support for the mother of the young child.

SUMMARY

In this chapter we sought to review the challenge of mothering the young child in the context of object relations theory. We attempted to emphasize the interactive aspect of this process although, clearly, our review of the effects of mother on the child was much more extensive than our review of the converse. This merely reflects the current state of the literature. Hopefully, the emerging systemic-ecological perspective in psychology will augment our understanding of this fascinating, crucial process of human development.

REFERENCES

Ainsworth, M. D. S. Infant-mother attachment. *American Psychologist*, 1979, *34*, 932–937.

Ainsworth, M. D. S. Patterns of attachment behavior shown by the infant in interaction with his mother. *Merrill-Palmer Quarterly*, 1964, *10*, 51–58.

Ainsworth, M. D. S. Object relations dependency and attachment: A theoretical review of the infant-mother relationship. *Child Development*, 1969, *40*, 965–1025.

Ainsworth, M. D. S. & Bell, S. M. Some contemporary patterns of mother-infant interaction in the feeding situation. In A. Ambrose (ed.), *Stimulation in early infancy*. London and New York: Academic Press, 1969.

Bandura, A. The self system in reciprocal determinism. *American Psychologist*, 1978, *33*, 344–358.

Bane, M. J. Marital disruption and the lives of children. *Journal of Social Issues*, 1976, *32*, 103–117.

Baumrind, D. Child care practices anteceding three patterns of preschool behavior. *Genetic Psychology Monographs*, 1967, *75*, 43–88.

Bowlby, J. *Attachment and loss, Vol. I, Attachment*. New York: Basic Books, Inc., 1969.

Bowlby, J. *Attachment and loss, Vol. II, Separation*. New York: Basic Books, Inc., 1973.

Bowlby, J. *Attachment and loss, Vol. III, Loss*. New York: Basic Books, Inc., 1980.

Brown, R. *A first language: The early stages*. Cambridge: Harvard University Press, 1973.

Caldwell, B. M. The effects of infant care. In M. L. Hoffman and L. W. Hoffman (eds.), *Review of child development research*, Vol. 1. New York: Russell Sage Foundation, 1964.

Chess, T. A. & Birch, H. *Temperament and behavior disorders in children*. New York: New York University Press, 1969.

Condon, W. Speech makes babies move. In R. Lewin (ed.), *Child Alive*, London: Temple Smith, 1975; New York: Doubleday, 1975.

Connell, D. B. Individual differences in attachment: An investigation into stability, implications, and relationships to the structure of early language development. Unpublished doctoral dissertation, Syracuse University, 1976.

David, H. P. & Baldwin, W. H. Childbearing and child development: Demographic and psychosocial trends. *American Psychologist*, 1979, *34*, 866–871.

Dennis, W. *Children of the Creche*. New York: Appleton-Century-Crofts, 1973.

Deutsch, H. Some forms of emotional disturbances and their relationship to schizophrenia. *Psychoanalytic Quarterly*, 1942, *11*, 301–321.

Dorr, D., Barley, W. D., Gard, B., & Webb, C. Understanding and treating borderline personality organization. *Psychotherapy: Theory, Research and Practice*, in press.

Fairbairn, W. R. D. A revised psychopathology of the psychoses and psychoneuroses. In *Psycho-Studies of the Personality* (an object-relations theory of the personality). London: Tavistock, 1952; New York: Basic Books, 1954.

Ferguson, L. R. The woman in the family. In E. Donelson and J. Gullahorn (eds.), *Women: A psychological perspective*. New York: John Wiley & Sons, 1977.

Fraiberg, S. *The magic years*. New York: Scribners, 1959.

Fraiberg, S. (ed.). *Clinical studies in infant mental health: The first year of life*. New York: Basic Books, 1980.

Goldfarb, W. Psychological privation in infancy and subsequent adjustment. *American Journal of Orthopsychiatry*, 1945, *15*, 247-255.

Hartley, R. E. Sex-roles from a child's viewpoint. Paper presented at the annual meeting of the American Orthopsychiatric Association, San Francisco, 1966.

Hartmann, H. The mutual influences in the development of the ego and id. In *The psychoanalytic study of the child*, Vol. 7. New York: International Universities Press, 1952.

Hartmann, H. *Ego psychology and the problem of adaptation*. New York: International Universities Press, 1939.

Hetherington, E. M., Cox, M., & Cox, R. The development of children in mother headed families. In H. Hoffman and D. Reiss (eds.), *The American family: Dying or developing?* New York: Plenum, 1978.

Hill, R. & Aldous, J. Socialization for marriage and parenthood. In D. A. Goslin (ed.), *Handbook of socialization theory and research.* Chicago: Rand McNally, 1969.

Hock, E. Working and nonworking mothers with infants: Perceptions of their careers, their infants' needs, and satisfaction with mothering. *Developmental Psychology*, 1978, *4*, 37-43.

Hoffman, L. W. Effects of maternal employment on the child: A review of the research. *Developmental Psychology*, 1974, *10*, 204-228.

Hoffman, L. W. Changes in family roles, socialization, and sex differences. *American Psychologist*, 1977, *32*, 644-657.

Jürgens, H. W. Social psychological aspects of population decrease (in German). *Materialien zur Bevölkerungswissenschaft*, 1978, *5*, 149-169.

Kagan, J., Kearsley, R. B., & Zelazo, P. R. The effects of infant day care on psychological development. *Educational Quarterly*, 1977, *1*, 109-142.

Kernberg, O. F. Borderline personality organization. *Journal of the American Psychoanalytic Association*, 1967, *15*, 641-685.

Kernberg, O. F. The treatment of patients with borderline personality organization. *International Journal of Psycho-Analysis*, 1968, *49*, 600-619.

Kernberg, O. F. Factors in the psychoanalytic treatment of narcissistic personalities. *Journal of the American Psychoanalytic Association*, 1970, *18*, 51-85.

Kernberg, O. F. Early ego integration and object relations. *Annals of the New York Academy of Sciences*, 1972, *193*, 233-247.

Kernberg, O. F. Transference and countertransference in the treatment of borderline patients. *Journal of the National Association of Private Psychiatric Hospitals*, 1975, *7*, 14-24.

Kernberg, O. F., Goldstein, E. G., Carr, S. F., & Blumenthal, R. Diagnosing borderline personality. *Journal of Nervous and Mental Disease*, 1981, *169*, 225-231.

Lasch, C. *The culture of narcissism*. New York: W. W. Norton, 1979.

Mahler, M. S. Thoughts about development and individuation. *Psychoanalytic Study Child*, 1963, *18*, 307-324.

Mahler, M. S. *On human symbiosis and the vicissitudes of individuation*, Vol. I. New York: International Universities Press, Inc., 1968.

Mahler, M. S. A study of the separation-individuation process and its possible application to borderline phenomena in the psychoanalytic situation. In *The psychoanalytic study of the child*, Vol. 26. New York: Quadrangle, 1971.

Mahler, M. S., Pine, F., & Bergman, A. *The psychological birth of the human infant*. New York: Basic Books, Inc., 1975.

Mahler, M. S. & LaPerriere, R. Mother-child interactions during separation-individuation. *Psychoanalytic Quarterly*, 1965, *34*, 483-489.

Masterson, J. F. *Treatment of the borderline adolescent: A developmental approach*. New York: John Wiley & Sons, Inc., 1972.

Masterson, J. F. *Psychotherapy of the borderline adult*. New York: Bruner/Mazel, 1976.

Petrie, A. *Individuality in pain and suffering*. Chicago: University of Chicago Press, 1967.

Piaget, J. *The origins of intelligence in children*. New York: International Universities Press, 1952.

Piaget, J. *The child's conception of the world*. London: Routledge, 1960.

Schaefer, E. S. A circumflex model for maternal behavior. *Journal of Abnormal and Social Psychology*, 1959, *59*, 226-235.

Sears, R. R., Maccoby, E. E., & Levin, H. *Patterns of child rearing.* Evanston, IL: Row, Peterson, 1957.
Spitz, R. A. *The first year of life* (a psychoanalytic study of normal and deviant development of object relations). New York: International Universities Press, 1965.
Thomas, A., Chess, S., Birch, H., Hertzig, M., & Korn, S. *Behavioral individuality in early childhood.* New York: New York University Press, 1964.
White, B. L. Critical influences in the origins of competence. *Merrill-Palmer Quarterly*, 1975, *21*, 243–266.
Winett, R. A., Neale, M. S., & Williams, K. R. The effects of flexible work schedules on urban families with young children: Quasi-experimental, ecological studies. *American Journal of Community Psychology*, 1982, *10*, 49–64.
Winnicott, D. W. *Mother and child.* New York: Basic Books, Inc., 1957.
Winnicott, D. W. *The maturational processes and the facilitating environment.* New York: International Universities Press, Inc., 1965.
Woods, N. B. The unsupervised child of the working mother. *Developmental Psychology*, 1972, *6*, 14–25.
Yarrow, M. R., Campbell, J. D., & Burton, R. V. *Child-rearing: An inquiry into research and methods.* San Francisco: Jossey-Bass, 1968.

4

Black Women in American Society

A Resource Development Perspective

LaRue Allen
University of Maryland

David W. Britt
New York Institute of Technology

There are alarming parallels between black women's position in American society and their place in social science research and literature. Black women have gone largely ignored by scholars who speculate upon or investigate ways to prevent psychological disorder. And black women are largely ignored by policy analysts who assess the impact of high rates of unemployment on society. They are largely overlooked by researchers who evaluate the impact of unemployment on its victims, as well. The unemployment of women in general, but most especially, the unemployment of black women, has not been considered a social problem. Two political and curricular efforts that might have been great sources of support for black women have not always come through. The Civil Rights movement and its academic counterpart, Black Studies, have focused largely on the problems and concerns of black men. The Women's Liberation Movement and its counterpart in the academy, Women's Studies, have been for and about white women. An informal survey of a half dozen psychology of women textbooks, for example, revealed a ceiling of three pages devoted to black women.

In the face of racism, classism and sex discrimination it is a wonder that black women have not become extinct. Their neglect by political movements and social science investigators parallels the evidence from numerous social and economic indicators that black women are neglected by society as a whole. They earn less than white men, white women or black men (Statistical Profile of the Black Woman, 1981). The maternal mortality rate for Black females has always exceeded that for white females. Black women, in self reports of psychological well-being, are below black men, white women and white men in the extent of their feelings of well-being. Race, class and sex discrimination seem to work together in a triple whammy (or "Triple jeopardy" as Staples, 1973, labels it) to oppress and deny opportunities to black women. Despite these adverse circumstances, black women continue. It would seem that social scientists could learn a great deal from black women of all classes about mechanisms of survival.

RESOURCES—AMMUNITION
AGAINST DOWNWARD SPIRALS

Black women have continued, since the seventeenth century, to be individuals who can persist despite a harsh environment. This persistence is not without cost of course, to black women and to their oppressors. We believe that the resourcefulness of black women has aided in their survival. First we will discuss how and why resources can make a difference in an individual's development. Then we will discuss literature on some of the problems of black women from the perspective of how different kinds of resources are related.

In a recent discussion of the implications of social class for prevention of psychological disorder, Allen and Britt (in press) emphasized the importance of resources of various types in interrupting the destructive relationship between the incidence of stressful life events and the occurrence of psychological disorder in an individual. We can see how that argument applies to the present subject with a brief review. Black women experience many stressful life events, some because they are people, some because they are black, some derived from their gender and some because they are not as monied as those around them. From what is known about the relationship between stressful life events and psychological disorder (e.g., Dohrenwend, 1981) we would predict that, for black women, this high incidence of stressful life events would lead to high rates of psychological disorder. High rates of disorder will increase the chances that they and others see them as a disturbed group. These perceptions of self and outsiders' perceptions of the self, can constitute additional stressful life events, and this in turn can lead to more disorder. Once this relationship between the two variables is established, stressful life events and psychological disorder spiral downward, each breeding more of the other. The two variables can also be described as enjoying a *feedback* relationship because changes in each of the variables feed back on, or influence, the other variable.

What can prevent stress and disorder from spiralling downward into disaster for the individual, according to Allen and Britt (in press), is the presence of resources that can be brought to bear to minimize the negative consequences of stressful life events. Allen and Britt consider resources of three types and define them as conceptually distinct but overlapping and interrelated constructs. The three types of resources are economic, personal and social.

The term economic resources refers to the relative capacity to fulfill economic needs that are determined largely by the requirements of one's chosen (or imposed) style of life. Economic resource vulnerability is the degree to which the economic resources system is threatened with collapse or malfunction. For a middle class black woman, invulnerable economic resources may mean that she can put together the capital for a townhouse downpayment through friends, savings, relatives and a credit union loan. Economic resource invulnerability for a lower class black woman may mean that she can make arrangements to pay her gas bill in installments, and then meet the payments.

Sylvia Porter (1980) provides a convenient starting point for a more inductively derived definition of economic resources. She discusses the things lenders consider when deciding whether or not you are a good credit risk, or the three C's of credit. The three C's are character (which we will discuss later as a personal resource), capacity, and capital. Capacity refers to the financial ability to repay a loan, and is affected by such things as earnings, kind of job and your prospects for advancement. More formally, capacity refers to how stable your income generation has been, your current level of income generation, and your future prospects for generating income. Capital refers to assets which could serve as collateral, and would include such things as valuable paintings, cars, homes, stocks and bonds, and of course, bank accounts. But in assessing the vulnerability of someone's economic resources, we must emphasize that it is essential to also note how an individual's resources compare with those of others who share her lifestyle. Not having the capacity to secure a five hundred dollar loan might be more devastating in some circles than an inability to repay a million dollar loan in another. Less dramatically perhaps, not being able to send your child to the kind of camp endorsed by your social group, could be a stressor. Such invidious comparison, and consequent stress, may occur at any absolute level of economic resources.

Turning to social resources, we find that studies of social resources have focused on factors such as primary and secondary interpersonal relationships (e.g., Schwab & Schwab, 1973) and neighborhood and community attachment (e.g., Lin et al., 1979), often organized under the rubric social networks (Mitchell, 1974). These resources differ in, among other things, emotional support, informational value and esteem provided (Cobb, 1976), and in their components (Tolsdorf, 1976). Some of these are clearly structural; others refer to the things which social resources provide. Community interventionists consider building and strengthening social support systems important preventive tools (Dohrenwend, 1978) and assume that, by some still little understood mechanism, support systems can be good for people.

Personal resources may refer to how you would perform as a borrower (e.g., honesty, sense of responsibility, soundness of judgment—all qualities which are attributed to good credit risks [Porter, 1980]), your intelligence level (Yando et al., 1979), the degree to which you are fatalistic (Wheaton, 1980), your self-esteem (Rosenberg, 1965), coping styles (Mechanic, 1975), political cynicism (Greenberg, 1971), or communication skills (Dohrenwend & Dohrenwend, 1969). The list of personal resources could be extended much farther, but these examples should serve to make the point; these are all attributes of persons rather than of groups. They are distinguished from economic resources in being more or less stable personality characteristics which might lead to the generation of income rather than having immediate monetary value.

Kinzer (1978) presents the case of a poor black woman who faces difficult odds with her religious faith—for her a highly developed personal resource—as armor and ammunition. "Ruby" works hard to support her two sons, holding down two and sometimes three low paying, low status jobs. Despite the highly unfavorable odds, Ruby is certain that her two boys will go to college and make something of themselves. The boys' success, along with the church, are the focal points of Ruby's life. Ruby's faith is a personal resource; her peace of mind comes from prayer and religious devotion. Ruby's involvement with the church also represents a well developed social resource. Priests serve as father substitutes for the boys. The personal resource (her faith) was instrumental in the development of the church family as a strong social resource.

All three types of resources—economic, social and personal—may be placed on a continuum labelled "vulnerability to disruption" and examined for their relative strengths and weaknesses. While it is traditional to attribute strength or weakness to persons, the Allen and Britt model uses vulnerability as a property of each of these resources rather than as attributes of individuals. Thus, the emphasis is moved from the person as the only possible locus of intervention, to the person and her context as sites for fruitful activity.

The three resources, as they are defined, are conceptually distinct but overlapping. How strongly these variables are interrelated may change with different populations. Race and gender differences, for instance, may make economic resources a buffer for some groups and social resources the buffer for another in protecting them from the negative consequences of having to endure high levels of stressors. Although this assertion requires further empirical data, we will bolster our theoretical argument in the remaining sections of this chapter by discussing the current plight of black women with regard to economic, social and personal resource vulnerability. The idea that the three types of resources may be correlated differently among different demographic groups has implications for understanding differences among these groups, as stated above. The suggestion that relationships in the model may have different values for different subgroups also has implications for intervention strategies. Black women as a group are lower in social class, have a higher incidence of stressful life events and suffer higher rates of psychological disorder than many others. If we demonstrate the logic of assuming that greater use of even minimal resources helps to keep the disorder rate among black women from spiralling out of control, we would be likely to plan interventions at the individual, community and policy level to shore up these resources. So the discussion of current knowledge about the status of black women from a resource vantage point can have implications for theory and research as well as action.

ECONOMIC RESOURCES

When the three variables economic, social, and personal resources are taken together, and evaluated from one demographic group to another (white men to white women, to black men and so on) we would hypothesize that black women as a group have the most vulnerable economic resource network. As women who are also ethnic minorities, access to the opportunities to make money, generate capital, collateral, develop relationships with banks and so on, are very limited. Two factors that could make a difference are educational opportunities and the type of labor force participation that black women engage in. We conceive of these as economic resources and see them as pivotal because of their importance in enabling women to develop other economic resources.

It has sometimes been argued that black women have been favored over black men in having educational opportunities made available to them. Available statistics do not fully support this conjecture. In 1970, black males averaged 9.6 years of schooling while black females averaged 10.2 years (Rodgers-Rose, 1980). However, such a small difference may not translate into much of a competitive advantage or handicap in the job market. For persons over 25, there is little difference in numbers between black males and females for those who graduated from college (Rodgers-Rose, 1980). In 1979, 17 percent of working women from this age group and 23 percent of working men had a college degree (Statistical Profile of the Black Woman, 1981). Those who argue that black females have been favored and given preferential access to higher education within black families use the following line of reasoning: In the black community the rates of completion of college fluctuate from year to year, but keep black males and females about equal. Since women from the black community are not discriminated against as often as white women are, they are "favored." Such reasoning would conclude that white men and black women are the most favored of the four groups. At the very least, such a conclusion, accepted without challenge, could confuse black women about how to understand the distance between their alleged favored status and the reality of their existence. Such myths could create conflicts over false issues between black men and women, threatening the quality of black male-female relationships—a social resource.

This threat to a social resource because of perceived strength in the economic resource network can be used to illustrate how relationships between these resource variables can differ for different race or gender groups. The case of labor force participation can provide another arena for examining the impact of economic resource strength on a social resource like male-female relationships. Although black women are not, in fact, displacing men in the labor force, another myth is that such is indeed the case. The fact is that black women have a higher un-employment rate than black men (13.1 percent versus 10.9 percent in 1978) and that women are not threatening men's jobs because women tend to be concentrated among a small number of occupations (Statistical Profile of the Black Woman, 1981). But, given the perception that black women are better off, we can infer that an economic resource such as employment status may have significant impact on a social resource like male-female relationships. For black women, being employed could be a threat to the quality of relationship enjoyed with a black male. For males, employment and quality of relationship are more likely to be positively correlated. Although the conjectured relationship would not hold among all black couples, the examples do illustrate how relationships among the resources may vary for different subgroups, in this case, black men and black women.

When black women do enter the labor force as employed people they get lower status jobs than their white counterparts. This difference in entry level job status remains even when social origins and educational level are held constant (Treas, 1978). Since entry level job status is a good predictor of career success across the years, this gap has both negative short and negative long-term implications. Black women narrow the race gap in occupational status over the course of their careers, but they never overcome the handicap imposed by their manner of entry into the labor force (Treas, 1978).

At all ages, the differences in rate of labor force participation persist between black and white women. During the childbearing years (25-34) there is a sharp drop in white women's labor force participation and an increase in black women's. As children age, white women are employed more, but never reach the rate of employment of black women working in the same age group (Perlo, 1975).

Across classes, women differ in their employment patterns in what may be counter-intuitive ways. Landry and Jendrek (1978) found that black middle class wives are employed at higher rates of participation than white middle class or even black lower class wives. And the reasons for their employment vary in both the cross race (black middle class vs. white middle class) and cross class (black middle class vs. black lower class) comparisons. Across classes prior participation in the labor force was the only variable among those studied that was predictive of employment for both classes of black women; the women's age had a curvilinear effect on labor force participation for working class black women only. Landry and

Jendrek (1978) conclude that black middle class women are less likely to be influenced by variables measuring husbands' income or attitude than either black lower class or white middle class women are because of the economic need in these middle class black families.

Five factors affected white female participation in the labor force. Presence of young children, presence of older children, and husband's income and attitude inhibited their participation, and prior employment facilitated participation. For black women this last variable, extent of prior employment, was the only predictive variable.

Among black women who are not married, employment rates are very high and income levels are very low. For instance, 38 percent of all black families are headed by women. Further, 44 percent of all black children live in female headed families. And, at $5900, the median income of these female headed families is below the poverty line of $6700 for an urban family of four (Simmons, 1979). Black women are more likely than white women to be working while they are heads of households and are more likely to work full-time than to work part-time.

So with regard to two economic resources, education and labor force participation, we can conclude that black women are sometimes equal to black men and sometimes equal to white women on predictor variables, but never equal on outcome measures. That is, they may start off equal to white women in preparedness for a job, but end up with a lower status entry level position. Or, black women work more consecutive years than white women, but are unable to retire as early as white women do. So the two factors that, as economic resources, could have been theoretically related to even greater economic resource strength, do nothing to eradicate our initial impression that black women are not at all well off. If they are to continue, as indeed they do, then they must be better off on some resource if our theory is to be of any value to us. We turn next to social resources (and to those blends of economic and social resources that cannot be easily placed in one category or another) for evidence of a more hopeful prognosis for black women.

SOCIAL RESOURCES

Social resources such as family, friends, medical advisors, colleagues, neighbors and so on, can provide a woman with various kinds of help in averting the negative consequences of high levels of stress. Friends can give you advice on how to cope, family can protect you when you are feeling especially weak, neighbors can give advice on how to get plumbing work done and not overpay. Black women in political, familial and career settings have sought the support of those around them. This section discusses the degree to which these various searches have been successful.

It is our view that the position that black women are in with regard to both white women and black men is a classic instance of a mirage in the desert. Both groups have appeared to be available—as potential allies and sources of support. But both groups have turned to thin air when asked for support. Black women have been caught between black men and other women in demands on their loyalty: they have historically been supported well by neither group. Attitudinally, they seem to support the causes of both women's liberation and black liberation. But behaviorally, it seems that black women are more often more likely to devote their energies to the black cause.

Reports on black women's attitudes toward feminist issues suggest that it is not because of lack of sympathy for the goals of Women's Liberation that black women are more likely to lend their physical support to the Civil Rights Movement. It appears, rather, to be a case of limited energies that have to be given to the highest priorities. Hemmons (1980) questioned a sample of 45 black women and 37 white women about their attitudes toward the Women's Movement, and found that there were no race differences in acceptance of the ideals of Women's Liberation. Middle class women were slightly more receptive than lower class women. Within races, only small differences occurred between the black social classes, but black lower class women did show a tendency to be more receptive to female liberation than black middle class females.

Femininity, thought by some to be antithetic to female liberal attitudes, was endorsed by about two-thirds of the black women and about two-fifths of the white women. But the two races endorsed social liberalism in approximately equal percentages. With regard to class differences within races, both black and white middle class women endorsed less feminine items and more racial liberalism compared to their lower class counterparts. But black women were more likely than white to maintain these clashing values (38 percent of blacks and 20 percent of whites were high on femininity and high on liberation). It was also true that women who embraced racial equality embraced the ideals of equality for women as well.

Results of national surveys have shown similar patterns. For instance, in 1972 62 percent of black women were found to be more supportive of efforts to strengthen or change women's status in society as compared to 45 percent of white women (Frieze et al., 1978). Black women are also more supportive of the Women's Liberation Movement (67 percent vs. 35 percent). Findings like these are important for two reasons. First they indicate that black women endorse feminine values without being antiliberation, a very real difference from white women. It would appear that it has been clear to black women that access to economic opportunities did not require that you become a man or even act like one; white women seem to be just struggling with this issue.

Second, black women are not avoiding women's liberation groups because black women do not endorse their goals. It seems rather that the symptoms of inequality that white women are fighting are not high priority ones for black women. White women have wanted to leave the home to find meaningful work. They have met to increase their awareness of themselves as individuals with rights of their own; neither of these are new goals for black women. White women do not seek to remedy racist oppression, or to improve educational access for all who want career training; those are things that numbers of black women would be more likely to spend time on.

Hood (1978) states the matter more explicitly when she says that it is because white women are unwilling to confront the special problems of black women that black-white feminist coalitions are unlikely. What all of this means from the point of view of resource development is that what could be a large network of men and women for social support is instead a source of conflict for black women. Those who choose to visibly ally themselves with the feminist cause probably do so at considerable cost in inner conflict and uncertainty about whether the rest of their world perceives them accurately. Staples (1973) and Hare and Hare (1978) feel that black women's primary objection to Women's Liberation is that it may distance and estrange black men and women when unity to fight black oppression is so important. Others have argued that women's liberation is necessary to insure success of the black movement and all other movements designed to eliminate discrimination (Chisholm, 1972). A variant on that argument advanced by Murray (1973) suggests that because black women are discriminated against in the Civil Rights Movement (note, for example, that no woman spoke at the historic march on Washington) and in view of the high probability that a black woman will be financially responsible for herself and maybe even a family, black women cannot afford to ignore sexism when it obstructs employment opportunities. Murray exhorts black women to fight racism and sexism simultaneously.

Social resources of many kinds are vital for survival on an ambitious career ladder. The overload on the demands for black women's time and attention from Black and Women's Liberation groups is seen in a negative way in most career settings. That is, the *over* demand for time is accompanied by an *under* emphasis on providing support and guidance to black females from black men, white women and white men as well. We have spoken above of the relatively limited opportunities for black women to achieve high status jobs. The small number who do reach high professional levels are subjected to innumerable stressful life events and must develop some substantial support mechanisms in order to persist (Alperson, 1975). One potentially large source of stress is the discrepancy between their high status as professionals and their low status as women and blacks in American society.

Leggon (1980) discusses this problem of status discrepancy among black female professionals as a situation that arises when these professionals do not conform with traditional images of what professionals are like. For in addition to having achieved statuses such as lawyer or psychologist, people are categorized by their ascribed statuses such as race or gender. Leggon finds that there is a status hierarchy in which ascribed statuses are noted first, then achieved statuses are added. Further, her respondents, from top achieved status positions, noted that there was a hierarchy of ascribed statuses—with race ranking above sex. Her pilot sample of 25 Chicago professional black women shows that they did experience more discrimination on the basis of race than sex, although several respondents said that it is often difficult to tell the difference between the two. As in our discussion of the relative lack of involvement of black women in the Women's Movement, Leggon's respondents, of all ages, felt that the Black Liberation Movement was more relevant to resolution of their problems than the Women's Liberation Movement. They did not deny that sex discrimination caused them problems, but felt that the Women's Liberation Movement was not as good at addressing either their sex or race discrimination problems as the Black Movement.

Among these professional women, it was evident that black women may need their own reference group because they have problems unique to their subgroup. Glenn (1960) reports that black men are dispersed throughout the professions more so than black women, with women highly concentrated in a few occupations. So they may share problems of racism in general with black men, but seem to have some race-gender interaction problems that distinguish them from black men. And as we stated above, black females share problems with other women, but have some that distinguish them from the rest of their gender. First, black women work after marriage and childbirth more years for less money than their white counterparts. And second, work for black women is not an option as it is for upper and middle class white women, but rather a necessity (Lerner, 1972).

Another report of results of interviews with high status black female professionals also considered the impact of multiple negative statuses on an individual, but with more questionable conclusions (Epstein, 1976). Epstein's results lead her to suggest that persons with multiple negative statuses tend to suffer from a cumulative negative effect: "The costs of having several negatively evaluated statuses are very high and lead to social bankruptcy when people simply cannot muster the resources to pay them" (p. 183). Epstein concludes from her interviews with 31 high powered professional black women that the costs of negative status are not that high for black women, allowing them to succeed. More particularly, one "pattern" is said to have emerged in which black women have one negative status canceled by the presence of another. She suggests, by way of illustration that black women do not suffer as much sex discrimination in their professions as white women do. This is said to be because the white males who control these institutions do not view black females as females or sex objects, but only as blacks. So, Epstein argues, being black would cancel the chances of being perceived as having either feminine or female characteristics.

To conclude that black women in these settings must suffer less discrimination because they were able to succeed is circular reasoning. And to state that white males do not view black females as women flies in the face of evidence accumulated from the seventeenth century to the present. State miscegenation laws are one pointed example of the extent to which some felt that mingling of blacks and whites in sexual relationships represented an issue. After the United States became a nation, 33 states eventually outlawed black-white intermarriage (Porterfield, 1978). While it might be comforting to some to believe that black women are no sexual threat, such a belief does not help to advance our understanding of how black women get ahead. Leggon (1980) also takes exception with Epstein's argument that black women may not suffer from sex discrimination because they are not perceived as sex objects. Her pilot interviews provided data to refute that argument, in their documentation of the extent to which professional black women in Chicago see themselves as victims of sexism as well as racism.

Another group of professional women who have gone wanting for support are women at all levels of the academic hierarchy—from coeds to administrators. According to Mosley (1979), black women who are administrators in higher education are an endangered species. The 232 black women on campuses across the country who responded to her survey reported that neither affirmative action nor the Women's Movement has been a source of support for them as black women. In the former case it appears that there have been more affirmative actions than affirmative results. The number of black administrators on white campuses has not increased substantially, leaving Mosley's respondents feeling isolated and stereotyped. They also feel that publicized efforts to attract minority candidates are often just a law-appeasing smokescreen for business as usual.

The lack of relevance or support from campus women's groups echoes a refrain often sounded by black women that women's lib is for middle class white women— not for lower class women and certainly not for blacks. Only four women in Mosley's sample felt that the women's movement represents the interests of all women. The majority of this group felt that the Women's Movement is about power for white women rather than about reducing oppression in society. Thus, their perception was that sources of support for these women seem limited. Students were reported to treat them equitably, particularly black students, but their colleagues were reported as less evenhanded. The majority felt that they were treated best by white women, worst by white men, with black men in between in terms of the amount of respect and support accorded them. Mosley emphasized in her discussion that she does not intend to convey the impression that all black women are relatively wary of all black men, but that the women did feel that their assertiveness and ambition were, at times, not well received by black male colleagues or by black men at home.

Mosley concludes that without substantive changes in higher education, black women may disappear from this arena entirely. Alperson (1975) paints a similar gloomy picture for black women who are higher education professors. Inundated with responsibility for all minority (and sometimes women) students, assumed to be experts only on black issues, these women become alienated and burned out at a rapid pace.

Scott and Horhn (cited in Smith, 1982) report that women from the other end of the hierarchy, female undergraduates, felt that they were less well accepted by faculty and students than either black men or white women. These respondents from a pilot sample of women in areas of study not traditionally considered female indicated feelings of isolation and alienation in their classrooms, but refused to allow these negative experiences to discourage their plans for independence in multiple roles as wives and career women.

So far it seems that professional and aspiring professional black women feel that they get little support from other groups within their professional setting in meeting their career goals. What may be a saving grace then, is the fact that professional black women have a higher regard for one another than white professional women do (Epstein, 1976). Perhaps their best hedge against the negative consequences of a stressor like alienation is that they have each other. In forming this community, black women may benefit from both the unique qualities they bring as blacks and the unique qualities they bring as women, e.g., the high rate of friendliness, eye contact and greeting among blacks, combined with the feminine ability to establish close relationships, and desire to be helpful to one another. A social resource that black women are instrumental in maintaining is an extended family support network (McAdoo, 1980; McCray, 1980). These family matrices consist of ties along which money, aid and services are directed from those who have, to those who need. Stack, an anthropologist who studied poor black families, found that it was relationships among the women that formed the basis of these networks (Stack, 1974).

Turning directly to kinship, McAdoo (1980) reports that involvement in the kinship network does not diminish as blacks achieve upward mobility. Additionally she has found that no significant differences exist between single mothers and married mothers in the extent to which they are involved in a kinship network, nor in the type of help that they give or receive. Clearly relationships with a family (and relationships with one another mentioned above) have enormous potential as a buffer in times of distress.

The question of why there are so many single mothers who use this network support is an important one for those who aim to improve the quality of life for black women. It is important at the same time to note that female-headed households are not the norm (in the statistical sense) in the black community. During the seventies, forty percent of black families could be classified as female headed compared to twelve percent of white families (Statistical Profile of the Black Woman, 1981). Despite this social difference, we can conclude that the stable husband-wife family remains the rule rather than the exception (Levitan et al., 1975). Since 1960, however some of the changes in black marital and family status have not been positive, threatening to increase the percentage of female-headed households.

Some of the real threats to the stability of the black male-female unit include the fact that the divorce rate has increased since 1960; and that nonwhite birthrates exceed white birthrates. Thus, there are more mouths to feed in black families (Levitan et al., 1975) and fewer wage earners to feed them. These indicators of instability have risen even as black income and education attainment have increased. Several factors contributed to these trends.

Demographic characteristics of the black population, for one, may influence the possibility of a black woman's finding a suitable partner. Since 1840, census figures have shown more black females than black males. The 1979 figures show that, in the 18- to 34-year-old age group, black females are 53 percent of the total black population. Among whites in the same age range, females are 50 percent of the total population (U.S. Bureau of the Census, 1980). Repeated undercounting of black males may have exaggerated the size of the difference in numbers (Rodgers-Rose, 1980), but the perception of a large difference in ratio is quite common among black women. Second, it is true that black women outlive black men, serving to increase the uneven sex ratio. Third, more black men than women are victims of homicide or are incarcerated for criminal activities, further decreasing the pool of eligible males or disrupting ongoing male-female bonds.

One alleged factor that contributes to the number of female heads of households is the myth of lax attitudes toward marriage among black women. This myth, perpetrated over the last century or so, was said to explain why there were so many black women who had families without benefit of marriage—before it became popular to do so. Some of this misinformation may be confusion about the fact that black women during slavery were often not in a position to marry the fathers of their children. Sometimes this was because slave-masters forbade it; sometimes it was because the slave-master himself was the father and unable or unwilling to marry.

The appearance of relaxed attitudes may have been furthered by the realistic stance that black women take toward prospective suitors, even as teenagers. Ladner (1972) says that girls desire interpersonal relationships as a way of affirming their womanhood. But their attitudes toward men, by age eighteen, can best be described as ambivalent. Through vicarious experience with men as abandoning husbands, runaway brothers-in-law and so on, these young women come to believe that the dream man who will join them in creating a stable marriage family situation is just a dream. The nonexistence of dream men is not considered by these women to be a flaw of the men, but rather to reflect the damage that the oppressive political and economic system inflicts on black men (Ladner, 1972).

Economic need may be another determinant of the large number of female-headed households. Over the $3,000 income level, black families are headed by males (Staples, 1973), but under $3,000, females predominate as heads of black families (Simmons, 1979). It may be economic need that contributes to the disruption of family stability, whether through the desire to comply with welfare regulations, or to reduce tensions created by arguments over finances, or because the man cannot face the fact that he is unable to provide as the family needs.

It is in these female-headed households that another myth can be exploded. That myth is the "myth of the matriarchy" (Hood, 1978) which has also been termed a "cruel hoax" (Staples, 1973). The myth of the matriarchy serves as a sexist, racist tool obstructing black women's access to needed resources by engendering hostility in those who are the alleged victims of these "powerful" mother figures. Writings on black men hating their mothers or black males being afraid of black women create unnecessary tension (Wilkinson & Taylor, 1977). If there were going to be matriarchs, they would be most likely to emerge from female heads of households. But these women are largely poor and oppressed (Staples, 1973), heading families out of necessity rather than choice. "The concept of the privileged, domineering black women only serves to mask the real economic and social deprivation of the black female underclass. The economic order, in conjunction with racism and sexism, has placed the black women in triple jeopardy, forced to face the machinations of capitalism, racism and sexism by herself" (p. 23).

The polar opposite of the castrating, emasculating matriarch image is another myth, that of the sole-support-of-family-full-time-worker-pillar-of-the-church-best-mother-on-the-block paragon. This elevation of black women to superhuman status is destructive of their relationships with black men (and anyone else who feels awed by the presence of a minor deity). McCray's (1980) call for a more balanced approach to studies of black women and black men, if answered, would serve as a source of relief for black women burdened by myths of omnipotence not of their own creation.

The factors which we have discussed as concomitants or determinants of unstable male-female relationships all converge on the boundary between social and economic resources. As with the friend who lends you money (Is that a social or an economic resource?), it is not always possible, nor even necessary, to make razor sharp distinctions among different resources. Being a single parent carries with it, by definition, certain threats to economic and social resource invulnerability. For example, a single parent has child care problems that make it more difficult to hold a job. Jobs that require travel demand unusual feats in social and economic resource mobilization. But this occasional meeting at the boundaries does not threaten the conceptual independence of these resources. We can see this clearly when we consider how major stressors might affect resources of combined types (e.g., economic/social). Suppose a young woman becomes pregnant and is abandoned by the father-to-be. This represents an assault on economic and social resources. But for poor black teenagers, the impact on economic resources is likely to be more severe and enduring. For upper class white or black teens, the event may represent more of a social demise than an economic threat.

Despite a situation which is tough on relationships, and a propensity for realistic appraisal of their prospects, black women continue to endorse the wife and mother roles. As we suggested in our sections on the Women's Movement and on professional women's issues, black women consider the blending of careers and family life an attainable goal. Research on sex role attitudes of black and white women supports a general conclusion that black women do not see traditional values, such as femininity, and freedom as mutually exclusive (Gump, 1975). Contrary to the predictions of those who view black women's equal participation in family leadership as negative and indicative of power hungry emasculation drives, Gump's data showed that black women were more likely than white women to have home-centered and submissive sex role attitudes. Black women were also the more likely of the two groups to derive their identity from the wife and mother roles.

Also contrary to the views of those who view black women's equal participation in family leadership and decision-making as a black family weakness are Fichter's findings, cited by McCray (1980). Fichter reported that black husbands accept their wives' working more readily than white husbands do. It was further reported that attitudes toward marriage, child rearing and wife's occupational role were more similar in black couples than white ones. In a similar vein, Beckett (1976) suggested that black women were more likely to work, whether it was necessary or not, than white women; and their husbands were more accepting of this fact than the white husbands. Their acceptance was more than cerebral; black men were more willing to accommodate themselves behaviorally to the needs created by their wives' employment. Black men are likely to have been trained at an early age, to care for younger children, prepare meals, keep their own clothes cleaned and ironed. They are likely as adults, to be willing to join their wives in the practice of these skills.

Fichter's results may help to explain some later research on women's satisfaction with their roles as a function of husbands' approval/disapproval of their roles. White middle class women who stay at home are more satisfied with their role if they feel that their husbands approve. White middle class women who work seem to be less dependent on the husband's approval of their role, but still there was a significant correlation between husband's perceived attitudes toward the wife's roles and the wife's satisfaction with her roles (Barnett & Baruch, 1978). Among black women across three income groups, wives' satisfaction with worker roles was independent of husband's perceived approval (Harrison & Minor, 1978). In traditional social science procedure one might be tempted to look for explanations for the "deviant" pattern among black wives. The search for such explanations has most often been cast in negative, deficiency hypotheses [as had research on black families until scholars like Robert Hill (1972) and Herbert Gutman (1976) began to contribute to the literature]. But reflecting on these findings on role satisfaction with Fichter's research and the work of Hill (1972) and others in mind, we might note that role flexibility has been a strength of black families with positive adaptive consequences. Perhaps the black women of all classes know that it does not matter what their husbands "attitudes" are since they can be expected to be accepting and supportive of the wife's working role.

Family relationships, for married and unmarried women, provide women with support for career development, support as mothers, as socially effective beings and in many other roles that they wish to pursue. Relationships with friends, especially other black women, are also a significant source of support. The balance sheet on social resources shows a profit. Myths and historically tense issues involving black males sap the social resource pool; mutual support among black women and the extensive kinship network are very large assets. But the ability to use the help offered by those around you also requires a certain level of skill and resource development. In this instance, personal resources such as one's own self evaluation would determine how well one could construct and mobilize a rich social network.

PERSONAL RESOURCES

Personal resources may refer to how you would perform as a borrower such as honesty, sense of responsibility, soundness of judgment—all qualities of good credit risks (Porter, 1980), your intelligence level (Yando et al., 1979), your self-esteem

(Rosenberg, 1965), coping styles (Mechanic, 1974; 1975; 1977), or communication skills (Dohrenwend & Dohrenwend, 1969). These and other personal resources are all characteristics of individuals, and differ from economic resources in being characteristics which might *lead to* the generation of income rather than having immediate monetary value. They differ from social resources in that personal resources may influence your chances of generating a viable support network, without actually constituting a social resource. Inversely, an adaptive support network may mean that you get better feedback on various dimensions of your personal resource repertoire. This would allow for adjustments in those personal resources that are subject to an individual's control.

Americans have come to realize over the last decade just how important a personal resource good health is, and that health problems can, to a large extent, be controlled. Smoking less, exercising more, controlling one's diet are all personally controllable factors that can have a substantial impact. The health of black Americans is not as good as that of whites, though black women are better off than black men. Of the two conditions especially prevalent among black women, hypertension and diabetes mellitus, hypertension is definitely subject to individual control. Excessive weight, tobacco smoking, exercise and cholesterol or fat in the diet are all factors that increase the risk of hypertension or high blood pressure. Two surveys in the last decade have shown no decrease in hypertension rates among black females (Statistical Profile of the Black Woman, 1981). It seems that widespread public education efforts have not reached black women or have gone unheeded.

Obesity is a major risk factor in diabetes as well as hypertension. Black women of all ages are heavier than white women and more are considered obese. However, there is no race difference in the prevalence of smoking in women, another contributor to hypertension. The implications for intervention seem apparent although health education efforts, a prevalent intervention in the past, must be closely evaluated.

Turning from physical to mental health, a finding of the Health and Nutrition Examination Survey made available in the early through mid 1970s indicated that there may be a significant difference between black men and women in self-reported psychological well-being. Black women's self reports were significantly lower than those of black males and white females. The latter two groups reported themselves to be at about the same level of well-being. Black women's reported level of well-being was, in fact, the lowest across the gender and age groupings, with 63 percent noting moderate to severe levels of distress (Statistical Profile of the Black Woman, 1981). Rates of self-reported illness interact with social resources to either increase or decrease a woman's sense of well-being. In related studies, Lemert (1962) and Mechanic (1962) have suggested that the more different an individual is, the more likely she will be ostracized by the group. Members tend to close ranks *against* the bizarrely-acting member, treating her as an outsider, defining her symptoms as internal ("Why is she so paranoid?"), and reducing the sufferer's chances of access to help in developing strategies for reducing the severity of her symptoms. The more fully the disordered member is integrated into the group, on the other hand, the greater the chance of the group's closing ranks *around* her, protecting her from outsiders, defining her symptoms as "only temporary," attributing the symptoms to external causes ("She's been under a lot of pressure lately."), and both generating and implementing coping strategies. If these strategies are adaptive, or if the fact of being emotionally supported is itself anxiety reducing, then the symptoms should stabilize or even become less pronounced as the feedback cycle is dampened. For self-reported symptoms, feedback from one's support network that one's self perceptions are accurate or inaccurate can reduce or increase symptoms over time, thus influencing the feedback from the social network, which will influence self perception, and so on.

Personal resources of another type are those that may be characterized as personality traits. Racism, classism, and sexism have all helped to shape black women's personalities (Staples, 1973), but in little understood ways. Empirical data on the personalities of black women is scarce at best. Major textbooks on personality theory omit mention of ethnic validity, and frequently gender validity, in critiquing a given theory. Work that has been done in testing theories on varied populations has usually suffered from bias in conceptualization and sampling problems (e.g., comparing small groups of lower class blacks with middle class whites is an often made error, confounding race with class differences). Data from white populations is of limited value because black girls of all ages are socialized differently than white girls (Ladner, 1972). From studies focused on other aspects of their lives we can infer that, while there are many black women who evidence symptoms of disorders, there are also many who operate in high stress situations for years with aplomb. Some of this is due to economic resources, of course, although for black women, economic resources are least likely to be the strong suit. Some of the ability to prevent high levels of stress is attributable to the intervention of a resilient social resource network. But much of the variation in the relationship between high stress and the presence or absence of symptoms of disorder is attributable to the relative vulnerability of a women's personal resource network.

We observed, with the undergraduate black females in nontraditional programs (Scott & Horhn, cited in Smith, 1982), that a perceived hostile environment did not dampen their motivation and aspirations for a family life and rewarding career. Epstein (1976), too, notes that black female professionals have more self-confidence than white females do. That kind of confidence may well have contributed to experimental results indicating that black women in competitive situations worked longer at an anagrams task that black women in a non-competitive situation (Jackson, 1982). Those in the competitive setting also produced more words on the anagram task and reported themselves as more self-confident than women in the non-competitive condition.

An essential personal resource is a positive self concept. For black women, with attitudes toward blacks and toward women being prevalent and negative, forging a positive self concept is a formidable task indeed (Jackson, 1982). The black female subjects of the experiment also worked longer at the task when competing with a white or black male confederate than when competing with a white or black female confederate, giving no evidence of the existence of a fear of success motive in black women. A negative self concept would seem in fact, to be a reasonable response to media promulgation of white middle class standards of beauty, the myth of the matriarchy that implies that black women enjoy some advantages that they certainly do not perceive; the myth of the superwoman that leaves us all feeling inadequate, and pressures to disprove the myth of the matriarchy by taking a submissive role to black men (Copeland, 1977). And it is true that some black women suffer from low self esteem and other depressive symptoms. But evidence from the lay press as well as scholarly sources supports the notion that, despite all odds, despite discrimination in multiple settings and for multiple reasons, many black women have maintained a positive self concept.

In a paradoxical way, it may be the universal hostility of much of her external environment that makes the black women's self confidence durable. In a world that is totalling ungiving, like a black women's work setting, any gains can be attributed to the self. Interaction with an environment that makes it clear that there is no reinforcement possible for your gender/race group makes it easier to attribute the variance for personal achievement correctly. This explanation is incomplete because it cannot account for the signs of helplessness in the matter of curing obesity and curbing the smoking impulse. But it is a start if it gets students, scholars and practitioners thinking about attributes and behaviors of black women as contextual problems—as questions regarding interactions between women and their wider environments.

DISCUSSION

The mechanisms of survival of black women in American society form a provocative social science puzzle. Some of the pieces fit, but perhaps not in the way envisioned by mainstream social scientists. We should not be surprised that white males—in the aggregate—have fairly resilient personal resources, healthy social networks, and strong economic resources. These puzzle pieces fit intuitively. What may be puzzling is that in spite of continuing discrimination from a variety of sources, black females seem to have much better personal and social resources than would be expected on the basis of their relatively weak economic resources.

What can we glean, then, from our discussion of the admittedly sparse literature on resource utilization among black women? And what implications do our conclusions have for the discovery of fruitful avenues for change?

The picture that we get from examining available data on economic resources among black women is that even as they enter the job market they are already at a disadvantage. They take lower status jobs, for less pay, and work longer years than other major groups in society. For the majority of black women, then, economic resources will never be an adequate buffer against high levels of stress until some way of breaking this depressed career chain is found. One possible way of breaking the chain would be marshalling resources to equalize entry level jobs for blacks and whites. This would require such forces as consumer pressure to increase the demand for changes in career counseling in high schools, the development of opportunities for more active involvement in work settings during the student phase, and the development of more on-the-job training opportunities to increase exposure to career options.

Kinship ties and a mutual respect among black females have been the primary bases for social support. A number of studies have supported the idea that having people around you on whom you can count to share your burdens helps one to cope with stress. And if any idea has held truth for black women, it has been this one. But social support can become a growth inhibitor if the skills and resources of at least some of the network members are not compatible with the emerging goals of the individual. So no matter how supportive friends or family are of the general idea of career development, the network should include those who have the skills—of whatever race or gender—if you want to acquire those skills.

There is evidence to suggest that the self concept of black females is more positive than would be predicted given the multiple discriminations to which they have been exposed. This counter-intuitive state of affairs is even more puzzling given the degree to which American society instills economic success benchmarks as major criteria for personal evaluations. If black women are able to maintain positive self concepts in the face of relatively impoverished economic resources, it may be that they have detached themselves from the benchmarks used by the rest of society, and evaluate themselves on different sets of criteria. Given that the large majority of black women must contribute to their own economic well being, it is in their best interest to have their jobs become more salient to their view of themselves. First, they need the ammunition for success (such as good entry level jobs), then they need to buy into the notion that this kind of success is important, if they are to become better able to develop a broad based economic resource network. The mutually reinforcing nature of these resources suggests that some momentum could be sustained once action on the economic resource front began— even in the face of continued discrimination.

REFERENCES

Allen, L. & Britt, D. W. Social class and mental illness: The impact of resources and feedback. In R. D. Felner, L. A. Jason, J. N. Moritsugu, & S. S. Farber (eds.), *Preventive psychology: Theory, research and practice in community intervention.* Elmsford, N.Y.: Pergamon Press, Inc., in press.

Alperson, E. D. The minority woman in academe. *Professional Psychology*, 1975, *6*, 232–256.

Barnett, R. C. & Baruch, G. K. Women in the middle years: A critique of research and theory. *Psychology of Women Quarterly*, 1978, *3*, 187–197.

Beckett, J. Working wives: A racial comparison. *Social Work*, 1976, *21*, 463–471.

Chisholm, S. Sexism and racism: One battle to fight. *Personnel and Guidance Journal*, 1972, *51*, 123–125.

Cobb, S. Social support as a moderator of life stress. *Psychosomatic Medicine*, 1976, *38*, 300–314.

Copeland, E. T. Counseling black women with negative self-concepts. *Personnel and Guidance Journal*, 1977, *55*, 397–400.

Dohrenwend, B. S. Social stress and community psychology. *American Journal of Community Psychology*, 1978, *6*, 1–14.

Dohrenwend, B. S. & Dohrenwend, B. P. Life stress and psychopathology. In *Risk factor research in the major mental disorders*, (DHHS Publication No. (ADM) 81-1068). Washington, D.C.: U.S. Government Printing Office, 1981.

Dohrenwend, B. P. & Dohrenwend, B. S. *Social status and psychological disorder: A causal inquiry.* New York: Wiley-Interscience, 1969.

Epstein, C. F. Positive effects of the multiple negative: Explaining the success of black professional women. In F. L. Denmark (ed.), *Women—Volume I: A PDI research reference work.* New York: Psychological Dimensions, Inc., 1976.

Fichter, J. *Graduates from predominantly Negro colleges: Class of 1964.* Washington, D.C.: U.S. Government Printing Office, 1969.

Frieze, I. H., Parsons, J. E., Johnson, P. B., Ruble, D. N., & Zellman, G. L. *Women and sex roles: A social psychological perspective.* New York: W. W. Norton & Co., 1978.

Glenn, N. Some changes in the relative status of American non-whites: 1940–1960. *Phylon*, 1960, *24*, 443–448.

Greenberg, E. S. Models of the political process: Implications for the black community. In E. S. Greenberg, N. Milner, & D. J. Olson (eds.), *Black politics.* New York: Holt, Rinehart and Winston, Inc., 1971.

Gump, J. P. Comparative analysis of black women and white women's sex-role attitudes. *Journal of Consulting and Clinical Psychology*, 1975, *43*, 858–863.

Gutman, H. *The black family in slavery and freedom, 1750–1925.* New York: Pantheon Books, 1976.

Hare, N. & Hare, J. Black women 1979. *Transaction*, 1978, *8*, 65–69.

Harrison, A. O. & Minor, J. H. Interrole conflict, coping strategies, and satisfaction among black working wives. *Journal of Marriage and the Family*, 1978, *40*, 799–805.

Hemmons, W. M. The women's liberation movement: Understanding black women's attitudes. In L. F. Rodgers-Rose (ed.), *The black woman*. Beverly Hills, Calif.: Sage Publications, Inc., 1980.

Hill, R. *The strengths of black families*. New York: Emerson Hall, 1972.

Hood, E. Black women, white women: Separate paths to liberation. *The Black Scholar*, 1978, *9*, 45–56.

Jackson, A. Militancy and Black women's competitive behavior in competitive versus non-competitive conditions. *Psychology of Women Quarterly*, 1982, *6*, 342–353.

Kinzer, N. S. *Stress and the American woman*. New York: Ballantine Books, 1978.

Ladner, J. *Tomorrow's tomorrow: The black woman*. Garden City, N.Y.: Doubleday, 1972.

Landry, B. & Jendrek, M. P. The employment of wives in middle-class black families. *Journal of Marriage and the Family*, 1978, *40*, 787–797.

Leggon, C. B. Black female professionals: Dilemmas and contradictions of status. In L. F. Rodgers-Rose (ed.), *The black woman*, Beverly Hills, Calif.: Sage Publications, Inc., 1980.

Lemert, E. M. Paranoia and the dynamics of exclusion. *Sociometry*, 1962, *25*, 2–20.

Lerner, G. (ed.) *Black women in white America*. New York: Pantheon Books, 1972.

Levitan, S., Johnston, W. B., & Taggart, R. *Still a dream: The changing status of blacks since 1960*. Cambridge, Mass.: Harvard University Press, 1975.

Liem, R. & Liem, J. Social class and mental illness reconsidered: The role of economic stress and social support. *Journal of Health and Social Behavior*, 1978, *19*, 139–156.

Lin, N., Simeone, R. S., Ensel, W. M., & Kuo, W. Social support, stressful life events, and illness: A model and an empirical test. *Journal of Health and Social Behavior*, 1979, *20*, 108–119.

McAdoo, H. P. Black mothers and the extended family support network. In L. F. Rodgers-Rose (ed.), *The black woman*. Beverly Hills, Calif.: Sage Publications, Inc., 1980.

McCray, C. A. The black woman and family roles. In L. F. Rodgers-Rose (ed.), *The black woman*. Beverly Hills, Calif.: Sage Publications, Inc., 1980.

Mechanic, D. Some modes of adaptation: Defense. In A. Monat & R. S. Lazarus (eds.), *Stress and coping*. New York: Columbia University Press, 1977.

Mechanic, D. Sociocultural and socio-psychological factors affecting personal responses to psychological disorder. *Journal of Health and Social Behavior*, 1975, *16*, 393–404.

Mechanic, D. Social structure and personal adaptation: Some neglected dimensions. In G. V. Coelho, D. A. Hamburg, & J. E. Adams (eds.), *Coping and adaptation*. New York: Basic Books, 1974.

Mechanic, D. Some factors in identifying and defining mental illness. *Mental Hygiene*, 1962, *46*, 66–74.

Mitchell, J. C. Social networks. *Annual Review of Anthropology*, 1974, *3*, 279–300.

Mosley, M. H. Black women administrators in higher education: An endangered species. In W. D. Smith, K. H. Burlew, M. H. Mosley, & W. M. Whitney (eds.), *Reflections on black psychology*. Washington, D.C.: University Press of America, Inc., 1979.

Murray, P. Jim Crow and Jane Crow. In G. Lerner (ed.), *Black women in white America*. New York: Pantheon Books, 1972.

Perlo, V. *Economics of racism, USA: Roots of black inequality*. New York: International Publishers Co., 1975.

Porter, S. *Sylvia Porter's new money book for the 80's*. New York: Avon, 1980.

Porterfield, E. *Black and white mixed marriages: An ethnographic study of black-white families*. Chicago: Nelson-Hall Publishers, 1978.

Rodgers-Rose, L. F. (ed.) *The black woman*. Beverly Hills, Calif.: Sage Publications, Inc., 1980.

Rosenberg, M. *Society and the adolescent self-image*. Princeton: Princeton University Press, 1965.

Schwab, J. & Schwab, R. *The epidemiology of mental illness*. Paper presented at the American College of Psychiatrists, Sixth Annual Seminar for Continuing Education of Psychiatrists, New Orleans, 1973.

Scott, P. & Horhn, M. A pilot study of black female undergraduates enrolled as majors in nontraditional curricula at the University of Tennessee, Knoxville. Unpublished study, 1975.

Simmons, J. The black women's burden. *Black Enterprise*, 1979, *10*, 57–60.

Smith, E. J. The black female adolescent: A review of the educational, career and psychological literature. *Psychology of Women Quarterly*, 1982, *6*, 261–288.

Stack, C. B. *All our kin.* New York: Harper & Row, 1974.

Staples, R. *The black women in America: Sex, marriage, and the family?* Chicago: Nelson Hall, 1973.

Statistical profile of the black woman. *Urban Research Review*, 1981, 7, 1–4.

Treas, J. Differential achievement: Race, sex and jobs. *Sociology and Social Research*, 1978, 62, 387–400.

Tolsdorf, C. C. Social networks, support, and coping: An exploratory study. *Family Process*, 1976, 15, 407–417.

U.S. Bureau of the Census. *Statistical abstracts of the United States: 1980* (101st edition). Washington, D.C.: U.S.Government Printing Office, 1980.

Wheaton, B. The sociogenesis of psychological disorder: An attributional theory. *Journal of Health and Social Behavior*, 1980, 21, 100–124.

Wilkinson, D. Y. & Taylor, R. L. *The black male in America: Perspectives on his status in contemporary society.* Chicago: Nelson-Hall, 1977.

Yando, R., Seitz, V., & Zigler, E. *Intellectual and personality characteristics of children: Social-class and ethnic-group differences.* Hillsdale, N.J.: Lawrence Erlbaum Associates, 1979.

II

SOCIAL PROBLEMS
OF WOMEN

This part deals with some of the social problems women in our society face and attempt to cope with. As in the previous section, a wide variety of topics are sampled, and the implications of current research for the prevention of, early intervention into, or specific treatment for these problems are discussed.

Gerrard, McCann, and Geis, in Chapter 5, address the problem of unwanted or unplanned pregnancy. The increase in the incidence of premarital sexual intercourse in the United States over the last decade is well known. However, even with an increase in the availability of birth control information and contraceptive technology over the past five years, there has been a decrease in the use of reliable contraception by sexually active women. An estimated 20 percent of the unmarried women who are sexually active at age 19 have conceived at least once, and evidence suggests this figure may be an underestimate. There are basically four choices open to the unmarried women who conceives: abortion, giving the child up for adoption, keeping the child without marrying, and marriage. All four options are likely to result in stressful, if not traumatic, psychological and/or economic consequences.

The effects of this social problem of unwanted pregnancy can be greatly reduced if sexually active women consistently use a reliable contraceptive method; researchers estimate a possible 40 percent or more reduction in premarital pregnancies is possible. The authors review the research pertaining to the antecedents of contraceptive behavior, and outline the demographic, social, and personality factors related to unwanted pregnancy, pointing out that contraceptive risk takers differ from reliable contraceptive users on a number of demographic, dispositional, and attitudinal variables. The pattern of relative contributions of these variables to contraceptive behavior is, however, very complex.

The authors describe three types of intervention programs currently available: the walk-in clinic, the milestone intervention, and the outreach intervention, and present research conducted to evaluate the effectiveness of these three programs. Future directions for research are also suggested.

Chapter 6 addresses the roles and status of a growing segment of our population—the divorced woman. As Allen and Britt in Chapter 4 identified stressful life events as being characteristic of the lives of black women, the authors of Chapter 6 deal with a specific stressful life event, divorce. Caldwell, Bloom, and Hodges explore the antecedents and consequences of the divorce process as they differentially affect women and men.

Chapter 4 noted black women's ability to handle stresses upon their economic, social, and personal resources; Caldwell, Bloom, and Hodges point out women's ability to handle the stress of divorce. The stereotype of the woman as a helpless victim in a divorce situation is challenged.

Divorced women, compared to divorced men and married women, tend to face more economic difficulties that result in several stressful situations. However, when comparing divorced women with married women and with widows, some investigators report that divorced women mention significantly more positive life changes. For the most part, however, men and women report experiencing the same negative effects, and to the same degree. The process of divorce appears to take its toll on both males and females, and both genders are equally able to bounce back and attain some degree of emotional stability.

Since men and women tend to react similarly to the divorce process in terms of the amount of psychological distress experienced, the most important predictor of successful adaptation is not sex, but the presence of other moderating variables. Among those characteristics that predict successful adjustment are an egalitarian sex role orientation, the availability of an emotional support system, and an amicable relationship between ex-spouses. The implications for crisis intervention and for prevention of traumatic divorces are noteworthy. With the increasing number of divorces in our society, treatment to ease the usual accompanying stress warrants careful consideration.

Focusing again on women with fewer resources and more stresses as high risk for social problems, Chapter 7 looks at recent intervention strategies for promoting parenting skills in lower socioeconomic families. Often these families are single parent, where the responsibility for child rearing is doubly felt. In this chapter, Shure presents highlights of her research-based intervention program. The goal of this program is to train parents to teach their preschool children effective ways of solving problems; in so doing, parents often enhance their own adjustment. Parents are not trained to modify their children's behavior, but rather to teach them how to think in more socially adaptive ways. In particular, Shure has identified four interpersonal cognitive skills that are absent in deficient problem-solving preschoolers: alternative solution thinking, consequential thinking, causal thinking, and sensitivity to interpersonal problems.

In order to make the teaching process interesting for the children, many of the training sessions developed by the author are in the form of games that the child and parent play together. In addition, parents are taught to encourage their children, through instruction and modeling, to use these skills in the face of real-life daily problems that require interpersonal problem-solving skills.

Shure's chapter is an excellent example of data-based psychological research addressing social problems. It is at the level of primary prevention that large-scale social and psychological problems must be attacked. Shure's successful results with her target population of low-income families and preschool children suggest the possibility of generalizing her program to other groups, such as older children of school age, retarded children, learning-disabled children, and possibly parents who abuse their children. Future applications, especially to problem groups, are promising.

Widespread and increasing fear of crime constitutes a major social problem, and the burden of this fear falls disproportionately on women. Riger and Gordon, in Chapter 8, outline the unique nature of crime against women and proceed with a detailed description of women's attitudinal and behavioral reactions to crime. Psychosocial and environmental factors that affect women's responses to crime are reviewed.

This chapter focuses again on the interface between psychological and social factors in the understanding of a female problem area. Women's reactions to crime are shaped by both types of factors. Based on data from the U.S. Census Bureau's National Crime Survey and the authors' own study launched in 1977, findings are reported on the extent and distribution of women's fear of rape and other crimes, the major determinants of fear, and the strategies women use to cope with the threat of victimization.

It is not simply rates of victimization that generate women's fears, but also the nature and perceived likelihood of that victimization. In addition to women's estimates of their own risk of danger, their perceptions of their physical competence and their sense of attachment to the neighborhood have an impact on their levels of fear. For example, women who perceive their risks as high, who see themselves as slow and weak, and who have marginal ties to their neighborhood are especially fearful.

Although relatively low victimization rates for women seem paradoxical with women's high fear levels, methodological practices may account for the discrepancy. The underreporting of violence by known assailants may be the cause of serious underestimation of crime rates against women. Also, the authors' research suggests that the nature of the crime, rape in particular, may be especially fear inducing. In fact, *men's* fear levels are also associated with their perceptions of a *woman's* risk of being raped in their neighborhoods.

After identifying those groups of women at highest risk for fear of victimization, Riger and Gordon outline various precautionary strategies taken. These strategies are described and the distribution of usage among demographic subgroups identified. Attitudinal and perceptual variables were found to be more powerful predictors of women's fears and of women's use of precautionary strategies than were either demographic variables or actual crime rates.

The distribution of fear appears to follow existing social cleavages delineated by gender, age, race, and social class—factors that mark status and power inequalities in our society. What can be done to reduce fear of crime and the behavioral restrictions women incorporate into their lives? Several intervention strategies are suggested both on an individual level and on a group, social policy level.

Concern about the contribution of health professionals to the quality of women's lives has been growing over the last 15 years. This concern has paralleled the development of the holistic and preventive medicine movements, and has been spurred by the recognition that some female medical problems have not been adequately dealt with by the medical professions. Chapter 9 addresses the relationship between society's reactions to women's health issues and the quality of women's lives. Although women have a lower mortality rate than men, they experience a greater amount of acute health problems during their lives. Thus, women utilize medical services more frequently than men; however, women rarely have a voice in initiating and developing health care policies.

Albino and Tedesco discuss some of the psychosocial reasons why women in our society experience more health problems than men. They include the multiple roles women play and the special health hazards associated with stereotypically feminine occupations. To compound this susceptibility to health problems, women often have neither the time nor the services available to them for adequate preventive measures. Again, as we have seen in other chapters, the identified social problem is particularly salient for minority and low-income women.

The authors identify other contributors to women's health issues. In particular, primary health care deliverers, i.e., doctors, tend to be male and many retain biases toward their female patients' complaints. Reported symptoms such as dysmenorrhea and nausea during pregnancy are frequently dismissed as being psychogenic in origin, not medical.

In conclusion, Albino and Tedesco offer several intervention strategies for a health care system that is currently fragmented and, hence, less than adequate for many women, especially those of low income who most need it. Unlike Chapter 7, which offers a *prescription* for enhancing low-income mothers' child-rearing skills, Chapter 9 calls attention to the epidemic proportions of another social problem, which again requires special intensive care for low-income women. Perhaps by taking this first step of alerting us to the severity of the problem, Albino and Tedesco have begun the process of discovering prescriptive interventions.

The section concludes with an appropriate topic: support and advocacy roles for women. The sampling of social problems presented in this volume, while complex and diverse, all are reflective of an underlying male-dominated core of our society. Until women wrest away from men a larger, more equitable share of power and, thus, are in a position to mold social policy, many of the social problems of women identified here will persist.

Chapter 10 deals with the issue of women advocating for power and of women helping women. The authors have chosen to study how women function in the role of advocate by using a case study approach. A feminist battered women's shelter and a woman's organization for the training and placement of volunteers are described. Following Reinharz' more theoretical chapter, which portrayed women as community builders, Bond and Kelly offer us a closer look at the factors which enable women to function effectively in advocacy roles.

The term "advocacy" is defined by the authors as "influence efforts to allocate community resources to meet the goals of an organization." While Gilbert's earlier chapter on achievement was directed at an *individual's* attainment of career goals, the process of advocacy implies an individual acting in the role of "achiever," "goal-obtainer," or "advocate" for a *group's* interests.

According to Bond and Kelly, effective advocacy is based on an interrelation between an individual's influence style and the particular organizational setting. In general, the literature on influence and advocacy portrays one style as most effective, that is, a male style. The authors conclude that women need to develop different strategies and styles of influence beyond those dictated by society to those derived from the task requirements.

A conceptual framework is presented which illustrates the interaction of support networks, advocacy, and organizational setting. A woman who is effective in advocacy work is assumed to have a social support network that will (1) facilitate her staying with the work, (2) give her tools to do the work, and (3) provide her with energy and commitment to complete the work. In contrasting these two organizations, the battered women's shelter and the organization for training and placing women volunteers, the authors reveal how the differing organizations' goals affect the advocate's role in each organization.

5

The Antecedents and Prevention
of Unwanted Pregnancy

Meg Gerrard
University of Kansas

Lisa McCann
Capitol Regional Mental Health Center, Hartford

Bill D. Geis
University of Kansas

The contraceptive revolution began a little more than two decades ago with the introduction of oral contraceptives and the development of antiseptic plastic and stainless steel intrauterine devices (IUD). These events heralded the beginning of a new reproductive age, and many scientists believed that it was only the beginning, that the development of the perfect contraceptive—effective, safe, acceptable, inexpensive, and simple to use and distribute was close at hand (Atkinson et al., 1980). It is now generally acknowledged that the search for a single universally acceptable, safe, effective method was naive, and that a variety of birth control methods are necessary for the variety of birth control life styles and circumstances we live under. The scientific community and a more sophisticated public have now recognized that each method has advantages and disadvantages, and that it will always be necessary to weigh the effectiveness of a given method against its risks.

In spite of the fact that birth control information and sophisticated contraceptive technology are readily available to most women today, substantial numbers of sexually active women use an unreliable method of contraception (e.g., foam, withdrawal, or rhythm), or no method at all (Zelnick & Kantner, 1977, 1980). It is estimated that at least 20 percent of the unmarried women who are sexually active at age 19 have conceived at least once (Zelnick et al., 1979), and recent reports would indicate that since the use of *reliable* methods of birth control among those women who use contraception has been gradually declining over the past 5 years (Zelnick & Kantner, 1980; Gerrard, 1982), this figure can be expected to rise.

It could be argued that recent increases in unwanted pregnancy and abortion are due to the increase in the last ten years in the proportion of teenage women who are sexually active. Zelnick and Kantner (1977, 1980) assessed the premarital sexual experience of metropolitan area teenage women and found that the proportion who reported engaging in sexual intercourse rose from 30 percent in 1971, to 43 percent in 1976, to 50 percent in 1979. Among metropolitan males between the ages of 17 and 21, 70 percent of those surveyed in 1979 reported having engaged in sexual intercourse. However, the increase in pregnancy rates can not be solely attributed to the increase in sexual activity. As noted, use of highly reliable methods of birth control (e.g., the pill, IUD or diaphragm) appears to be declining (Gerrard, 1982; Zelnick & Kantner, 1980), and this decline may be due in part to an increased number of women who have both realistic and exaggerated concerns about the undesirable side effects of the pill and IUDs (Atkinson et al., 1980; Benditt, 1980).

While much of the research on the antecedents and consequences of birth control has focused on teenagers and members of racial minority groups, the trends in contraceptive use indicate that the danger of unwanted pregnancy exists for most women throughout the child bearing ages of 13 to 45, for white and middle class women as well as minority women and women from the lower SES levels.

CONSEQUENCES

There are basically four choices open to the unmarried woman who conceives: abortion, giving the child up for adoption, keeping the child without marrying, and marriage. While there is little data on the mental health consequences of giving a child up for adoption, there is no doubt that the experience is at the very least upsetting, and may cause long-term trauma (Niswander et al., 1972). While induced abortion is less traumatic, both physically and psychologically, than carrying a pregnancy to term, it is clear that many women suffer from long-term depression following the procedure (Brewer, 1978).

The social, economic and psychological consequences of single motherhood are clearly documented for both teenagers and older women. The most frequently cited problems are delayed or truncated educational and social activities, unemployment, and role overload resulting from the responsibility of caring for a child without the support of a spouse (Furstenberg et al., 1981). Brazierman et al. (1971) report that children born to unwed mothers are more likely to be born prematurely and to experience health problems. Kempe and Helfer (1968) have also noted that child abuse is more prevalent for children who are the result of an out-of-wedlock pregnancy.

The pregnant teenager who does marry has a 50 percent probability of divorce within four years (Semens, 1970), and even if the couple does stay married they suffer some adverse consequences. A recent 15-year longitudinal study of 129 continuously married couples who had carried a premarital pregnancy to term and kept the child, (compared with a matched sample of non-premarital pregnancy married couples) revealed several significant differences between the groups (Freedman & Thornton, 1979). Specifically, it was found that couples with a premarital pregnancy achieved lower educational and family income levels, and had higher rates of unemployment and more subsequent unwanted pregnancies than couples who had not had a premarital pregnancy. Finally, if there is any remaining doubt about the social and emotional risks attendant to unplanned pregnancy, one need only examine the suicide rate among teenage mothers. Data presented in a 1968 report by the *Commission on Population and the American Future* indicated that the suicide rate among teenage mothers is ten times that of the general population (cited in Cvetkovich et al., 1975).

However this problem need not be so bad. Zelnick & Kantner (1978) estimate that it would be possible to reduce the number of premarital pregnancies, and presumably their psychological and economic consequences, by at least 40 percent if all sexually active young women were to use a method of contraception and use it consistently. Furthermore, if the majority of all sexually active women were to use the most reliable methods of contraception, the unwanted pregnancy rate would be reduced even more dramatically. However, reliable contraceptive behavior involves a complex sequence of psychological and behavioral events including a) awareness of the risk of becoming pregnant, b) obtaining adequate information about contraception, c) making a decision about contraceptive use, d) acquiring contraception, and e) regular and consistent use of a reliable contraceptive method.

ANTECEDENTS OF CONTRACEPTION

In the last 10 to 15 years, researchers have become increasingly interested in understanding the antecedents of contraceptive behavior with the goal of reducing unwanted pregnancies. Progress has been made in understanding the psychological and demographic correlates of contraceptive risk taking, and in demonstrating the effectiveness of a variety of interventions aimed at decreasing the incidence of unwanted or unplanned pregnancy by increasing the use of reliable contraception.

Demographic Factors

Some researchers reviewing contraceptive behavior and the importance of demographic factors such as age, race, religion, education, and social class have assigned them little meaningful influence (Fishbein, 1972; Mindick et al., 1977). However, there is a vast literature documenting the relationship between contraceptive behavior and variables such as ethnicity, social-economic level, and age (e.g., Zelnick et al., 1979; Dryfoos, 1982). In general, members of racial minority groups, the lower SES classes and Catholics are unlikely to use the most effective methods of birth control. Moreover, significant correlations have been found between an individual's age at first intercourse and their use of more effective forms of contraception at the time of that event, and between current age and use of contraception with the most recent sexual intercourse (Foreit & Foreit, 1978). These findings, however, point to a problem with such variables, i.e., they are often more descriptive than explanatory. For example, the fact that age may be associated with contraceptive behavior probably reflects an experience factor rather than any specific effect of chronological age. Indeed, experiential factors may have more predictive power than demographic variables.

Experiential Factors

Foreit and Foreit (1978) also report a significant relationship between frequency of intercourse and effective contraceptive behavior. However, as with age, it is not clear how an individual's frequency of intercourse relates to actual contraceptive practice. Is an older individual who has had more sexual experience more likely to have improved his or her contraceptive behavior on the basis of a pregnancy scare? Or, is it the case that the older and more experienced individual has been exposed to more birth control information and altered his or her behavior accordingly? Since the nature of this research has dictated correlational designs, these questions have been difficult to answer.

Related to this research on age is a body of literature investigating the relationship between the nature of the sexual relationship and contraceptive use (Cvetkovich & Grote, 1983, Fisher et al., 1979). Specifically, the type of relationship (e.g., casual, steady, engaged) appears to affect the use of contraceptives—the more serious the relationship, the more likely the couple is to use effective contraception. Hypothesizing about these findings, Fisher et al. (1979) have suggested that individuals in steady relationships may feel more comfortable discussing contraception, and/or have sex on a more predictable schedule, thus have more time and latitude to implement a contraceptive strategy. Moreover, Foreit and Foreit (1978) suggest that the nature of the relationship has much more to do with the use of effective contraception than do factors such as personality traits or attitudes.

Personality Correlates

Research guided by the dispositional model assumes that certain traits or personality characteristics predispose individuals to contraceptive risk taking behavior. A large number of studies have investigated relationships between dispositional variables and aspects of contraceptive behavior since the early 1970s, with a somewhat smaller number of findings turning up consistently across studies. In this brief overview we will focus on the areas of research which have produced the most consistent and promising results.

One of the first personality variables to be examined closely in terms of its relationship to effective birth control was locus of control. In two early studies, MacDonald (1970) and Lundy (1972) found significant correlations between contraception and internal locus of control. As with many studies in the early 1970s, Lundy's study may be criticized, however, for considering all women who reported using any form of contraception—regardless of the contraceptive's effectiveness—as members of the same contraceptive group.

In fact, more recent research has failed to replicate the significance of locus of control (Oskamp et al., 1978; Gough, 1973a; Harvey, 1976). However, Mindick and his colleagues have pointed out that although differences on Rotter's (1966) Locus of Control Scale are far from significant, when the items are broken down into factors (cf., Mirels, 1970), ineffective contraceptors do, in fact, report greater feelings of helplessness in their dealings with societal organizations and institutions than do effective contraceptors (Oskamp et al., 1976; Mindick et al., 1978).

Another set of variables, which is conceptually related to locus of control, has consistently been shown to differentiate between effective and ineffective contraceptors. This set includes planfulness (Mindick et al., 1978), future time perspective (Oskamp et al., 1978; Mindick et al., 1977; Oskamp et al., 1976), and socialization (Gough, 1973b; Oskamp et al., 1976). Harvey (1976) compared sexually active women using the pill or IUD with those using the diaphragm, foam, jelly, condom, rhythm, or no contraception, and found that pill and IUD users demonstrated higher levels of striving for the present and the future than did the less effective contraceptive group. In general, then it appears that ineffective contraceptors are less socialized, less future oriented, less planful, and have a lower level of striving than effective contraceptors.

This profile may well be related to risk taking behavior in general. Zuckerman et al. (1972), have reported that subjects with high scores on the Sensation Seeking Scale have had more sex partners and engage in sex more frequently than low or moderate sensation seekers. Since Foreit and Foreit (1978) have presented evidence that the use of ineffective contraceptive methods is more common in casual relationships, and that individuals with high sensation seeking scores are more likely to have multiple or casual relationships (Zuckerman et al., 1972), it could be expected that individuals scoring high on the Sensation Seeking Scale would use less effective contraception than individuals who score lower on the scale. However the one study that has examined the relationship between contraceptive use and a general tendency to take risks, using Kogan and Wallach's Choice Dilemmas Questionnaire (1964), did not find support for this hypothesis (Rader et al., 1978).

Taking a different approach to risk taking, sociologist Luker (1975) has proposed that contraceptive behavior is no different from other risk taking behaviors such as smoking, skiing, and not using seat belts, but that it is determined specifically by attitudes toward contraception and conception.

Attitudes toward Contraception

Luker argues that contraceptive behavior is a result of a rational decision-making process in which the costs of contraception (e.g., medical side effects, loss of spontaneity) are weighed against the potential benefits of pregnancy (e.g., proof of femininity and fertility). Conversely, the rewards of contraception (e.g., freedom from worry about conception) are weighed against the costs of contraceptive failure (e.g., psychological strain resulting from an unplanned child, abortion, or adoption). In this essentially cognitive model she suggests that "unwanted pregnancy is the end result of an informed decision making process" (p. 32).

One of the obvious problems with Luker's model of contraceptive behavior however is that it does not take into account the impact of irrational beliefs. As noted earlier, many women express exaggerated concerns and negative beliefs about the side effects of the pill and IUD, and it is believed that this may explain the general decline in the use of these methods. These concerns, often stimulated by sensational news coverage, appear to affect some women much more than others, and a woman's reaction or overreaction, to such concerns appears to be related to her contraceptibe behavior. For example, ineffective or unsuccessful contraceptors are more likely to hold negative attitudes and irrational beliefs such as "If you use the pill too long it will make you sterile." (Gerrard et al., in press).

Fishbein (1972) has presented a model of the role of attitudes and beliefs which is more sophisticated than the Luker model in that it recognizes the importance of these negative attitudes and irrational beliefs. According to this model, a woman's intention to use contraception is a function of 1) her beliefs about the consequences of contracepting or not contracepting, i.e., her subjective judgement of the probability that practicing birth control will lead to certain consequences and that not practicing birth control will lead to certain other consequences; and 2) her beliefs about what others expect her to do and her desire to comply with these expectations. Thus, this model incorporates a belief such as "the pill causes cancer" into the decision making process. Davidson and Jaccard (1975) found support for this model using a formula which multiplied beliefs about the consequences of birth control by the evaluation of these consequences, and beliefs about the norms for contraception by motivation to comply with these norms. This formula predicted 60 percent of the variance in intentions to contracept, and correlated with use of birth control pills. In a related study Insko et al. (1970) reported that women who use contraception not only have more positive attitudes and beliefs about contraception than do non-users, but that users also display more consistency within their attitude and belief systems.

While these examinations of the relationship between attitudes toward contraception and contraceptive behavior have been very productive, a number of authors have suggested that contraceptive behavior is mediated by attitudes toward sex in general as opposed to specific attitudes toward contraception.

Sex Related Attitudes and Emotions

An early study by Goldsmith et al. (1972) indicated that unsuccessful contraceptors are significantly less accepting of their sexuality than are successful contraceptors. This finding has now been replicated a number of times with a variety of instruments (cf. Gerrard, 1977), and has been expanded to include not just contraceptive successes and failures, but effective and ineffective contraceptors as well.

Byrne and his associates have studied individual attitudinal differences in emotional orientation to sexuality using the Sexual Opinion Survey (White et al., 1977), a measure of a dimension they call erotophobia-erotophilia. Erotophiles are purported to respond positively to sexual topics, issues, and practices whereas ertophobes hold generally negative attitudes toward all matters pertaining to sex. In addition, and perhaps more importantly, erotophobes have been shown to know less than erotophiles about the factual details of sexuality including information about conception and contraception (Byrne et al., 1977). This group is also less likely than erotophiles to use a campus contraception clinic, to use contraception consistently (Fisher et al., 1979), or to use *any* contraception during intercourse (Fisher, 1978).

Mosher (1973) has presented evidence that high-sex-guilt males hold less favorable attitudes toward the widespread availability of sex information, contraceptives, or abortion. Similarly, Gerrard (1982), found a significant negative correlation between sex guilt and frequency of contraception, and that women using no contraception or ineffective methods had significantly higher sex guilt scores than women using effective methods.

Mosher and Cross (1971) have argued that in addition to inhibiting sexual activity, sex guilt interferes with sex related cognitive processes. In a seldom replicated study Schwartz (1973) provided evidence of this cognitive interference in that individuals who were high in sex guilt had difficulty retaining birth control information. In a study of sex guilt in abortion patients, Gerrard (1977) provided support for these findings. Not only did the abortion patients have higher sex guilt than the sexually active control subjects, but within each contraceptive use group, the sex guilt scores of the abortion patients were higher than those of the control group. This suggests very strongly that women with high sex guilt are often not successful at applying effective contraceptives even when they do attempt to use them. Taken together these studies support Mosher's contention that sex guilt can interfere with cognitive processes related to sex.

Summary

In conclusion, the research on the antecedents of contraceptive use indicates that contraceptive risk takers differ from reliable contraceptors on a number of demographic, experiential, dispositional, and attitudinal variables. One particularly promising line of research points to the importance of attitudes toward sex and contraception, and emotional predispositions toward sex. Characteristics such as sex guilt and erotophobia appear to inhibit sexual activity. However if a woman who scores high on one of these traits does engage in sexual intercourse, she tends not to use adequate contraception. It is interesting to note that mean sex guilt levels remained relatively constant during the 1970s while the number of young women engaging in intercourse rose dramatically (Gerrard, 1982). Is is not surprising then that the level of sex guilt sufficient to inhibit sexual activity in the early 1970s was no longer a sufficient deterrent in the late 1970s (Gerrard, 1982). However, an anomaly appears to exist here. That is, even when the level of sex guilt is not high enough to preclude sexual intercourse, it often operates to inhibit use of effective contraception, perhaps as a result of the interference with rational cognitive processes suggested by Mosher and Cross (1971).

It must be noted that to date much of this research has been more descriptive than predictive, and although some of it's results are helpful in planning preventive interventions, there is still a large gap between the basic research cited above and the applied field of designing interventions into contraceptive behavior. Having laid this groundwork in defining what psychology has contributed to the understanding of the correlates of unplanned pregnancy, we will now turn our attention to interventions designed to prevent such pregnancies by increasing the use of effective contraception.

INTERVENTIONS

A perusal of the literature indicates that all contraceptive interventions are based on one or more of the following assumptions:

1) Unwanted pregnancies and abortions occur because of ignorance about contraception or lack of adequate and complete information about sexuality and contraception. This approach suggests that men and women would engage in reliable contraceptive behavior if they were knowledgeable, and that the problem of unwanted pregnancies could be substantially reduced if all sexually active people were adequately educated about sexuality and contraception.

2) Lack of access to contraceptive devices and prescriptions is a contributing factor in unplanned pregnancies. Consequently, an increase in the availability of contraceptives is thought to result in a decrease in the incidence of unplanned pregnancy.

3) Contraceptive risk taking reflects dispositional and attitudinal biases which interfere with a person's ability to make logical and informed decisions concerning contraception. This approach suggests several therapeutic possibilities for changing contraceptive behavior which are often used in combination with knowledge and access interventions.

Although all interventions have one or more of these assumptions in common, they can be best classified in terms of the characteristics of their target groups rather than the assumptions underlying the program. We will discuss three major kinds of interventions: 1) the *walk-in clinic*, aimed at providing contraceptive counseling and devices to anyone who identifies themselves as being at risk of unplanned pregnancy and seeks services, i.e., women who are self-motivated to avoid pregnancy; 2) the *milestone* intervention, aimed at providing birth control services to people at some specific point in their lives (e.g., women after their first birth or abortion, students in junior high, high school or college); and 3) the *outreach* intervention which attempts to identify individuals at risk and provide information, counseling, or contraceptive devices to contraceptive risk takers who have not identified themselves as being vulnerable, or at least have not presented themselves for services.

While these approaches are not mutually exclusive (e.g., walk-in clinics can be located in schools, and milestone interventions can be aimed at either self-identified risk takers or women at risk who do not recognize their vulnerability to conception), this classification highlights the distinctions between both the approaches and provides a framework for the examination of relevant social policy and research issues.

Walk-in Clinics

The most common type of intervention is the walk-in clinic where the goal is to "enable American families freely to determine the number and spacing of their children" (Senate Committee on Labor and Public Welfare, 1971). In 1979, 4.5 million women received services from organized family planning programs such as these across the United States; 3.9 million of these women were from low or marginal income families. These organized programs are operated by hospitals, Planned Parenthood affiliates, health departments, and voluntary organizations at 5195 clinic sites (Tores et al., 1981), serving at least two-thirds of all counties in the U.S. (Alan Guttmacher Institute, 1976). These clinics typically offer medical contraceptive services to any women who walks in the door, with a priority assigned to providing these services for low-income women.

The primary goal of organized family planning programs is to provide contraceptive devices and prescriptions to those who request birth control. However, prior to the recent cuts in federal funds, some sites offered very limited outreach services in an effort to attract clients who do not perceive themselves to be at risk (Dryfoos, 1982).

One of the most sophisticated evaluations of the impact of Family Planning Clinics was conducted by Cutright and Jaffe (1976). This evaluation compared the fertility rates of women with access to organized family planning programs with census data on the fertility rates of women of childbearing age who were from the same socioeconomic backgrounds but did not have access to such services. Noting that organized family planning programs increased during a period of overall decline in U.S. fertility, and that the decline in fertility was greatest among the very groups that were targeted by the programs (i.e., blacks, and women with little education), Cutright and Jaffe raised the question of how much of the reduction in unwanted pregnancies was attributable to the family planning movement, and how much was caused by concurrent social and economic changes. To answer this question they examined the effects of differences in family planning program enrollment in 1968–1969 on differences in fertility in 1969–1970, when sociodemographic factors are controlled. Fertility rates were computed for a sample of counties served by family planning clinics and for a matched set of counties without clinics. Simultaneous multiple regression was used to determine the relative influence of the rate of enrollment in these clinics, educational level, mobility, marital status, and employment on fertility rates. The results of these analyses were very clear and consistent. As the authors wrote:

Under rigorous statistical controls, it has been shown that the larger the proportion of lower SES women enrolled in organized family planning programs, the lower their fertility. Program effects, independent of other social, economic and cultural factors were shown for lower SES whites and blacks, and for most age groups . . . . The program works because it gives women of lower socioeconomic status access to modern and effective methods of contraception that they would not otherwise have. (p. 110)

Finally, it should be pointed out that this evaluation was conducted on 1969–1970 fertility rates, using estimates of clinic use in 1968–1969. At this time, the family planning movement was in its infancy. Undoubtedly the effects of these walk-in clinics upon the fertility of the nation has increased dramatically since the late 1960s.

Milestone Interventions

The milestone approach differs from the walk-in clinic in that its major assumptions are that there are certain periods in a person's life when they are most likely to be responsive to contraceptive information and services, and that prevention of unwanted pregnancy can be accomplished most efficiently when the target group is easily accessible. The most common site for milestone programs is the school system, although maternity wards and abortion clinics have also been used.

The St. Paul Maternal and Infant Care Project (MIC) provides an excellent example of such a program aimed at providing educational and counseling services, as well as increased access to contraceptive devices (Edwards et al., 1980). This program, situated in two senior high schools (grades 9–12), was part of a comprehensive health care program which provided immunizations, dental check-ups, health examinations for jobs, college and sports, in addition to pregnancy tests, contraceptive education and counseling, referral to a special evening adolescent clinic at a local hospital for contraceptive devices, and day care for adolescent parents.[1] Each school had its own health care team consisting of a family planning nurse practitioner, a social worker, an obstetrician-gynecologist, a pediatrician and pediatric nurse, a dental hygeinist, nutritionist, health educator, and day care director. This wide range of services allowed students to enter the clinic under circumstances which protected their anonymity and confidentiality, an important concern for most adolescents.

A six year evaluation of the effectiveness of this program proved very encouraging. The 403 students who received initial family planning, educational, medical, counseling or referral services at the MIC clinics were followed until they were 18 years old or had graduated from high school. In the last year of the evaluation period 75 percent of the entire student body at the two schools attended the clinic at least once, and the 12 month continuation rate for contraception was 92.8 per 100 women. More importantly, the fertility rate for the schools fell from 79 per 1000 to 35 per 1000.

A number of factors are apparently responsible for the success of this program in recruiting patients, promoting continued contraception, maintaining low attrition, and decreasing pregnancy rates. Foremost among these were confidentiality, the anonymity provided by the large number of services offered and the lack of need to communicate with the students through their homes. Another contributing factor was the ability of the family planning nurse practitioner to contact the patients within one week of their initial visit, and later on a monthly basis, to

---

[1] Since some community members objected to dispensing contraceptives in the school, members of the school clinic staff were available at the evening teenage clinic for this purpose.

discuss such issues as contraceptive problems, accessibility of free contraceptive devices and prescriptions, and the provision of educational and counseling services.

The Outreach Approach

While there are innumerable examples of walk-in clinics and milestone interventions currently operating across the country, there are few outreach programs aimed primarily at identifying and providing services to women who are not motivated to seek them on their own initiative. A recent study by McCann (1981, reported in Gerrard et al., 1983) is an evaluation of an outreach program aimed at ineffective contraceptors. This study was designed to compare the effectiveness of a contraceptive information intervention with that of a cognitive restructuring intervention. The approach is different from the walk-in and milestone programs presented above in a number of important ways. First, the cognitive restructuring intervention tested in the McCann study was based on cognitive models of contraceptive decision making (i.e., those presented by Luker, 1975, and Fishbein, 1972). As such, it is the first attempt to examine the use of a cognitive approach to change contraceptive behavior. The second important distinction is that the target population was sexually active women who had not evidenced motivation to obtain or use effective contraception. The choice of this population reflects the assumption that sex related attitudes and emotions can interfere with rational thinking about contraception in such a way that they might inhibit a woman's motivation to initiate effective contraceptive behavior no matter how accessible the services are. And the third major distinction between the McCann intervention and the programs described above is that it was primarily designed to serve a research function rather than a service function. Because of these differences, we will elaborate on the design of the study as well as describe the intervention and the results of its evaluation.

In this study sexually active unmarried college women who were using either an ineffective method of contraception or no method at all were assigned to one of three conditions: an information only intervention, a cognitive restructiring intervention, or a no-treatment control group. Subjects in the two treatment groups completed pretest instruments at the beginning of the first treatment session, whereas control subjects completed the pretest instruments during a session designed specifically for administration of the instruments. The two treatment groups then listened to a lecture on contraception and returned one week later for a discussion group session. Subjects in all three conditions returned approximately four weeks after the pre-test session to complete post-test instruments designed to assess current level of sexual activity and contraceptive use. In addition, a follow-up telephone interview was conducted three months later in which all subjects were asked about their current sexual activity and current use of contraceptives.

Subjects in the two treatment conditions listened to an hour long structured lecture on the use and effectiveness of available contraceptive methods. The didactic material was combined with demonstrations on the actual use of various contraceptives. Lectures in both treatments contained the same content regarding contraceptive use and effectiveness, designed to increase the subject's knowledge of the risk of conception and available means of preventing conception. However, the two lectures differed in the emphasis placed on challenging negative attitudes and beliefs about effective contraception. Specifically, the cognitive restructuring lecture focused on common negative attitudes and beliefs about effective contraception and then actively challenged these attitudes and beliefs. In contrast, the information only lecture presented factual information about contraception without actively attempting to change negative attitudes or beliefs. In the discussion groups (one week after the lectures), subjects were encouraged to raise any questions or concerns that were stimulated by the lecture. These sessions were designed to enhance the impact of the lecture by providing the opportunity to clarify and discuss the material presented in the lecture. The cognitive restructuring discussion group was focused on changing misconceptions and negative attitudes toward effective contraceptive use while the information only discussion group clarified factual information about various contraceptives.

The results of the analysis of the contraceptive use data demonstrated that at the one month follow-up, subjects in both the information only condition, and the cognitive restructuring condition, had increased their use of effective methods of contraception significantly more than had the subjects in the no treatment control condition. Analysis of the three month follow-up data revealed that the cognitive restructuring intervention was still significantly different from the no treatment intervention, while the information only condition showed only a trend towards significance.

This investigation provides support for the utility of an intervention designed to change cognitions which inhibit effective contraception, and demonstrates the potential of a proactive approach which identifies women at risk of unplanned pregnancy and provides them with services which will decrease the probability that they will conceive.

IMPLICATIONS FOR SOCIAL POLICY

These three examples of interventions illustrate a number of dimensions along which interventions can vary. These dimensions in turn, represent many of the social policy decisions that are inherent in designing birth control programs. An examination of the characteristics of these three illustrative approaches will serve as a framework for discussion of these issues.

Target Population

The vast majority of all organized interventions fall under the rubric of walk-in clinics such as those operated by Planned Parenthood. These programs are designed primarily to provide contraceptive devices and prescriptions to women who do not get them from a private physician, but who are motivated to avoid unwanted or mistimed pregnancies. The assumption behind such clinics is that women are motivated to avoid such pregnancies, and that providing access to services will increase a woman's ability to control her fertility. Moreover, the location of the clinics implies additional assumptions about the characteristics of the population in need of such services. In the case of federally funded programs, the target group is typically identified as being members of lower socioeconomic classes, the poorly educated, and minority groups who have traditionally not used private physicians and have historically had higher fertility rates than the population in general.

Implicit in the milestone approach is a different set of assumptions about the appropriate target group. Foremost among these are the assumptions that there are times in a woman's life when she is most open to contraceptive services (e.g., after an abortion, or following delivery of a baby); that there are times when she is most in need of such services (e.g., when she first becomes sexually active); or that there are locations where it is easy to serve women at risk of unwanted pregnancy (e.g., abortion clinics, maternity wards, schools). In contrast to the walk-in clinic approach, milestone interventions do not assume that women are not motivated to seek contraceptive services, but instead, assume that they will accept such services if the services are brought to them.

The outreach approach represents yet another set of assumptions about appropriate target groups. It suggests that identified risk takers (e.g., women who have experienced an unwanted pregnancy such as abortion patients, or women who are sexually active but not using effective contraception) are appropriate target groups, and that interventions designed for this group should not assume motivation to avoid pregnancy or even knowledge of the risk. These assumptions are fundamentally different from those underlying the walk-in clinic and the milestone interventions in that they imply that knowledge and/or personality factors influence the amount of initiative a woman will take to prevent conception. Given these assumptions interventions should be directed at (a) educating women as to the risks of sexual intercourse without contraception, and (b) helping women overcome their dispositional and attitudinal blocks to effective contraception.

While it is obvious that the assumptions behind these approaches do not define mutually exclusive target groups, it is equally obvious that they guide the implementation of the interventions. For example, Planned Parenthood clinics could provide more outreach services if they were not built on the assumption of self motivation. Similarly the McCann outreach intervention would only have provided education if it were not based on the assumption that attitudinal and dispositional biases contribute to a woman's inability to make rational decisions about contraception.

Comprehensiveness

The assumptions behind the intervention, the purpose of the intervention, and the resources available to the program all influence the decisions about the comprehensiveness of the services to be provided. The resources of the MIC program were allocated in such a way that it provided every service which could reasonably be assumed to increase the program's effectiveness in two high schools. This is in direct contrast to the family planning approach which provides less comprehensive services to more people, and the McCann study which was designed specifically to test the effectiveness of a cognitive restructuring intervention.

The most comprehensive of the interventions described earlier is the MIC school-based program. This program provided education about sex and contraception, counseling, access to contraceptive devices and prescriptions, follow-up counseling and medical examinations and even pregnancy tests. The only service it did not provide was early identification of women at risk. The least comprehensive approach (in terms of range of services) described above was the McCann intervention which provided education and group counseling but not access to contraception or follow-up.[2]

---

[2] Although the follow-up contacts with the subjects in this study may have had the effect of facilitating continued contraceptive use, they were designed primarily to assess the effectiveness of the group intervention.

Intensity

The issue of the intensity of the program is closely related to the issue of comprehensiveness. Here again the MIC program provided more intense individual counseling and continuation services than either the Planned Parenthood program or the Gerrard et al. program. A particularly useful aspect was the provision of a one week follow-up to the initial visit where the nurse practitioner discussed any problems the client might have encountered with the contraceptive method she chose, and monthly follow-up appointments with all clients until their 18th birthday or graduation from high school. Although many organized family planning services schedule such follow-up appointments, few have the advantage MIC did of knowing where and how to locate the clients when they missed follow-up appointments.

Cost Effectiveness

While a comprehensive analysis of the cost effectiveness of the different approaches to decreasing unplanned or mistimed pregnancies is beyond the scope of this chapter, some cost effectiveness issues are inherent in the comparison of these three programs. Of the three approaches described above, only the McCann study was designed primarily to meet research goals. As such, it was never intended to be cost effective in terms of preventing pregnancies. However it was based on the assumption that early identification and treatment of contraceptive risk takers is cost effective, as well as an effective strategy in the primary prevention of the stress and trauma attendant to an unwanted conception.

A comparison of the cost effectiveness of the Planned Parenthood vs. MIC programs raises several difficult but important questions. First among these is whether an effective, intensive, and comprehensive intervention early in young women's sex lives is likely to reduce unwanted conceptions throughout the clients' lives. If so, is this approach more cost effective than less targeted, less comprehensive, and less intensive interventions which reach more women? With shrinking federal funds for both intervention programs and research, are these funds best spent on research designed to demonstrate that the effectiveness of previously demonstrated programs can be increased, or on research aimed at refining programming and answering questions about the relative contributions of various aspects of effective programs? The evidence indicates that walk-in programs like Planned Parenthood are effective in reducing fertility among targeted subgroups, *and* that comprehensive and intensive milestone programs can be effective in the short term. This suggests that optimal cost effectiveness would be attained through research designed to determine which elements of these programs are producing the effects, and continued basic research into the antecedents of contraceptive risk taking.

FUTURE DIRECTIONS FOR BASIC RESEARCH

Since family planning services have made contraceptives as available to the low income, uneducated, and minority groups in our population as they are to the patients of private physicians, the question has now become whether different intervention strategies and possibly different methods of contraception are appropriate for different groups, rather than which groups should be targeted. In this view, one relatively neglected area of research is the contraceptive practices and preferences of men. While the overwhelming method of choice among urban teenage males is the condom, a recent study of college men indicated that in this older, better educated population, men reported that the pill and the condom were equally popular (Geis & Gerrard, in press). In addition to the obvious need for additional research on the antecedents of male contraceptive behavior, the results of the Geis and Gerrard study suggest several potentially fruitful lines of research.

First, relatively little research has addressed the role of the sexual partner in contraceptive decision making. Since with the exception of vasectomies, the most effective methods are of necessity initiated and applied by the woman, male use of effective contraception is largely determined by association with women who use effective methods. It has been shown that some women are more easily influenced by their partner's preferences than are others (cf. D'Augelli & Cross, 1975).

If these women are also more vulnerable to their partner's contraceptive preferences, then the characteristics of the male and the dynamics of the relationship become important topics for future research. We can only speculate as to whether the dearth of research on the relationship between the dynamics of the couple's relationship and their contraceptive decision making is due to the fact that women are the target of most research because they bear most of the consequences of unwanted pregnancies, because the most effective methods require female initiation, or because women's contraceptive use is easier to study. Regardless, it is time to turn our attention to the antecedents of male contractive preferences, but also to the impact of both partners on contraceptive decision making.

Second, but perhaps more important is need for more sophisticated longitudinal studies of contraceptive use. While increased age is clearly associated with effective contraception, and poor early contraception is predictive of continued poor contraception (Freedman & Thornton, 1970), longitudinal or retrospective studies of the evolution of contraceptive behaviors which examine the development of behaviors *and* attitudes are nonexistent. Such research could not only answer questions about individual continuation or discontinuation of effective birth control, but if it started tracking young women before they became sexually active, it could potentially shed some light on the antecedents of contraceptive risk taking present even before the decision to become sexually active. Since the vast majority of all research on the correlates of contraceptive risk-taking is conducted on women who have already become pregnant, and women who have sought contraceptive services, very little is known about either the relationship between the decision to become sexually active and contraceptive use, or about women who are sexually active but not motivated to seek contraceptive services. While the longitudinal work of researchers such as Mindick and his colleagues on the continuation of contraception has been very valuable (e.g., Oskamp et al., 1978), a number of important questions can only be addressed by studying those women who never present themselves for help.

The Dependent Variable Problem

One methodological problem that has plagued research in the area involves the definition of appropriate dependent variables. Some studies have ranked birth control methods in an ordinal scale of increasing use effectiveness (e.g., (1) no contraception, (2) withdrawal, (3) condom, (4) the pill) and sampled use at a specific point in time (c.f., Foreit & Foreit, 1978). Others have attempted to assess the consistency of contraceptive use, but have made no provision for judging the reliability of the methods used (c.f., Fisher et al., 1979).

However none of these methods provides an overall picture of an individual's contraceptive behavior. An accurate assessment of contraceptive behavior would need to include measures of (1) the use effectiveness of the method(s) used, (2) the consistency with which these methods have been used, and (3) the initiative taken in planning for contraception. Such an assessment method is definitely needed if the focus of contraceptive research is going to shift to an assessment of the probability of unwanted or mistimed conception during an individual's or couple's *entire* sexual history.

SOME CONCLUDING OBSERVATIONS

The literature on the psychological antecedents of contraceptive behavior clearly characterize ineffective female contraceptors as being unaccepting of their own sexuality (Goldsmith et al., 1972) and having negative attitudes toward most matters pertaining to sex (White et al., 1977). Their attitudes and emotions include irrational fears about specific contraceptives (Gerrard et al., 1983), conflicting attitude and belief systems about birth control in general (Insko et al., 1970), and guilt (Gerrard, 1977; 1982). Implicit in this profile is an inability to think rationally about the high probability that unprotected sex will result in conception, and an inability to engage in rational decision making about birth control. When this interference with cognitive processes related to contraception is combined with lack of socialization (Oskamp et al., 1976), planfulness (Mindick et al., 1978), and future time perspective (Oskamp et al., 1978), it is not surprising that these women often fail to use services which are easily accessible, and fail even when they attempt to use contraceptives (Gerrard, 1977).

However, our review of the prevention programs currently available reveals that the vast majority are designed to serve the self-motivated woman. Given that these programs have already been demonstrated to be effective, it is time to turn our attention to exploring ways to reach those women who will not take adequate precautions without first experiencing changes in their attitudinal and emotional respones to sex. Given the current need to conserve financial resources, it is important that programs pay attention to the results of the last 10 to 15 years of basic research on the antecedents of contraception, and take a more proactive approach to the primary prevention of unwanted pregnancies.

REFERENCES

Alan Guttmacher Institute, *Data and Analyses for 1976 Revision of DHEW Five-Year Plan for Family Planning Services*, New York, 1976.

Atkinson, L., Schearer, S. B., Harkavy, O., & Lincoln, R. Prospects for improved contraception. *Family Planning Perspectives*, 1980, *12*, 173–192.

Benditt, J. M. Current Contraceptive research. *Family Planning Perspectives*, 1980, *12*, 149–155.

Brazierman, M., Sheehan, C., Ellison, D. B., & Schlessinger, E. R. *Pregnant Adolescents: A Review of Literature with Abstracts 1960-1970*. Washington, D.C.: Consortium on early childbearing and childrearing. Research Utilization and Sharing Project, 1971.

Brewer, C. Induced abortion after feeling fetal movements: Its causes and emotional consequences. *Journal of Biosocial Science*, 1978, *10*, 203–208.

Byrne, D., Jazwinski, C., DeNinno, J. A., & Fisher, W. A. Negative sexual attitudes and contraception. In D. Byrne and L. A. Byrne (eds.), *Exploring Human Sexuality*. New York: Harper and Row, 1977.

Cutright, P. & Jaffe, F. S. Family Planning Effects on the Fertility of Low-Income U.S. Women. *Family Planning Perspectives*, 1976, *8*, 100–110.

Cvetkovich, G. & Grote, B. Adolescent development and teenage fertility. In D. Byrne and W. A. Fisher (eds.), *Adolescents, sex, and contraception.* New York: Lawrence Erlbaum, 1983.

Cvetkovich, G., Grote, B., Bjorseth, A., & Sarkissian, J. On the psychology of adolescents' use of contraceptives. *The Journal of Sex Research*, 1975, *11*, 256.

D'Augelli, J. F. & Cross, H. Relationship of sex guilt and moral reasoning to premarital sex in college women and in couples. *Journal of Consulting and Clinical Psychology*, 1975, *43*, 40–47.

Davidson, A. R. & Jaccard, J. J. Population Psychology: A New Look at an Old Problem. *Journal of Personality and Social Psychology*, 1975, *31*, 1073–1082.

Dryfoos, J. G. Contraceptive use, pregnancy intentions and pregnancy outcomes among U.S. women. *Family Planning Perspectives*, 1982, *14*, 81–94.

Edwards, L. E., Steinman, M. E., Arnold, K. A., & Hakanson, E. Y. Adolescent Pregnancy Prevention Services in High School Clinics. *Family Planning Perspectives*, 1980, *12*, 6–14.

Fishbein, M. Toward an understanding of family planning behaviors. *Journal of Applied Social Psychology*, 1972, *2*, 214–227.

Fisher, W. A. *Affective, attitudinal, and normative determinants of contraceptive behavior among university men.* Unpublished doctoral dissertation, Purdue University, 1978.

Fisher, W. A., Byrne, D., Edmunds, M., Miller, C. T., Kelley, K., & White, L. A. Psychological and situation-specific correlates of contraceptive behavior among university women. *Journal of Sex Research*, 1979, *15*, 38–55.

Foreit, K. G. & Foreit, J. R. Correlates of contraceptive behavior among unmarried U.S. college students. *Studies in Family Planning*, 1978, *9*, 169–175.

Freedman, D. S. & Thornton, A. The long-term impact of pregnancy at marriage on the family's economic circumstances. *Family Planning Perspectives*, 1979, *11*, 6–21.

Furstenberg, R. R., Lincoln, R., & Menkern, J. (eds.), *Teenage sexuality, pregnancy and childbearing.* Philadelphia: University of Pennsylvania Press, 1981.

Geis, B. D. & Gerrard, M. Predicting male and female contraceptive behavior: A discriminant analysis of high, moderate, and low contraceptive effectiveness groups. *Journal of Personality and Social Psychology*, in press.

Gerrard, M. Sex guilt in abortion patients. *Journal of Consulting and Clinical Psychology*, 1977, *45*, 708.

Gerrard, M. Sex, sex guilt, and contraceptive use. *Journal of Personality and Social Psychology*, 1982, *42*, 153–158.

Gerrard, M., McCann, L., & Fortini, M. Prevention of Unwanted Pregnancy. *American Journal of Community Psychology*, 1983, *11*, 153–168.

Goldsmith, S., Gabrielson, M., Gabrielson, I., Matthews, V., & Potts, L. Teenagers, sex, and contraception. *Family Planning Perspectives*, 1972, *4*, 32–38.

Gough, H. G. A factor analysis of contraceptive preferences. *Journal of Psychology*, 1973, *84*, 199–210. (a)

Gough, H. G. Personality assessment in the study of population. In J. R. Fawcett (ed.), *Psychological perspectives of population.* New York: Basic Books, 1973. (b)

Harvey, A. L. Risky and safe contraceptors: Some personality factors. *Journal of Psychology*, 1976, *92*, 109–112.

Insko, C. A., Blake, R. R., Cialdini, R. B., & Mulaik, S. Attitude toward birth control and cognitive consistency: Theoretical and practical implications of survey data. *Journal of Personality and Social Psychology*, 1970, *16*, 228–237.

Kempe, R. R. & Helfer, C. H. *The Battered Child.* Chicago: University of Chicago Press, 1968.

Kogan, N. & Wallach, M. A. *Risk taking: A study of cognition and personality.* New York: Holt, Rinehart & Winston, 1964.

Luker, K. C. *Taking Chances: Abortion and the decision not to contracept.* Berkeley: University of California Press, 1975.

Lundy, J. R. Some personality correlates of contraceptive use among unmarried female college students. *Journal of Psychology*, 1972, *80*, 9–14.

MacDonald, A. P. Internal-external locus of control and the practice of birth control. *Psychological Reports*, 1970, *83*, 1975–1982.

McCann, L. Information Only and Cognitive Restructuring Interventions with Contraceptive Risk Takers. Unpublished Master's Thesis, University of Kansas, 1981.

Mindick, B., Oskamp, S., & Berger, D. E. Prediction of success or failure in birth planning: An approach to prevention of individual and family stress. *American Journal of Community Psychology*, 1977, *5*, 447.

Mindick, B., Oskamp, S., & Berger, D. E. Prediction of Adolescent Contraceptive Practice. Paper presented at American Psychological Association Convention, 1978.

Mirels, H. L. Dimensions of internal versus external control. *Journal of Consulting and Clinical Psychology*, 1970, *34*, 226-228.

Mosher, D. L. Sex differences, sex experiences, sex guilt, and explicitly sexual films. *Journal of Social Issues*, 1973, *29*, 95-112.

Mosher, D. L. & Cross, H. Sex guilt and premarital sexual experiences of college students. *Journal of Consulting and Clinical Psychology*, 1971, *36*, 27-32.

Niswander, K. R., Singer, J., & Singer, M. Psychological reaction to therapeutic abortion. *American Journal of Obstetrics and Gynecology*, 1972, *114*, 29.

Oskamp, S., Mindick, B., Berger, D., & Motta, E. A longitudinal study of success versus failure in contraceptive planning. *Journal of Population*, 1978, *1*, 69-83.

Oskamp, S., Mindick, B., Hayden, M., & Pion, G. Contraceptive Attitudes and Behavior of Several Groups of Women. Paper presented at American Psychological Association Convention, 1976.

Rader, G. E., Bekker, L. D., Brown, L., & Richardt, C. Psychological Correlates of Unwanted Pregnancy. *Journal of Abnormal Psychology*, 1978, *87*, 373-376.

Rotter, J. B. Generalized expectancies for internal versus external control of reinforcement. *Psychological Monographs*, 1966, *80*.

Schwartz, S. Effects of sex guilt and sexual arousal on the retention of birth control information. *Journal of Consulting and Clinical Psychology*, 1973, *41*, 61-64.

Semens, J. P. Marital sexual problems of teenagers. In J. P. Semens and K. E. Krants (eds.), *The adolescent experience*. London: MacMillan, 1970.

Senate Committee on Labor and Public Welfare, *Report to the Secretary of Health, Education and Welfare Submitting Five-Year Plan for Family Planning Services and Population Research Programs*. U.S. Government Printing Office, Washington, D.C. (GPO), 1971.

Torres, A., Forrest, J. D., & Eisman, S. Family Planning Services in the United States, 1978-1979. *Family Planning Perspectives*, 1981, *13*, 133-141.

White, L. A., Fisher, W. A., Byrne, D., & Kingma, R. Development and validation of a measure of affective orientation to erotica: The Sexual Opinion Survey. Midwestern Psychology Association, Chicago, May 1977.

Zelnick, M. & Kantner, J. F. Sexual and contraceptive experience of young unmarried women in the United States, 1976 and 1971. *Family Planning Perspectives*, 1977, *9*, 55.

Zelnick, M. & Kantner, J. F. Contraceptive patterns and premarital pregnancy among women aged 15-19 in 1976. *Family Planning Perspectives*, 1978, *10*, 135.

Zelnick, M. & Kantner, J. F. Sexual activity, contraceptive use and pregnancy among metropolitan-area teenagers: 1971-1979. *Family Planning Perspectives*, 1980, *12*, 230.

Zelnick, M., Kim, Y. J., & Kantner, J. F. Probabilities of intercourse and conception among U.S. teenager women, 1971 and 1976. *Family Planning Perspectives*, 1979, *11*, 177-183.

Zuckerman, M., Bone, R. M., Neary, R., Mangelsdorff, D., & Brustman, B. What is the sensation seeker?: Personality trait and experience correlates of sensation-seeking scales. *Journal of Consulting and Clinical Psychology*, 1972, *39*, 308-321.

6

Sex Differences in Separation and Divorce

A Longitudinal Perspective

Robert A. Caldwell
Michigan State University

Bernard L. Bloom and William F. Hodges
University of Colorado

One of the most significant changes in American society in the past two decades has been the dramatic increase in the number of separations and divorces. Between 1962 and 1981, the number of divorces in the United States tripled (National Center for Health Statistics, 1982). From 1970 to 1977, the divorce rate in the United States increased 79 percent (Camara et al., 1980). In the past several years, however, while the number of divorces has continued to increase, the divorce rate has stabilized. Nevertheless, there are currently over one million divorces granted annually in the United States. Since there is an average of one child per divorcing couple, these divorces represent a serious disruption in the lives of more than three million people every year (Bloom et al., in press). Current projections suggest that the near future will be little different from the recent past, and that about one-third of married persons between 25 and 35 years of age in 1975 will divorce (Camara et al., 1980).

Social scientists have not ignored this phenomenon. There is a growing literature on the relationship of marital status to psychological well-being and a substantial number of empirical studies now exist on the effects of marital disruption, particularly in the case of women. While there is general agreement that separation and divorce is nearly always profoundly stressful (Bloom et al., 1978), there is less agreement regarding sex-specific differences in either the process of, or reactions to, this stressful life event.

Existing studies that focus on marital disruption can be arranged to reflect the chronological process that men and women go through during separation and divorce. It is reasonable to assume that there may be sex-specific differences in the experience of each of the major phases in the divorce process—the preseparation period, the decision-making process, and postdivorce adjustment.

This report is based, in part, on work supported by the National Institute of Mental Health, through Grant No. MH 26373 (Preventive Intervention for Newly Separated Persons), Bernard L. Bloom and William F. Hodges, co-principal investigators. We are pleased to acknowledge this support.

THE PRESEPARATION PERIOD

Several studies suggest that the preseparation period may be more stressful to women than to men. Albrecht and Kunz (1980) examined questionnaire responses from a sample of 500 divorced persons in the western United States. The sample, obtained following a screening questionnaire mailed to over 11,000 randomly selected households, consisted of 293 (59 percent) women and 207 (41 percent) men. The questionnaire that was subsequently distributed to all persons who had indicated in the initial survey that they had at some time been divorced, sought to learn about the process through which these persons reached the decision to obtain a divorce. While those views were undoubtedly tempered over time (average time since divorce in this sample was 14 years), there are some notable sex differences.

When subjects were asked to contrast their former marital satisfaction with that of other couples they had known at the time, women in the study generally reported less relative satisfaction than men. While 65 percent of women saw themselves as less satisfied than other couples they knew, only 49 percent of men made the same observation. On the other hand, when respondents were asked to contrast their former marital satisfaction with what they had anticipated at the time of entering the marriage, there were no significant sex differences. Among both men and women, about 80 percent felt that their marriages turned out to be worse than expected. While both men and women described the preseparation period as more difficult than the postseparation period, men reported that the best times in their marital histories were before the decision to divorce, while women indicated that the best times for them were after divorce.

Bloom and Caldwell (1981) examined adjustment as a function of sex and stage in the divorce process in four different samples of men and women who were undergoing marital disruption. Their measure of adjustment was derived from a factor analysis of four scales commonly used for the assessment of psychological well-being in community surveys. In contrasting the preseparation and immediate postseparation period, they found that prior to separation, women reported significantly more severe psychological symptoms than did men. In contrast, during the early postseparation period, men reported significantly more severe symptoms than did women. They concluded that

> the preseparation difficulties of married women may be associated with their greater dissatisfaction with the marital relationship. . . . Shortly after separation, however, while women may be feeling the positive effects of their separation, men may be just beginning to come to grips with the loss of their spouses and with the personal cost that loss entails. (p. 700)

The general premise that marriage may be more stressful to women than to men has been investigated from another perspective. Gove (1972) analyzed a series of previously published studies in order to highlight sex by marital status measure of mental disorder.

Analysis of these studies suggests that mental disorder rates are more powerfully associated with marital status than with sex, although sex by marital status interactions can be noted. Gove hypothesized, however, that married women were particularly vulnerable to mental disorder, largely as a consequence of the stressful nature of their marital roles.

Similarly, Bernard (1972) has taken the position that women who enjoy the highest levels of personal well-being are in the never-married category, while men who enjoy the highest levels of personal well-being are in the married category. Bloom et al. (1978) applied statistical tests to four survey study results used by Bernard in arriving at her hypotheses and found no significant sex-specific differentials in reported well-being.

However, not all research supports the view that being married is more satisfying to men than women. Warheit et al. (1976) conducted a large epidemiological community study in southeastern United States, and examined self-report measures of psychopathology as a function of sex and marital status, and found that females tended to report more pathology than males in all marital status categories. In addition, persons currently separated reported significantly more pathology than those in all other marital status categories, regardless of sex.

Moving from an emphasis on pathology to a focus on the positive experience of marriage, White (1979) examined global happiness as a function of sex and marital status, based on data obtained from a sample of 1085 Nebraska adults under age 60 who were currently either married, divorced, or remarried following a divorce. Married persons of both sexes reported higher overall happiness than those persons who were divorced. But while more women than men among persons in first marriages reported being very happy, more remarried men than women reported being very happy. Among men, those who were remarried were significantly happier than those in first marriages, while the opposite was true in the case of women.

White attempted to explain these findings regarding differential happiness by marital status by examining recruitment into the remarried-following-divorce category, and by exploring the possibility that the experience of remarriage might be very different for women than for men. As for recruitment, there is some evidence that remarriage tends to attract the least financially secure divorced women while attracting the most financially secure divorced men. This differential financial security could serve as an explanation of the findings regarding sex differences in global happiness among the remarried.

THE DECISION TO SEPARATE

The decision to end a marriage is often difficult and complex. It is an action motivated by individual dissatisfactions experienced within a larger social context. Several investigators have attempted to disentangle the multiple factors that influence this decision.

Examining the decision to separate from the perspective of the individuals involved, Kitson and Sussman (1982) explored patterns of marital complaints in a sample of 209 divorcing men and women in metropolitan Cleveland in order to determine if these patterns differed as a function of a number of demographic variables including sex. In addition, they sought to determine whether these complaints differed from those identified in similar studies conducted more than three decades earlier.

Differences in types of complaints mentioned by men and women were found to be smaller than was the case three decades earlier. There was no difference between the sexes in number of complaints. As for type of complaint, there were a number of significant sex differences in their sample. These included: (1) not sure what happened—mentioned by 18 percent of husbands and 2 percent of wives; (2) drinking—mentioned by 7 percent of husbands and 21 percent of wives; (3) over-commitment to work—mentioned by 13 percent of husbands and 4 percent of wives; (4) untrustworthiness and immaturity—mentioned by 10 percent of husbands and 21 percent of wives; (5) out with the boys/girls—mentioned by 8 percent of husbands and 20 percent of wives; (6) extramarital sex—mentioned by 11 percent of husbands and 21 percent of wives; (7) financial and employment problems—mentioned by 7 percent of husbands and 15 percent of wives; (8) emotional and personality problems—mentioned by 5 percent of husbands and 12 percent of wives; and (9) external events, such as a death in the family—mentioned by 5 percent of husbands and 1 percent of wives.

As for differences in types of marital complaints between the current study and those studies conducted 30 years earlier, an analysis was made of those complaints in a sample of mothers age 38 and under (in order to keep the samples comparable across the two time periods). In comparison with earlier studies, significantly more complaints are now made in the areas of personality, home life, and values. Significantly fewer complaints are now made in the areas of drinking, non-support, physical illness, and desertion. Kitson and Sussman suggest that marital complaints made three decades ago might be considered to be more serious than those identified today, and that "marriages were perhaps more unhappy and marital situations more desperate before a couple decided to divorce. . . . If so, this may have made adjustment to divorce more difficult as well" (p. 96).

Albrecht and Kunz (1980) also examined the complaints that divorced men and women had about their marriages. With regard to the most important reasons for marital failure, few sex differences emerged. The most common reasons cited were infidelity, loss of love, and emotional problems. Only two reasons appeared to be differentially reported by men and women—physical abuse was reported by 10 percent of the women and none of the men, and alcohol-related problems were reported by 7 percent of the women and only 2 percent of the men.

Important sex differences were found in the case of reported barriers to obtaining a divorce, however. Nearly half of the women, in contrast to fewer than 10 percent of men identified financial difficulties as a barrier. The presence of children constituted a barrier by 26 percent of men but only by 16 percent of women. Religious beliefs were more commonly reported as barriers by women (25 percent) than by men (14 percent). As for the factors that played a significant role in the decision to go ahead with the divorce, personal unhappiness was mentioned by 20 percent of women but only by 9 percent of men. Children's desires figured more importantly in women's decisions than in men's (11 percent vs. 2 percent), while opportunities for alternative sources of financial support figured more prominently in the case of women than in the case of men (13 percent vs. 5 percent).

POSTDIVORCE ADJUSTMENT

Once the separation from a marital partner takes place, a process beings that has a variety of consequences, both positive and negative. Several research studies have examined these consequences. Longitudinal studies of samples of American families have consistently shown that divorced persons, particularly women, function under substantially more economic hardship than persons in intact marriages (see Hoffman & Holmes, 1976). For example, Espenshade (1979) reported that between 1968 and 1974, "the real income of married couples increased 21.7 percent, in contrast to *decreases* of 29.3 percent for divorced women and 19.2 percent for divorced men" (p. 617). When family needs are taken into account in evaluating income, divorced women had a 6.7 percent drop in standard of living over that same time period, while divorced men had an increase of 16.5 percent and married couples an increase of 20.8 percent. In 1977, female-headed families comprised 14 percent of all families, but nearly half of families in poverty.

Brown et al. (1976) examined the costs and benefits of divorce in a sample of 30 Boston-area mothers who had been divorced between one and five years and who had minor children. The authors suggest that while their sample of mothers were no better prepared for divorce than they were for marriage, they generally felt relieved about being on their own. Most reported that their lives were easier than had been the case when they had been with their husbands.

The most common problem that this sample of divorced mothers noted was the increased responsibility associated with the fact that activities formerly undertaken by two parents now needed to be carried out by only one. Specifically identified were the difficulties in combining the role of parent and wage-earner, arranging for child care, and carrying out housework, repairs, and maintenance. Many mothers mentioned problems associated with continuing financial dependence on the ex-spouse, and problems of stigma and discrimination that they faced as divorced persons.

In spite of these difficulties, most women were able to identify a number of benefits associated with the divorce. Among those most commonly mentioned were freedom from restrictive domestic routines, lack of interference in the establishment of parent-child relationships, increased personal autonomy, and an increased sense of personal competence and control over their lives. Few women in this sample were interested in remarriage, although most were in a close relationship with a man.

Sex Differences in Divorce Adjustment

It is clear that the transition from being married to being separated or divorced is a stressful one. Several studies have examined sex differences in postseparation adjustment. Hackney and Ribordy (1980) examined emotional reactions to divorce by contrasting 74 subjects who were divided into four groups—happily married; persons undergoing marriage counseling; persons who had filed for divorce; and persons who had been divorced between 6 and 12 months previously. While numerous problems were identified in the case of the divorced and divorcing samples, no sex differences were noted. Hackney and Ribordy noted, "men and women reported experiencing the same negative effects and to the same degree. Thus, it seems that the process of divorce takes its toll on both males and females and that both are equally able to bounce back and attain some degree of emotional stability" (p. 110).

Defrain and Eirick (1981) contrasted coping patterns and adjustment to divorce in a sample of 33 custodial fathers and 38 custodial mothers in Nebraska, and found virtually no significant sex differences. The questionnaire was designed to examine six areas—the history of the divorce process; feelings as a single parent; child-rearing issues; the children's feelings and behaviors; relations with the ex-spouse; and forming new social relationships. Of the 63 questions that were explored, only one significant difference was obtained when contrasting custodial fathers and custodial mothers. Since this finding represents fewer differences than one would expect simply by chance, these authors concluded that lifestyle and divorce-related issues being dealt with in these two samples of custodial parents were remarkably similar to each other.

Ahrons (1981) examined the coparental relationship, that is, the relationship between divorced spouses that permits them to continue their child-rearing responsibilities, in a sample of 54 couples who had been divorced for about one year, and for whom the mother was the custodial parent. Coparenting was the rule rather than the exception—85 percent of the former couples continued to maintain some contact with each other. In about half of the cases, this interaction concerned itself with child-rearing issues. Coparental communication often was conflictual in nature, although at the same time, it was often seen as supportive. Those parents who reported supportive and cooperative coparenting relationships interacted more with each other regarding issues unrelated to parenting.

While few significant sex differences were found, men tended to perceive themselves as being more involved in sharing child-rearing concerns and in general interaction with their former spouses than did women. In addition, men tended to be more satisfied with the coparenting relationship than women.

Ahrons has suggested that coparenting involves the establishment of two interdependent households—maternal and paternal—into a binuclear family system. Sex differences in attitude toward coparenting may reflect differing expectations of the parenting role after divorce. There may be an underestimation of shared child-rearing on the part of women and an overestimation on the part of men. In any case, clinicians who work with divorced couples with children can be helpful by identifying differing perceptions of the coparenting role and by helping divorced couples maintain their child-rearing responsibilities while terminating their marital relationship.

Generally, research examining sex differences in postdivorce adjustment has uncovered few significant consistent findings. What differences appear to exist seem to be related to parenting issues and to the differences between custodial and noncustodial parental roles and responsibilities.

Moderators of Postdivorce Adjustment

Some people fare better than others in the adjustment process following divorce. The search for factors that influence postdivorce adjustment has occupied several investigators. Granvold et al. (1979) searched for factors associated with postdivorce adjustment in a sample of 53 women who had been divorced within the previous five years and had not remarried. A number of these women were clients in community human service agencies. Women with more egalitarian sex role expectations were found to be significantly better adjusted than women who were less egalitarian. Availability of friends or family with whom the divorce could be discussed was found to be significantly related to adjustment. Those women with more sources of social and emotional support were better adjusted.

Chiriboga and Thurnher (1980) studied a sample of 298 persons who had filed for divorce in two counties in California. No one in the study had been separated longer than eight months. Included among the items in the interview were a number of questions regarding former marital lifestyle—division of labor, authority relationships, use of leisure time, and reliance on the spouse.

Adjustment at the time of the interview was significantly associated with many aspects of reported former marital lifestyle. For men under age 40, better adjustment was associated with an egalitarian relationship with the wife and at the same time, with a strong social network outside of the marriage. In the case of women under age 40, better adjustment was found among those who had been more pragmatic, assertive, and independent during their marriages. In the case of persons above age 40, adjustment among men was better in the case of those who had been nonauthoritarian, helpful around the house, and somewhat passive. Among older women, adjustment was better in the case of those who had found ways of achieving a balance of dependence and control via traditional sex role behaviors.

With regard to factors associated with adjustment following divorce, Nelson (1981, 1982) found that the best predictors of psychosocial adjustment were age, and current relationship and current feelings about the ex-husband. Adjustment was significantly better in the case of younger than older women. In the case of attitudes toward the ex-husband, adjustment was better for those women who had more positive feelings and a better current relationship with their former husbands. Nelson concluded that "an important target for interventions with divorced families would be an attempt to . . . promote civil relationships between the ex-spouses following divorce" (p. 82).

Brown and Manela (1978) examined the relationship between sex role attitudes and psychological adjustment following divorce in a sample of 253 divorcing women all of whom had at least one minor child. Sex roles among married women have been conceptualized to vary along a continuum from traditional to nontraditional. Traditional female sex roles are those that place special virtue on staying at home, child rearing, providing psychological support to the husband, and on the husband being gainfully employed. Nontraditional sex roles are those that place special value on equity between husband and wife, and on equal importance of employment outside the home as on activities inside the home. Brown and Manela found that there was a significant relationship between sex role beliefs and adjustment to divorce, specifically, that adjustment was superior among women whose sex role orientations were nontraditional.

In summary, marital disruption appears to be a life stressor of the first magnitude and the preponderance of evidence would suggest that marital status is more important than sex in determining psychological well-being. That is, regardless of sex, persons who are in intact marriages generally report higher levels of psychological well-being than persons in any other marital status category.

Even though the nature of marital dissatisfaction has undergone a radical transformation in the past generation, sociocultural and psychological characteristics of our society dictate that the experience of marital disruption can be very different in the two sexes. What remains unclear is the extent to which these different experiences are due directly to sex or indirectly to factors associated with sex. For example, mothers become custodial parents far more often than fathers, and thus, any stresses associated with having custody of children will fall disproportionately on mothers. Yet in studies contrasting custodial mothers and custodial fathers, few sex differences in adjustment are found. Accordingly, it appears likely that custodial status may be a more important variable than sex in determining adjustment to marital disruption among parents.

One area in which there do seem to be significant sex differences is in the type of dissatisfactions that lead men and women to end their marriages. Further, the social context that legitimizes these reasons as appropriate for ending marriage appears to be changing. Finally, adjustment to marital disruption in both men and women is clearly related to a number of mediating variables. Among the more important of these mediating factors should be mentioned the nature of the social support system, marital sex role orientation, characteristics of the marriage, and the nature of the continuing relationship between the former spouses.

The rest of this chapter will report on a study that sought to learn more about the natural history of the separation and divorce experience. The design of this study provides an examination of both women's and men's paths through the separation process and into the first 20 months after separation. While the emphasis of this report will be on women, as will be seen, the separation experience is often no different for them than for men.

STUDY DESIGN

A sample of 28 women and 21 men—all once-married and newly separated—comprise the subjects for this study. These subjects served as the no-treatment control group for a preventive intervention program for the newly separated conducted at the University of Colorado (see Bloom et al., 1982). Since marital separation is not a legally reportable event, there is no certain way of identifying the entire population at risk. The procedure that was followed in this study was to use the mass media (newspapers, radio stations, posters in supermarkets, laundromats, etc.) and direct mailing to human service providers to publicize the program. Although the program was open to both the husband and wife of a separated couple, the 49 people in this sample participated without their spouse. The subjects were interviewed by advanced clinical psychology graduate students at three points in time: approximately 2 months after their separation (the initial interview), six months later (the 6-month interview), and one year later (the 18-month interview). The initial and 6-month interviews were virtually identical but the 18-month interview was abbreviated. Only two subjects, from the original control group of 51, were lost during the 18 months of this study. All 49 subjects were followed through all three interviews, regardless of their subsequent marital histories. Most of the questions were precoded, but there were opportunities for the study participants to respond to open-ended questions as well.

The interviews were designed to collect self-report data about problems and functioning in several different areas including: the separation experience, social support, finances, the relationship with the ex-spouse, benefits of the separation, new relationships, helpseeking behavior, attitudes about remarriage, single parenting, career and employment, and housing and homemaking. Additionally, a symptom checklist (Bloom & Caldwell, 1981) was completed at each interview. Two questionnaires were administered only once—the Male Female Role Research (MAFERR) sex role orientation scale (Steinman & Fox, 1974) which was administered at the initial interview, and a portion of the Quality of Life Scale (Andrews & Withey, 1976) which was administered at the 18-month interview. For a more complete account of the interview procedures and subject selection see Bloom and Hodges (1981).

The women in the sample were on the average 32 years old, had been married an average of 12.5 years before the separation. Slightly over half ($n = 15$) of the women had children with an average of 2.0 children per mother. The current separation was the first one for three-quarters of the women and it had lasted, on the average, two months at the time of the initial interview. Half of the women had moved between the separation and the initial interview, most of them (83 percent) only once. The women were all Anglo and were well educated (average education = 15.3 years). The 21 men in the sample were slightly younger, had not been married quite as long and were slightly better educated. None of these differences was statistically significant. Thus, the two groups were well matched demographically.

By the time of the 6-month interview over half of the women (61 percent) had obtained a divorce. About a third (32 percent) were still separated, and 7 percent had reconciled. Of the women who had divorced, one had already remarried. Fewer men (38 percent) had divorced and none had reconciled or remarried.

By the time of the 18-month interview virtually all (96 percent) of the women had divorced. Two had remarried and one was still reconciled. In contrast, 81 percent of men had divorced. Men were more likely than women to still be separated.

RESULTS

The Preseparation Period and the Decision to Separate

During the six month period that preceded the separation, women and men retrospectively reported many psychological and psychosomatic symptoms on the Composite Symptom Checklist. Half or more of the women in the sample experienced weight change, upset stomach, general pains, fatigue, headaches, the feeling that they might have a "nervous breakdown," inability to "get going," nightmares, sleep disturbances, and nervousness or tenseness. Men also reported experiencing these same psychological and psychosomatic problems, however, and there were no statistically significant differences in the frequencies with which the two groups reported these symptoms.

Study participants were asked to rate 18 different sources of marital dissatisfaction in terms of the extent to which they existed and played a role in the decision to separate. While there were no significant differences in the degree to which men and women experienced these dissatisfactions, there were some interesting differences in the relative importance the two groups attributed to each of these dissatisfactions. As can be seen in Table 1, while communication difficulties and life styles and values were ranked first and second on both lists, women ranked infidelity and interest in another person higher on their list of complaints about their spouse than did men. Men, on the other hand, ranked job or school commitments and lack of love higher on their list of complaints about their spouses than did women.

While the decision to separate from a marriage is usually a stressful one for both partners, there were clear differences between men and women in terms of who initiated the separation. While about one-third of men and women reported that the decision was shared mutually with their spouse, women in this sample were nearly three times more likely than men to report initiating the separation themselves.

Table 1 Ranking of sources of marital dissatisfaction (complaints about spouse) for women and men

Complaints made	
By women	By men
1. Communication difficulties	Communication difficulties
2. Life styles, values	Life styles, values
3. Infidelity	Lack of love
4. Interested in another person	Job or school commitments
5. Boredom	Boredom
6. Verbal abuse	Suspiciousness, jealousy
7. Lack of love	Verbal abuse
8. Sexual difficulties	Sexual difficulties
9. Financial problems	Interested in another person
10. Neglect of home	Infidelity
11. Neglect of children	Neglect of children
12. Nagging, bossiness	Nagging, bossiness
13. Other problems with children	Other problems with children
14. Suspiciousness, jealousy	Financial problems
15. Drinking, drug abuse	Neglect of home
16. Job or school commitments	In-law trouble
17. Physical abuse	Drinking, drug abuse
18. In-law trouble	Physical abuse

Attitude toward the Separation

Women, unlike men, remained consistently positive in their evaluation of the separation over the time of the study. Men, initially negative, tended to become more positive in their evaluations over time. Between the initial and 6-month interviews, men continued to become somewhat more favorable in their attitudes so that by the 6-month interview the two groups were both positive and nearly equal in their evaluations.

With regard to women's attitudes toward remarriage, there was a gradual change over the 18 months of the study in a more favorable direction. At the initial interview 35 percent of the women felt that they did not want to get remarried, but by the 18-month interview only 16 percent had such a negative attitude, while 68 percent thought that they might like to get remarried, and 16 percent were not sure. At the time of the 18-month interview, about the same proportion of men felt negatively about remarriage (18 percent), but, in contrast, only 48 percent felt positively, with 35 percent being unsure about their attitudes toward remarriage.

Relationship with the Ex-spouse

During the 18 months of the study the relationship of women to their original husbands improved and also became less intense. At the time of the initial interview 29 percent of the women reported having a good relationship with their husbands, 18 percent had a bad relationship, and the rest reported either an ambivalent or minimal relationship. These figures remained unchanged at the time of the 6-month interview. By the time of the 18-month interview, however, 36 percent reported a good relationship with their now ex-husbands, 8 percent reported that they had a bad relationship, and 56 percent reported an ambivalent or minimal relationship. At all three data points, men reported very similar experiences as women regarding their relationships with their spouses.

At the time of the initial interview, women saw their husbands on the average of about once a week. This figure dropped to about once a month by the time of the 18-month interview. These contacts were most often related to working out separation details and to issues regarding children (where there were children). Most women (75 percent) had stopped sexual contact with their husbands by the time of the initial interview and this figure remained approximately the same at the 6-month interview. In the case of men, at the time of the initial interview, 81 percent reported that they did not have sexual contact with their wives. At the 6-month interview, however, this figure had dropped to 62 percent.

Heterosexual Involvement

Involvement with persons of the opposite sex sometimes began before the separation and steadily increased over the course of the study. At the time of the initial interview, 39 percent of the women were involved with a man other than their husband. Almost two-thirds (64 percent) of these women had begun this involvement prior to their separations. While about the same proportion of men were heterosexually involved at the time of the initial interview (33 percent), slightly less than a third (29 percent) of these involvements had predated the separation. By the time of the 6- and 18-month interviews, respectively, 54 percent and 82 percent of the women were involved in heterosexual relationships. The comparable figures for men were 67 percent and 90 percent. In nearly all cases these relationships included sexual contact with the new person.

Social Support

There was some evidence of loss of social support after the separation, but in general, friends and family were supportive, especially to women. Both women and men felt that they could talk about their problems with friends and family members, but women found friends to be significantly more supportive than did men on all three interviews ($p < 0.05$ in all three cases). Both men and women saw their friends on the average of several times a week and their families several times a month. Both groups felt that they had either the same number or more friends by the initial interview as compared to the time before the separation. There were, however, changes in the frequency with which the subjects saw their friends. At the time of the initial interview 75 percent of the women saw their old friends either as frequently or more often than before the separation. Six months later this figure had dropped to 43 percent. The figures for men are very comparable. Although the separated women had lost some old friends by the time of the 6-month interview it was as often by their own choice as by their friends' decision. The friends that remained were described as moderately or very supportive in almost all cases.

Most women (61 percent) were comfortable with the amount of "alone time" they had and only a quarter reported moderate or frequent loneliness at the time of the 6-month interview. Men were substantially more lonely. Only 38 percent were comfortable with their amount of "alone time," and nearly half (48 percent) reported moderate or frequent loneliness.

Separation-Related Problems

As might be expected, these newly separated study participants experienced many separation-related problems, and in some areas women reported significantly more problems than men. The participants were asked to rate each of 18 different areas in which separated persons might be expected to experience problems from (1) not a problem to (5) extreme. This list was given at both the initial and 6-month interviews and the mean ratings for men and women are presented in Table 2. There was only one significant difference at the initial interview between men and women with women experiencing more severe financial problems than men, $t(47) = 1.99$, $p < 0.05$. At the 6-month interview, however, women reported significantly more problems than men in the areas of homemaking ($t(47) = 2.04, p < 0.05$), parental relationships ($t(47) = 2.28, p < 0.05$), and guilt and self-blame ($t(47) = 3.02$, $p < 0.05$).

Between the initial and 6-month interviews, substantial sex-related changes were found in reported problems associated with the separation. In the case of men, financial and legal problems increased while problems in their relationships with their children decreased, as did loneliness, the sense of guilt and self-blame, feelings of incompetence, and problems with sexual satisfaction. In the case of women, several problems became more severe. Problems with employment, career planning, homemaking difficulties, social relationships, relationships with their parents, guilt and self-blame, and sexual satisfaction were all exacerbated, while only problems associated with relationships with the spouse decreased.

Table 2 Mean ratings by sex of separation-related problems on the initial and 6-month inteviews*

Problem area	Initial interview means			6-Month interview means		
	Total	Men	Women	Total	Men	Women
1. Ex-spouse relationship	3.4	3.6	3.3	3.1	3.4	2.9
2. Loneliness	3.1	3.4	2.9	2.7	2.5	2.9
3. Mental health	2.8	2.7	2.8	2.6	2.3	2.9
4. Financial	2.7	2.2	3.0	2.9	2.8	2.9
5. Personal failure	2.7	2.5	2.9	2.7	2.4	2.9
6. Guilt, self-blame	2.7	2.4	2.9	2.6	2.0	3.1
7. Housing	2.4	2.0	2.7	2.3	2.0	2.5
8. Sexual satisfaction	2.4	2.8	2.1	2.4	2.1	2.6
9. Feeling incompetent	2.4	2.3	2.5	2.2	1.9	2.5
10. Child rearing	2.1	2.4	1.9	2.1	2.0	2.2
11. Career planning	2.1	2.3	2.0	2.5	2.4	2.6
12. New relationships	2.1	2.2	2.1	2.4	2.1	2.6
13. Legal	2.1	1.9	2.3	2.4	2.5	2.4
14. Child relationship	2.1	2.6	1.8	1.8	1.9	1.8
15. Homemaking	2.0	1.9	2.0	2.3	1.9	2.6
16. Physical health	1.9	1.7	2.1	2.1	1.9	2.2
17. Employment	1.8	2.0	1.7	2.1	1.9	2.2
18. Parental relations	1.7	1.6	1.8	2.1	1.6	2.4

*1 = none; 2 = mild; 3 = moderate; 4 = considerable; 5 = extreme.

On the 18-month interview the format for asking about these potential problem areas was somewhat different. The 18 specific problem items from the initial and 6-month interviews were combined into 9 general problem area questions. There were no significant differences in the proportions of men and women reporting problems in the nine general areas that were identified. For the participants in this study, the areas that were most problematic were personal feelings, such as low self-esteem, feelings of guilt, or a sense of personal failure; social problems, such as relations with friends or family and loneliness; and financial problems. These problem areas are similar to the types of problems that study participants had noted on both the initial and 6-month interviews (see Table 2). Interestingly, even at the 18-month interview, between one-half and three-quarters of the study participants attributed these problems to the separation that had taken place on the average of 20 months earlier.

In the area of finances, women consistently reported having a smaller income than did men. Over the course of the three interviews the average income for women increased more rapidly (35 percent increase in a year and a half) than it did for men (26 percent increase) but even by the 18-month interview women's income was only 83 percent that of men.

On both the initial and the 6-month interview, regardless of sex, over three-quarters of the study participants reported that their income was barely or not at all adequate to meet their expenses. Half of the women had to seek financial aid within the first two months of the separation, but only three of these women reported any problems in obtaining the aid. Womens' financial problems persisted, however, and 54 percent sought financial aid between the time of the initial and 6-month interviews. This figure compares to 24 percent of the men who sought aid over that same time period. In the year between the 6- and 18-month interviews, 45 percent of the women and 36 percent of the men sought aid, again with very few problems. Employment was the major source of income for women as opposed to child support, maintenance, or welfare.

Eighty-nine percent of women were employed either full- or part-time at the time of the initial interview. They held predominantly professional (54 percent) or clerical (38 percent) positions. This figure was up from 75 percent who had been employed at the time of the separation. Over the three interviews the proportion of employed women dropped slightly to 82 percent at the 6-month interview and to 72 percent at the 18-month interview. Among men, the proportion employed was similar initially, but did not drop over time. By the 18-month interview only 45 percent of the working women still held the same job that they had at the time of their separation. In the case of men, this figure was 63 percent. The most frequent problems that both women and men reported were fatigue on the job and trouble concentrating. On the other hand women initially reported that they obtained significantly more pleasure and satisfaction from their work than men did. This difference disappeared, however, by the time of the 6-month interview.

Helpseeking

Given the stressful nature of the separation experience and the problems that these women continued to have over the year and a half of the study, it is not surprising that their level of helpseeking behavior was rather high. Nearly half of the women (43 percent) had been in couples treatment with their husbands before the separation. An additional third (36 percent) reported that they had wanted to be in couples treatment but that their spouse had refused. Additionally, over half (54 percent) had been in individual therapy, most with private sector mental health professionals. Most found the individual sessions to be more helpful than the couples treatment.

This high level of helpseeking continued after the separation. At the time of the initial interview, 61 percent of the women were in individual treatment of some sort and were finding it helpful. As time went on, the proportion of women in treatment decreased somewhat but never went below 50 percent.

At each interview there was a smaller but still substantial proportion of men in treatment. Over half (52 percent) of the men were in individual treatment at the time of the initial interview. This proportion decreased to 43 percent by the time of the 18-month interview.

Separation-Related Benefits

While the separation experience is often stressful and negative, there are also benefits that can be derived from the experience. The participants in this study were asked to rate to what extent they had experienced personal growth, increased happiness, increased independence, freedom from responsibility, and relief from conflict. Although there were no statistically significant differences between the level of benefits experienced by men and women at any of the interviews, women nearly always reported more benefits than did men. Men reported more benefits on only 1 of the 14 comparisons.

Parenting Issues

Over 90 percent of the women with children in the sample had custody of their children. This proportion remained virtually unchanged over the three interviews. Women were relatively satisfied with their relationship with their children, somewhat less satisfied with their parenting, occasionally felt their children to be a burden but often enjoyed their time with the children. Equivalent information collected from fathers (most of whom were noncustodial) revealed very similar ratings.

Psychological Adjustment and Well-Being

At the time of the 6-month interview, the study participants were asked to rate the frequency with which they had experienced 20 psychological and psychosomatic symptoms, this time for the preceding six months, using the Composite Symptom Checklist (Bloom & Caldwell, 1981). At the 18-month interview they rated the same list of symptoms and completed the Andrews and Withey Quality of Life Scale for the period between the last two interviews. In addition to the individual item scores, the Symptom Checklist provides a score on a Neurasthenia subscale, an Anxiety subscale and a Total symptom score, while the Quality of Life scale yields one total score.

There were no significant differences between women and men on the two Composite Symptom Checklist subscales or the Total symptom score at either the 6-month or 18-month interviews. There was, however, evidence that the preseparation disruption had continued, unabated, to the time of the 6-month interview. All but one of the symptoms experienced by at least 50 percent of the women prior to the separation were again reported by more than 50 percent at the time of the 6-month interview. Additionally, the problems of loss of appetite and health interfering with work were reported by at least half of the women at 6 months.

By the time of the 18-month interview, significant improvement had taken place on the Composite Symptom Checklist measure. For women, 14 symptoms (out of 20) were reported with less frequency than on the 6-month measure, 3 symptoms remained at their 6-month level and 3 symptoms (all reflecting anxiety) were worse. On the 18-month Quality of Life Scale there was no significant difference between men and women.

Moderators of Adjustment

In previous studies, several variables have been shown to have an effect on post-separation adjustment among women, including age (Granvold et al., 1979; Nelson, 1981), adequacy of income (Espenshade, 1979), changes in income (Mott & Moore, 1979), current relationship with ex-spouse (Ahrons, 1981; Nelson, 1981), and sex role (Brown & Manela, 1978; Granvold et al., 1979).

Correlations between the Composite Symptom Checklist subscales (Neurasthenia and Anxiety), the Total symptom score, the Quality of Life score and measures of six possible moderator variables were calculated for women. These results are presented in Table 3.

Perceived income adequacy was modestly related to the number of symptoms women reported at the 6-month interview in the expected direction, that is, Neurasthenia, Anxiety and Total symptom scores increased with decreases in income

Table 3 Correlations between women's adjustment at 6- and 18-month interviews and moderator variables

Adjustment measures	Moderator variables					
	Age	Income decrease	Income adequacy	Relationship with ex-spouse	MAFERR self realization score	MAFERR family orientation score
Neurasthenia (6-month)	−0.19	0.05	−0.26	−0.12	−0.02	0.04
Anxiety (6-month)	0.13	−0.01	−0.40*	−0.22	−0.31*	0.43**
Total symptom (6-month)	0.02	0.02	−0.25	−0.15	−0.14	0.22
Neurasthenia (18-month)	−0.12	0.03	−0.04	−0.34*	−0.38*	0.25*
Anxiety (18-month)	0.11	0.01	−0.05	−0.40*	−0.52**	0.20
Total symptom (18-month)	0.03	0.02	−0.13	−0.38*	−0.44*	0.35*
Quality of life	−0.34*	−0.32*	0.25	0.20	0.49**	−0.58**

*$p < 0.05$.
**$p < 0.01$.

adequacy. Endorsement of traditional marital sex role attitudes and values (high family orientation and low self realization) was related to more symptomatology at 18 months. Similar relationships, but to a lesser degree, were found at the 6-month interview. Quality of Life scores were higher for younger women, for the women who did not display traditional sex role attitudes and values, and for women whose income had increased.

In the case of men, no significant moderators were found, although two important near significant relationships ($p < 0.10$) were noted. First, as in the case of women, quality of life scores were lower in those men whose incomes had shown the greatest decrease. Second, in contrast to women, those men who reported better relationships with their spouses also reported higher levels of psychological symptoms at the time of the 18-month interview.

CONCLUSIONS

While this chapter focuses on sex differences in the process of separation and divorce, it is important not to lose sight of those aspects of the process that do not differentiate men from women. Few differences in the nature of marital dissatisfaction exist. Preseparation psychological symptoms are equally high for both men and women, and in both sexes tend to remain high for the next six months before beginning a slow decrease. Among problems that newly separated persons face, many are no more common in women than in men, and formal helpseeking is remarkably common in both men and women.

On the basis of the analysis of the data from this sample of newly separated men and women, the most striking difference between the two sexes is in their attitudes toward the ending of the marriage. Women are more often initiators of the separation; during the early months of separation they feel more favorably toward the separation than do men; they consistently see more benefits to themselves as a consequence of the separation; and they devote far less energy in efforts to delay the ending of the marriage.

Men struggle to remain attached to their spouses to a much greater extent than women, and while they ultimately come to feel about as positively about the separation as do women, they are not as willing as women to go beyond that, such as by considering remarriage. The greater reluctance on the part of men toward the ending of their marriage can be understood in the context of the differential rankings of sources of marital dissatisfaction. The most striking sex differences in this ranking reflect the greater need on the part of men to be cared for by their spouses. Thus, men complain of lack of love and of job and school demands on their wives that take their wives away from them. In fact, while women who have better relationships with their spouses tend to have better levels of psychological adjustment, men who report better relationships with their spouses tend to have poorer levels of adjustment. That is, the change in attitude toward separation expressed by men may be more one of resignation than affirmation.

Like all stressful life events, marital disruption has the potential to bring about both problems and benefits (Brown et al., 1976). Compared to men, women in this sample experience more of both. Women, more often than men, identify the separation as the source of benefits as well as problems. Many of the benefits that are mentioned are consistent with benefits reported by women interviewed by Brown et al. (1976), and Nelson (1981). Even in the face of significant problems, women are more able than men to appreciate the benefits of living outside a failed marriage.

One aspect of marital separation that is often mentioned is the disruptive effect that the event has on a person's social network (Weiss, 1975). For women in this study, there is little evidence of loss of social support. Over time, women's relationships with their spouses improve considerably, a large proportion become involved with new men, and women feel close to and supported by their friends and family. In contrast, men perceive less support from their social network. This difference takes on added importance in light of the fact that social support has been shown to moderate the effects of separation stress on adjustment (Granvold et al., 1979).

There are some personal characteristics that seem to promote better adjustment to separation. As in several other studies, women who are younger and who hold non-traditional sex role attitudes seem to achieve better adjustment than women who are older and who hold more traditional attitudes. This relationship seems to become stronger as time goes on with sex role attitudes being more powerfully associated with 18-month symptomatology than with the 6-month measures. This finding is consistent with previous results that have also shown a relationship between non-traditional sex role attitudes and positive adjustment to divorce (Brown & Manela, 1978; Chiriboga & Thurnher, 1980; Granvold et al., 1979). It is clear from these data, however, that these findings apply only to women. In the case of men, disengagement from the spouse is the most striking correlate of better adjustment to the marital disruption. Thus, Nelson's (1981) suggestion that interventions designed to promote better relationships between ex-partners would be likely to improve postseparation adjustment has not been corroborated.

Based on the results of this study, interventions aimed at influencing sex role orientation in the nontraditional direction would seem to be much more likely to have an impact on adjustment to marital disruption in the case of women, and interventions designed to facilitate appropriate distancing from the spouse, and to build stronger social support networks outside of the family on the part of men would seem more likely to have a positive impact on their adjustment to marital disruption.

Marital disruption is clearly a difficult and stressful life experience, with long-term consequences for both women and men. Our data suggest that women have to cope with some problems that men do not face, but also receive greater support and perceive more separation-related benefits than do men. In general, the most appropriate conclusions to draw from these data are that there are few sex differences in the *magnitude* of the difficulties faced by women and men undergoing marital disruption. On the other hand, sex differences are clearly present in the *nature* of those difficulties, and there is evidence that women appear to resolve them more rapidly than men.

REFERENCES

Ahrons, C. R. The continuing coparental relationship between divorced spouses. *American Journal of Orthopsychiatry*, 1981, *51*, 415–428.

Albrecht, S. L. & Kunz, P. R. The decision to divorce: A social exchange perspective. *Journal of Divorce*, 1980, *3*, 319–337.

Andrews, F. M. & Withey, S. B. *Social indicators of well being: American's perceptions of life quality*. New York, Plenum Press, 1976.

Bernard, J. *The future of marriage*. New York: World Press, 1972.

Bloom, B. L., Asher, S. J., & White, S. W. Marital disruption as a stressor: A review and analysis. *Psychological Bulletin*, 1978, *85*, 867–894.

Bloom, B. L. & Caldwell, R. A. Sex differences in adjustment during the process of marital separation. *Journal of Marriage and the Family*, 1981, *43*, 693–701.

Bloom, B. L. & Hodges, W. F. The predicament of the newly separated. *Community Mental Health Journal*, 1981, *17*, 277–293.

Bloom, B. L., Hodges, W. F., & Caldwell, R. A. A preventive program for the newly separated: Initial evaluation. *American Journal of Community Psychology*, 1982, *10*, 251–264.

Brown, C. A., Feldberg, R., Fox, E. M., & Kohen, J. Divorce: Chance of a new lifetime. *Journal of Social Issues*, 1976, *32*, 119–133.

Brown, P. & Manela, R. Changing family roles: Women and divorce. *Journal of Divorce*, 1978, *1*, 315–328.

Camara, K. A., Baker, O., & Dayton, C. Impact of separation and divorce on youths and families. In P. M. Insel (ed.), *Environmental variables and the prevention of mental illness*. Lexington, MA: D. C. Heath, 1980.

Chiriboga, D. A. & Thurnher, M. Marital lifestyles and adjustment to separation. *Journal of Divorce*, 1980, *3*, 379–390.

Defrain, J. & Eirick, R. Coping as divorced single parents: A comparative study of fathers and mothers. *Family Relations*, 1981, *30*, 265–273.

Espenshade, T. J. The economic consequences of divorce. *Journal of Marriage and the Family*, 1979, *41*, 615–625.

Gove, W. R. The relationship between sex-roles, marital status, and mental illness. *Social Forces*, 1972, *51*, 34–44.

Granvold, D. K., Pedler, L. M., & Schellie, S. G. A study of sex role expectancy and female postdivorce adjustment. *Journal of Divorce*, 1979, *2*, 383–393.

Hackney, G. R. & Ribordy, S. C. An empirical investigation of emotional reactions to divorce. *Journal of Clinical Psychology*, 1980, *36*, 105–110.

Hoffman, S. & Holmes, J. Husbands, wives and divorce. In G. J. Duncan & J. N. Morgan (eds.), *Five-thousand American families: Patterns of economic progress*. Vol. IV. Ann Arbor, MI: Institute for Social Research, 1976.

Kitson, G. C. & Sussman, M. B. Marital complaints, demographic characteristics, and symptoms of mental distress in divorce. *Journal of Marriage and the Family*, 1982, *44*, 87–101.

Mott, F. L. & Moore, S. F. The causes of marital disruption among young American women: An interdisciplinary perspective. *Journal of Marriage and the Family*, 1979, *41*, 355–365.

National Center for Health Statistics. Births, marriages, divorces, and deaths for 1981. *Monthly vital statistics report*, 1982, *30* (No. 12), 1–12.

Nelson, G. Moderators of women's and children's adjustment following parental divorce. *Journal of Divorce*, 1981, *4*, 71–83.

Pearson, W., Jr. & Hendrix, L. Divorce and the status of women. *Journal of Marriage and the Family*, 1979, *41*, 375–385.

Steinmann, A. & Fox, D. J. *The Male Dilemma*. New York: Jason Aroson, 1974.

Warheit, G. J., Holzer, C. E., Bell, R. A., & Arey, S. A. Sex, marital status, and mental health: A reappraisal. *Social Forces*, 1976, *55*, 459–470.

Weiss, R. S. *Marital Separation*. New York: Basic Books, 1975.

White, L. K. Sex differentials in the effect of remarriage on global happiness. *Journal of Marriage and the Family*, 1979, *41*, 869–876.

7

Enhancing Childrearing Skills in Lower Income Women

Myrna B. Shure
Hahnemann University

There are many ways parents can affect the behavior of their children. They can demand, suggest, and even explain why their suggested idea is a good one. They can praise a child who complies, or discipline one who does not. While momentary needs may be satisfied, often more those of the parent than of the child, the parent is either thinking for the child, or urging desired behavior with no thought at all.

This chapter will describe a different approach. It is an approach that helps parents help their children learn *how* to think, not what to think, so that when typical interpersonal problems arise, the children can decide for themselves what to do, and whether or not *their* idea is a good one. We took this approach because we learned that children who can think through and solve problems for themselves are better adjusted in school than children who cannot. And we learned that lower income inner-city black mothers, two-thirds of whom were raising their children without a consistent male father figure could successfully transmit these skills to their children, children as young as four years of age.

Specific discussion will focus on: a) why problem solving intervention for use by parents is valued, b) the specific cognitive skills that appear to be most relevant to the child's social adjustment, c) highlights of the intervention itself, and d) how parents, in helping their child learn to think, also acquire skills to help themselves. Our research with parents has been with those of normal, but high-risk four-year-olds who display varying amounts of behavioral difficulties in school. Recent evidence from problem solving research suggests implications for parents of older children, and of children with more severe behavior problems as well.

WHY PROBLEM SOLVING INTERVENTION

As interest in promoting parenting skills increases, so too does the variety of ways to enhance them. Some educational programs help parents learn to show their children affection, to apply nonrestrictive but firm control, and to encourage verbal interaction, particularly reasoning and explanation for instructions, commands, and discipline (called induction). These attitudes and strategies, applied by

The ICPS research of the author was supported in part by the National Institute of Mental Health (#20372), 1971–1975.

researchers such as Johnson et al. (1976) with Mexican-American parents of one-year-olds, and by Wittes and Radin (1969) with parents of preschoolers were based on investigations which have linked these techniques with healthy impulse control and mature moral development, (Hoffman, 1970; Sears et al., 1957). Thus, the goal was to reduce the use of physical punishment and verbal coercion, practices which are commonly linked with the child's frustration, anger, and aggression.

Beyond warmth and affection, even when combined with reasoning and explanations of behavior consequences, Baumrind (1967) found that parents who encourage their children to express their *own feelings* and opinions have more socially competent children than parents who do not. Children's expression of feelings and opinions, advocated by Gordon (1970) as one communication technique of Parent Education Training (PET), used primarily in the middle class, does not just happen; it is the result of acquired skills. We learned that by age four, some lower income children have these skills and others do not. When asked for an *opinion* about what to do if they found themselves in conflict with another child, some of these children typically responded simply, "I don't know." Some children with such cognitive deficits often reacted impulsively to frustration (such as to hit a child who would not give up a toy), then resisted when told a "better" way, even when it was explained that "Jonny doesn't like that," or "you might lose a friend." Others would walk away in defeat and avoid the problem entirely. We then asked ourselves: If children could learn to think for themselves, and parents could teach them to do that, to what extent would such cognitive capacity play a role in the behavior and social adjustment of the young child?

The Problem Solving Training Model

Instead of focusing on the *content* of what children should or should not do, and why, the problem solving model focuses on a *process*, or style of thinking that allows children to decide for themselves what and what not to do, and why. When for example, a child in pursuit of a toy belittles another by calling him or her a name, the child is asked about what happened, what the other child did or said, and whether or not calling the child a name was a good idea. If the child replies that "he hit me," the parent may say, "Calling him a name is *one* thing you can do," and then ask: "Can you think of something different you can do so he won't hit you and so you can still get a chance to play with the toy?"

Focusing upon process, not content seemed reasonable because both adjusted and socially aberrant children could think of forceful ways to obtain a toy, but the adjusted also had a wider repertoire of rational, thoughtful, and nonaggressive strategies (Spivack & Shure, 1974). Thus, our approach was not to take away from poor problem solvers what they already knew, but to help them to think about what they do and then to discover there is more than one way. It seemed reasonable to believe that good problem solvers would more likely succeed because if their first attempt should fail, they could turn to a different, perhaps more effective way to solve the problem.

William, age four, exemplifies what a good problem solver can do. He wanted his six-year-old brother Darren to let him run the switch (on his trains) one day. First he asked, but Darren refused. William then tried, "I'll just run them for a little while." "Don't bug me!" shouted Darren. Recognizing Darren's anger, William waited a while, then tried again. "Why can't I run the switch?" Darren answered,

" 'Cause everytime I want to you keep on switching (running the switch)." "I'll just switch a little while. I'll switch two times and you switch two times, how's that?" "O.K.," said Darren, "but I will be the captain." "O.K.," said William. In finding out about Darren's feelings, William was able to incorporate them into a solution that ended up successful. Like other good problem solvers, he may have *thought* about hitting, or just running the switch without asking, and he also may have been able to anticipate the consequences of such acts. But most importantly, his ability to wait for a better time (when Darren calmed down), then think of other options prevented William from experiencing frustration and failure.

The resourcefulness of good problem solvers not only helps them when they can obtain their wish, but helps them to cope with the frustration when they cannot. JoAnn, when told she could not fingerpaint now because her grandmother was coming for dinner, and that it would make a mess, did not whine and nag. Instead she thought, "I'll color (with my crayons) in my coloring book." Had her mother, concerned about the mess from the finger paints suggested JoAnn use the crayons, JoAnn might well have resisted, "But I want to finger paint!" JoAnn felt good about her own idea and didn't need to nag. Any potential mother-child power play became unnecessary. JoAnn could think for herself.

If advice and explanations often fall on deaf ears, would children who are encouraged, and able to think of their own ways be more likely to carry them out? Would a child's own ineffective solution to a problem prompt him or her to evaluate it more readily, and decide on a "better one"? If the child were encouraged to think what way, would he or she in fact take action that would consider the needs and feelings of others?

For parents to guide their children to problem solve, some of them must first acquire skills themselves. When, for example, Corey's mother saw him grabbing a truck from Keith, he told him to give it back. When Corey answered, "But it's mine," his mother suggested he play with his blocks. When Corey predictably replied, "But I want my truck," his mother, now angry, shouted, "How many times have I told you to share your toys! Grabbing is not nice. If you keep grabbing things, you won't have any friends. Tell him you're sorry."

While this mother did explain the consequences of her child's action, she did nothing to help him think about the problem, or what he did. She was thinking about what was important to her, not what was important to him. And when her suggestion to play with his blocks was met with resistance, she continued to impose her own point of view. Had this mother elicited her child's point of view, she might have learned that he had shared his truck, and now wants it back. The conversation might then have shifted from the act of grabbing, to ways the child could get it back. In that case, the mother and child would now be trying to solve the same problem, and thus facilitate the process of communication.

For children, the goals were to help them: 1) learn to think through and solve problems and not to give up too soon, 2) take into account other people's feelings and desires, and 3) recognize when they can and cannot have what they want. For mothers, the goals were: 1) to increase sensitivity that the child's point of view may differ from her own; 2) to heighten awareness that there is more than one way to solve a problem; 3) to think about what is happening, because in the long run, it may be more beneficial than immediate action to stop it; and 4) to provide a model of problem solving thinking—a thinking parent might inspire a child to think.

THE THINKING SKILLS

For parents and children to talk *with* each other, and not just to each other when daily problems arise, the acquisition and use of certain cognitive skills can aid in that process.

For Children

To date, our research has identified four interpersonal cognitive problem solving skills (called ICPS) that distinguish competent from deficient problem solvers in lower income children by age four: 1) alternative solution thinking, 2) consequential thinking, 3) causal thinking, and 4) cognitive sensitivity to a problem as interpersonal.

A child's ability to generate in his or her own mind different options (solutions) that could solve a problem defines his or her capacity for *alternative solution thinking*. For a four-year-old, a boy may want his friend to let him play with his toy. He may ask him, but his friend may refuse. Of interest is whether the boy who wants the toy would think of another way to try (as did William, described earlier), or whether he would react impulsively by hitting the child or grabbing the toy. Perhaps, in the absence of other options, the boy might merely retreat, and walk away from the problem entirely.

If a child does think of different solutions to the problem, the question becomes whether he/she can evaluate whether the idea is a good one, based partly on what the other child might do or say, whether a figure of authority might intervene etc. Having considered potential *consequences*, a child who hits or grabs to obtain a toy may not be merely reacting to feelings of frustration, but may have thought about it and decided that such actions were a good way to get the toy. If these were not the only ways the child could think of, consideration of how these acts may affect the thoughts and/or actions of another might change his or her course of action.

In addition to solution and consequential thinking, good problem solvers tend to consider that there might be a reason a friend might have refused him or her a toy. The boy might recognize that perhaps his friend said no "because I wouldn't let him play with my new ball," or "because he's afraid I might break it." Such recognition, or *causal thinking* can open up solution strategies that might not otherwise be considered.

Finally, if the boy who wanted the toy were aware that a problem or potential problem could develop once he first asked for the toy, his behavior and/or problem solving strategies may differ from what might ensue in the absence of such sensitivity. Further, if he were also sensitive to the fact that a new problem might emerge should he hit his friend, his behavior and/or problem solving strategies may differ from his course of action in the absence of such sensitivity. Such *interpersonal sensitivity* involves the cognitive ability to perceive a problem when it exists, and the tendency to focus on those aspects of interpersonal confrontation that create or could create a problem for the individuals involved.

In lower-income children, each of these four cognitive skills are correlated with each other, suggesting that each plays a role in the total ICPS chain. Causal thinking and cognitive interpersonal sensitivity however, are not enough to guide the child's behavior. While further research is needed, it is possible that these skills enhance solution and consequential thought, ICPS skills which in turn do relate to the child's level of adjustment as observed in school (Granville & associates, 1976; Shure et al., 1973). Importantly, deficient solution skills are most intimately related to both impulsivity and inhibition in black inner-city four- and five-year-olds. Solution and consequential skills, in *combination*, best identify the inhibited (Spivack et al., 1976). Although impulsive youngsters may be aware they might get hit back if they hit a child, perhaps they continue to pursue their desire with the limited repertoire of solutions they have. Perhaps inhibited children, relatively poor at considering either solutions or consequences, simply retreat from people and from problems they cannot solve. Whether ICPS skills affect behavior or the reverse is not yet known. However, positive impact from training which focuses upon enhancing a child's cognitive capacity, rather than direct modification of behavior itself will give us some clues in that regard.

For Parents

Our childrearing research (Shure, 1979; 1981a; 1981b; Shure & Spivack, 1978; 1979) has identified three ICPS skills that distinguish good from poor problem solvers in black inner-city mothers, and how these skills help these mothers teach their child how to think.

Above and beyond considering discrete types of categories of solution, such as making friends by "having a party," or "help a neighbor whose sick," or, "start talking to someone at the store" (alternative solution thinking), a second skill, called means-ends thinking requires sequenced planning, step-by-step, how to reach an interpersonal goal. Such planning includes insight and forethought to forstall or circumvent potential obstacles and, in addition, having at one's command alternative means if an obstacle is realistically or psychologically insurmountable. The process implies an awareness that goals are not always reached immediately and that certain times are more advantageous than others for action. For example, in planning steps to make friends in a new neighborhood, a hypothetical woman (Mrs. X) might "invite a neighbor for coffee" (*a mean*), but the neighbor might not be friendly and might not come (*potential obstacle*). Mrs. X was afraid to invite her (*obstacle*) but if she waits 'till later 'cause she might be eating dinner now (*recognition of time*), maybe she'll be nice and come. But the neighbor was busy (*obstacle*), so Mrs. X joined the PTA (*mean*) and worked with some mothers on a project (*mean*). It turned out her neighbor (who was busy) was one of those mothers. After several weeks (*time*), they got to know each other and then she asked her to her party (*mean*). That's how she could make friends."

In addition to means-ends thinking about problems which occur between adults (called adult-related problems), means-ends thinking about mother-child or child-child (called child-related) problems (e.g., a child keeps saying 'no' to her mother; two kids are fighting) was measured to evaluate its importance for the ICPS approach to childrearing.

Before training, these skills appear to have a differential effect on the child's ICPS skills, some more direct than others. In both mothers of boys and of girls, a series of partial correlations showed that a mother's ability to solve hypothetical adult-related problems related to her ability to solve hypothetical child-related ones, which in turn related to her style of communication when real problems came up. Thus, ability to solve adult-type problems appears to have an indirect, though not direct affect on how she handles actual problems with her child. We learned that in general, high ICPS mothers tended to suggest solutions and explain consequences to their children when real problems arose—in contrast to low ICPS mothers who tended to apply abrupt commands without explanation. Though very few mothers asked their children for their ideas about what to do or what might happen next, the techniques used by high ICPS mothers did represent the most sophisticated style of communication before training.

Regarding impact on the child, the behavior of black inner-city four-year-olds related to the childrearing practices of the mother, but mainly when the child was a girl. We also discovered that before training, use of induction, suggestions, demands and the like related to the daughters' but not sons' ICPS skills as well (a finding replicated by Flaherty, 1978). Because boys, who were no more ICPS-deficient than girls, and because the child's ICPS skills related to behavior in both sexes, it would be important to learn whether boys, when trained by their mothers would benefit from ICPS intervention to the same extent as would girls.

THE TRAINING PROGRAM

The curriculum (taught in weekly group meetings) is designed so that both mother and child learn to problem solve, and to use their newly acquired skills when real problems arise. Thus, the program differs from earlier described ones, wherein the child responds to what the parent learns to do; children exposed to ICPS intervention actively acquire problem solving skills of their own. The format of the program is a script (in Shure & Spivack, 1978), adapted from our teacher-trained curriculum (in Spivack & Shure, 1974) for use with a single child or with small groups.

What Children Learn

For about three months, parents teach their four-year-old (and other children who wish to participate) a series of daily 20-minute sequenced lessons in game form. The first 24 lesson-games teach skills judged to be prerequisite to the final problem solving skills to be learned, followed by 12 hypothetical problem situations designed to teach the two ICPS skills found to be most intimately related to children's behavior: alternative solution and consequential skills. In addition to the formal structure of the lesson-games, parents are instructed in how to guide their children to use the prerequisite and problem solving concepts outside of the formal teaching time, as situations allow during the day.

Prerequisite Problem Solving Concepts

The first six to eight weeks focus upon word concepts which can be associated with later problem solving, building to games which focus upon recognition and awareness of the children's own and others' feelings and preferences. For example, to help children develop the habit of thinking, "There's more than one way," a process of thought which underlies alternative solution skills, the words "same" and "different," are taught, first through simple distinctions as "stamping my foot is *different* from tapping my knee." These words also help children later recognize that "hitting and kicking" are kind of the *same* because they are both "hurting," and they are encouraged to think of a way that is *different* from hurting. As a precursor to later consequential thinking, the words "not" and "might" are included, beginning with simple statements as "My name is _____; my name is *not* _____." "Donald *might* be cold; he might *not* be cold." To later decide whether an idea is or is *not* a good one, a child can consider, "If I hit him, he *might* hit me back."

As the children learn to identify people's feelings (through pictures, puppets, facial expressions), it is possible to teach that *different* people feel *different* ways about the *same* thing (e.g., "When I mess my room, my mother is *mad*; I am not"), and that there is more than one way to find out how people feel—by hearing what they say, watching what they do, and asking them if they are not sure.

Outside of the formal structured lesson-games, mothers can take advantage of any number of opportunities during the day to reinforce use of the prerequisite problem solving skills (e.g., when a brother is crying). Children enjoy using word concepts they have learned, and informal use of them can begin to sensitize the child to what others are doing, how they are feeling, and ways to help them feel better at times when that would be appreciated.

Problem Solving Concepts

By about the eighth week of the program, children are ready for games and dialogues that focus upon the final solution and consequential skills to be learned. Using pictures and puppets, problem situations are created, first by the mother, later by the child. For example, one picture was depicted as: "This girl wants that boy to sit down so she can see the picture book." The mother asks, "What can the girl do or say so the boy will sit down?" All ideas are accepted equally, whether they be force (e.g., "Push him out of the way") or nonforce (e.g., "Ask him nicely to sit down). In subsequent games, the child will evaluate the merits of each idea. Regardless of solution content, the mother follows the child's first solution with, "That's one way. The idea of this game is to think of lots of *different* ways the girl can get the boy to sit down." IF needed, the mother might pick up a puppet character and, in the puppet-character's voice, say, "I wish I could think of an idea. Can you help me?" Sometimes the child enjoys "being the puppet." Should the child offer an enumeration of an earlier offered solution (e.g., hit him, kick him), the mother responds, "Hitting and kicking are kind of the same because they are both hurting. Can you think of something different from hurting?" To avoid focus on negative types of responses, nonforceful enumerations as "give him candy," and "give him gum," are also classified (in this case, as "giving something"), and the child is asked for an idea that is different.

Following free flow of solutions, children are guided to think about "what might happen next," or, "what the other child might do or say" if a particular solution were carried out (consequential thinking). All solutions are evaluated *by the child*, as the mother probes for multiple consequences for any given solution. By the end of the third month, children engage in solution-consequence pairing, wherein the children offer one solution, one possible consequence of that solution, another solution to the same problem and its possible consequence. Such pairing helps a child think, "If I do this, that might happen; if I do that, this might happen." With the skills the children develop, they can decide whether an idea *is* or is *not* a good one because of what might happen next.

No matter what the child says, at no time does the mother, or puppet character as played by the mother, offer solutions to a problem or consequences to an act.

For children who offer only one or two, ample opportunity is provided in subsequent lesson-games to expand. While it is tempting to help by giving the child ideas, we have learned that most children offer more solutions and consequences as the program progresses.

Just as prerequisite skill concepts are reinforced informally during the day, so too are problem-solving ones. To do this, the mother learns a problem solving style of communication, a style we call "dialoguing." In the same way children are asked for their idea for how a pictured child (or puppet) could "get another child in the way to sit down," children are asked (not told) what they could do if their sister, or friend is, for example, blocking the TV set. Consistent with the formal structured lesson-games, the mother guides the child to see the problem ("What happened," "What's the matter?"), helps the child to see how he/she and others feel about what happened, guides the child to evaluate his or her action, and encourages the child to think of other ways to solve the problem. To do this without just memorizing a series of questions, applies in a mechanical way, some parents have to acquire problem solving skills which underlie this kind of communication, and then to apply those skills to dialogues.

What Parents Learn

To help mother appreciate the thinking skills her child learns, to provide her with greater insight when her child experiences difficulty, and to help her acquire skills for perceptive use of dialoguing techniques, exercises are strategically inserted into the program script to parallel concepts she teaches her child (illustrated in full in Shure & Spivack, 1978).

As mothers help their children think about their own and others' feelings, and how to consider the effect of their actions on others, mothers are encouraged to think about feelings and how what *they* do affect others, including their child. As a mother learns to guide her child to think of solutions to problems relevant to that child, and consequences to acts he or she might pursue, each mother considers solutions and consequences to problems relevant to herself, particularly when a child creates a problem for her. In addition, the mother is guided to think through sequenced steps to reach her goal, obstacles that could interfere, and to consider the time it might take to succeed. She is then helped to incorporate these skills in practice dialogues, so that she and her child can engage in a problem solving style of communication at home (an example is given in the following section).

PROGRAM EFFECTS

Over a two-year period, 40 black inner-city mothers demonstrated they could successfully apply the ICPS program script with their child.

In the first (pilot) year, 20 of 94 mothers who participated in the correlational study implemented the structured lesson-games with their child. They also learned to dialogue with their child when real problems came up, but were not given ICPS training of their own. In addition to evaluating our adaptation of the nursery-teacher program script for use by parents, children were tested for ICPS and behavior change as observed by their teachers in school (federally funded day care). We learned that although ICPS skills and behavior of initially aberrant children improved, the improvement of solution skills was less than that of earlier groups of children trained by their teachers in school. Suspecting that teachers may have had greater natural understanding of, and sensitivity to the concepts being taught than the mothers (of whom many were ICPS deficient before training), parents were taught to problem solve in Year 2, through exercises discussed earlier in the program section describing what parents learn.

In the second year, 20 of 80 correlational-study mothers were trained (10 whose four-year-old was a boy; 10 whose four-year-old was a girl), chosen because their child was ICPS deficient and/or behaviorally aberrant. Because of the need to test a large number of mothers and their children for correlational purposes, to conduct the training sessions, and to retest trained and control mother-child pairs (matched as closely as possible for mother's ICPS skills, and child's age, sex, ICPS skills and behavior), it was not possible train more than 20 mothers during the time limits imposed by the school year. To evaluate any program impact, it seemed important that mothers selected should be those whose children stood to benefit the most.

Impact on the Child

As measured by the Preschool Interpersonal Problem Solving, or PIPS test (Shure & Spivack, 1974a), trained youngsters, compared to controls, gave more different, relevant solutions to hypothetical child-child and parent-child-type problems after training than before it, problems concerning one child wanting a toy from another, and how to avert mother's anger after having damaged an object $[F (7, 36) = 32.28, p < 0.001]$. They also gave more potential consequences to acts such as grabbing a toy, and taking an object from an adult without first asking as measured by the What Happens Next Game, or WHNG (Shure & Spivack, 1974b), $F (1, 36) = 11.54, p < 0.002$. In behavior, 12 of 17 (71 percent) of those whose behavior could improve were, after training, rated by their teachers within a nominally defined normal range on the Hahnemann PreSchool Behavior (HPSB) rating scale (see Spivack & Shure, 1974) a percentage significantly different via a difference-of-proportions test from the 5 of 16 (31 percent) behaviorally comparable controls $(Z = 2.26, p < 0.05)$. Importantly, no sex differences emerged, suggesting that both sexes could benefit the same. As in our teacher-training research, trained youngsters who improved in behavior also improved in their solution skills more than youngsters whose behavior did not $[t (15) = 2.62, p < 0.025$ (one-tailed)]. That such a linkage did not occur for consequences gain confirms our earlier findings that solution skills may be the strongest ICPS mediator of behavior measured to date.

Impact on the Mother

When given the beginning and end of a story, and asked to "fill in the middle," or, "tell everything that happens in between" (means-ends thinking), trained mothers of both boys and girls gained more than controls on child-related problems, $F (1, 36) = 25.32, p < 0.001$, but not adult-related ones (Shure & Spivack, 1978). For example, when a story mother found her two children fighting (the beginning) and the children end up happy (the ending), a trained mother gave this account:

First she tells them she is sorry they are so upset. She asks one of them to tell her what happened. The older boy said his brother lost his racing car. So she asked, "Why don't you make a game of it and look for it together." The older boy said, "Yeah, and whoever finds it first wins a prize." The mother agreed to go along with this, and they both looked for it. Finally the younger boy found it. The mother didn't want another fight over the prize, so she gave a treat to both of them, letting the younger one have first choice. That was fair. She asked them if they were happy now, and they said yes. (Shure & Spivack, 1978, pp. 174–175)

This trained mother focused on the problem is stated. She conceptualized a solution given *by the child* (whoever finds it wins first prize), and accepted that reasonable solution. In contrast, nontrained mothers more typically were preoccupied with their own needs (to stop the fighting), not on the story goal (the children end up happy). Trained mothers who most improved their hypothetical child-related means-ends skills were also most likely to apply problem solving dialogues with their child, $r(18) = 0.54$, $p < 0.05$. For example, one child was experiencing rejection by his brothers.

Child: Robbie and Derek won't let me play.
(Trained) Mother: What are they doing?
C: They're cowboys. They chased me away.
M: Do you want to play their game?
C: Yeah!
M: What did you say to them?
C: I'm a cowboy, too.
M: Then what happened?
C: Derek said, "You're too little. You can't play."
M: What did you do then?
C: Nothing.
M: Can you think of something different you can do or say so they will let you play?
C: I can say, "I'm a big cowboy."
M: What might happen if you do that?
C: They's say, "No you're not."
M: They might say that. What else can you say or do?
C: I could tell them Indians are coming. I could help catch them.
M: That's a different idea. Try your ideas and see what happens. (Shure & Spivack, 1978, pp. 114–115)

This mother encouraged her child to think about the problem, ways to solve it, and the potential consequences of what he might do. Had his brothers continued to refuse, the mother could have guided him to think of (but not suggest) something else he could do, to lessen the momentary frustration. While trained mothers learned to do this, control mothers did not, and demands and suggestions continued to be met with resistance, power plays, and frustration.

Effect of Parent Skills on the Child

A series of analyses (detailed in Shure & Spivack, 1978) revealed that it was the combination of mothers' hypothetical child-related means-ends thinking and dialoguing skills that best predicted the child's enhanced ICPS skills, especially alternative solution skills, the latter of which best predicted the child's behavioral adjustment. We also learned that regardless of the child's sex, children of Year 2 (ICPS-trained) mothers improved in their solution skills significantly more than those of Year 1 (non ICPS-trained) mothers, $t(38) = 2.19$, $p < 0.05$. Although

Year 1 trained mothers had children whose solution skills improved more than earlier teacher research controls, it appears that at least with respect to that important ICPS behavioral mediator, training impact on the child is even greater when both mother and child are taught how to problem solve.

Comments on Training Impact

Although mothers' ability to solve hypothetical adult-related problems showed little, or less consistent change, the importance of them for helping their child is still unknown. Had the training put further emphasis on adult-type problems, the earlier described indirect effect on dialoguing techniques could have been ascertained. It was particularly encouraging that inner-city mothers, some of whom were ICPS-deficient at the start, could improve in some ICPS skills of their own, and enhance those of their child in only three months time. Importantly, the behavior of children, trained at home, improved their behavior as observed by teachers in school, teachers who were unaware of the training procedure or its goals. Perhaps this occurred because children, not having been told what to do (at least not as often), acquired skills that enabled them to generalize when confronted with new problem situations.

In light of the earlier described pretest studies showing correlations between mothers and their daughters, but not sons, it was particularly encouraging that boys could benefit as much as girls. It seems reasonable to assume that trained mothers acquired cognitive skills and dialoguing techniques above and beyond those which even the most inductive pretrained mothers applied. With nearly all trained mothers having been more likely to elicit the child's thoughts, it is possible that boys, perhaps naturally more resistant, were less so when guided, then freed to think for themselves.

It is possible that children improved in their ICPS skills and behavior because of the special attention their mother's gave them. But children whose mothers received the added ICPS skill training improved more than those trained by mothers who did not, even though the latter children received the same amount of attention from their mothers during the training months. Perhaps the added skill training did give mothers more insight into the concepts they taught to their children, enabling them to more effectively guide their child toward more independent problem solving through dialogues.

Other Applications of ICPS Training
with Lower Income Women

The intervention described in this chapter was conducted with black parents of inner-city four-year-olds who were normal, yet displayed varying amounts of behavioral difficulties in school. Although to our knowledge, ICPS participation by parents of other children has been rare, research and/or service applications suggest it has possibilities for childrearing in other groups as well: older children, children with special needs (e.g., disturbed, learning disabled, retarded); abused children; and children in families experiencing other troubles (e.g., divorce).

ICPS for Older Children

Interviews with parents of elementary school-aged children have provided insight about how seldom the problem solving approach is used. Although the content of the problems, and what parents do or say may differ, the extent to which parents encourage independent problem solving thought does not (Shure, 1981a). In lower income children, ICPS skills and behavior are correlated phenomena in normal first- to third-graders (McKim et al., 1982), and in normal third- to sixth-graders (Pelligrini, 1980). Although these relationships are not limited to the lower class (e.g., Arend et al., 1979; Elias, 1978; Ford, 1982; Johnson et al., 1981; McKim et al., 1982; Richard & Dodge, 1982; Schiller, 1978), and some lower class youngsters are more ICPS-competent than some of their middle-class counterparts, it does appear that as a group, lower income youngsters do stand to gain the most (McKim et al., 1982) and indeed, can be trained.

In lower or mixed income groups, teacher-trained elementary school-aged children learned ICPS skills and how to use them (Camp & Bash, 1981; Elardo & Caldwell, 1979; Elias, 1980; Gesten et al., 1982; Shure, 1980; Weissberg et al., 1981). Although both ICPS and behavior gains were observed in each of these studies, relatively weak ICPS/behavior change linkages suggests that it may take somewhat longer than three to four months of training for older children to associate their newly acquired thinking skills directly with what they do, and how they behave. Or, perhaps training both teachers *and* parents would be optimal. Although ICPS/behavioral linkages were not examined, Larcen (1980) did find that three months following a six week intervention, third- and fourth-graders trained by parents who supplemented teacher training (by applying informal dialogues at home) increased their ICPS skills even more than did youngsters trained only by their teachers. Although behaviorally aberrant children trained at ages four and five can begin school from a better behavioral vantagepoint, the evidence to date suggests the elementary school years are not too late. The reciptivity to it by parents who participated in the Larcen study sparks enthusiasm for training older children at home.

ICPS for Special-Needs Children

Within homogeneous groups of children with special needs, the more behaviorally troubled, and/or those with poor peer relations are also more ICPS deficient. Among emotionally disturbed eight- to 13-year-old boys, those least liked by their peers were also least able to plan means toward an interpersonal goal (Higgens & Thies, 1981). Among educable-mentally retarded six- to 12-year-olds, high-impulsive children, those judged to be least aware of and/or concerned for peers in distress, and those least liked by their classmates were also least able to think of solutions to problems and consequences to acts (Healey, 1978). Within-group ICPS and behavioral differences notwithstanding, Higgens and Thies found that even their best liked boys did not generally fare as well as normals, differences not accounted for by IQ. As early as kindergarten, Friedenthal (1981) noted that youngsters with normal IQ, but "at risk" for later perceptual and/or attentional learning disabilities have more behavior problems, poorer peer relations, and greater solution and consequence ICPS deficits than did their non at-risk agemates. In lower middle class 11- and 12-year-old boys (girls were not measured), comparable ICPS distinctions remain. School-identified learning disabled (LD) youngsters scored significantly lower on tests of solution, consequential, and means-ends thinking than did their normal (similar IQ) counterparts (Berg, 1982). Whether LD-associated short-attention span, distractibility, and relatively greater impulsive behaviors predispose cognitive deficits or the reverse is unknown. In our own study of trained normal urban ten-year-olds (Shure, 1980), enhanced ICPS skills had a direct impact on some measures of adjustment, which in turn related to improved academic achievement. It is possible that once behaviors mediated through ICPS skills do improve, youngsters can better absorb the task-oriented demands of the classroom, and subsequently do better in school. Although the cognitive and behavioral associates in LD youngsters are no doubt more complex, it would be interesting to learn if similar patterns of relationships would occur in these youngsters as well.

Although we are unaware of any attempt to train younger children with special needs, it appears that school-aged learning-disabled (Weiner, 1981), disturbed (Natov, 1981), as well as the educable-mentally retarded (Healey, 1977) can benefit from ICPS intervention at school. Because ICPS skills and behavior are correlated phenomena, and given that children with special needs can be trained, important implications for childrearing appear. In fact, Herman (1979) has learned that retarded nine- to 11-year-olds who have mothers who allow their children to make their own decisions are better problem solvers than those whose mothers are more restrictive. Herman's finding that children's ICPS skills are associated with maternal freedom of independent decision-making adds credence to the ICPS approach for their parents.

ICPS for Child Abuse

As a service to parents who harmed their children, or feared they might, workers on a telephone hotline service applied ICPS dialoguing in an informal way (Gonzales, personal communication). Although it was not possible to train a parent to use structured lesson-games, or to dialogue in a manner that would teach their *child* to think, the workers could talk with the parents in a way that would stimulate *them* to think. After waiting for these parents (mostly mothers) to calm down, the worker helped them to focus on their feelings, and then, how they thought their child might feel about the situation (the latter, rarely considered). By guiding the parents to recall, step-by-step, what happened that might have made them angry, some came to see the situation as a problem to be solved, and not just one to vent emotion on their child. Others came to understand that sometimes, their children may have been fighting or engaged in other obstreperous behaviors because they were in conflict with each other, and were not behaving in ways to deliberately annoy them. By helping these parents see the problem in a new way, several called back to express some relief. If they were not yet able to take positive action, at least they were, at times, able to restrain themselves from imposing physical harm.

Reports from parents on the telephone hotline are only suggestive, and these were parents who called for help. Although there are, to be sure, a multitude of reasons parents abuse their children, there would seem good reason to believe that adding the ICPS approach to existing child abuse therapy groups could alter the behavior of parents who participate in them. Having learned that six- to 15-year-old abused youngsters can improve their ICPS skills and (parent perceived) behaviors when trained by their therapists, and even more so when trained by their parents (Nesbitt et al., 1980), it seems fruitful to explore the cognitive benefits for an ICPS-receptive parent as well as the child who is being abused. Although parent perceptions may have created a behavioral rater bias, it would be important to examine whether such perceptions, real or apparent, would at least translate to lower incidence of abuse.

ICPS for Other Troubled, Distressed Families

The perception of child behavior as deliberate annoyance is not uncommon in other families experiencing insufferable childrearing practices. Silver (personal communication) reported how the ICPS approach helped one family, about to place their three children into a foster home. In addition to formal group ICPS meetings, this family was urged to record interpersonal problems that arose at home, how (and if) they applied dialogues, and the success or failure of the outcome. Having learned to better appreciate their childrens' point of view, including the perception that children have problems too, the enhanced problem solving skills of both the parents and their children prevented outside placement of the children.

When skills of children in troubled-distressed families are measured, clear ICPS deficiencies are revealed. For example, Perez et al. (1981) found ICPS deficiencies in third-graders whose families experience one or more family background problems, especially separation or divorce, or lack of educational stimulation at home. Whether lack of educational stimulation preceeds or follows separation and divorce in homes where they coincide, and whether such emotional turmoil creates dynamics which restrict the child's opportunity to acquire ICPS skills is not known. In either case, to the extent that ICPS skills mediate adjustment, and to the extent that ICPS training can help people build coping stretegies in these high risk families, training parents and children the ICPS approach has potential to reduce, even prevent more severe behavioral dysfunction.

REFLECTIONS ON THE ICPS APPROACH

To the extent that ICPS skills mediate behavior, they uncover a unique area of thought processes that suggest important implications for social adjustment and interpersonal competence. In the context of interpersonal problem solving, these processes involve a *style* of thought, which, as described throughout includes considering multiple options, consequences, means-ends thinking, and the like. We believe that a readiness to problem solve is more adaptive than repetition of any one strategy, or a limited few, behavior which can be perceived as nagging, no matter what the content.

Focus on the process however, does not suggest indifference to *what* people think. In the long run, style and content are usually not independent. All, or nearly all children can *think* about forceful ways to obtain a toy, and most can think to ask for it. The difference is that high-ICPS children have a greater repertoire of options from which to choose. In our experience, children who can think of solutions which take into account the feelings and/or thoughts of others can think of more solutions than children whose solutions focus primarily on the self. For example, the quality of solutions give by our initially aberrant parent-trained four-year-olds typically included "ask" for a toy; "take it," or "grab it." After training, these solutions were supplemented (but not replaced) with more reciprocal ones: "Let him ride his bike" (form of trade); "Say, I'll give it right back" (a loan); and "Tell him he'll be his friend if he lets him play with the truck" (interpersonal reciprocation).

Regarding content, childrearing practices have an effect. Jones et al. (1980) found that regardless of social class, four-year-olds of restrictive mothers (concerned with the child's adherence to adult-imposed rules and expectations) offered evasion strategies to the PIPS mother-type problem (e.g., Say, "I didn't break [the vase]"; "hide it"), strategies that Jones et al. interpret to require no attempt to deal with the thoughts, feelings and needs of the other. In contrast, children of nurturant mothers who were warm, involved, and recognized the child's desires and emotional needs offered more solutions of personal appeal and negotiation (e.g., "Mom, don't be mad," or, in the peer-type story, "I'll give the truck right back"), reciprocal solutions that recognize others' thoughts, feelings, and wishes. Not unexpectedly, the tendency to think of force to obtain a toy was independent of childrearing practice, just as we have found it to be independent of the number of ideas conceptualized.

The question becomes whether one "good" solution might really be better than several different ones, including less effective ones. In this regard, we have learned that youngsters who can only offer one nonforceful solution, such as "say please," are often behaviorally inhibited, but just as maladaptive as children who offer only "grab," or "hit," to obtain a toy (Shure & Spivack, 1970). If only a few solutions are learned from parents who stress *specific* content, what can a child who is not stimulated to think do if those solutions should fail at any given time? That is why we believe it is the process of thought that encourages a child to not give up too soon, a flexibility that allows him or her to generalize from one problem situation to another. In the short run, one "good" solution may indeed, solve a problem. In the long run, we believe that alternative solution skills generate the kinds of thought that results in resiliency instead of frustration. (For further discussions of this, see Shure, 1981b; 1982.)

Guiding children to think for themselves does not imply that parents should always allow children to do what they want. A parent who wants her child to clean his or her room does not give her child that choice. An ICPS parent does, however, guide her child to think about how he or she can go about doing that (see Shure & Spivack, 1978 for examples). And, such guidance does not imply that parents should never show anger to their child. Anger is a problem in itself that a child has to learn to cope with, *if* he or she is encouraged to think that way—and if anger and emotional outbursts are not the predominant forms of coping with a problem.

Parents we trained responded very favorably to the program. Perhaps this was because it is flexible. It does not teach people what to do to solve their problems. It teaches them a way to think so they can solve problems important to them, in ways that are relevant for them. As one mother put it, "It doesn't tell me *what* to do. It helps me think better when I have my own problems," and another, "After a while, I could make up my own games. That made me feel smart." One mother was especially thrilled when her child, in response to having asked him, "How do you think it makes me feel when you make so much noise when I'm trying to watch my TV show" answered, "Sad, mommy. I'll think of a different place to play." And especially heartening, still another told us, "Jerome likes to solve his own problems now. He likes to say, "Mommy, that was my idea."

We know that the cognitive and behavioral effects of teacher training can last at least one full year (Shure & Spivack, 1982). We also learned that trained youngsters who showed no observable behavioral difficulties in nursery were less likely than nontrained youngsters to begin showing them in kindergarten, findings which support Perez et al.'s suggestion of the utility of the ICPS approach for primary prevention. If teachers can play a significant role in affecting children's adjustment while they are in school, it appears that parents, in a unique position to affect ICPS development can have an even more enduring impact if they apply problem solving techniques at home.

REFERENCES

Arend, R., Gove, F. L., & Sroufe, A. L. Continuity of individual adaptation from infancy to kindergarten: A predictive study of ego-resiliency and curiosity in preschoolers. *Child Development*, 1979, *50*, 950–959.

Baumrind, D. Child care practices anteceding three patterns of pre-school behavior. *Genetic Psychology Monographs*, 1967, *75*, 44–88.

Berg, F. L. Psychological characteristics related to social problem solving in learning disabled children and their non-disabled peers. Doctoral dissertation, University of Michigan, Ann Arbor, 1982.

Camp, B. W. & Bash, M. A. *Think Aloud: Increasing Social and Cognitive Skills—A Problem Solving Program for Children, Primary Level.* Champaign, IL: Research Press, 1981.

Elardo, P. T. & Caldwell, B. M. The effects of an experimental social development program on children in the middle childhood period. *Psychology in the Schools*, 1979, *16*, 93–100.

Elias, M. J. The development of a theory-based measure of how children understand and attempt to resolve problematic social situations. Unpublished masters thesis, University of Connecticut, Storrs, 1978.

Elias, M. J. Developing instructional strategies for television-based preventive mental health curricula in elementary school settings. Unpublished doctoral dissertation, University of Connecticut, Storrs, 1980.

Flaherty, E. Parental influence on children's social cognition. Final Summary Report, No. 29033. Washington, D.C.: National Institute of Mental Health, 1978.

Ford, M. Social cognition and social competence. *Developmental Psychology*, 1982, *18*, 323–340.

Friedenthal, M. S. Relationship of attentional and/or perceptual impairment to the social problem solving abilities of kindergarten children. Unpublished doctoral dissertation, Fordham University, New York, 1981.

Gesten, E. L., Rains, M., Rapkin, B., Weissberg, R. G., Flores de Apodaca, R., Cowen, E. L., & Bowen, G. Training children in social problem-solving competencies: A first and second look. *American Journal of Community Psychology*, 1982, *10*, 95–115.

Gonzales, R. Personal communication, June 1977.

Gordon, T. *Parent Effectiveness Training.* New York: Peter H. Wyden, Inc., 1970.

Granville, A. C., McNeil, J. T., Meece, J., Wacker, S., Morris, M., Shelly, M., & Love, J. M. *A process evaluation of project developmental continuity interim report IV, Vol. 1: Pilot year impact study—Instrument characteristics and attrition trends.* No. 105-75-1114, Washington, D.C.: Office of Child Development, August 1976.

Healey, K. An investigation of the relationship between certain social cognitive abilities and social behavior, and the efficacy of training in social cognitive skills for elementary retarded educable children. Unpublished doctoral dissertation, Bryn Mawr College, 1977.

Healey, K. N. Social problem solving skills in retarded educable children. Paper presented at the meetings of the American Psychological Association, Toronto, August 1978.

Herman, M. S. The interpersonal competence of educable mentally retarded and normal children and its relation to the mother-child interaction. Paper presented at the meeting of the Society for Research in Child Development, San Francisco, March 1979.

Higgins, J. P. & Thies, A. P. Problem solving and social position among emotionally disturbed boys. *American Journal of Orthopsychiatry*, 1981, *51*, 356–358.

Hoffman, M. L. Moral development. In P. H. Mussen (ed.), *Carmichael's Manual of Child Psychology*, Vol. II. New York: Wiley, 1970.

Johnson, D. L., Kahn, A. J., & Leler, H. *Houston Parent-Child Development Center.* Final Report DHEW-90-C-379. Houston: Office of Child Development, 1976.

Johnson, J. E., Roopnarine, J. L., & Serlin, R. E. Relations of social problem solving, referential communication, and intelligence test scores with peer status and social behavior within a mixed-age classroom. Manuscript submitted for publication, 1981.

Jones, D. C., Rickel, A. U., & Smith, R. L. Maternal childrearing practices and social problem-solving strategies among preschoolers. *Developmental Psychology*, 1980, *16*, 241–242.

Larcen, S. W. Enhancement of social problem solving skills through teacher and parent collaboration. Unpublished doctoral dissertation. University of Connecticut, Storrs, 1980.

McKim, B. J., Weissberg, R. P., Cowen, E. L., Gesten, E. L., & Rapkin, B. D. A comparison of the problem-solving ability and adjustment of suburban and urban third grade children. *American Journal of Community Psychology*, 1982, *10*, 155–169.

Natov, I. An intervention to facilitate interpersonal cognitive problem-solving skills and behavioral adjustment among emotionally handicapped children. Unpublished doctoral dissertation, Fordham University, New York, 1981.

Nesbitt, A., Madsen-Braun, J., Bruckner, M., Caldwell, R., Dennis, N., Liddell, T., & McGloin, J. Children's Resource Center: "A problem solving approach;" Final Evaluation. Report to LEAA No. 77-2A(1)-3C-52, Washington, D.C.: and Adams County Department of Social Services, Commerce City, Co.: 1980. (Available from Draft Aid Reproductions, 1088 S. Gaylord, Denver, Co. 80209.)

Pellegrini, D. Social cognition, competence, and adaptation in children under stress. In N. Garmezy (Chair), *Studies of stress and coping in children.* Symposium presented at the meeting of the American Psychological Association, Montreal, September 1980.

Perez, V., Gesten, E. L., Cowen, E. L., Weissberg, R. P., Rapkin, B. D., & Boike, M. Relationships between family background problems and social problem-solving skills of young normal children. *Journal of Prevention*, 1981, *2*, 80–90.

Richard, B. A. & Dodge, K. A. Social maladjustment and problem-solving in school-aged children. *Journal of Consulting and Clinical Psychology*, 1982, *50*, 226–233.

Schiller, J. D. Child care arrangements and ego functioning: The effects of stability and entry age on young children. Unpublished doctoral dissertation, University of California, Berkeley, 1978.

Sears, R., Macoby, E. E., & Levin, H. *Patterns of Child Rearing.* New York: Harper & Row, 1957.

Shure, M. B. Training children to solve interpersonal problems: A preventive mental health program. In R. E. Munoz, L. R. Snowden, & J. G. Kelly (eds.), *Social and psychological research in community settings.* San Francisco: Jossey-Bass, 1979.

Shure, M. B. Interpersonal problem solving in ten-year-olds. Final Report No. MH-27741, Washington, D.C.: National Institute of Mental Health, 1980.

Shure, M. B. A social skills approach to childrearing. In Argyle, M. (ed.), *Social skills and health.* London: Methuen and Co. LTD, 1981. (a)

Shure, M. B. Social competence as a problem solving skill. In J. Wine & M. Smye (eds.), *Social competence.* New York: Guilford Press, 1981. (b)

Shure, M. B. Interpersonal problem solving: A cog in the wheel of social cognition. In Serafica, F. (ed.), *Social Cognition and Social Development in Context.* New York: Guilford Press, 1982.

Shure, M. B., Newman, S., & Silver, S. Problem solving thinking among adjusted, impulsive and inhibited Head Start children. Paper presented at the meeting of the Eastern Psychological Association, Washington, D.C.: May 1973.

Shure, M. B. & Spivack, G. Problem-solving capacity, social class and adjustment among nursery school children. Paper presented at the meetings of the Eastern Psychological Association, Atlantic City, April 1970.

Shure, M. B. & Spivack, G. *Preschool interpersonal problem-solving (PIPS) test: Manual.* Philadelphia: Department of Mental Health Sciences, Hahnemann Medical College 1973. (a).

Shure, M. B. & Spivack, G. *The What Happens Next Game (WHNG); Test and Scoring Instructions.* Philadelphia: Department of Mental Health Sciences, Hahnemann Medical College and Hospital, 1974. (b) [mimeo]

Shure, M. B. & Spivack, G. *Problem solving techniques in childrearing.* San Francisco: Jossey-Bass, 1978.

Shure, M. B. & Spivack, G. Interpersonal problem solving thinking and adjustment in the mother-child dyad. In M. W. Kent & J. E. Rolf (eds.), *The Primary Prevention of Psychopathology.* Vol. 3: *Social Competence in Children.* Hanover, N.H.: University Press of New England, 1979.

Shure, M. B. & Spivack, G. Interpersonal problem solving in young children. *American Journal of Community Psychology*, 1982, *10*, 341–356.

Silver, S. Personal communication, June 1977.

Spivack, G., Platt, J. J., & Shure, M. B. *The problem solving approach to adjustment.* San Francisco: Jossey-Bass, 1976.

Spivack, G. & Shure, M. B. *Social adjustment of young children.* San Francisco: Jossey-Bass, 1974.

Weiner, J. A theoretical model of the affective and social development of learning disabled children. Unpublished doctoral dissertation, University of Michigan, Ann Arbor, 1978.

Weissberg, R. P., Gesten, E. L., Carnrike, C. L., Toro, P. A., Rapkin, B. D., Davidson, E., & Cowen, E. Social problem-solving skills training: A competence-building intervention with second- to fourth-grade children. *American Journal of Community Psychology*, 1981, *9*, 411–423.

Wittes, G. & Radin, N. *Helping Your Child to Learn: The Reinforcement Approach.* San Rafael, Calif.: Dimensions Publishing Company, 1969.

8

The Impact of Crime on Urban Women

Stephanie Riger
Lake Forest College

Margaret T. Gordon
Northwestern University

INTRODUCTION

Although crime in the United States is so widespread that it affects a third of
the nation's households (Bureau of Justice Statistics Bulletin, 1981), this figure
still underestimates the true consequences of crime because the social, emotional
and economic costs affect even more people than those directly victimized. Observers for more than a decade have recognized that widespread and increasing
fear of crime constitutes a major social problem (e.g., Maltz, 1972). Many people
suffer from anxiety in anticipation of victimization, and modify their lives to
avoid crime in ways that cost them lost social and work opportunities (McIntyre,
1967; Biderman et al., 1967). The self-imposed isolation of people seeking to
prevent victimization also costs their communities in terms of participation in
volunteer, leisure and other activities.

The burden of this fear of crime falls disproportionately on women. In a national poll conducted in 1972, over half the women surveyed, compared to 20
percent of the men, said they were afraid to walk alone in their neighborhoods
at night (Erskine, 1974). Gender is a consistent and powerful predictor of fear
in a variety of studies and it appears to be more important than other sociodemographic predictors such as age, race, and income (Cook et al., 1982).

Women's high levels of fear of crime seem inconsistent with their generally low
rates of victimization. Observers attempting to reconcile this apparent paradox have
suggested two types of explanations: either women's reactions are inappropriate
and based on such factors as socialization for timidity, or women are especially
vulnerable because of their risk of a particularly heinous crime—rape—and their
inability to defend themselves against male attackers (see DuBow et al., 1979,
and Riger et al., 1978, for reviews).

It is the contention of this chapter that women's reactions to crime are shaped
by a number of factors residing both in themselves and in the environments in
which they live. It is not simply *rates* of victimization that generate women's

The research on which this article is based was conducted at the Center for Urban Affairs
and Policy Research at Northwestern University and partially supported by grant #R01 MH-
2960 from the National Institute of Mental Health. This chapter summarizes data and arguments presented in earlier papers.

fear, but also the *nature* and perceived likelihood of that victimization. Further, most women are victimized by men (Dodge et al., 1976), which links criminal encounters to more general patterns of interaction between the sexes. Women are more likely to know their attackers than men, and are more often subject to crimes such as rape and wife abuse which affect not only their bodily safety, but also their social identity and emotional well-being (U.S. Department of Justice, 1980b; Table C and 1980a; Weis and Borges, 1973). In addition to women's estimates of their own risk of danger, their perceptions of their physical competence and ties with their neighborhood have an impact on their levels of fear and the extent of precautions they take. Women who perceive their risks as high, who see themselves as slow and weak, and who have marginal ties to the locality are especially fearful; and high fear contributes to frequent use of self-protective behaviors (Riger and Gordon, 1981).

Our chapter begins by delineating the unique nature of crime against women and proceeds with a detailed description of women's attitudinal and behavioral reactions to crime. Then we review a variety of sociopsychological and community-related factors that affect women's responses to crime.

The chapter concludes with a discussion of some implications of women's reactions to crime for the quality of their lives. Feminists have long contended that the threat of crime, especially rape, acts as an instrument of social control over women, encouraging them to restrict their behavior and depend on men for protection (Brownmiller, 1975; Griffin, 1979). The research findings reviewed here suggest further than the restrictive effects of crime do not fall equally on all women; those who appear to have the fewest resources are most affected.

In writing this chapter we rely primarily on two sources: the U.S. Census Bureau's National Crime Survey reported by Hindelang et al. (1978) and others, and our own study launched in 1977 designed to assess the extent and distribution of women's fear of rape and other crimes, to explore major determinants of fear, and to examine strategies that women use to cope with the threat of victimization. We conducted extensive interviews with nearly 300 women in urban neighborhoods in Chicago, Philadelphia, and San Francisco.[1] This article reviews the findings of that study in the context of previous research and discusses some implications of those findings. (The methods and results of the study are presented in detail in Gordon and Riger, 1978; Gordon et al., 1980; LeBailly, 1982; Riger & Lavrakas, 1981; and Riger et al., 1981.)

[1] In conjunction with the Reactions to Crime Project (Lewis, 1978) at Northwestern University's Center for Urban Affairs and Policy Research, we conducted a telephone survey in 1977 of 1620 people living within the city limits of Philadelphia, San Francisco and Chicago. In each city we interviewed 540 adults selected through random-digit-dialing. The sample was weighted to correct for the number of telephone lines per household, since that affected people's chances of being contacted. The weighted $N = 1389$. (This sample is referred to hereafter as the "3-city aggregate sample.") An additional 3400 respondents, randomly selected from ten neighborhoods within the three cities, were interviewed by telephone in order to permit an in-depth examination of how crime affects community life. A more complete discussion of the methodology of the telephone interview is given in Skogan (1978), and findings are presented in Lewis and Salem (1980), Podalevsky and DuBow (in press), and Skogan and Maxfield (1981). At the end of the telephone interview, respondents in six of the ten neighborhoods were invited to participate in an in-person interview about their fear of crimes including sexual assault; the 299 women and 68 men interviewed in person comprise the core sample for our study. We deliberately oversampled women so that the causes and consequences of their greater fear of crime could be explored in depth. An examination of the reliability and validity

VICTIMIZATION OF URBAN WOMEN

Although not without flaws, the National Crime Survey constitutes the best available body of information about victims and their experiences with crime (see Skogan, 1977). When we compare rates of criminal violence against women with those against men, these data reveal that men are victimized about twice as often as women, with two exceptions: rape and personal larceny with contact (see Table 1). In 1978, the most recent year for which data are available, the rate of crimes of violence against men was 45.7 per thousand, while the comparable rate for women was 22.8 per thousand. For crimes of theft, the ratio was closer to unity; men experience about 20 percent more victimizations than do women.

In general, more serious crimes occur less often, and murder is the least frequently occurring crime (Skogan & Maxfield, 1981). Since victimization survey data are based on self-reports of victims, murder statistics come from police files. According to FBI data reported by Bowker (1978), women constitute 24 percent of all reported murder victims.

Among violent crimes, the most likely to happen to women, as to men, is assault, followed by robbery. Rape is the violent crime that occurs least often to both sexes. Women's rates of theft also parallel men's rates, with personal larceny without contact much more frequent than that with contact. The two crimes which women suffer *more* often than men, rape and personal larceny with contact (primarily purse-snatching), are also among the least frequently occurring crimes. In 1978, the rate of rape for women was 1.7 per thousand, while the comparable rate for men, (0.2 per thousand) was based on so few cases that the figure is statistically unreliable.

Between the years of 1964 and 1975, crime in the United States rose dramatically. Much of the increase was in violent crime, with rates of assault, robbery, rape and burglary rising up sharply (Skogan, 1978b). Since 1975, most victimization rates in cities have remained relatively constant, although the rates for assault increased by about 8 percent between about 1973 and 1978 and the rate for robbery fell 13 percent during this time (U.S. Department of Justice, 1980a). Violence against men increased by about 3.6 percent between 1973 and 1978, while the parallel increase against women was 5.5 percent. Rates of rape reported to the census takers appear to have remained fairly constant during this time, while police data have shown a sharp increase in rapes since 1933 (Hindelang & Davis, 1977).

But data about the prevalence of victimizations do not tell the whole story of

---

of responses from persons included in both the telephone and in-person surveys is presented in LeBailly, 1979.

A comparison of the 367 persons interviewed in-person with the 3-city aggregate telephone sample indicated no statistically significant differences in their area of residence or race. However, the in-person respondents were younger, better educated, and wealthier than the randomly-selected telephone sample. Two percent of the women in the 3-city aggregate sample reported ever having been raped or sexually assaulted. Among the women who were interviewed both in person and on the telephone, 6 percent reported on the phone that they had been raped or sexually assaulted, while almost twice as many (11 percent) mentioned such an assault when interviewed in person. (Note that this incidence data is considerably higher than that reported in other victimization surveys, e.g., McDermott, 1979; this may be because the question asked about sexual assault as well as rape, and because the time frame was not limited to the past six or twelve months, as is typical in many surveys.) These data raise serious questions for epidemiological studies of rape, since methodological artifacts may contribute considerable error to rape rates reported in such studies.

Table 1 Victimization rates in the U.S., 1978, by gender and for females by race or Hispanic origin, age, and marital status[a]

	Crimes of violence	Rape	Robbery	Assault	Crimes of theft	Petty larceny With contact	Petty larceny Without contact
Males	45.7	0.2	8.3	37.2	105.6	2.7	102.9
Females	22.8	1.7	3.7	17.2	88.7	3.5	85.1
Race/Ethnicity							
White	22.0	1.4	3.4	17.2	90.0	3.1	87.0
Black	29.7	3.8	6.4	19.6	80.2	6.8	73.4
Hispanic	23.0	1.0[*]	5.3	16.7	92.4	7.5	84.9
Age							
12–15	37.7	2.3	2.7	32.7	126.6	0.7[*]	125.9
16–19	51.6	4.6	8.3	38.9	139.0	2.0	136.9
20–24	44.4	3.8	7.2	33.4	135.1	5.2	129.8
25–34	25.7	2.0	3.8	19.8	111.1	3.5	107.6
34–49	14.7	0.7	2.9	11.1	88.2	3.2	85.0
50–64	7.8	0.5[*]	1.5	5.8	52.7	5.1	47.7
65 or more	6.4	0.2[*]	2.6	3.6	18.6	3.5	15.4
Marital status							
Married	11.7	0.7	2.0	9.0	73.3	2.6	70.7
Widowed	9.1	0.0[*]	3.9	5.3	37.7	4.0	33.7
Never married	38.7	3.2	5.2	30.3	130.5	3.8	126.7
Separated/ Divorced	62.5	5.2	10.0	47.3	125.0	8.5	116.5

Source: U.S. Department of Justice, Bureau of Justice Statistics, *Criminal Victimization in the U.S.: 1973-78 Trends.* Washington, D.C.: U.S. Government Printing Office, 1980 (Tables 3, 4, and 5).
[a]Rates per 1,000 persons age 12 and over.
[*]Rate, based on about 10 or fewer sample cases, is statistically unreliable.

crime against women. Table 1 shows that black women are more likely than white or Hispanic women to be victims of violent crime, although they are the *least* likely of these three subgroups to experience theft. Age 24 seems to demarcate risk levels for women, with those younger being in generally greater danger than those older than 24 years. Women who have never married and those who are separated or divorced have considerably higher rates of victimization of both violence and theft than married or widowed women. Thus, with the exception of age, the heaviest burden of violent crime falls on those women who appear least likely to have resources with which to cope with victimization.

The apparent paradox between women's high fear levels and low victimization rates presumes that victimization surveys accurately reflect the actual incidence of crime against women. Is this so? Methodological investigations have been conducted to assess how many crimes reported to police are also reported to survey interviewers. The results indicate that certain classes of crime events sometimes are not reported to survey interviewers, most often rape and nonstranger crime (Skogan, 1977). Females are more likely to be victims of rape and to know their attackers than males; about 56 percent of those victimized by known attackers are female, while about 44 percent are male (U.S. Department of Justice, 1980b). Within the category of marital violence, the sex ratios are even more skewed, with women constituting 94.6 percent of those victimized by a spouse or ex-spouse. Thus the underreporting of violence by known assailants may result in serious underestimation of the extent of crime against women.

While many more crimes are reported to survey interviewers than to police, the *pattern* of distribution of crime is generally similar in both police and survey data (Skogan, 1977). However, both police data and victimization surveys include only violent behavior that fairly closely fits legal definitions of crime. In recent years, feminists have called attention to certain kinds of incidents occurring to women which may be threatening or fear-provoking, but which are not classified as violent crime, such as obscene telephone calls, sexual harassment at work, or verbal abuse on the street (Medea & Thompson, 1974). Although these incidents could generate fear and leave women feeling victimized, the National Crime Survey does not ask about them and neither their prevalence nor women's reactions to them have been systematically assessed. In addition, the National Crime Survey does not ask victims directly if they have been raped, but rather, asks if assaults that occurred to them were rapes. Thus it is possible that many rapes are not mentioned by respondents or are misclassified as assaults by the surveyors (McDermott, 1979).

In 1979, over 192,000 women reported rapes during the preceding twelve months to the victimization surveyors (an increase of 47,000 or 24 percent over the 1976 figures). Many analysts estimate that since many victims don't report their rapes to surveyors or anyone else, these figures may represent only 10 to 25 percent of the rapes that actually occur. The figures also indicate that the incidence of rape is much higher in large urban areas in the U.S., than in rural ones. Taken together, these data mean that if a woman lives in a large U.S. city for 25 years, she has a 1-in-12 chance of being raped during that time. If the rates are actually higher, her chances of being raped are still greater.

To summarize, the pattern (although not the magnitude) of criminal violence against women is generally similar to that against men, with certain important exceptions which are likely to have a strong impact on women's reactions to crime. Women are subject to rape and are more likely than men to know their attackers. Among those assaulted by their spouses, women constitute the majority of victims. And most female victims are attacked by male offenders. Thus, patterns of crime against women strengthen the inequitable gender distribution of power in society by reinforcing male dominance with actual or threatened violence.

We believe that women's greater vulnerability to rape is central to both their fear and reactions to crime. Apart from murder, rape is the most fear-inducing crime (Brodyaga et al., 1975). Rapes often take place over several hours or days, and there is more opportunity for injury (Stinchcombe et al., 1980). In the National Crime Survey, proportionately more rape victims (48 percent) reported being otherwise injured than those in any other crime category (Hindelang et al., 1978). While most of these injuries are minor (e.g., cuts and bruises), they occur in addition to emotional damage. The National Crime Survey measures only bodily injury, yet a survey of citizens' fear of crime found that 53 percent of the females and 36 percent of the males interviewed believed that the worst aspect of a rape was the emotional damage to the victim (Riger et al., 1978). Studies of the after-effects of rape indicate that it is one of the most traumatic of crimes, with many victims developing symptoms of emotional distress which last for several weeks or even years after the attack (Burgess & Holmstrom, 1974; Katz & Mazur, 1979). In addition to the damage occurring from the rape itself, attribution of blame to the victim by friends, co-workers and actors in the criminal justice system may leave her feeling doubly victimized (Berger, 1977; Medea & Thompson, 1974). To some extent this may happen to all crime victims, since most people seem to want to believe in a world where people get what they deserve (Lerner, 1980). By blaming the victim we preserve our belief in justice (Ryan, 1971). However, researchers have found that such "blaming" reactions are particularly likely to occur in the case of rape (Feild, 1978; Jones & Aronson, 1973; Krulewitz, 1977). And men are more likely to attribute responsibility to the rape victim than are women (Feild, 1978; Selby et al., 1977).

Rape may be especially fear-inducing because of widespread beliefs that it is linked with gratuitous violence (in addition to the rape itself), and that is is nearly impossible to resist successfully. In fact, the statistical profile of rape derived from the National Crime Survey indicates that despite the common presence of more than one offender or the use of a weapon, most victims actively resist or attempt to escape (Hindelang & Davis, 1977; McDermott, 1979). Victims who resisted in some manner increased the chances that the rape would not be completed; however, injury (in addition to the rape itself) is more frequent among those who resisted (McDermott, 1979). Most of the injuries take the form of bruises, cuts, scratches, and black eyes, rather than more severe stabbings or capricious beatings. Since these data are correlational in nature, identification of the causal sequence is impossible. That is, we do not know if these women were injured because they resisted, or if they resisted because they were being injured. Two recent studies comparing women who were raped with those who managed to deflect an attack found that successful resisters were those who from the moment they realized they may be in danger used a multiplicity of self-protective strategies, for example, physical resistance, screaming and trying to flee, and the like (Bart, 1981; McIntyre et al., 1979). Active, forceful fighting at the onset of an attack rather than passive pleading or screaming appears to be more successful in warding off attackers (Bart, 1981; Sanders, 1980). In addition to thwarting the assault, resistance may help some women to preserve their self-esteem and lessen the psychological damage done by rape (Sanders, 1980).

In our study, we asked women to estimate their chances of being raped and otherwise assaulted in their neighborhoods. Women who perceive a high risk of rape in their neighborhoods are more fearful than those who think such risk is low. Surprisingly, *men's* fear levels also are associated with their perceptions of a *woman's* risk of being raped in their neighborhoods. And men's estimates of women's risks of rape are higher than those reported by women themselves (Riger & Gordon, 1981).

In short, rape may be a "bellwether" crime against which both men and women judge the general criminal environment in their communities. When rape does occur it may signal that other crimes are likely to happen, too. The high correlation in the FBI Uniform Crime Reports between the rates of rape and rates of other violent crimes (e.g., for 1976, the Spearman rank-order correlation was 0.68; Bowker, 1978: 120) indicate this is a reasonable speculation. Women's estimates of their risk of rape are associated with their perceived risk of other violent crimes, and this index of the combined risks of violence is strongly related to fear (Riger et al., 1981). This suggests that women fear a multiplicity of crimes involving personal confrontations, leading them to experience their environment as a whole as a dangerous place to be.

WOMEN'S RESPONSES TO URBAN CRIME

To what extent is fear of crime commensurate with the patterns of victimization outlined above? This section describes in greater detail the distribution of the fear of crime by gender and among women and men of varying demographic characteristics. Table 2 is based on 1975 National Crime Survey data from the nation's five largest cities—New York, Los Angeles, Chicago, Philadelphia, and Detroit (Garofalo, 1977).

About 7 out of 10 men (68.3 percent) in this survey reported feeling "very" or "reasonably" safe in response to the question, "How safe do you feel or would you feel when out in your neighborhood alone at night?" In contrast, only about 4 out of 10 of the women (38.9 percent) interviewed reported feeling safe. Women were almost three times as likely as men to report feeling "very unsafe." When we look at the distribution of fear by race, marital status, and age, we find that the overall pattern is similar for males and females, but that the reported amounts of

Table 2 Percentage distribution of feeling of personal safety when out alone in the neighborhood at night by gender, race/ethnicity, marital status, and age

		Very safe	Reasonably safe	Somewhat unsafe	Very unsafe	N
Gender	Male	21.8	46.5	19.2	12.5	5230
	Female	7.7	31.2	28.1	33.0	6368
Race						
Male	White	24.7	47.5	18.2	9.7	3773
	Black	13.8	43.3	22.2	20.8	1337
	Other	21.5	50.5	17.8	10.2	121
Female	White	8.7	33.3	29.1	28.9	4322
	Black	5.3	26.3	25.6	42.8	1924
	Other	8.5	35.6	32.6	23.3	122
Marital status						
Male	Married	2.0	47.0	19.9	13.1	3252
	Widowed	11.1	35.1	27.0	26.8	182
	Never M.	27.1	48.2	16.7	8.0	1434
	Sep/Div.	21.2	41.2	19.6	18.0	344
Female	Married	7.6	32.2	30.1	30.1	3303
	Widowed	6.5	24.9	24.4	44.1	922
	Never M.	8.9	34.6	28.0	28.5	1365
	Sep/Div.	6.8	28.9	24.4	39.9	761
Age						
Male	16–19	26.8	49.7	16.2	7.2	553
	20–24	30.1	51.5	13.1	5.3	612
	25–34	27.1	51.2	15.1	6.6	1006
	35–49	21.5	47.3	20.7	10.5	1146
	50–64	17.2	43.1	22.3	17.3	1212
	65 or more	11.4	37.2	25.1	26.4	701
Female	16–19	10.9	35.4	27.5	26.2	607
	20–24	9.3	36.5	28.2	26.0	734
	25–34	7.9	34.5	28.9	28.7	1214
	35–49	8.6	34.6	29.3	27.5	1427
	50–64	6.3	27.2	29.6	36.9	1384
	65 or more	5.0	21.7	23.6	49.7	1003

Source: 1975 National Survey, five-city sample.

fear differ sharply. In general, blacks report more fear than persons of other races or ethnicities; those widowed or separated or divorced report more fear than the never or currently married; and older people report more fear than younger people. Within each of these demographic categories, however, women report more fear than men. Blacks, whether male or female, appear to be the most fearful of any ethnic or racial subgroup, but about twice as many black females report high fear as black males. More of those widowed, separated, or divorced report high fear than the never married or currently married, yet a higher percentage of females than their male counterparts within each of these marital categories falls into the high-fear-level. Gender differences in fear by age are especially pronounced: the lowest proportion of women describing themselves as feeling very unsafe (26.0 percent of those 20–24 years) is about the same as the highest proportion of men who feel afraid (26.4 percent of those 65 or over). Close to half (49.7 percent) of the women aged 65 or over reported feeling "very unsafe"; these women are the most fearful of any demographic subgroup.

Critics have pointed out a multitude of problems with the way fear is measured in the National Crime Survey (e.g., Baumer, 1978; Garofalo, 1979). Yet the consistency across a number of surveys of the finding that women fear crime more than men prevents its dismissal as a mere methodological artifact. In addition to greater fear, studies of behavioral reactions to the threat of crime indicate that women employ more precautions than do men (Baumer, 1978). In the National Crime Survey, for instance, more females (52 percent) than males (37 percent) said they had limited their behavior because of crime (Garofalo, 1977).

Feminists have argued that rape and the fear of it it is central to the tendency of women to impose these limitations on their own behavior. In *Against Our Will: Men, Women and Rape*, Susan Brownmiller (1975) argued that rape is an instrument of social control, "a conscious process of intimidation by which *all* men keep all women in a state of fear" (p. 15). While her attribution of conscious collusion in rape by all men evoked a storm of controversy (see Geis, 1977), Brownmiller emphasized that rape is a crime which affects all women, *regardless of whether they are actually victimized*. By limiting women's freedom and making them dependent on men for protection, the threat of rape provides support for a social system based on male dominance. Griffin (1979) verbalized what many women experience: "I have never been free of the fear of rape. From a very early age I, like most women, have thought of rape as part of my natural environment— something to be feared and prayed against like fire or lightening" (p. 3). "The fear of rape keeps women off the streets at night. Keeps women at home. Keeps women passive and modest for fear that they be thought provocative" (p. 21).

Such fear can induce a continuing state of stress in women and can lead to the use of safety precautions that severely restrict women's freedom, such as not going out alone at night or staying out of certain parts of town. Ironically, taking these precautions does not always provide the protection they promise, since women's own homes are the single most frequent site (about 33 percent) of rape victimizations (McDermott, 1979).

PRECAUTIONARY STRATEGIES

In a discussion of strategies that people use when interacting with their environment, Cobb (1976, p. 311) distinguishes between adaptation ("changing the self in an attempt to improve person-environment fit") and coping ("manipulation of the environment in the service of self"). This distinction is loosely reflected in one made by DuBow et al. (1979) between avoidance and self-protective behaviors in response to the threat of crime. "Avoidance refers to actions taken to decrease exposure to crime by removing oneself from or increasing the distance from situations in which the risk of criminal victimization is believed to be high" (p. 31). Avoidance behaviors, such as not going out at night or staying out of certain parts of town, limit one's exposure to dangerous situations. In contrast, self-protective behavior, such as self-defense tactics or asking repair persons to show identification, has the goal of minimizing the risk of victimization when in the presence of danger. While avoidance may require changes in one's daily behavior to *reduce exposure* to risks, self-protection tactics permit the *management* of risks once they occur (Skogan & Maxfield, 1981). The analytical distinction between avoidance and self-protection has been empirically supported through factor analysis of a variety of data sets (Keppler, 1976; Lavrakas & Lewis, 1980; Riger & Gordon, 1979).

Women in our own survey used two basic types of precautionary strategies in response to the threat of crime; we have labeled them "isolation" and "street savvy." Isolation includes avoidance tactics, designed to prevent victimization by not exposing oneself to risk (e.g., not going out on the street at night). Street savvy, on the other hand, includes tactics intended to reduce risks when exposed to danger, such as wearing shoes that permit one to run, or choosing a seat on a bus with an eye to who is sitting nearby.

When we asked women in the in-person interview sample how frequently they used these precautionary strategies, about 41 percent said they used isolation tactics "all or most of the time" or "fairly often," while about 59 percent said they "seldom" or "never" did these things (see Table 3). In contrast, 71 percent of

Table 3 Demographic distribution of the frequent use of precautionary behaviors, by gender

Category	Isolate (% Often)		Street savvy (% Often)	
	Men	Women	Men	Women
Sample	10.3 (68)*	41.5 (299)	29.4 (68)	73.9 (299)
Age				
18–26	5.3 (19)	37.3 (102)	15.8 (19)	74.5 (102)
27–33	5.6 (18)	35.7 (56)	33.3 (18)	75.0 (56)
34–51	16.7 (18)	38.8 (98)	38.9 (18)	75.5 (98)
52–93	15.4 (13)	64.3 (42)	30.8 (13)	66.7 (42)
Race/Ethnicity				
Black	9.1 (11)	45.0 (100)	36.4 (11)	78.0 (100)
White	4.9 (41)	33.3 (159)	22.0 (41)	68.6 (159)
Hispanic	11.1 (9)	69.2 (26)	22.2 (9)	80.8 (26)
Income				
< $6,000	14.3 (7)	38.0 (50)	28.6 (7)	84.0 (50)
$6,000–9,999	0 (9)	40.7 (54)	33.3 (9)	77.8 (54)
$10,000–14,999	18.8 (16)	52.5 (61)	31.3 (16)	77.0 (61)
$25,000 and over	11.1 (27)	38.7 (106)	33.3 (27)	67.0 (106)
Education				
< H.S.	15.4 (13)	59.1 (66)	53.8 (13)	71.2 (66)
H.S. Grad	22.2 (9)	44.3 (88)	33.3 (9)	81.8 (88)
> H.S.	6.5 (46)	31.7 (145)	21.7 (46)	70.3 (145)

*Numbers in parentheses indicate *N*'s.

the men we interviewed said they rarely avoided exposure to risk. (Note that since few men were included in the in-person survey, data on men's coping strategies are presented for illustrative purposes only, as statistical tests would be unreliable.) Among demographic subgroups of women, Hispanic (69 percent) and elderly (64 percent) women and those with less formal education (59 percent) rely even more often on isolation tactics. Conversely, the lowest levels of use of isolation prevailed among highly educated women (only 32 percent used them frequently) and among those who are white (33 percent). As was the case with the distribution of fear, areal effects may be operating: residential segregation of ethnic and racial minorities into high crime neighborhoods could prompt greater use of isolation tactics.

The distribution of the use of street savvy tactics did not differ significantly among demographic subgroups of women. Overall, about 74 percent of the women in our sample reported frequent use of street savvy tactics while 26 percent seldom used them. However, 90 percent of men we interviewed said they rarely used these tactics. Among women, the elderly used street savvy tactics least often (33 percent responding "seldom" or "never"), while black, Hispanic and poor women used them frequently.

Although one might expect local crime rates to be the best predictor of the use of these self-protective behaviors, we found fear of crime to be the best predictor of both the use of isolation behaviors and street savvy tactics (Riger et al., 1982). Women who assess their neighborhoods as unsafe and women who perceive themselves to be less physically competent are especially likely to rely on isolating tactics as a means of protecting themselves. Race and amount of formal education also were significant predictors of isolation in the directions described above. Although differences among age levels were significant in bivariate analyses, age was not related to the use of isolation when the effects of all variables were controlled simultaneously.

Finally, we asked women in our study how frequently they engaged after dark in each of a series of everyday but potentially dangerous activities, such as being home alone, using public transportation, or walking through public parks (Gordon et al., 1980). In every instance, how often our respondents reported doing something was significantly and negatively related to their levels of worry about possible harm when doing those activities. People did least often the things that worried them most. Especially important for understanding the impact of fear on the quality of women's lives, activities done least often by women in our sample are those associated with the most choice, such as going out for entertainment alone at night. Activities which seem less discretionary, such as using public transportation to go to work, were avoided less than social or leisure activities.

MITIGATING CIRCUMSTANCES

Following an analysis of data from four Chicago neighborhoods, Lewis and Maxfield (1980) suggest that fear also is a function of the presence of signs associated with danger and social disorder, such as graffiti, abandoned buildings, and teenagers hanging out on street corners. Such disturbing (although not necessarily criminal) behavior seems to heighten fear, since perceptions of the frequency of such phenomena were related to increased use of street savvy tactics. Signs of such social disorganization suggest that local mechanisms of social control are not operating, indicating that, in the aggregate, a community is unable to regulate behavior within its boundaries.

Why should such signs of incivility lead women to fear crime more than men? If such signs are cues for danger, then in their presence women may be afraid because of the serious consequences victimization has for them. As noted above, women run the risk of rape while men usually do not, and the trauma inflicted by this crime can be severe. In addition, women may feel less able to defend themselves against attack. We found that 41 percent of the women we interviewed believed they could successfully defend themselves against attack, in contrast to 54 percent of the males. We also asked people how strong they thought they were and how fast they thought they could run, compared to the *average man* and the *average women*. This index of physical competence was a significant predictor of fear levels. On the average, women believe themselves to be weaker and slower than both men and *other women* (Riger & Gordon, 1978). As Stinchcombe et al. (1980) point out, the physical differences between the sexes are magnified by social conditioning; running fast, fighting, and self-defense are not part of traditional female sex-role socialization.

In our study of women's fear of crime, we found that although signs of incivility or social disorder were associated with fear levels in bivariate analyses, this relationship was not significant in multivariate analyses. However, the perception of signs of local disorder was related to women's use of precautionary behavior, as discussed above.

Other community-related attitudes may have an impact on women's reactions to crime. Women's feelings of attachment to their community are related to their fear levels (Riger et al., 1981). Those who find it easy to distinguish local residents from strangers, who know neighborhood children by name, and who feel a part of their area rather than think of it just as a place to live, tend to report less fear. This suggests that some degree of attachment to community may be a prerequisite for perceiving the impact of social control processes. Those who do not feel a part of the neighborhood may incorrectly perceive lack of order there; and the presence of neighborhood bonds may permit the exercise of informal social control mechanisms that reduce the frequency of criminal (or noncriminal but deviant) acts that generate or heighten fear.

Discussion or gossip about crime in the neighborhood may also affect women's fear levels. Talk about crime seems to be stimulated by the perception that the local crime problem is serious, and those with strong local ties tend to speak more frequently with neighbors about such problems (Skogan & Maxfield, 1981). Stories that circulate about crime tend to concern women and the elderly, although as Table 1 demonstrated, these people are the least frequently victimized. Skogan and Maxfield speculate that such stories about crime become the focus of discussion because they are norm-breaking, and hence newsworthy. These stories may also indice greater fear because they may seem to indicate lack of social control in the community. After all, when even those traditionally deemed the recipients of society's protection—women and the elderly—are victimized, then the community's lack of control may be particularly pronounced. In addition, theories about social comparison processes suggest that crime stories tend to generate greater fear in persons who see themselves as similar to victims (Heath et al., 1981). Women and the elderly may hear or read more about victims like themselves, and hence be more fearful and have an exaggerated view of the likelihood of victimization (Skogan & Maxfield, 1981).

Media reports about crime present a distribution of victims similar to that in discussions among neighbors (i.e., more women and elderly), and may also contribute to fear (Skogan & Maxfield, 1981). In a study of the presentation of rape in major metropolitan newspapers, Heath et al. (1981) found that newspapers report thirteen *completed rapes*, often with sensational and grisly details, to every one *rape attempt*, although victimization survey data show a ratio of three attempts for every completed rape. Such a skewed media presentation of rape may elevate women's fear and risk estimates, and lessen their belief that they can successfully resist an attack. (See also Gordon & Heath, 1981.)

While signs of incivility, neighborhood ties, perceptions of risk, and other factors all affect fear levels, they do not necessarily determine who gets victimized. In an extensive analysis of data from the National Crime Survey, Hindelang et al. (1978) suggest that victimization is related to lifestyles, since "lifestyles are related to the probability of being in places (streets, parks, and other public places) at times (especially nighttime) when victimizations are known to occur" (p. 255). Likewise, structural constraints and role obligations dictated by lifestyles circumscribe people's ability to use precautionary tactics, particularly those which involve avoiding dangerous areas. For example, the demands set by occupational schedules may necessitate exposure to risk, and indeed employed women report less avoidance behavior than those who do not work outside the home (Furstenberg, 1972).

Women may not go out alone at night because of sex-role expectations or childcare obligations, or because of fear. Whatever the reason, the result of circumscribing their activities means that women are less exposed to the possibility of being victimized, since it is likely that rate of exposure affects the victimization level. According to Balkin (1979), the actual rate of crime generates fear in people; fear leads people to reduce their exposure to risk, which in turn lowers the frequency of victimization. Our study of women's reactions to crime partially confirms this hypothesis, since we found that fear is the best predictor of women's use of both broad categories of precautionary behaviors (Riger & Gordon, 1981).

Since the data in all of these studies are correlational, it is not possible to determine causal directions between attitudes and behavior. Fear may lead to the use of self-protective behavior or the use of self-protective behavior *may* lead to fear (Bem, 1970). In the latter case, the employment of precautionary behavior could lead people to infer that they must be afraid. The result of the relationship between fear and precautionary behavior, whatever its causal direction, means that fewer women are exposed to risk and hence are less available as victims of crime. But the relatively high frequency with which women are victimized within the home by known assailants, and the fact that more rape attempts that occur within the home are completed (McDermott, 1979) raises the question of whether restricting one's movements through public places really keeps women safe. While this may keep women safe from some attacks by strangers, it may not prevent their victimization from other forms of violence.

CRIME AND QUALITY OF LIFE FOR WOMEN

Feminist analyses of the effect of the threat of rape on women assert that it operates as an instrument of social control, encouraging women to restrict their behavior and keeping them in a state of stress (Brownmiller, 1975; Griffin, 1979). A sizeable proportion of women in our study report high fear of crime. Those with the fewest resources to cope with victimization—the elderly, blacks and Hispanics, women with low incomes and less formal education—are those who bear the heaviest burden of fear. Although the pattern of fear among women is similar to that among men, women's fear is significantly greater. Thus the distribution of fear appears to follow existing social cleavages delineated by gender, age, race and social class, that mark status and power inequalities in our society.

Although fear appears disproportionate to the risks women face as measured by victimization and reported crime data, women's fear is proportionate to their *own* estimates of risk. It is understandable that women perceive themselves to be at risk of rape, and that these risk perceptions affect their levels of fear. What is intriguing is that women perceive themselves to be at greater risk of robbery and assault than men, even though all available statistics indicate that men are most frequent victims of these crimes. A conclusive test of the relationship among fear, victimization, and risk awaits improvements in methods of measuring the "true" amount of crime and some non-self-report ways of measuring fear and precautionary behavior.

It is possible that women's high perceived risk produces fear and consequent precautionary behavior, which in turn leads to low rates of victimization (Balkin, 1979). Since their estimates of risk of robbery and rape are highly correlated, women may perceive a general threat of personal violence from any of a multitude of crimes. The original feminist formulation of rape as a means of controlling women may need to be expanded to include other crimes of violence. Bowker (1978) suggest that wife-beating may be a better example than rape of forces of social control that affect women. Since our study focuses on street crime, we did not include domestic violence in our calculations of women's fear. Whatever the causes of violence, the effects may be to reinforce constraints already operating on low status victims, and, hence, further encourage them to restrict their behavior.

The sizeable proportion of women who use isolation tactics regularly gives support to the argument that the impact of the threat of crime on many women is restrictive. Numerous studies have found that women use avoidance behaviors more than men (summarized in DuBow et al., 1979). The social and work opportunities lost to women because of the threat of crime seem likely to very much reduce the overall quality of their lives. Although the precautionary strategies employed by women may not involve significant monetary expenditures, these strategies are undoubtedly costly in terms of personal freedom.

Hindelang et al. (1978) argue that shifts in behavior due to fear of crime are subtle. They assert that people don't change *what* they do, only *how they do it;* for example, they might drive instead of walk to their destination. Our findings suggest that for women, the *sum* of these subtle shifts may exert a considerable toll on their time, effort and freedom. When we asked our respondents how often they avoided doing necessary activities such as shopping or errands because of fears for their safety, 78 percent of the men but only 32 percent of the women responded "never." Thirty-four percent of women in our sample said they avoided doing these things because of fear for their safety "fairly often" or "most of the time." When we asked about behavior that didn't involve necessary tasks but rather consisted of things they wanted to do, such as visting friends or going to movies, 75 percent of males but only 30 percent of females reported they never let fear deter them. Thirty-six percent of females said they often avoided doing such activities because of fear of harm.

Other data suggest that the price paid by women for safety is greatest in the area of behaviors involving the most discretion, such as visiting friends or going out for evening entertainment (Gordon et al., 1980). High fear seems to shrink the scope of women's choices about their lives by restricting their movement through time and space, giving credence to feminist arguments that the threat of criminal victimization severely limits women's freedom.

The important role of self-assessments of physical competence in determining women's reactions to crimes, both in fearful attitudes and in isolation behavior, raises intriguing questions for future research. What are the socialization and situational factors that induce women to believe that they are less physically powerful not only than men but also *than most women*? How do feelings of physical competence affect women's beliefs about potency in other areas of their lives, such as work and family interactions? And are perceptions of physical competence related to women's likelihood of resisting attack? Larwood et al. (1977) suggest that the "social inhibition" that suppresses the expression of physical aggression by females can be disinhibited under certain circumstances. Cohn et al. (1978) found that after taking a self-defense training course, women reported feeling stronger, braver, more active, more in control, bigger, safer, and more efficacious in a variety of arenas.

UNDERSTANDING THE IMPACT OF CRIME ON WOMEN

To summarize, victimization rates are an inadequate explanation for women's reactions to crime. Rather, in order to understand women's high fear and frequent use of precautions, it is necessary to look at women in the context in which they live. That is, women's perceptions both of themselves and of the world they live in shape their reactions. Women live in a world that is filled not only with danger but also with resources with which to combat that danger. Out of that world and the constraints imposed by lifestyles, women create ways of coping with the stresses in the environment. The salient factors in understanding women's reactions to crime, then, become women's perceptions of the dangerousness of their neighborhoods and the strength both of their ties to that locality and of themselves. If they perceive that the neighborhood is filled with risks, then women are fearful, and their fear is related to their use of behavioral strategies to cope with danger. Lack of local social control, as perceived through signs of disorder such as graffiti and vandalism, prompt the use of risk-management tactics (i.e., street savvy) in the face of possible danger. Women who feel that they are slow and weak attempt to enhance their safety by restricting their movement through time and space. In imposing restraints on themselves, women are not simply reacting to crime, but working actively to shape their environments in order to balance the demands of their lives with the avoidance of danger.

Although the self-protective strategies that women use more than men do not necessarily cost money, they may cost time, effort, and freedom. Discretionary activities appear to be most restricted in response to the threat of criminal victimization. Women forego leisure and social opportunities because of the fear of crime, an intangible cost that is hard to measure but that may have a significant impact on the quality of their lives. Hindelang et al. (1978) assert that the fear of crime has a subtle impact on behavior, and that people don't change what they do because of crime, but rather how they do it. For example, they might drive instead of walk to their destination. Surveys indicate that women make these changes more than men, and the sum of these changes may be considerable.

The causes of crime against women, as against men, are multiple. Bowker (1978) suggests that rape is the result of several factors: urbanization and the associated geographic mobility, impersonality, anonymity, and bystander apathy; an abundance of available victims; and personal problems in the rapist. He rejects the feminist belief that rape is a means of social control of women, since rapists do not mention this as a motive. But this may be confusing cause with effect. Whatever the causes of rape and other violence against women, a major effect of these crimes on even non-victims may be self-imposed restrictions. That men are more frequent victims of every violent crime except rape while they do not seem to react by restricting their behavior, suggests that something more than crime is implicated. Rarely are men warned not to go out alone at night because they will be victimized, even though they are victimized more often than women. It seems that crime against women, whatever the motivation of the individual criminal, has the cumulative effect of reinforcing social norms. Women who are victimized, especially by rape, are blamed for that victimization (Feild, 1978; Jones & Aronson, 1973; Krulewitz, 1977). This is not only because of belief in a "just world," (Lerner, 1980) but also because in being victimized women are breaking social norms, and blame acts as a cautionary warning to other women not to do likewise.

Perhaps the central question to be answered by research on precautionary behavior is whether the use of such restrictive behaviors, in fact, keeps women safe from crime. There were too few victims in our sample to sufficiently and directly test this question. Other analyses of nation-wide data sets suggest that it is *rates of exposure* to crime, rather than *degree of precaution*, which determine victimization. Hindelang et al. (1978) hypothesize that the probability of being in dangerous places (e.g. streets and public parks) at times (especially nighttime) when crimes are likely to occur is strongly related to victimization rates. Women are often assaulted in their homes, and are more likely than men to know their attacker (Bowker, 1978). These findings suggest that while limiting exposure to street crime may keep women safe from some attacks by strangers, it will not prevent their victimization from a myriad of other forms of violence.

What can be done to reduce these restrictions, these indirect effects of crime on women? Since women's fear is not simply a function of crime rates, reducing crime, while a top priority, will be only a partial solution. Two additional alternative approaches are likely to be useful. First, efforts should be made to increase women's sense of themselves as physically powerful and competent. A second strategy would be to increase women's attachments to their neighborhoods. Since those who feel more attached are less fearful, strategies to enhance neighborhood integration may be successful in reducing fear.

But these are individual responses, designed to increase the safety only of those who employ them. If successful, they may simply defer victimization onto others (Cohn et al., 1978). Since crime is a problem that affects many women, a more effective strategy would involve collective efforts. In the late 1970s a new kind of political demonstration occurred in the United States. Throughout the country, women (and men) marched through city streets with chants of "take back the night" accompanied by cries of "stop rape now!" These marches heralded women's refusal to accept the restrictions on their lives advocated as protection against the threat of rape and other forms of criminal victimization. Unwilling to go out alone only in daylight, unwilling to hide behind locked and barred windows and doors or to live in a constant state of anxiety over the possible depredations of criminals women acted to change the situation documented in the research described above—that fear of crime has particularly deleterious effect on the lives of women living in American cities.

Although it is impossible yet to determine if such actions have had an impact on rates of rape and other crimes against women, we suggest they may have increased women's sense of control of their lives. That is, by refusing to live in fear, women are taking control of a situation that has long plagued them. Such active resistance may be critical to maintaining a sense of well-being and self-esteem. Of course crime should be reduced. But as Maltz (1972) has said, "unless the public feels safer in proportion to its increased actual safety, the full potential" of an effective crime control program will not have been reached.

The freedom to walk safely through city streets should be a right enjoyed by every citizen in this country. This freedom is denied to too many women, albeit often through the use of self-imposed behavioral restrictions. The threat of crime, by creating a constant state of apprehension about possible victimization in many women and by leading to the self-imposition of these behavioral restrictions, has the effects that feminists decry: It limits women's opportunities to be active participants in public life. It is destructive of the social fabric of our nation. Until the full weight of a range of social institutions can be brought to bear in order to generate the pressures and conditions capable of drastically reducing violent crime, the burden of fear of crime and its consequences will fall disproportionately on women, and, among women, on those with the fewest resources for coping with it.

REFERENCES

Balkin, S. Victimization rates, safety and fear of crime. *Social Problems*, 1979, *26*, 343-358.

Bart, P. Women who were both raped and avoided being raped. *Journal of Social Issues*, 1981, *37*(4), 123-137.

Baumer, T. L. Research on fear of crime in the United States. *Victimology: An International Journal*, 1978, *3*, 243-264.

Bem, D. J. *Beliefs, attitudes and human affairs*. Monterey, CA: Brooks/Cole, 1970.

Berger, V. Man's trial, woman's tribulation: Rape cases in the courtroom. *Columbia Law Review*, 1977, *7*, 1-103.

Biderman, A. D., Johnson, L. A., McIntyre, J., & Weir, A. W. Report on victimization and attitudes toward law enforcement. Washington, D.C.: Government Printing OFfice, 1967.

Bowker, L. H. *Women, crime, and the criminal justice system*. Lexington, MA: D. C. Heath, 1978.

Brodyaga, L., Gates, M., Singer, S., Tucker, M., & White, R. Rape and its victims: A report for citizens, health facilities and criminal justice agencies. Washington, D.C.: U.S. Government Printing Office, 1975.

Brownmiller, S. *Against our will: Men, women and rape*. New York: Simon & Schuster, 1975.

Burgess, A. W. & Holmstrom, L. L. *Rape: Victims of crisis*. Bowie, MD: Brady, 1974.

Chappell, D. & Fogarty, F. *Forcible rape: A literature review and annotated bibliography*. Washington, D.C.: U.S. Department of Justice, 1978.

Cobb, S. Social support as a moderator of life stress. *Psychosomatic Medicine*, 1976, *38*, 300-314.

Cohn, E., Kidder, L. H., & Harvey, J. Crime prevention vs. victimization prevention: The psychology of two different reactions. *Victimology: An International Journal*, 1978, *3*, 285-296.

Cook, F. L., Skogan, W. G., Cook, T. D., & Antunes, G. E. *Setting and reformulating policy agendas: The case of criminal victimization of the elderly*. New York: Oxford University Press, 1982.

Dodge, R. W., Lentzner, H., & Shenk, F. Crime in the United States: A report on the National Crime Survey, in W. G. Skogan (ed.), *Sample Surveys of the Victims of Crime*. Cambridge, MA: Ballinger, 1976.

DuBow, R., McCabe, E., & Kaplan, G. *Reactions to crime: A critical review of the literature.* Washington, D.C.: U.S. Department of Justice, 1979.

Erskine, H. The polls: Fear of crime and violence. *Public Opinion Quarterly*, 19xx, *38*, 797–814.

Feild, H. S. Attitudes toward rape: A comparative analysis of police, rapists, crisis counselors and citizens. *Journal of Personality and Social Psychology*, 1978, *36*, 156–179.

Furstenberg, F. F., Jr. Fear of crime and its effect on citizen behavior. In A. Biderman (ed.), *Crime and justice: A symposium.* New York: Nailburg, 1972.

Garofalo, J. Victimization and the fear of crime. *Journal of Research in Crime and Delinquency*, 1979, *16*, 80–97.

Garofalo, J. *Public Opinion about Crime: The Attitudes of Victims and Nonvictims in Selected Cities.* Washington, D.C.: U.S. Government Printing Office, 1977.

Geis, G. Forcible rape: An introduction. In D. Chappell, Geis, R., & Geis, G. (eds.), *Forcible rape: The crime, the victim, and the offender.* New York: Columbia University Press, 1977.

Gordon, M. T. & Heath, L. The news business, crime and fear. In Lewis, D. A. (ed.), *Reactions to Crime.* Beverly Hills, CA: Sage Publications, 1981.

Gordon, M. T. & Riger, S. The fear of rape project. *Victimology: An International Journal*, 1978, *3*, 346–347.

Gordon, M. T., Riger, S., LeBailly, R. K., & Heath, L. Crime, women and the quality of urban life. *Signs: Journal of Women in Culture and Society*, 1980, *5*, S144–S160.

Griffin, S. *Rape: The power of consciousness.* San Francisco: Harper and Row, 1979.

Heath, L., Gordon, M. T., & LeBailly, R. K. What newspapers tell us (and don't tell us) about rape. *The Newspaper Research Journal*, 1981.

Hindelang, M. J. & Davis, B. L. Forcible rape in the United States: A statistical profile. In Chappell, D., Geis, R., & Geis, G. (eds.), *Forcible rape: The crime, the victim, and the offender.* New York: Columbia University Press, 1977.

Hindelang, M. J., Gottfredson, M. R., & Garofalo, J. *Victims of personal crime: An empirical foundation for a theory of personal victimization.* Cambridge, MA: Ballinger, 1978.

Jones, C. & Aronson, E. Attribution of fault to a rape victim as a function of responsibility of the victim. *Journal of Personality and Social Psychology*, 1973, *26*, 415–419.

Katz, S. & Mazur, M. A. *Understanding the rape victim: A synthesis of research findings.* New York: John Wiley & Sons, 1979.

Keppler, H. Dimensions of reactions to crime: A cluster analysis. Evanston, IL: Center for Urban Affairs and Policy Research, Northwestern University, 1976.

Krulewitz, J. E. Sex differences in rape attributions. Presented at the annual meetings of the Midwestern Psychological Association, Chicago, May 1977.

Larwood, L., O'Neal, E., & Brennan, P. Increasing the physical aggressiveness of women. *Journal of Social Psychology*, 1977, *101*, 97–101.

Lavrakas, P. J. & Lewis, D. A. The conceptualization and measurement of citizen crime prevention behaviors. *Journal of Research in Crime Delinquency*, 1980, *17*, 254–272.

LeBailly, R. K. Method artifacts in telephone and in-person interviews: An examination of bias and consistency. Evanston, IL: Center for Urban Affairs and Policy Research, Northwestern University, 1979.

Lerner, M. J. *The belief in a just world: A fundamental delusion.* New York: Plenum, 1980.

Lewis, D. A. The reactions to crime project. *Victimology: An International Journal*, 1978, *3*, 344–345.

Lewis, D. A. & Maxfield, M. G. Fear in the neighborhoods: An investigation of the impact of crime. *Journal of Research in Crime and Delinquency*, 1980, *17*, 160–189.

Maltz, M. D. *Evaluation of crime control problems.* Washington, D.C.: Law Enforcement Assistance Administration, 1972.

McDermott, M. J. *Rape victimization in 26 American cities.* Washington, D.C.: U.S. Department of Justice, 1979.

McIntyre, J. Public attitudes toward crime and law enforcement. *Annals of the American Academy of Political and Social Science*, 1967, *41*, 34–36.

McIntyre, J., Myint, T., & Curtis, L. Sexual assault outcomes: Completed and attempted rapes. Presented at the annual meetings of the American Sociological Association, San Francisco, 1979.

McPherson, M. Realities and perceptions of crime at the neighborhood level. *Victimology: An International Journal*, 1978, *3*, 319–328.

Medea, A. & Thompson, K. *Against rape.* New York: Farrar, Straus and Giroux, 1974.

National Criminal Justice Reference Service. *Rape.* Washington, D.C.: U.S. Department of Justice, 1981.

Riger, S. & Gordon, M. T. The structure of rape prevention beliefs. *Personality and Social Psychology Bulletin*, 1979, *5*, 186–190.

Riger, S. & Gordon, M. T. The fear of rape: A study of social control. *Journal of Social Issues*, 1981, *37*(4), 71–92.

Riger, S., Gordon, M. T., & LeBailly, R. K. Women's fear of crime: From blaming to restricting the victim. *Victimology: An International Journal*, 1978, *3*, 274–284.

Riger, S., Gordon, M. T., & LeBailly, R. K. Coping with urban crime: Women's use of precautionary behaviors. *American Journal of Community Psychology*, 1982, *10*, 369–386.

Riger, S. & Lavrakas, P. J. Community ties: Patterns of attachment and social interaction in urban neighborhoods. *American Journal of Community Psychology*, 1982, *9*(1), 55–66.

Riger, S., LeBailly, R. K., & Gordon, M. T. Community ties and urbanites' fear of crime: An ecological investigation. *American Journal of Community Psychology*, 1981, *9*(6), 653–665.

Ryan, W. *Blaming the victim.* New York: Vintage Press, 1971.

Sanders, W. B. *Rape and woman's identity.* Beverly Hills, CA: Sage, 1980.

Selby, J. W., Calhoun, L. G., & Brock, T. A. Sex differences in the social perception of rape victims. *Personality and Social Psychology Bulletin*, 1977, *3*, 412–415.

Skogan, W. G. Dimensions of the dark figure of unreported crime. *Crime and Delinquency*, 1977, *23*, 41–50.

Skogan, W. G. The Center for Urban Affairs random digit dialing telephone survey. Evanston, IL: Center for Urban Affairs and Policy Research, Northwestern University, 1978.

Skogan, W. G. Crime in contemporary America. In Graham, H. & Gurr, T. R. (eds.), *Violence in America* (2nd ed.). Beverly Hills, CA: Sage, 1978.

Skogan, W. G. Coping with crime: Fear and risk management in urban communities. Presented at the annual meetings of the American Society of Criminology, Dallas, November 1978.

Skogan, W. G. & Maxfield, M. G. *Coping with crime: Victimization, fear, and reactions to crime in three American cities.* Beverly Hills, CA: Sage, 1981.

Stinchcombe, A. L., Adams, R. C., Heimer, C. A., Scheppele, K. L., Smith, T. W., & Taylor, G. E. *Crime and punishment-changing attitudes in America.* San Francisco: Jossey-Bass, 1980.

U.S. Department of Justice. *Criminal Victimization in the United States: 1973-78 Trends.* Washington, D.C.: U.S. Government Printing Office, 1980. (a)

U.S. Department of Justice. *Intimate victims: A study of violence among friends and relatives.* Washington, D.C.: U.S. Government Printing Office, 1980. (b)

U.S. Department of Statistics, *Bulletin*, Bureau of Justice Statistics, U.S. Government Printing Office: 1981, 0-344-894:QL3.

Weis, K. & Borges, S. S. Victimology and rape: The case of the legitimate victim. *Issues in Criminology*, 1973, *8*, 71–115.

9

Women's Health Issues

Judith E. Albino and Lisa A. Tedesco
State University of New York at Buffalo

Issues related to women's physical health and health care reflect the broader concerns of women who must function within systems that have been constructed by and for men. The health care system in this country is still very much a male-dominated institution in which the demands on women to fit a male model are especially cogent (Lee, 1975). Because women traditionally have had primary responsibility for the care of children and for the ill and aging in their families, they typically assume greater responsibility in health matters than do men. Yet there is evidence that women as a group, and particularly women of limited educational, social, and economic resources, encounter significant obstacles to obtaining adequate diagnosis and treatment of medical disorders. From a prevention perspective also, less attention has been paid to the health risks of women than to those of men.

This chapter will begin with a brief report on the general status of women's health risks and their relationships to lifestyles and social responsibilities of women. The remainder of the chapter will be devoted to a consideration of the health and illness behaviors of women, including patterns of health care utilization and the barriers to care that are experienced by women. Finally, attention will be given to some current efforts to enhance women's health and health care.

THE HEALTH STATUS OF WOMEN

During this century, and even within the last two decades, health statistics have reflected dramatic improvements in the health status of American women (Rice & Cugliani, 1980). While mortality is higher for men, women generally experience the same health problems that account for the majority of deaths in men. American white women can expect a life span of 77.3 years, or about eight years longer than American white men. Non-white American women have a life expectancy of 73.1 years, or eight and one-half years longer than non-white American men (National Center for Health Statistics, 1977). The primary killer of women, as well as men, is cardiovascular disease, including chronic heart and arteriosclerotic conditions that have been shown to be related to work stresses and other lifestyle factors (Martin, 1978). Recent data indicate that these risks may be related to the stresses of traditional female lifestyles and responsibilities, as well as to those of male-dominated occupations (Haynes & Feinleib, 1980; Ortmeyer, 1979).

Cancer is the second leading cause of death for both men and women, but the mortality rate for men is about one-third greater than for women. The cancers most frequently affecting women are breast, colon/rectal, and cervical, while for men the three most common are cancers of the lung, prostate, and colon/rectum (American Cancer Society, 1980).

The smoking behavior of women during the last 25 years has been associated with increased illness and death of women due to lung cancer and respiratory and cardiovascular diseases (Pomerleau, 1976; Fogel, 1981a; Ortmeyer, 1979; Rice & Cugliani, 1980). Female deaths attributable to lung cancer rose between 1950 and 1975 from four per 100,000 population to 13 (Ortmeyer, 1979). Male deaths from lung cancer increased from 18 to 53 per 100,000 during the same time period. While reports indicate that the smoking rate has declined for both men and women, the decline for women has been less than for men. In fact, smoking has increased among teenage girls and older women (Rice & Cugliani, 1980; Ortmeyer, 1979). Data from the 1978 Surgeon General's report show that women are beginning to smoke earlier and that they continue the habit longer (Fogel, 1981a). Attempts to equate women's liberation with smoking or to present smoking as a sophisticated and feminine behavior have only tended to equalize the related health risk factors for men and women.

Despite their lower mortality rates, epidemiological data reflect higher morbidity, or instances of illness, for women than for men (Woods, 1981). For example, women 17 years of age and over in the labor force had 202.1 acute conditions per 1000 persons and made 4.8 physician visits per year, compared with 151.8 acute conditions and 3.1 visits for men. For women not in the labor force these figures dropped to 153.8 conditions and 4.9 visits, compared with 109.1 conditions and 3.3 visits for men (Rice & Cugliani, 1980).

The overall incidence of acute conditions is approximately 10 percent greater for females than for males. Women report slightly more infections, respiratory problems, and digestive conditions, while men experience about 37 percent more injuries, including fractures, dislocations, sprains, and lacerations (Woods, 1981). With the exceptions of arthritis, rheumatism, and diabetes mellitus major chronic conditions occur less frequently in women than in men (Ortmeyer, 1979; Johnson, 1977; Verbrugge, 1976).

In summary, women as a group live longer than men, but they appear to experience more health problems while living. There are, of course, a number of health problems for which women are uniquely at risk simply because they are women. Furthermore, minority women and women of lower socioeconomic status (Coe, 1978) experience certain medical problems more often than do white, middle income women. An understanding of the health risks of women requires that we look beyond morbidity and mortality data to a consideration of social, behavioral, and economic variables that affect health and the etiology and course of disease.

Health Risk Factors for Women

While scientific, technological, and social progress have provided women with greater reproductive freedom, health problems related to contraception, childbirth, abortion, and venereal disease persist. Prolonged use of oral contraceptives has been linked to hypertension and thromboembolitic conditions, while intra-uterine contraceptive devices are associated with abnormal bleeding patterns and disorders of the uterine walls. Genitourinary problems occur nine times more frequently for women then for men (Fogel, 1981b).

Since the mid-1970s, there has been an increase in vaginal and cervical cancer in young women. This phenomenon has been linked to the drug diethylstilbestrol (DES) prescribed for their mothers during pregnancy. Complications of pregnancy occur in 20 to 30 percent of obstetrical cases, while complications of abortion occur in less than two percent of the 1.27 million performed (Fogel, 1981c; Bracken et al., 1982). These conditions represent a major cause of death for white women only among 15 to 24-year-olds, while for black women complications of pregnancy and abortion are among the top ten killers from 10 until 30 years of age. There are indications that deaths related to childbirth are underreported (Rubin et al., 1981).

The social context of women's health is critical when considering risk factors. Unique to women is the fact that reproductive functions, including such issues as contraception that do not actually represent health problems, are commonly dealt with through the medical system. Similarly, many primary prevention measures, such as testing for cervical cancer, require medical visits. Although Rice and Cugliani (1980) have suggested that the decreased birth rate and the increased availability of abortion reflect greater control by women of their reproductive roles, these changes have not decreased significantly the dependence of women on the medical system. Their ability to control their bodies remains critically linked to their access to health services.

Health problems shared by men and women include chronic diseases that are related to behavior and lifestyle. Unfortunately, much of the research in this area has not included female subjects. This has been true of the studies of hypertension and cardiovascular disease, in which a high risk "Type A" coronary-prone behavior profile has been described (Rosenman et al., 1975). This pattern of behavior is characterized by competitiveness, impatience, aggression, and is common among men in high pressure occupations. Women in the work force may exhibit these same behaviors, but Hayes and Feinleib (1980) have suggested that women also respond to the stresses associated with maintaining multiple roles in family and society.

Work-Related Risk Factors

In the past fifteen years the occupational status of women has again changed dramatically. More than half of all women over 16 are in the labor force, and married women comprise three-fifths of all women workers. Marriage and child-rearing no longer necessitate leaving jobs, and in fact, a third of working women have children of preschool age (U.S. Department of Labor, 1978).

Many women today are exposed to the same occupational hazards as men and simultaneously face the pressures of serving as primary, often sole, caregivers to children (Stellman, 1977). Constant financial concerns are frequently added to the lifestyle pressures experienced by women. Community or employer assistance with day care arrangements is not common. Women often enter the work force later with less formal training than men and generally have less earning power.

While men have a higher incidence of coronary heart disease than women, available data reveal no clear differences in overall health risks either between men and women, or between employed and unemployed women (Rice & Cugliani, 1980; Haynes & Feinleib, 1980; Waldron, 1980; Stellman, 1978). However, the fact that women working outside the home are at substantially lower risk for mental health problems than are those at home suggests that the relationship between women's social roles and their health is a complex one.

Recent longitudinal data from the Framingham Heart Study have provided a sharper focus on the psychosocial risks associated with coronary heart disease in men and women (Hayes & Feinleib, 1980). Study participants were followed for eight years and included 350 women not employed outside the home, 387 employed women, and 580 men, all assumed to be employed. All were 45 to 64 years of age and free of coronary heart disease at the beginning of the study. Baseline data included measures of personality type, situational and somatic stresses, occupational and family responsibilities, and socio-cultural mobility, as well as health assessments.

Men and employed women reported more Type A coronary prone behavior and more marital disagreement than did women not employed outside the home. Regardless of their work status, women reported more general tension and anxiety than men, but women employed outside the home reported more daily stress, marital dissatisfaction, aging worries, and inability to display anger than either men or women working at home. Working women also had greater occupational mobility, more job changes, and fewer promotions than men during the course of the study. However, standard coronary risk factors, such as blood pressure, serum cholesterol, cigarette smoking, and glucose intolerance, were similar for women employed outside the home and those at home. Men in the study had significantly higher blood pressures, but this difference may have been related to the smaller number of men taking antihypertensive medications. Men also consumed more cigarettes, while women had higher serum cholesterol levels.

When the employment status of women, psychosocial factors, and standard coronary risk factors were considered together, the Framingham data strongly suggested that the development of coronary heart disease was associated with psychosocial variables as a function of employment status. After controlling for standard hereditary and physical risks, Type A behavior and suppressed hostility were the psychosocial risk factors associated with coronary heart disease of working women over 45 years of age. The same pattern occurred for men and was particularly notable among those in white collar and professional positions. For women not employed outside the home, coronary heart disease was associated with easygoing behavior, display of tension, and Type A behavior.

In summary, the processes defining psychosocial etiologies demonstrate different patterns related to occupational status and sex. Both men and women experience occupation-specific demands and stresses. Women remain sex-segregated in stereotyped occupations, and when they do cross the barriers into traditionally male occupations, the pay is frequently less than that received by their male colleagues (Stellman, 1977; 1978). These facts of life may produce additional stresses in the form of job-dissatisfaction.

Chemical and physical hazards of work both inside and outside the home place women at special risk for reproductive problems and unhealthy pregnancies, as well as for the respiratory ailments (asthma, byssinosis, emphysema), skin disorders, and cancer to which male workers are also susceptible (Stellman, 1973; 1978). Exposure to chemicals is common in such female-dominated occupations as clothing, laundry, and textile work, cosmetology and even clerical and health care occupations. Dental hygientists and x-ray technicians are exposed to radiation, meat packers and frozen food workers to cold and dampness, and factory workers and flight attendants to noise and vibration. Some data suggest that sitting or standing for long periods of time, as secretaries, telephone operators, waitresses, and machine operators do, places workers at risk for circulatory disorders and back problems (Stellman, 1978). In addition, Stellman (1978) states that women are at risk in the workplace for injuries from poorly designed hand tools, safety equipment, and instrument panels that do not conform to the average smaller size of a woman's body. Risk of infection is also present in female-dominated occupations. Health care workers, social workers, and laundry workers, for example, are at risk for hepatitis, tuberculosis, and other infectious diseases. Daily contact with children places school teachers and child care workers at risk for respiratory infections, viruses, flus, and colds.

Two points are important to the understanding of the social context of women's occupational risks. First, as Stellman (1977) suggests, if health risks exist from work hazards for pregnant women, then the same hazards place their non-pregnant colleagues at risk. Sex should not be used to lessen the impact of work hazards, by diverting attention to pregnancy risks alone. Second, and most important to women's health issues, is the double jeopardy for exposure to health hazards that women experience when they are employed outside the home and also have primary responsibilities for maintaining a household. Just as the psychosocial risk factors appear to increase when work responsibilities must be met at home and on the job, this same role density, or role proliferation (Woods & Hulka, 1979), maintains women's double exposure to stressful chemicals and physical demands. Stellman (1978) has pointed out that injuries frequently occur when housework is done with muscles already fatigued from work outside the home, and in fact, data reveal that women have more accidents at home than on the job.

Environmental pollutants also affect the health of women. Pesticides and chemicals used without safeguards in farming and industry have been associated with physical, genetic, and neurological impairment. Reports have indicated that lactating mothers in rural Mississippi and Arkansas had DDT concentrations in their milk 10 times greater than the limits established by the World Health Organization for livestock (Sablosky & Studley, 1976). This is even more alarming since the use of DDT has been banned since 1973. Improper disposal of toxic industrial chemical wastes, has affected the health of the general population, including increases in miscarriages and other complications of pregnancy and childbirth (Brown, 1981). Higher rates of birth defects related to environmental toxins create additional stress on the mother who provides care for these children.

Socioeconomic Risk Factors

Social class and race, probably the most potent socioeconomic factors related to women's health risks, reflect differences in employment, income, education, preventive orientation, and access to health care. In general, chronic diseases, and physical disabilities occur more frequently in poverty groups than in middle and upper income groups (Coe, 1978). Women with higher levels of education tend to have better health and to be employed outside the home (Waldron, 1980). With the number of one-parent families headed by women at an all-time high (U.S. Department of Commerce, 1980) and with gaps in income increasing between white and black families (Edelman, 1980), women, and black women in particular, appear to be at high risk for health problems related to socioeconomic factors.

Black women are at higher risk for sudden death by heart attack than any other segment of society. Hypertension is more severe in black women than black men, a pattern the reverse of that in the white population; yet, less than one-third of black women with hypertension are under treatment (Rodgers-Rose, 1975). Cirrhosis and homicide—both of which are correlated with behavioral and lifestyle phenomena—cause more deaths among black women between 35 and 45 years of age than does cancer.

Conditions of poverty, especially the lack of health resources, appear to contribute to the disproportionate deaths of black women from anemias and complications of pregnancies and abortions (Martin, 1978). Black women receive less prenatal care and begin it later in their pregnancies than white women (Bullough, 1972; Edelman, 1980). The typical high risk pregnancy involves a non-white, low-income woman who is unmarried, poorly nourished, and has a history of alcohol, drug, or tobacco dependence, and chronic illness (Fogel, 1981d).

Socioeconomic factors are also associated with the development of eating and drinking disorders. The reasons women give for excessive drinking include unemployment, deficient job skills, lack of economic resources for educational improvement, primary childcare responsibilities, sex-role conflicts, and crises related to divorce or children (Fishel, 1981). Alcohol-related health disorders are greater for women than for men (Fishel, 1981), and women in lower socioeconomic groups have about six times greater incidence of obesity than those in upper socioeconomic groups (Fogel, 1981e). Obesity places women at risk for a myriad of other health problems including hypertension, coronary heart disease, menstrual irregularities, diabetes, gallbladder disorders, arthritis, varicosities, and foot problems, as well as social isolation, despondency, and other psychological problems.

BEHAVIORS RELATED TO HEALTH
AND ILLNESS

The lower mortality rates of women compared with men often have been assumed to reflect superior resistance to disease processes affecting both sexes, and there is some evidence for this (Verbrugge, 1979). The consistently higher morbidity rates of women, however, have prompted researchers to explore other explanations, including sex differences in psychological and social responses to health and illness.

The term "health behavior" has been used to refer to those actions taken by individuals in an effort to maintain health and avoid illness, while "illness behavior" indicates actions taken in response to symptoms of illness. "Sick-role behavior" designates those activities directed at treating medical disorders and regaining health. Interestingly, there are documented sex differences related to each of these behaviors that conceivably could affect either mortality or morbidity data.

Health Behaviors of Women

Women make greater use of professional health care than do men, including both physician visits and number of hospitalizations, although men tend to stay longer when they are hospitalized (Aday & Eichhorn, 1972). While these data have been interpreted as indicating higher morbidity, they may reflect preventive uses of health services. Feldman (1966) reported that women have more knowledge of and interest in health matters. Women have more eye examinations and glaucoma tests, and they make more preventive dental visits. They also make frequent use of preventive services for detection of cervical cancer and for prenatal monitoring (Woods, 1981).

Women's greater use of health services may result in earlier diagnosis and more effective treatment of the chronic diseases that result in higher death rates for men. Primary prevention, however, is closely associated with higher socioeconomic status and education. Women of low income continue to use health services primarily on an emergency basis, rather than out of a prevention orientation (Bullough, 1972). Since public assistance for health care rarely covers preventive procedures, health professionals may less frequently suggest such procedures to low-income patients, but preventive activities not requiring professional services also are less common among the poor (Bullough, 1972; Feldman, 1966). Healthy diet, adequate exercise, and rest, and sanitary living conditions are not typical aspects of the lives of poor women.

Illness Behaviors of Women

Explanations for sex differences on physician visits and hospitalization have also been viewed as differential responses to symptoms of illness. It may be more socially acceptable for women to respond to pain or discomfort (Mechanic, 1976; Nathanson, 1975; Verbrugge, 1979), while reporting illness or seeking medical help is more likely to be perceived as weakness in men. It is also possible that women are simply socialized to deal more directly with symptoms of illness than are men. In most families, mothers have taken primary responsibility for the health care of children and more frequently are concerned about attempting to assess and manage symptoms of illness. These behaviors may simply reflect one part of the female role that women learn.

Mechanic (1976) and Verbrugge (1979) have suggested that sex differences in reports of illness may be artifacts of interviewing techniques. For example, proxy reports tend to underrepresent episodes of illness, and such reports are most frequently accepted for male subjects. Furthermore, people tend to remember best those problems for which they sought help, and since women seek medical services more frequently, they would be likely to remember more episodes of illness.

Nathanson (1975) has viewed women's higher morbidity as a reflection of the more stressful roles and responsibilities of women working in the home. She suggested that their work is generally less satisfying and less prestigious than that of men and that women have more time to be concerned about their health. According to 1977 statistics (Rice & Cugliani, 1980), however, women in the labor force make the same number of physician visits as those working at home. Women working outside the home do experience slightly fewer days of disability or restricted activity, are hospitalized less often, and stay shorter periods of time when hospitalized. These figures may reflect a response to the demands of employment rather than a health advantage, of course. Although none of the data considered included reports related to childbirth, it is important to note that the differences between men and women on these measures are greatest during the years from 17 to 44, suggesting illness or disability related to reproductive or childbearing functions.

Woods and Hulka (1979) found significant relationships between the number of symptoms reported by women and number of responsibilities shouldered, number of children, lower socioeconomic status, and illness in the family. As women take on more responsibilities both inside and outside the home they appear to become more vulnerable to health problems.

Sick-Role Behaviors of Women

Mechanic (1976) has suggested that environmental demands and social role prescriptions are used by individuals to interpret their internal or personal experiences, including symptoms of illness. Thus, women may be more prepared and more willing to respond to illness by taking medication, remaining in bed, or seeking treatment and complying with medical treatment. Women take more prescribed medications than men (Lebowitz, 1980), and they stay in the hospital and away from work longer when ill (Lebowitz, 1980; Rice & Cugliani, 1980). These variables may be more related to differences in the treatment decisions made by physicians for women and for men. There is no consistent pattern of sex differences in compliance with medical recommendations that would indicate otherwise.

DiMatteo and DiNicola (1982) have reported that social class is a far more potent variable than sex in predicting response to medical treatment. Individuals from minority and poverty groups generally experience more competing demands on their time, energy, and financial resources—demands at the subsistence, or survival level. Furthermore, for those in poverty environments, the mechanisms available for coping with these life demands—such as smoking and use of addictive substances—are unlikely to facilitate either maintenance of health or recovery from illness (Syme & Berkman, 1976).

Others (Suchman, 1967; Langlie, 1977) have suggested that the relatively ineffective health, illness, and sick role behaviors of poverty groups are related to social structures. That is, compliance with health care recommendations may be in conflict with ethnic or social group norms. There may be traditions of self-reliance, use of folk remedies, or unwillingness to use public agencies and services. The impact of these social pressures on women coping with illness, often while trying to continue functioning as mothers and income producers, can only be imagined. The working class woman with limited financial resources and a family to support faces a dilemma—she has both the most to lose and the most to gain as a result of making a full commitment to engaging in time-consuming and costly medical treatment. Unfortunately, she is often forced to make the decision in terms of what she believes she can afford to lose.

BARRIERS TO HEALTH CARE FOR WOMEN

Women's greater use of health services and their lower mortality suggest that women have better access to and receive better health care. A closer look at the provisions for and management of women's health care reveals that this is not the case, however. There are two major related issues here. One is the treatment of women within the health care system, including the attitudes, perceptions, and training of health care professionals. The other is the planning of health care services, and the extent to which this is accomplished with the needs of women in mind.

Problems Related to Health Care Providers

Although women are being accepted into medical schools in record numbers and now account for about 20 percent of new graduates, the medical establishment continues to be dominated by men and by traditional male attitudes toward women patients. Howell (1974) reviewed what medical schools teach about women and concluded that the special problems of women are frequently considered "psychological" in origin or too unimportant to discuss. Male faculty continue to make jokes at the expense of women, and generally promulgate demeaning attitudes toward women.

Lennane and Lennane (1973) focused more sharply on medical teaching and practice regarding four disorders of women: primary dysmenorrhea, nausea of pregnancy, pain in labor, and infant behavior disorders. Citing standard medical texts, they pointed out that each of these health problems is routinely purported to be of psychogenic origin, although there are no data or other evidence to support such explanations. In each case, moreover, there are sound reasons for accepting an alternate explanation.

Armitage et al. (1979) analyzed the charts of 52 married couples seeing nine family physicians. The visits analyzed comprised 90 male and 91 female illness episodes. The primary complaints in each case were back pain, headache, dizziness, chest pain, or fatigue. For all complaints, physician workups were more extensive for men than for women, although this difference was most striking for low back pain and headache. Although these differences might be influenced by the more frequent physician visits of women (1.5 visits to 1 for men), or by differential risks suggested by some symptoms, stereotyped views of women as hypochondriacal were apparent to the authors.

As part of a federally funded study of information processes in medical care, Wallen et al. (1979) analyzed 336 tape recorded doctor-patient interactions and assessed differences in information seeking and responding for 184 male and 130 female patients. They found that the 34 male physicians involved in this study spontaneously offered information equally frequently to males and females. Women asked significantly more questions, however, and consequently were the recipients of a greater total number of informative statements. When total time spent explaining rather than the absolute number of explanations was assessed there was no difference for male and female patients. This seems to indicate that men were receiving fewer, but fuller, explanations without asking as many questions.

The general level of technicality of responses was not different for male and female patients. However, the level of technicality of physician's responses to the questions of women was frequently mismatched, with responses tending to be lower in level than the questions asked. The physicians apparently "talked down" to their female patients. While they perceived female and male patients as equally desirous of information, the physicians perceived the psychological components of illness as significantly more important for female patients. Finally, physicians were more pessimistic about the prognoses of female patients than those of male patients, again reflecting their view of women as hypochondriacal.

Lorber (1975) studied perceptions of patients by hospital staff and found that the consequences of being perceived as a "problem patient" included early discharge, referral for psychiatric help, neglect, or prescription of tranquilizers. "Good patients," on the other hand, were defined as those who did not question, complain, or otherwise interfere with routines by requiring more time than the staff expected to devote. Although Lorber did not report her data by sex of patient, if hospitalized women behave similarly to the female outpatients described by Wallen et al. (1979), we would expect women disproportionately to be the recipients of "problem patient" remedies.

In a final discussion of their data, Wallen et al. (1979) pointed out that when information is limited, patients—and women patients in particular—are forced to remain dependent on the medical care system. Their ability to make autonomous decisions and to select from a number of health care options is decreased. This maintenance of a male power advantage through withholding information reflects what Ehrenreich and English (1973) have described as the white male middle-class monopoly on medical knowledge and practice. The problem for women is not one simply of gaining access to health care, but rather of gaining full benefit from health care.

Health Care Policy and Planning

Muller (1976) has described health policy problems for women in terms of two issues: (1) distorted views of reproductive processes and their relationship to health care, and (2) negative perceptions of the value of women's time.

Data reflecting hospitalization or disability for childbirth or problems of reproductive functioning are frequently deleted from statistics on the comparative morbidity or mortality of men and women. Although this is intended to provide a fair evaluation, Muller (1976) suggested that the practice actually results in discriminatory policy. Obstetrical discharges comprise a fifth of all female hospital discharges. Their exclusion from statistical reports misrepresents the economic impact of reproductive processes on the provision of health care and results in inadequate responses to the need for public support and insurance coverage for women's health care costs.

The failure to place dollar value on the time of women, or to consider the child care and transportation in evaluating the cost-effectiveness of health programs, places unfair burdens on women, particularly on those in poverty groups (Muller, 1976). When neighborhood health centers are eliminated in favor of central sites, for example, it is women in their childbearing years who are most likely to suffer. Ironically, this is the group that will cost society the most through related decreases in reproductive efficiency. The lack of convenient and affordable health services will be reflected in both maternal and child mortality, in complications of pregnancy and delivery, birth defects, and later health problems of both mothers and their children.

Women who are employed outside the home face additional problems in achieving access to health services. When health services are not available after working hours, obtaining care can mean lost work time and lost income. The block scheduling used in some public clinics requires patients to spend many hours waiting to see a health care provider. Since women must generally take responsibility for getting their children to health care facilities, time lost from work due to health problems can be multiplied for mothers. Indeed, women 25 to 34 have the highest work absenteeism for health reasons (Lebowitz, 1980).

Problems faced by rural women, and particularly poor rural women, may include absence of health services, as well as the same transportation and communication problems faced by women in towns and cities. The specialized services available in cities do not exist at all in most rural areas. Doctor-patient ratios in rural areas may be as high as 1 : 2000 (Coe, 1978). Many children are born at home without the attendance of even a minimally trained midwife, and infant mortality rates are up to twenty times higher than in cities.

Finally, women in poverty circumstances almost inevitably suffer from fragmentation of health services. A report by the Children's Defense Fund (1976) provided the following illustration. A woman receiving Aid to Families with Dependent Children, often receives most of her care for acute health problems through a hospital emergency room. When pregnant she may seek prenatal care in a health department clinic, but her baby will be delivered in a public hospital that is, administratively, a separate entity. Her infant subsequently may be examined at still another health clinic, but if illness occurs the child may be referred to a private physician who sees welfare cases. If hospitalization is required, however, the hospital where that doctor practices may not accept her as a welfare patient, and another transfer would be made to another public hospital or specialized care facility. To make matters worse, medical records do not always follow the patient through such a fragmented system. The frustrations involved in pursuing health care certainly can be expected to discourage the efforts of patients with limited education, social and economic support, and skills for coping with the medical bureaucracy.

NEW DIRECTIONS IN WOMEN'S HEALTH CARE

Initiatives growing out of the women's movement, the recent focus on primary prevention in medicine, the self care movement in health education, and the development of health psychology as a discipline have resulted in attempts to increase the knowledge and responsibility of women with respect to their own health. While this empowerment is an important element in the improvement of health care, too little attention has been paid to the social context within which women act to pursue their health needs. In this section, some examples of approaches to improving health care for women will be discussed, with emphasis on social setting interactions and the mobilization of social support networks and other community resources.

Women's Self-Help Approaches

The work of the Boston Women's Health Collective (1976) is one of the best examples of the influence of the women's movement on empowerment in health care settings. Their efforts have included the formation of advocacy groups to help women assume an active role in their health care. Women are encouraged to obtain full information on tests, procedures, and drugs, to be aware of treatment consequences, to maintain the option of refusing treatment, and to seek complete access to their medical records.

Alternatives to the traditional health care system for women include a national network of Feminist Women's Health Centers that offer basic gynecology services, paramedical training, self-help, and counseling. Organizations such as the Women's Health Alliance of Long Island (Davey & Bruhn, 1981) have focused on education and provision of social support aimed at advocacy and empowerment of women, with special attention to health needs. Political action in the form of community surveys and guides to practitioners and services have also led to favorable changes in gynecological health care delivery for women (Reverby, 1973; Freudenberg, 1978).

Based on an analysis by class, sex, and occupation of who controls and who produces in the U.S. economy, and the health sector in particular, Navarro (1975) concluded that changes in responsiveness to women's needs will require changes in the control of our institutions. In the health sector, women comprise fewer than 7 percent of physicians, 8 percent of dentists, and fewer than 10 percent of scientists and administrators. On the other hand, women comprise over 95 percent of all nurses, 70 percent of health related technicians, and 76 percent of health-related therapists. In other words, women fulfill most of the support roles but few of the policy or decision-making roles within health care. The alienation of women from traditional male-dominated health care institutions is directly related to these conditions. While the women's movement has provided some alternatives, their influence is primarily among white, educated, middle-income groups. Well-baby clinics, family planning centers, and neighborhood screening clinics, are slender beginnings when considered in light of the total health problems of low-income women.

Outreach and the Promotion of Social Support

Women who live and work outside the mainstream of society, particularly those of minority racial or ethnic groups with strong traditions of social isolation, require more than clinics and low cost medical services. The use of outreach workers has provided one of the most effective approaches to easing entry into the health care system.

The Children's Defense Fund (1976) has recommended that outreach efforts should utilize trained individuals of the same ethnic or racial background as targeted clients. These health workers should reach members of the target population through personal contacts when possible, and their friends, family, and others in the community should be contacted and encouraged to strengthen the recommendations made or information given. Schools, neighborhood centers, and any other available settings can be used to make contacts and provide information. Finally, followup services should be a part of any outreach program. These follow-up contacts serve to reinforce the use of health services and help to overcome any obstacles encountered in seeking services, thereby discouraging attrition. Outreach efforts conducted in this manner have been used to bring clients in for such programs as the federally-funded Early and Periodic Screening, Diagnosis, and Treatment (EPSDT) initiatives, local family planning clinics, or maternal and child health programs.

Outreach workers have also functioned to disseminate information on prevention of disease or to accomplish health screening procedures. Artz et al. (1981) conducted a door-to-door hypertension screening program using trained community volunteers in city apartment buildings. They found this approach both more effective and less expensive than a control method using a central site for high blood pressure screening.

Experience with outreach workers underscores the fact that individuals are more likely to take health actions if others around them support that action (Levy, 1980). In addition, social support, in the form of relationships with others that are characterized by mutual concern and positive regard, may actually inhibit health problems through effects on the immune system. Pilisuk (1982) has pointed out that our current social milieu does not enhance the functioning of the traditional natural social ties involving the family, stable neighborhood associations, and other groups within the community. As a result of the deterioration of these natural support groups, there is an even greater need to provide formal social support for health-related activities that are not a part of the individual's prior experience. This means an expansion of outreach programs and energies directed at organizing support groups.

Support groups are becoming a particularly common mode of service delivery in prevention-oriented facilities such as health maintenance organizations. These institutions organize weight control groups, stress reduction groups, and others formed around specific health interests (Albino, 1983). Hospital-based programs for individuals recovering from myocardial infarction, or cornary artery bypass surgery, are also common, as are groups of cancer patients organized to provide one another with information and emotional support. Breast cancer patients, for example, help those with more recent surgeries to find and fit prostheses and provide empathic concern and support as they work through feelings of impaired identity and loss. Again, unfortunately, women may have more difficulty than men in availing themselves of even these forms of social support. The most successful programs are those that come to the women in need of their services.

Primary Prevention

Primary prevention for some of the health problems facing women exclusively include individual efforts such as family planning, breast self-examination, and regular screening for cervical cancer. These efforts, like making the changes in one's dietary and exercise patterns that are critical for men and women in the prevention of cardiovascular disease (Coates et al., 1981), require little beyond the understanding of appropriate actions and the desire and ability to act. Nevertheless, for women with families to care for and possibly outside employment as well, simply finding the time for primary prevention can be a major problem. Even if the time can be found, many will not have necessary child care services or the support within the family to implement dietary or other changes.

Green (1976) has recommended that multiple approaches be used to diseeminate and promote primary prevention programs and that these be directed at health and human service providers, as well as at individuals in the community at large. Communications through print and electronic media and also personal presentations can be coordinated through schools, clinics, pharmacies, work settings, and social gathering places. This multiple approach concept is especially important if primary prevention is to reach women since there is probably far greater variability in the patterns of women's lives and social roles than in those of men.

One of the aspects of primary prevention that distinguishes it from health care provided in response to disease is the difficulty of identifying outcomes. Since the objective is to achieve the *absence* of disease or dysfunction, there is no clear improvement from illness that would serve to reward or motivate and sustain new behaviors. Women whose energies are distributed over a number of activities and roles may find primary prevention particularly difficult. Just as illness in women cannot be separated from reproductive and family roles, so provisions for the enhancement of health must be developed with attention to the special demands of these social roles. Successful primary prevention programs require, above all, careful and complete analyses of both the needs of the community they are intended to serve and the resources available to support services designed to meet these needs.

A FINAL COMMENT

In studying the physical health of women, it is obvious that the problems of minority and poverty women are overwhelming in their magnitude. While women will experience the frustrations of dealing with fragmented services or biased attitudes toward their symptoms, it is the poor—those women living on the periphery of society—who suffer most from inadequate health care. When women suffer, their children also suffer, and costs to society of inadequate health care for women go far beyond the effects on these individuals.

For women of poverty and their families, the inability to obtain health care that is responsive to their needs is just one more cycle in an interminable downward spiral that has already included physical and material want, social alienation, powerlessness, and despair. The needs of poor women with respect to health are inextricably tied to their other human needs. It is indisputable that health suffers when nutrition is poor, when living conditions are crowded and unsanitary, when the environment is polluted, when there is no respite from noise, when there is no meaningful work, when there is continuing stress related to unequal social treatment, and there are few ties to other human beings who are able to provide comfort, esteem, and mutual support. Until we can begin to change this total situation, poor health will be just another symptom of poverty, and resources will continue to be poured into secondary and tertiary level care for chronic health problems that are to a high degree preventable.

REFERENCES

Aday, L. & Eichhorn, R. *The utilization of health services: Indices and correlates.* A research bibliography. Publication No. (HSM) 11-71-150. Washington, D.C.: Dept. of Health, Education and Welfare, 1972.

Albino, J. E. Health psychology and primary prevention: Natural allies. In R. D. Felner, L. A. Jason, J. N. Moritsugu, & S. S. Farber (eds.), *Preventive psychology: Theory, research, and practice.* Elmsford, N.Y.: Pergamon, 1983.

American Cancer Society. *Cancer facts and figures*, 1980.

Armitage, K. J., Schneiderman, L. J., & Bass, R. A. Response of physicians to medical complaints of men and women. *Journal of the American Medical Association*, 1979, *241*, 2186–2187.

Artz, L., Cooke, C. J., Meyers, A., & Stalgaitis, S. Community change agents and health interventions: Hypertensive screening. *American Journal of Community Psychology*, 1981, *9*, 361–370.

Boston Women's Health Book Collective. *Our bodies, ourselves.* New York: Simon & Schuster, 1976.

Bracken, M. B., Freeman, D. N., & Hellenbrand, K. Hospitalization for medical-legal and other abortions in the United States 1970-1977. *American Journal of Public Health*, 1982, *72*, 30–35.

Brown, M. *Laying waste: The poisoning of America.* New York: Pantheon, 1980.

Bullough, B. Poverty, ethnic identity and preventive health care. *Journal of Health and Social Behavior*, 1972, *13*, 347–359.

Children's Defense Fund. *Doctors and dollars are not enough: How to improve health services for children and their families.* Washington, D.C.: Washington Research Project, Inc., 1976.

Coates, T. J., Perry, C., Killen, J., & Slinkard, C. A. Primary prevention of cardiovascular disease in children and adolescents. In C. K. Prokop & L. A. Bradley (eds.), *Medical psychology: Contributions to behavioral medicine.* New York: Academic Press, 1981.

Coe, R. M. *Sociology of medicine.* New York: McGraw-Hill, 1978.

Davey, S. & Bruhn, M. Working for women's health: The Women's Health Alliance of Long Island, Inc. *Women and Health*, 1980, *5*, 39–46.

Di Matteo, M. R. & Di Nicola, D. D. *Achieving patient compliance: The psychology of the medical practitioner's role.* New York: Pergamon Press, 1982.

Edelman, M. W. *Portrait of inequality: Black and white children in America.* Washington, D.C.: Children's Defense Fund, 1980.

Ehrenreich, B. & English, D. *Witches, midwives, and nurses: A history of women healers.* Old Westbury, New York: The Feminist Press, 1973.

Feldman, J. J. *The dissemination of health information.* Chicago: Aldine, 1966.

Fishel, A. Mental health. In C. I. Fogel & N. F. Woods (eds.), *Health care of women: A nursing perspective.* St. Louis: The C. V. Mosby Company, 1981.

Fogel, C. I. Assessment of health status. In C. I. Fogel & N. F. Woods (eds.), *Health care of women: A nursing perspective.* St. Louis: The C. V. Mosby Company, 1981. (a)

Fogel, C. I. Fertility control. In C. I. Fogel & N. F. Woods (eds.), *Health care of women: A nursing perspective.* St. Louis: The C. V. Mosby Company, 1981. (b)

Fogel, C. I. Abortion. In C. I. Fogel & N. F. Woods (eds.), *Health care of women: A nursing perspective.* St. Louis: The C. V. Mosby Company, 1981. (c)

Fogel, C. I. High-risk pregnancy. In C. I. Fogel & N. F. Woods (eds.), *Health care of women: A nursing perspective.* St. Louis: The C. V. Mosby Company, 1981. (d)

Fogel, C. I. Nutrition. In C. I. Fogel & N. F. Woods (eds.), *Health care of women: A nursing perspective.* St. Louis: The C. V. Mosby Company, 1981. (e)

Freudenberg, N. Shaping the future of health education: From behavior change to social change. *Health Education Monographs*, 1978, *6*, 372–377.

Green, L. W. Educational strategies to improve compliance with therapeutic and preventive regimens: The recent evidence. In R. B. Haynes, D. W. Taylor, & D. L. Sackett (eds.), *Compliance in health care.* Baltimore: The Johns Hopkins Press, 1979.

Haynes, S. G. & Feinleib, M. Women, work, and coronary heart disease: Prospective findings from the Framingham Heart Study. *American Journal of Public Health*, 1980, *70*, 133–141.

Howell, M. C. What medical schools teach about women. *New England Journal of Medicine*, 1974, *291*, 304–306.

Johnson, A. Sex differentials in coronary heart disease: The explanatory role of primary risk factors. *Journal of Health and Social Behavior*, 1977, *18*, 46–54.

Langlie, J. K. Social networks, health beliefs, and preventive health behavior. *Journal of Health and Social Behavior*, 1977, *18*, 244–260.

Lebowitz, A. Overview: The health of working women. In D. C. Walsh & R. H. Egdahl (eds.), *Women, work, and health: Challenges to corporate policy.* New York: Springer-Verlag, 1980.

Lee, P. R. Questions for the future: Policy, women, and health: Same old system or something new? In V. Olesen (ed.), *Women and their health: Research implications for a new era.* NCHSR Research Proceedings Series, August 1–2, 1975. DHEW Publ. No. (HRA) 77-3138.

Lennane, K. J. & Lennane, R. J. Alleged psychogenic disorders in women—a possible manifestation of sexual prejudice. *New England Journal of Medicine*, 1973, *288*, 288–292.

Levy, R. L. The role of social support in patient compliance: A selective review. In R. B. Haynes, M. E. Mattson, & T. O. Engibretson (eds.), *Patient compliance to prescribed antihypertensive medication regimens: A report to the National Heart, Lung, and Blood Institute*, NIH Publ. No. 81-2102. Bethesda, MD: U.S. Dept. of Health and Human Services, 1980.

Lorber, J. Good patients and problem patients: Conformity and deviance in a general hospital. *Journal of Health and Social Behavior*, 1975, *16*, 213–225.

Martin, L. L. *Health care of women.* Philadelphia: J. B. Lippincott, 1978.

Mechanic, D. Sex, illness, illness behavior, and the use of health services. *Journal of Human Stress*, 1976, *2*, 29–40.

McKinlay, J. B. Who is really ignorant—physician or patient? *Journal of Health and Social Behavior*, 1975, *16*, 3–11.

Muller, C. Methodological issues in health economics research relevant to women. *Women and Health*, 1976, *1*, 3–9.

Nathanson, C. A. Illness and the feminine role: A theoretical review. *Social Science and Medicine*, 1975, *9*, 57–62.

Nathanson, C. A. Sex, illness, and medical care: A review of data, theory, and method. *Social Science and Medicine*, 1977, *11*, 13–25.

National Center for Health Statistics. Final mortality data–1977. Monthly Vital Statistics Report. Washington, D.C., 1977.

Navarro, V. Women in health care. *New England Journal of Medicine*, 1975, *292*, 398–402.

Ortmeyer, L. E. Female's natural advantage? Or, the unhealthy environment of males? The status of sex mortality differentials. *Women and Health*, 1979, *4*, 121–133.

Pilisuk, M. Delivery of social support: The social innoculation. *American Journal of Orthopsychiatry*, 1982, *52*(1), 20–31.

Pomerleau, C. Cardiovascular disease as a women's health problem. *Women and Health*, 1976, *1*, 12–15.

Reverby, S. Women in the health system: Challenges and changes. *Human Ecology Forum*, 1973, *4*, 4–5.

Rice, D. P. & Cugliani, A. S. Health status of American women. *Women and Health*, 1980, *5*, 5–22.

Rodgers-Rose, L. Relationships between black men and women: Toward a definition. In V. Olesen (ed.), *Women and their health: Research implications for a new era*. NCHSR Research Proceedings Series, August 1–2, 1975. DHEW Publ. No. (HRA) 77-3138.

Rosenman, R. H., Brand, R. J., Jenkins, C. D., Friedman, M., Straus, R., & Wurm, M. Coronary heart disease in the Western Collaborative Group Study: Final followup experience of 8½ years. *Journal of the American Medical Association*, 1975, *233*, 872–877.

Rubin, G., McCarthy, B., Shelton, J., Rochat, R. W., & Terry, J. The risk of childbearing re-evaluated. *American Journal of Public Health*, 1981, *71*, 712–716.

Sablosky, A. & Studley, J. A perspective on health care and women in the Mississippi Delta. *Women and Health*, 1976, *1*, 21–23.

Stellman, J. M. *Work is dangerous to your health*. New York: Random House, 1973.

Stellman, J. M. *Women's work, women's health*. New York: Pantheon, 1977.

Stellman, J. M. Forum on women's occupational health: Medical, social and legal implications. Occupational health hazards of women: An overview. *Preventive Medicine*, 1978, 7, 281–293.

Suchman, E. Preventive health behavior: A model for research on community health campaigns. *Journal of Health and Social Behavior*, 1967, *8*, 197–209.

Syme, S. L. & Berkman, L. F. Social class, susceptibility and sickness. *American Journal of Epidemiology*, 1976, *104*, 1–8.

U.S. Department of Commerce. Statistical Abstract of the United States, 101st edition. Washington, D.C., 1980.

U.S. Department of Labor. Women's Bureau: Women in the labor force–January 1976-1977. Washington, D.C.: U.S. Government Printing Office, 1978.

Verbrugge, L. M. Sex differentials in morbidity and mortality in the United States. *Social Biology*, 1976, *23*, 275–296.

Verbrugge, L. M. Female illness rates and illness behavior: Testing hypotheses about sex differences in health. *Women and Health*, 1979, *4*, 61–79.

Waldron, I. Employment and women's health: An analysis of causal relationships. *International Journal of Health Services*, 1980, *10*, 435–454.

Wallen, J., Waitzkin, H., & Stoeckle, J. D. Physician stereotypes about femal health and illness: A study of patient's sex and the informative process during medical interviews. *Women and Health*, 1979, *4*, 135–146.

Woods, N. F. Women and their health. In C. I. Fogel & N. F. Woods (eds.), *Health care of women: A nursing perspective*. St. Louis: The C. V. Mosby Company, 1981.

Woods, N. F. & Hulka, B. S. Symptom reports and illness behavior among employed women and homemakers. *Journal of Community Health*, 1979, *5*, 36–45.

10

Social Support and Efficacy in Advocacy Roles

A Case Study of Two Women's Organizations

Meg A. Bond and James G. Kelly
University of Oregon

Women's involvement in community activities in the United States is not new. Since the advent of indoor plumbing, running water, wash tubs, improved stoves and canning in the mid to late 1800s, an increasing number of women have reduced their full time domestic role to become active in their communities. While in the 1800s women were excluded from established clubs and organizations, they nevertheless began to organize their own groups from literary clubs to YWCAs. Women addressed topics ranging from child care to community standards for sanitation to admission of women to college. Isolated examples of community activity increasingly took the shape of more structured social movements: the temperance movement, the settlement house movement, the organization of women as consumers and the establishment of women's unions. These social movements became the major forum for the expression of both their leadership and their influence activities. There is, then, a long history of women in the U.S. organizing for influence—they have participated in their communities since the founding of the country.

In spite of this long history of women working together to help each other and creating organizations to do so, there are almost no published reports of how organizational variables affect the efficacy of women in influence roles. This chapter reports research that deals directly with this undeveloped topic.

No one would be surprised to find that women in a political caucus might exert their influence in a different manner than women in a museum guild. Such differences might be related to the personal qualities of organization members, to the

This chapter is an initial and partial report of doctoral dissertation research carried out at the University of Oregon by the first author (Bond, 1983). Grateful acknowledgement is made to the dissertation committee members: R. Dawes, chairperson, T. Bighan, B. Fagot, M. Goldman, and N. S. Sundberg. Appreciation is also acknowledged to Darien Fenn who carried out the data analysis.

Appreciation is acknowledged to the following women who devoted time and expressed committment by serving as research assistants and interviewers for this work: Lauren Herbert, Linda Nettekoven, Gerry Oldham, and Gretchen Studd. Data preparation and organization benefitted from the hard work of Meleta Jacobs. Barbara Honeyman provided invaluable collaboration in her roles as consultant and interview trainer/supervisor.

Meg A. Bond is now Postdoctoral Fellow, Institute for the Study of Developmental Disabilities, Chicago, and James G. Kelly is with the Department of Psychology, University of Illinois, Chicago.

nature of their task, and/or to the characteristics of the organizations with which they work. It might be expected, for example, that in a hierarchical organization with explicit assignments for work roles, women will carry out their work in structured and explicit ways. There will be little ambiguity about the tasks to be performed. At the same time, there may be few opportunities for women to express control and autonomy in how they carry out the work. In contrast, women working in an egalitarian organization may find that these dimensions are weighted in reverse, e.g., encouraging much autonomy with little explicit structure. The consequence is that as women increasingly work in more egalitarian organizations, where there are norms for the equal expression of power and influence, there may be increased demands for women to be advocates in the absence of clear guidelines and expectations. The implications of organizational structure and organizational mission for the performance of advocacy roles is, then, a topic of increasing salience for women.

Two questions have guided this work: 1) is there an interaction between the styles of women in advocacy roles and the characteristics of varied organizations in which they work? and 2) how does this interaction effect the efficacy of women in advocacy roles?

These questions were addressed by designing a case study of women who perform advocacy roles in two contrasting women's organizations. This chapter presents initial findings of the relationship between organizational setting, the use of social support, and effective advocacy for a sample of women in these two prototypic organizations. The work was carried out on the belief that clarifying how an organization limits or enhances advocacy work can reduce tendencies to "blame" an individual woman advocate for being ineffective. More importantly, this study may clarify how personal styles and organizational characteristics interact to contribute to improved advocacy performance.

The chapter will begin with a discussion of previous work related to women and advocacy. Then social support will be introduced as a topic relevant for women in influence roles. The organizations and the participants will be described, followed by a presentation of the methods and procedures. Specific hypotheses for the interaction between individual advocacy styles, social support functions and organizational characteristics will then be presented followed by the results. A closing discussion focuses on the practical implications of the findings.

WOMEN AND ADVOCACY

Advocacy is defined as: *Identifying and managing the use of* community *resources in a manner consistent with the goals and values of the organization.* Advocacy connotes aggressive, goal directed, even zealous activities that are determined as much by previous social status and personal characteristics as by current events or qualities of the specific organizational setting. In this work, however, the organizational setting is singled out as a primary defining element. The premise is that there are varied adaptive styles of advocacy and that these varied styles are affected by qualities of the organization. This premise is particularly salient for women given the possibility that styles developed by men who perform advocacy roles can predominate.

Singling out a preferred set of roles or skills is a latent problem. Women may be encouraged to take on specific strategies without an opportunity to assess the validity of other options. For example, there are a number of popular books that advise women who have never had access to influence strategies to adopt strategies that have historically been reserved for boys and men [e.g., "Games Mother Never Taught Me" by B. L. Harragan (1977); "Women and Power" by Jane Trahey (1977)]. Such advice can be valuable in helping women gain an understanding of a world of knowledge to which they have traditionally been denied access. However, these words of advice are limited for at least two reasons. One, they reinforce women's development of traditional strategies emphasizing individualistic values derived from the premise that there is a limited amount of power to be divided up among a select few. Secondly, and perhaps more importantly, these prescriptions perpetuate the notion that there is *one* strategy of influence effective in all settings regardless of a person's status, role, or access to resources. The unwitting implication is that if the strategy does not work, there is something deficient about the individual woman advocate.

Some attention has been given to the ineffectiveness of socially defined influence strategies for women. Johnson (1976) has built upon Tedeschi's (1972) categories of social influence—self confidence, expertise, social status, and access to resources. Using these categories, her thesis is that since women have less access to these four prerequisites for effective power, they are limited in the modes of influence available to them. Johnson (1976) argues that since women have historically had less access to concrete and economic resources, they have, instead, learned to use more personal resources (e.g., affection, approval, and acquiescence) as bases of influence. She asserts that instead of fighting the no-win battle of being recognized for their competencies, women have learned that acting helpless, for example, can yield results without the punishments that come from expressing an active role. The research of Broverman and colleagues is congruent with this interpretation. They have demonstrated that indirect rather than direct expressions of power are viewed, by men and women, as more acceptable for women (Broverman et al., 1972). The expectations are that women are supposed to act as if they are not using power even when in fact they are.[1] Unfortunately, these indirect styles of influence typically undermine the bases upon which women can build future influence efforts and can serve to reinforce the image of women as powerless.

Given women's historically limited access to resources coupled with the variety of new settings in which women are now beginning to exert influence it is important to assess the potential contribution of a diversified repertoire of styles and roles. A major challenge for women in assuming advocacy roles is to express influence in ways that are derived from personal preferences, the resources available, and the requirements of the task, independent of societal expectations for how a competent woman should behave.

SUPPORT NETWORKS

A major resource for advocacy highlighted by the women's movement is social support. Women's support groups, women's self-help movement and consciousness raising efforts all emphasize the importance of women being resources for one another. While much of the emphasis for women has been on the development of

---

[1] For an illustrative example of these dynamics, see Stein's (1971) description of the way in which female nurses influence the male physician in the hospital setting.

support networks to facilitate the feminist movement or as personal coping strategies, there is increasing recognition of the value of networking to increase womens' individual political and professional efficacy. Kanter (1976), for example, has emphasized the particular benefit of creating alliances as a method by which women can increase their base of influence in organizations.

This recognition of the diverse benefits of support networks increases the opportunity to relate an emerging literature in applied psychology with women's political development. The expanding literature on social support has explored its' function as a moderator of stress (Cobb, 1976; for review see Cohen and McKay, 1980) and as a facilitator of successful coping efforts (Hirsch, 1980; Tolsdorf, 1976, Gottlieb, 1976, 1979, 1981; Wilcox, 1981). There is almost no research literature which relates support networks to the acquisition of competencies, particularly competencies required of women in the effective performance of influence roles. Yet the relationship between social networks and political efficacy has a common sense appeal. It seems plausible that people are more effective in their work when provided with advice, help, and encouragement from others. However, beyond the initial assertion that social support and efficacy seem related, we know very little about the relationship between the two. Specifically, what are the mechanisms by which social support facilitates effectiveness for women advocates? What types of support are most important for women's competent advocacy in different social settings?

Despite recent attention given to the general concept of social support within the field of applied psychology, there is a striking lack of definitional clarity about what exactly *is* social support (Heller, 1979; Carveth & Gottlieb, 1979). Recently investigators have emphasized the importance of going beyond a general definition of social support to specify multiple types, sources, and network structures (Wilcox, 1981; Mitchell & Trickett, 1980; Heller, 1979). Here social support is defined as a multidimensional concept. *Social support is the composite of help and aid both emotional and instrument received from one's social environment.* A number of specific characteristics of social support networks are identified: 1) Multiple *sources* of social support, e.g., family, friends, coworkers; 2) Multiple *types* of social support, e.g., emotional support; task oriented assistance; specific and informed feedback; communication of shared expectations and a shared world view; access to new and diverse information; access to social contacts; and challenging support; and 3) Varied *structures* of social support networks; e.g., density (the extent to which networks members know and contact each other independently of the focal person). Two separate support networks were identified which were expected to aide the advocate's work. The first network includes those close friends and family members who provide life supports that directly and indirectly affect her work. This group of people is referred to as a "core support network." The second network, the advocate's "work network," consists of the advocate's coworkers. Since advocacy activities typically involve active collaboration with others working in a small group and networking to achieve political objectives, the relationship between the woman advocate and her coworkers is a critical issue.

ORGANIZATIONAL CONSIDERATIONS

Successful advocacy performance is expected to depend upon those qualities of the organization which sponsor and affirm advocacy roles. Some important considerations are: What is the nature of the organizational sponsorship for advocacy? How does the organization enhance persistence with advocacy tasks? How do organizational structures support commitment to advocacy? How can the necessary organizational resources needed for advocacy be identified and mobilized? Unfortunately, organizational research has not yet reported empirical investigations of the relationship between organizational structure, organizational role sets and advocacy performance. Decision making structures within an advocacy organization would seem particularly important for advocacy since the generic values underlying advocacy are so clearly egalitarian. Yet many organizations function in a relatively hierarchical fashion with clearly marked role functions and prerequisites. Little is known about how decision making or organizational structure of advocacy organizations affects the outcomes of the advocacy. Thus, the authors self consciously set out to select organizations which varied in terms of their organizational structure and style of decision making in order to develop a portrait of the interaction between organizational characteristics and advocacy.

The hypothesized mediating functions between organizational structure and efficacy are expected to be the social support activities discussed above. The present study was initiated to clarify how social support affects advocacy performance in two organizations which vary in how they define and structure advocacy tasks. Before developing specific hypotheses, the participants will be described.

THE ORGANIZATIONS

The two organizations studied were a feminist service delivery organization (FSO) and a women's organization for the training and placement of community volunteers (VO). These two organizations differ in mission, style and expectations for advocacy. The participants in the study were those women within each organization who work between the organization and the community advocating for activities or policies sanctioned by the organization.

FSO is in its fifth year of existence. It was spearheaded by a small group of feminists who took battered women into their own homes. It has grown into a confidential shelter with counseling services and community education functions. Their primary goal is: "to provide battered and abused women with options and to enable them to take control over their own lives." The organization has evolved from an informal collective. While decision making is becoming increasingly structured, FSO is maintaining a conscious commitment to a participatory democracy and a feminist ideology.

The VO is an entirely volunteer-run organization with 200 members established about 20 years ago. The primary focus is upon promoting volunteerism and developing the potential of organization members for volunteer participation in community affairs. The organization's impact in the community is felt in a broad spectrum of arenas as the membership has become involved in the delivery of services, and in the design of community programs and advocacy. The organization has local, state, regional, national and international activities and a strong hierarchical organizational structure. Members are consulted on most policy decisions, but decisions are ultimately made at the top of the organization and communicated downward. The members have traditionally been upper middle class, married, non-working mothers. Recently more single and professional women are joining the organization.

Women who perform advocacy roles in both organizations identify policy topics and activate these issues in a manner that is congruent with the purpose of the organization. Their work includes lobbying for legislative changes, fund raising, and networking with other community agencies.

At FSO, the advocacy function is primarily in the hands of the board of directors. The board consists of women who were recruited by the director and prior board members on the basis of diverse competencies and knowledge in such areas as accounting, organizational development and community organizing. The board members have multiple responsibilities related to the running of the shelter. They are involved in policy development and revision, personnel selection, finance, fund raising, and volunteer development. Members serve terms that range from one to three years in length. Advocacy is but one of their tasks and involves coordinating with other community groups, testifying at legislative hearings, fund raising, and educating the community about the shelter and the needs of battered women. Their interaction with the community is primarily aimed at generating the resources and rapport the organization needs in order to function effectively.

At VO, advocacy is delegated to a committee composed of women selected by the executive board. The women on the advocacy committee have typically been members of VO for several years during which they served on other committees and/or were involved in direct service delivery. While members of the advocacy committee, they are still typically involved in separate direct service delivery activities. However, for the one to three years that they serve on the committee, advocacy work is their primary commitment within the organization, and they receive training to prepare them specifically for this function. The mission of the committee is to study public issues related to the organization's purpose and program, and to organize and direct any related community action program decided upon by the organization's membership. The group has promoted such issues as mandated kindergartens, subsidized adoption, energy conservation, and historic preservation.

THE PARTICIPANTS

There were 10 FSO women and 11 VO women in the advocacy groups. Eight of the FSO women and seven women from VO participated in the study. Of the six women who chose not to participate in the study, one person was moving out of the city, a second person had a newborn child plus full-time work, three women cited time limitations due to family and work responsibilities and one woman had a recent death in her family.

The age range of the women at FSO was 28–58, while at VO ages ranged from 25 to 41. The family incomes of most women at FSO ranged from categories of less than $15,000 to between $30,000 and $50,000 with one woman earning over $50,000. At VO most family incomes were between $30,000–100,000, with one woman's family earning between $15,000 and $30,000, and one woman's family earning over $100,000. Five of the women at FSO worked full time, and six provided 50–100 percent of their family income. At VO only 1 of the 7 women worked full time, and six contributed less than 10 percent of their family income.

In essence the socioeconomic status of the women at VO is higher and more homogeneous; at FSO it is typically lower and more variable. These demographic differences suggest that the findings reported here relating organizational setting, social support and efficacy of advocacy work may be related to differences in the social and economic status of the participants from the two organizations.

RESEARCH PROCEDURES

A case study format was chosen to provide an initial statement of relationships between the organizational setting, social support, and efficacy in performing advocacy tasks. The choice of a case study was made for practical, philosophical and conceptual reasons. First, because of the absence of previous systematic inquiry regarding the advocacy process, we considered it important to identify variables that would enhance reporting the richness of the advocacy process, without presupposing that one or two major theoretical constructs could explain all of advocacy work. A case study seemed to meet this criteria. Secondly, it was desirable that the data gathering process make it possible for the participants to use the research activity as a resource for themselves and not just meet the needs of the researcher. This is a particularly salient point for research with women and women's organizations (Riger & Gordon, 1981). A case study seemed to best meet this criteria as well. Third, it was considered important to carry out the work, so that it could be provocative for a series of future research activities. It was considered more important to generate ideas, issues, and concerns about the relationship between the organizational setting, social support and advocacy, than to definitively test or delimit the issues. It was not clear to us that the most appropriate variables are yet known. Here again, a case study seemed most appropriate.

The limitations of a case study are apparent. The nature of the inquiry is correlational and time limited, and inferences about causes and effects can only be speculative rather than demonstrated. The descriptive, correlational nature of the data and the small sample size restrict the types of conclusions that can be drawn. Competing hypotheses in explaining results cannot be excluded. The small number of advocates available in each setting limits the validity of interpretation and emphasizes the tentative nature of summary comments.

Research procedures developed to facilitate the goals of an exploratory study involved an active engagement of participants. The methods were intended to be structured enough to reflect the unique role of social support for individual women within the organization. More specifically, the data gathering process was organized into three phases (see Table 1). During the first phase, participant observation and informal interviews with organization members provided us with an initial understanding of the organization and helped to promote rapport. The information gathered during this process provided the basis for identifying themes that guided further data collection. It was during this phase that particular attention was given to elaborating how the organizational settings varied and developing hypotheses about how the support activities for advocacy roles vary between the two organizations. During the second phase, questionnaires and semi-structured interviews were implemented to obtain more specific information about the functions and structures of individual women's social support networks. Coworker ratings of one another provided information about each advocate's efficacy. The final phase (Phase Three) involved sharing a summary of the data gathered in Phase Two with participants in order to explore their interpretations of the findings and thereby enhance our understanding of the results.

The choice of the case study then reflects practical, philosophical and conceptual criteria. The case study created here is not, however, a traditional case study of individuals, but a case study, employing hypotheses which focus upon the interactions between key persons, their social networks and their work setting. The method attempts to take account of naturalistic phenomena and, thereby, to

Table 1 Procedures

Phase I

Informal interviews
Participant observation
Documents
⟶ Develop hypotheses
Describe settings

Phase II

Social support measures
Core network questionnaire
Work network questionnaire
Situational analysis
Interview
Efficacy measures
Coworker ratings
⟶ Test hypotheses

Demographics
Beliefs
Social skills
⟶ Explore alternative explanations
Expand descriptions of settings
and participants

Ongoing descriptive data gathering
Elaborate variables
Check accuracy of observations

Phase III

Feedback to and from organizations
Evaluation of research procedure
⟶ Develop model of relationship between social support, effective advocacy and
organizational setting
Generate hypotheses for further study

increase the grounded quality of the data for future explorations (Glaser, 1978; Willems & Raush, 1969). The work derives from an ecological paradigm, where the relationship between the research staff and participants is as important as viewing the interdependence of women advocates and co-workers in their work setting (Kelly, 1968; Trickett et al., 1972; Muñoz et al., 1979; Trickett et al., 1983). The exploratory nature of the work derives from the newness of the topic. The selection of two representative organizations and the identification of multidimensional variables, is intended to focus upon person and setting relationships and to enhance the merits of the study.

THE CONCEPTUAL FRAMEWORK: ORGANIZATIONAL SETTING, SUPPORT NETWORKS, AND ADVOCACY ROLES–THE HYPOTHESES

To bring together ideas about organizational setting, support networks and advocacy roles, underlying assumptions about how social support affects advocacy will be laid out. Specific hypotheses will then be stated for how social support is expected to be expressed in each of these organizations. This is intended to illustrate the impact of organizational setting on the expression of social support.

What are the assumptions about *how* social support enhances women's social influence? That is, what specific function is a woman's social support network presumed to serve that will impact the effectiveness of her advocacy work? If these functions can be identified, then the specific types, sources and structural qualities of social support that serve the functions can be predicted.

The following functions of support networks are suggested as relevant for the expression of effective advocacy roles for women:

1. Enhancing persistence in advocacy work
2. Yielding access to multiple resources needed for the advocacy work
3. Reinforcing commitment to the advocacy role within the organization

Thus, a woman who is effective in advocacy work is presumed to have a social support network that will facilitate her staying with the work, give her the tools to do the work, and provide her with encouragement to carry out the work. The specific types and structures of social support which serve these functions discussed above are expected to be different in the two organizations. Hypotheses for how social support is expected to facilitate efficacy in the two organizations are developed below.

At the FSO, where participation is a dominant value and where the organization is still evolving, an advocate's efficacy is expected to be enhanced by social support that: 1) enables her to persist through *crises* within the organization; 2) provides her with resources from *outside* the organization that enable her to participate in a manner useful to the organization; and 3) reinforces her commitment to the *goals* of the organization.

In contrast, at VO where there is more clarity about roles and decision making and where resources are available for the work, an advocate's efficacy is expected to be enhanced by social support to the extent that it: 1) enables her to persist and maintain a steady level of involvement even when her work seems *routine*; 2) provides her with knowledge about and access to resources *within* the organization; and 3) reinforces her commitment to her *role* as an advocate.

As each of these three connections between social support and efficacy are discussed, specific hypotheses about the expression of support in the two organizations will be presented. The following discussion is outlined in Table 2.

1. Social Support Networks Function to Sustain Persistence

The role of social support in enhancing persistence is expected to vary with whether the advocacy task involves dealing primarily with crises, conflicts, or fluctuating demands (FSO) or with carrying out ongoing institutionally sanctioned work (VO). The task of persisting through crises or conflicts is expected to require active buffering; persisting through more routine work is expected to require reinforcement for the small victories and for working toward long term goals. Hypotheses about the different types of social support that enhance the persistence of FSO and VO advocacy committee members come out of differences in the nature of the advocacy tasks in the two organizations.

The challenge for FSO's advocates has primarily been to help the organization become respected and financially stable. Doing so has involved dealing with crises and conflicts within the organization surrounding finances, personnel, and policy development. Social support is expected to enhance the persistence of board members by buffering stress and facilitating a quick response to the crisis situation or event. Although the literature on the stress buffering role of social support has not typically delineated the specific *types* of support that will buffer stress (Cohen & McKay, 1981), it seems reasonable to expect that increased accessibility of network members and a willingness to call upon one's work network for help could facilitate dealing with the stressful job demands.

Women involved in VO deal with a different set of challenges with respect to persistence. Their task is to carry on a tradition of advocacy via an ongoing committee in the organization. This work may seem routine and, as a result, the participants may not be energized for ongoing work. Social support that facilitates the persistence of the women on the advocacy committee is expected to validate the importance of the advocacy work and to remind them about *why* they are doing the work (i.e., about the long term goals). This idea was operationally defined as the number of core network members who show interest in the work, ask about how the work is going, and/or share an understanding of long term goals. It also was predicted that the more VO members the advocate has in her "core" social support network, the more she would receive ongoing support for her involvement in advocacy.

2. Social Support Networks Function to Yield Access to Multiple Resources

The way in which a social support network can yield access to multiple resources to facilitate advocacy work is expected to vary according to the accessibility of resources. Especially relevant to the women in this study is whether the necessary resources need to be mobilized from sources outside of the organization (FSO) or whether the majority of needed resources are available from within the organization (VO).

Table 2 Social support and efficacy in two organizations: An hypothesized framework

Social support will enhance efficacy by	Social support will enhance efficacy of the FSO advocate by	Social support will enhance efficacy of the VO advocate by
I. Enhancing persistence	Enabling her to persist through *crises* within the organization	Enabling her to persist and maintain a steady level of involvement even when the work seems *routine*
	H1a: Effective FSO advocates will perceive work network members as more accessible. b: Effective FSO advocates will be more likely to utilize work network support.	H2a: Effective VO advocates will have a greater proportion of organization members in their core network. b: Effective VO advocates will have more core network members who express interest in their advocacy work.
II. Yielding access to multiple resources	Providing her with resources from *outside* the organization that enable her to participate in a manner useful to the organization	Providing her with knowledge about, and access to, resources *within* the organization
	H3a: Effective FSO advocates will have lower density core networks. b: Effective FSO advocates will have more connections to people outside the organization who have access to resources.	H4a: Effective VO advocates will perceive high status organization members as more likely to help them gain access to needed resources. b: Effective VO advocates will have more contact with high status organization members.
III. Reinforcing commitment to the advocacy work in the organization	Reinforcing her commitment to the *goals* of the organization	Reinforcing her commitment to her *role* as an advocate
	H5a: Effective FSO advocates will perceive more support for their beliefs about organizational goals. b: Effective FSO advocates will have more contact with nonadvocate organization members. c: Effective FSO advocates will have more nonadvocate organization members in their work network.	H6a: Effective VO advocates will perceive more support for their beliefs about advocacy issues. b: Effective VO advocates will have more contact with advocacy committee members.

The FSO does not have ready access to such resources as money, volunteers, and training. The organization provides advocates with a cause and an identified need, but the role of generating and gathering resources for running the organization and advocating for battered women belongs to the board. Thus, a primary function of social support networks for FSO advocates is to identify and mobilize multiple resources from throughout the community. It was, therefore, hypothesized that effective advocates would have social support networks that are broad, diverse, and that tap into a large variety of *community* resources. The more effective board member was hypothesized to have a low density network and to have a large number of connections to community members who can provide task-oriented assistance and/or access to new information or social contacts relevant to the goals of the organization.

In contrast to the FSO, VO is relatively rich in formal resources. For example, the organization provides the advocacy committee with both financial resources and training opportunities. Due to the organization's history of involvement in the community, the organization also offers advocates a considerable amount of credibility within the community. Social support that facilitates advocacy work at VO is expected to yield access to *organizational* resources and, more specifically, to be characterized by links to people in the organization who control the resources (e.g., "high status" members such as officers and committee chair people). Thus, the more effective advocate committee member is hypothesized to have more ties with those organization members who have control over resources.

3. Social Support Networks Function to Reinforce Commitment to Advocacy Work

Social support networks potentially enhance an advocate's efficacy by reinforcing her commitment to *both* the advocacy role *and* the goals of the organization.

FSO's advocates have taken on the task of identifying and mobilizing community resources out of a commitment to women's issues and out of a commitment to advocacy work. Most of these women became involved in the organization as a result of being recruited for the role of advocate. In a sense, these women's initial loyalty is to the role of advocate and their secondary commitment is to the organization. When they leave the role, most women predict that they will also leave the organization. Social support is expected to enhance the efficacy of advocates' work by increasing their identification with this particular oganization. The amount of contact between advocates and members of the organization is expected to facilitate commitment to the organization by increasing identification with and knowledge about the day-to-day workings of the organization. The extent to which board members feel an ideological identification with the organization is also seen as relevant to their commitment. Thus, the more effective board members were expected to have more contact with general organizational members and to perceive others as sharing their views about the purpose of the organization.

Women on the VO advocacy committee are members of the organization first and then members of the advocacy committee. They not only were members of the organization before they assumed the specialized role, but they also typically continue as members of the organization after they have moved on from their advocacy tasks to other commitments within VO. In order to facilitate commitment to the advocacy role, it was predicted that social support in VO would need to re-inforce and integrate their identification with the advocacy function with their sense of membership in the organization. Support from the advocacy group itself, in terms of frequent contact and as reciprocally supportive relationships with group members, was expected to solidify this commitment. Receiving support from others for their stance on specific advocacy issues was also expected to enhance commitment to the advocacy role and thus be associated with increased efficacy. Thus, VO advocates who have more contact with other advocacy committee mem-bers and who perceive support for their views on advocacy issues were hypothesized to be more effective members.

RESULTS

As the previous section indicated, there are three major themes around which the hypothesized relationships between social support, advocacy and organizational characteristics are organized. The results will be presented and discussed according to these same three topics. Table 2 summarizes the hypotheses, and Table 3 sum-marizes the results. The discussion will only focus upon those results which report correlations above 0.40, in order to reduce a premature assumption of an empirical connection between the two variables. Given the case study design, the small N and the socioeconomic differences, it is important to remember that all results are speculative and proposed as topics for future defining research.

Table 3 Correlates of efficacy

	F.S.O.	V.O.
I. Persistence		
H1a. Accessibility of support (FSO)	0.85	*
b. Likelihood of using support (FSO)	*	*
H2a. Proportion of organization members in core network (VO)	*	*
b. Interest in advocacy work expressed by core support network (VO)	−0.62	0.60
II. Resources		
H3a. Core support network density (FSO)	*	*
H4a. High status work network members' help in gaining access to resources (VO)	*	0.76
b. Amount of contact with high status organization members (VO)	*	0.88
III. Commitment		
H5a. Amount of contact with nonadvocate organization members (FSO)	−0.73	*
b. Number of nonadvocate organization members in work network (FSO)	−0.45	*
c. Support for beliefs about the goals of the organization (FSO)	0.55	*
H6a. Support for beliefs about advocacy (VO)	0.66	*
b. Amount of contact with advocacy committee members (VO)	*	*

*Correlation ≤ 0.40.

1. Social Support and Persistence

In support of the notion that a FSO advocate's efficacy is related to support that enables her to deal with crises, efficacy was found to be highly correlated with accessibility of coworkers ($r = 0.85$). Whereas at VO the correlation was close to zero ($r = 0.07$). An advocate's willingness to utilize support from coworkers was not highly correlated with efficacy in either organization (VO, $r = 0.33$; FSO, $r = 0.29$).

These results indicate that FSO advocates consider their network members easily accessible and yet do not request their support. It is as though the comfort and security of knowing that people are available is more important than the actual emotional or instrumental support they might offer. The stressful nature of the task at FSO is perhaps "buffered" by knowing that coworkers are standing by. This finding is in contrast to VO where knowledge of the availability of coworkers seems to have no relationship to efficacy. Given the lower level of crisis work at VO, this dimension may not be salient for VO advocates.

As predicted, efficacy of VO advocacy committee members was correlated with the amount of perceived support from core support network members for their advocacy work ($r = 0.60$). Interestingly, at FSO perceived interest of core network members in one's advocacy work was negatively correlated with efficacy ($r = -0.62$). The proportion of network members in one's core network was not highly correlated with efficacy at either VO ($r = 0.19$) or at FSO ($r = 0.08$). These results lend at least partial support for the notion that effective VO advocates experience more validation for their work from family and friends than their less effective counter parts and perhaps as a result feel the advocacy task to be better integrated into their lives.

In sum, some of the hypotheses generated about persistence in the two settings were supported and some were not. The constellation of correlations thus lends only tentative support for the specific initial expectations about what types of support would be congruent with efficacy. In general terms, it appears important that effective FSO members have a sense that support is available even though they might not be inclined to use it frequently. The lack of inclination toward asking for support and the negative correlation between efficacy and perceptions of interest of core network members suggests that reliance upon oneself is important for efficacy at FSO. Efficacy at VO on the other hand, is positively related to perceived interest on the part of others in one's work. As predicted, these findings suggest that the more effective VO advocacy committee members experience more validation for the importance of advocacy work than the less effective members.

2. Social Support and Access to Resources

The results do not clearly indicate that efficacy at FSO was associated with resources gained from friends outside the organization or the variety of distinct friendship circles (density)—both of which were expected to reflect access to resources outside the organization. The lack of correlation goes contrary to prediction. However, as suggested by Granovetter (1973), casual acquaintances with whom people have infrequent contact may be the key providers of resources. Particularly given the varied and crisis nature of FSO's organizational needs, it may be that informal connections are the critical links to community resources. Information about such connections is not reflected by the present measures of core and work networks which tend to tap more stable, close or long term associations.

As predicted, efficacy at VO was associated with access to the resources available within the organization. More specifically, it was found that efficacy was highly correlated with the amount of contact an advocate has with high status organization members ($r = 0.88$) and with their perception of the likelihood of receiving aid or support from these organization members when needed ($r = 0.76$). Neither of these measures correlated with efficacy at FSO.

The results provide partial support for the hypothesized relationship between organizational setting, social support and efficacy at VO. It appears that efficacy for VO advocates is indeed related to their access to resources internal to the organization. The relationship between efficacy at FSO and access to resources is more difficult to assess given the limitations of available measures.

3. Social Support and Commitment to Advocacy Work with the Organization

For FSO advocates, there is indeed a correlation between efficacy and perceived support for one's beliefs about the goals of the organization ($r = 0.55$)—in contrast to VO where no such correlation was found ($r = 0.07$). Indicators of an FSO advocate's integration into the organization, however, did not correlate with efficacy in the manner predicted. In fact, the number of work network members not on the board ($r = -0.73$) and the average amount of contact with these nonboard organizational members ($r = -0.45$) were negatively associated with effective advocacy. It may be that since advocacy is an identified function at FSO, ideological comitment to the total organization is more important while indices of integration (e.g., time spent with volunteers) detract from one's time or energy for the advocacy function per se.

Contrary to hypotheses, the amount of contact with advocacy committee members was not associated with effectiveness at VO ($r = 0.15$) nor were advocates' perceptions of support for their views on advocacy issues ($r = 0.19$). Whereas at FSO perceived support for beliefs about specific advocacy issues was highly correlated with efficacy ($r = 0.66$).

With respect to the topic of commitment and the manner in which it is facilitated by support networks, the results suggest a need for revision of the hypotheses. It appears that effective advocacy at FSO is correlated with perceived support for one's beliefs, both about the goals of the organization and about specific advocacy issues. Whereas the notion of ideologically based commitment appears less relevant to the advocate at VO. That is, commitment at VO may be more related to the cohesiveness of the advocacy group and to a loyalty between the individuals involved than to ideological beliefs as is the case at FSO.

SOCIAL SUPPORT AND EFFECTIVE ADVOCACY: SOME ADDITIONAL FINDINGS

In addition to hypotheses about the relationship between social support, advocacy and organizational setting, some questions about the support received in each setting were assessed on the premise that the more support an advocate receives, the more effective she will be. Seven types of support were defined: 1) task oriented assistance, 2) access to new and diverse information, 3) access to social contacts, 4) emotional support, 5) specific and informed feedback, 6) communication of shared expectations and a shared world view, and 7) challenging support. Advocates rated their coworkers on each of these types of support. The resulting correlations between support ratings and efficacy ratings are reported in Table 4.

At FSO, effective advocacy appears to be correlated with only one of the categories of support measured: communication of shared expectations and a shared world view. No correlations greater than 0.40 were observed between any other types of support and effective advocacy at FSO, whereas at VO, efficacy was correlated, to varying extents, with all the subcategories of support as well as being quite highly correlated ($r = 0.86$) with a summary measure of total amount of support received.

SUMMARY OF RESULTS AND DISCUSSION

More effective advocates at FSO consider network support from coworkers more easily accessible even though these same women are not necessarily more apt to call upon coworkers for support. Ideological support—in the form of support for beliefs about the goals of the organization and about the advocacy task as well as sharing a world view—is consistently associated with efficacy. Shared ideology stands out as the critical type of support associated with effective advocacy at FSO.

In contrast, effective advocacy at VO is correlated with a broad range of supports from family, friends and coworkers. The more effective advocates experience more support for their advocacy activities from their family and friends and also experience multiple types of supportive exchanges with their coworkers in the advocacy activities. They also appear to be more connected to the organization as a whole such that they have greater access to resources available within the organization, e.g., through their associations with high status organization members. Instrumental and emotional support as well as shared views of the world are all associated with efficacy at VO.

The fact that ideology is important in the work at FSO should come as no surprise. The goals and identity of the organization are based on a feminist ideology. Shared beliefs and a commitment to women's issues were typically reasons the women accepted or sought advocacy positions within this particular organization. However, it is less clear why a sense of ideological support would differentiate between the efficacy of the members. That is, why should *efficacy* be *correlated* with ideological support within this organization?

Table 4 Work network support and efficacy

Total support	F.S.O.	V.O.
Total support	*	0.86
Task-oriented assistance	*	0.41
Access to new and diverse information	*	0.56
Access to social contacts	*	0.85
Emotional support	*	0.63
Specific and informed feedback	*	0.52
Communication of shared expectations and shared world view	0.54	0.92
Challenging support	*	0.70

*Correlation ⩽ 0.40.

It is as if shared beliefs go a long way to aide the women in carrying out their work effectively. It is possible that shared beliefs are a sort of insurance policy: the greater one's sense of ideological support, the less relevant the need for either instrumental or emotional support. This may be particularly true for the types of women who chose to become involved in a feminist organization, while at the same time the importance of ideological support may also be intensified by the marginality of the organization in the community. Another interpretation is that for the effective advocate within FSO, the very act of advocacy increases her sense of ideological support.

The advocacy task of VO members does not revolve around a shared ideology nor did the members join on the basis of a highly salient political belief system. These factors most likely contribute to the lack of correlation between efficacy and support for beliefs about advocacy and the goals of the organization. The positive correlation between efficacy and support for one's view of the world may be indicative of the general notion that shared personal values increase the likelihood of social interaction (Cherniss, 1979). The importance of being socially integrated into VO is a consistent theme throughout our findings (e.g., through connections to high status organization members or through the receipt of support from advocacy coworkers). Effective advocacy is correlated with receiving all types of support from coworkers from task-oriented assistance to challenging support. Given the marginality of the advocacy task *within* VO it may thus be more essential that the advocacy group be interpersonally responsive and supportive of members.

In FSO where advocacy is critical to the survival of the organization it appears less critical that advocates be actively integrated into the organization through emotional or instrumental sharing. The importance of their task and their shared political beliefs may be integration enough. It does appear important that they feel that women within the organization are available to them, reflecting a sense of goodwill, a cooperative spirit, and shared commitment. This is so even though they do not actually call on them for practical types of support.

PRACTICAL IMPLICATIONS

In terms of advocacy, the requirements for social support appear to be dictated by the quality and quantity of resources available to advocates both inside their organizations and in their lives outside the organization. The characteristics of the organization, the structure of the advocacy role and the salience of advocacy in one's life activities *all* may have mediating effects on what is needed in terms of social support.

To facilitate advocacy work at FSO, the organization could take advantage of activities and resources which encourage the continued development of ideological commitments. The continued refinement of beliefs about the mission and the organization can potentially affect the effectiveness of advocates. If these beliefs erode or become less salient for persons in advocacy roles, the quality of their work would be expected to diminish.

A critical challenge for ideologically based organizations like FSO is to facilitate the expression of beliefs while allowing individual members to develop their own unique personal perspectives. An ideologically based organization may inadvertently support conformity, or a sort of "group think," and thus push out those members who may approach tasks differently. The risk is that the organization will have a lower personal resource base and be limited in attaining its goals. The challenge is to sanction and develop a clear ideology without becoming myopic. From a preventive point of view, the organization can benefit by focusing on how social support mechanisms can be generated and adapted to neutralize any conformity pressure while encouraging the clear expression of the differentiated ideologies.

For the individual advocate working at FSO, it may be important to integrate advocacy with other activities in her life. Given the intensity and level of involvement of the advocacy work, the FSO advocate may lack the time and energy she needs to carry out other life tasks. The advocacy work needs to be ideologically nourished, supported and replenished while also either being connected with other life tasks or allowing a woman access to outside people and resources which help meet her more personal needs. Support for outside activities could reduce her sense of marginality in her work and strengthen her core identity.

It appears that in VO, where there are clear mechanisms for doing the work and where there is a very rich resource base, the advocate's challenge is to integrate her advocacy work into a broader context. At VO the organization's leaders might enhance the effectiveness of the advocacy work by facilitating the advocate's sense of integration into the organization and aiding her access to high status members of the organization. The advocate in this type of setting seems to need to be plugged into the primary activities of the organization and may need to feel she has a personal impact upon the host organization as a result of her advocacy work. A potential danger is that she might feel that she is doing work that is not really acknowledged by her organization or that she is simply carrying out the preplanned intentions of the organization without much option for the expression of the advocate's own autonomy.

There also appears to be a clear value at VO on one's friends being involved with the advocate's work through their expression of interest, emotional or instrumental support. It may be that since the advocacy task is marginal to the organization, there is an increased risk of isolation which generates more desire to involve friends. Thus, it would seem appropriate for organizational leaders to applaud and acknowledge the support that the advocate receives from her friends and her family.

A danger of integrating advocacy work even more directly with personal networks is to remove the demands on the women to set and clarify their personal priorities. The risk is that the advocate can become so well "integrated" that she looses the opportunity to express explicitly individual needs. She can unwittingly take on a "super woman" role as she tries to do everything well. Organizations like VO allow women to express and develop competencies while reminaing in relatively traditional roles. Such organizations can benefit from focusing on how social support mechanisms can challenge women to clarify their particular values and priorities.

In sum, the report of this preliminary work suggests the importance of developing a diversified view of the relationship between social support and effective advocacy. Social support that reinforces beliefs and values about advocacy work is germane in one setting, whereas support that functions to enhance one's integration into her organization may be adaptive in another. Each type of support clearly can have both positive and negative impacts on advocacy work, and the development of a multi-faceted view of organizational impact on advocacy performance can have theoretical and practical benefits.

REFERENCES

Bond, M. A. *Social support and efficacy in advocacy roles: A comparative study of four women's organizations.* Unpublished doctoral dissertation. University of Oregon, 1983.

Broverman, I. K., Vogel, S. R., Broverman, D. M., Clarkson, F. E., & Rosenkrantz, D. S. Sex role stereotypes: A current appraisal. *Journal of Social Issues*, 1972, *28*, 59–78.

Carveth, W. B. & Gottlieb, B. H. The measurement of social support and its relation to stress. *Canadian Journal of Behavioral Science*, 1979, *2*.

Cherniss, C. *Staff burnout: Job stress in human services.* Beverly Hills, CA: Sage Publications, 1980.

Cobb, S. Social support as a moderator of life stress. *Psychosomatic Medicine*, 1976, *38*, 300–314.

Cohen, S. & McGay, G. *Social support, stress and the buffering hypotheses: Naturalistic studies.* Unpublished manuscript. Department of Psychology, University of Oregon, 1981.

Glaser, B. G. *Theoretical sensitivity.* Mill Valley, CA: The Sociology Press, 1978.

Gottlieb, B. H. (Ed), *Social networks and social support.* Beverly Hills, CA: Sage Publications, 1981.

Gottlieb, B. & Todd, D. Characterizing and promoting social support in natural settings. In R. F. Muñoz, L. R. Snowden, and J. G. Kelly (eds.), *Social and psychological research in community settings.* San Francisco: Jossey-Bass, 1979.

Gottlieb, B. H. Lay influences on the utilization and provision of health services: A review. *Canadian Psychological Review*, 1976, *17*, 126–136.

Granovetter, M. The strength of weak ties. *American Journal of Sociology*, 1973, *78*, 1360–1380.

Harragan, B. L. *Games mother never taught you.* New York: Warner Book Edition, 1977.

Heller, K. The effects of social support: Prevention and treatment implications. In A. P. Goldstein and F. H. Kanfer (eds.), *Maximizing treatment gains.* New York: Academic Press, Inc., 1979.

Hirsch, B. Natural support systems and coping with major life changes. *American Journal of Community Psychology*, 1980, *8*, 159–172.

Johnson, P. Women and power: Toward a theory of effectiveness. *Journal of Social Issues*, 1976, *32*, 99–110.

Kanter, R. M. *Men and women of the corporation.* New York: Basic Books, Inc., 1977.

Katz, D. & Kahn, R. L. *The social psychology of organizations.* New York: John Wiley and Sons, 1978.

Kelly, J. G. Towards an ecological conception of preventive interventions. In J. W. Carter (ed.), *Research contributions from psychology to community mental health.* New York: Behavioral Publications, Inc., 1968.

Kieffer, C. H. *The emergence of empowerment: Patterns and process in the evolution of participatory competence amongst lower income individuals.* Unpublished doctoral dissertation. University of Michigan, 1981.

Keiffer, C. H. *The emergence of citizen empowerment: Research findings and development implications.* Paper presented at National Conference on Lifelong Learning, University of Maryland, February 6, 1980.

Mitchell, R. E. & Trickett, E. J. Task force report: Social networks as mediators of social support. *Community Mental Health Journal*, 1980, *16*, 27–44.

Muñoz, R. F., Snowden, L. R., & Kelly, J. G. *Social and psychological research in community settings.* San Francisco: Jossey Bass, 1979.

Riger, S. & Gordon, M. T. *Dilemmas in the practice of feminist research.* Paper presented at the American Psychological Association, Los Angeles, August 1981.

Stein, L. Male and female: The doctor-nurse game. In J. P. Spradley and D. W. McMurdy (eds.), *Conformity and conflict: Readings in cultural anthropology.* Boston: Little and Brown, 1971.

Tedeschi, J. T. *The social influence processes.* Chicago: Aldine, 1972.

Tolsdorf, C. C. Social networks, support, and coping: An exploratory study. *Family Process*, 1976, *15*, 407–417.

Trahey, J. *On women and power.* New York: Avon Books, 1977.

Trickett, E. J., Kelly, J. G., & Vincent, T. The spirit of ecological inquiry in community research. In E. Susskind and D. C. Klein, *Knowledge-building in community psychology: Approaches to Research.* New York: Plenum, 1984.

Trickett, E. J., Kelly, J. G., & Todd, D. M. The social environment of the high school: Guidelines from individual change and organizational redevelopment. In S. Golann and C. Eisdorfer (eds.), *Handbook of community mental health*. New York: Appleton Century-Crofts,
1972.

Wilcox, B. L. The role of social support in adjustment to marital disruption: A network analysis.
In B. F. Gottlieb (ed.), *Social networks and social support in community mental health*.
Beverly Hills: Sage, 1981a.

Wilcox, B. L. *Assessing social support networks: A conceptual and methodological analysis*.
Unpublished manuscript, University of Virginia, Charlottesville, VA: 1981b.

Willems, E. P. & Raush, H. L. (Eds.), *Naturalistic viewpoints in psychological research*. New
York: Holt, Rinehart and Winston, 1969.

III

PSYCHOLOGICAL PROBLEMS AND WOMEN

We have thus far reported several social problem areas for women. It is interesting to note a recurring theme for prevention and intervention of these problems: the presence of a strong social support system. In some of the earlier theoretical chapters, a support network was seen to be a source of strength for the community builder and for the black woman. The lack of a social support system, and the lack of a mentor and role model, in particular, were seen as hindrances to the individual woman seeking career achievement. Again in the section on social problems, a support system was offered as an important ingredient of prevention. The divorced woman's adjustment was seen to be easier with adequate social supports; the woman less fearful of crime had a secure sense of belonging to her neighborhood; and the woman advocate was most successful when she possessed a strong supportive social network.

The aim in this section of the book is to examine specific psychological problems with which women may contend, and to explore the adaptiveness of coping mechanisms used by women. The intent is not to focus on deviant women, but to explore the social and environmental factors related to these psychological problems.

Chapter 11 addresses a special aspect of the most common psychological diagnosis for women—depression. There are approximately two depressive females to every one such male patient in the United States, and many have suggested that symptoms of depression may be considered as an intensification of what were traditionally considered normal female characteristics, such as dependency, helplessness, and passivity. Furthermore, the intensification of a traditional sex role has typically been more tolerated by society than the reversal of it. In fact, some mental health professionals have defined adaptation to sex roles, i.e., female dependency, for example, as the ultimate criterion for female mental health. It is not surprising, then, that a woman's complaints of depressive symptoms have not always been taken seriously and may even have been encouraged.

Atkinson and Rickel concentrate on one type of depression unique to women. Postpartum depression is a complex but little investigated topic of popular and professional literature. The popular literature cautions new mothers that they may experience the "baby blues," a mild depression, following the birth of their infant, but the standard device is to accept these "blues" as natural. An examination of the professional literature reveals much disagreement, not only in the etiology of postpartum depression, but also in the progression of the phenomenon. Many questions regarding postpartum depression are due to the lack of good experimentally controlled research. And perhaps the dearth of research focusing on postpartum depression stems from an attitude among professionals about women and depression in general, an attitude that parallels the one regarding postpartum depression found in the popular literature, i.e., that postpartum depression is a natural concomitant of childbirth which, if treated with benign neglect, will remit with time.

Atkinson and Rickel review the literature on postpartum adjustment and in so doing delineate the individual and socioenvironmental variables that contribute to this depression. Emphasis is placed on the social context of the acute crisis of caring for a newborn infant. Using theoretical premises similar to Mulvey and Dohrenwend in Chapter 12, Atkinson and Rickel conceptualize the process of postpartum depression as being a stressful life event that may be interpreted from classical theories of depression, viz., Beck, Seligman, and Lewinsohn. The specific theoretical model presented is unique not only for heuristic purposes, but also as a model for prevention and crisis intervention.

Chapter 12 by Mulvey and Dohrenwend deals with gender differences in response to stressful life events. Environmentally induced stresses as they relate to women and men in urban as well as rural settings are considered.

Mulvey and Dohrenwend, unlike past researchers who have investigated sex differences by focusing on personality traits that tend to dichotomize and define the *differences* between the sexes, have objectively measured men's and women's lives in such a way as to yield both similarities and differences. They pursue this goal through the measurement of stressful life events, which are defined as disruptive occurrences in the usual day-to-day patterns of activities.

Using data from a stressful life events measure, the authors challenge some commonly held beliefs regarding differences between sexes. Previous literature on gender roles has suggested that women's lives are less varied and less meaningful than men's and particularly, that women perceive themselves as being helpless while men are "in control." Mulvey and Dohrenwend reveal data that both dispute these ideas and illustrate the inadequacy of a simple male-female dichotomy in explaining sex differences. Rather a more complex interaction of gender, marital status, and age must be used to understand differences in perceived control over stressful life events.

This chapter illustrates the value of data-based research programs in understanding psychological problems. As Mulvey and Dohrenwend's research reveals, the meaning and influences of gender should be studied in the context of the complex social structure in which women and men go through various life stages, rather than in the context of an intrapsychic developmental process of personality change associated with natural gender differences. The interface of psychological and social factors seen in earlier chapters are again apparent in Chapter 12.

In Chapter 13 we are presented with a discussion of psychology's most often used type of crisis intervention—psychotherapy. "Differential Needs and Treatment Approaches for Women in Psychotherapy" begins by stating that there is no such thing as *"Women* in psychotherapy"; rather, *individuals* enter psychotherapy. Lorian and Broughan debunk the "uniformity myth," touted by many who extend this premise to viewing all women with psychological problems as manifesting symptoms of a sick society, i.e., a male-chauvinistic world. They decry the uselessness of male therapists who can never really treat female issues. The authors of this chapter, in addressing the mental health professional, emphasize the need for careful individual diagnostic work-ups that go beyond political rhetoric to the individual patient's needs.

Based on experience from their clinical practices, these therapists describe some of the various types of female clients they have seen. These categories are not meant to label or classify clients, but rather are offered to show the diversity of problems women present in therapy. The "Lolita Syndrome" and the "Empty Next Syndrome" are two examples.

Of special interest to professional therapists and other mental health workers is the authors' exposition of various treatment modes for therapy: individual, group, marital/conjoint-marital, and family therapy. The authors also present a variety of treatment variables that encompass issues of not only mode of treatment, but who should treat. Having had extensive experience as male-female team therapists, Lorian and Broughan conclude their chapter with an explication of the team approach. Women in therapy are viewed from the female therapist's perspective, the male therapist's perspective, and from the male-female therapists' team viewpoint. The insight offered by these practicing clinicians is most illuminating.

Bry in Chapter 14 addresses the problem of substance abuse by women. While dispelling the misconception that women's abuse of alcohol is now converging with men's higher abuse rate, this chapter points out the prevalence of alcohol abuse among women and the unique consequences for women.

Of all substances abused, alcohol is the most frequently misused among women, with an estimated seven percent incidence. In relationship to men, women abuse alcohol less, in a ratio of 1 woman to every 4–5 men. In contrast with abuse of alcohol, women use psychotropic drugs (tranquilizers, stimulants, and sedatives) more frequently than men. This finding does not separate out use from abuse, however.

Bry details many of the serious consequences to women who abuse drugs. These include reproductive disorders, pregnancy and childbirth problems, fetal and neonatal difficulties, and parenting deficiencies. With such grave consequences possible, investigation of the etiology of substance abuse is critical, and the author recounts the quest for the variables which would explain the "addictive personality." Various theoretical models have been proposed with recent research suggestive of a complex, multidimensional model unique for each individual.

Although this idiographic approach to understanding substance abuse may be most accurate, its implications for treatment are staggering, suggesting that no one treatment program will be found. Lest we become too discouraged at the awesome task before us, Bry discusses some conditions or precursors that are known to increase the probability of substance abuse. This knowledge, combined with knowledge of linking processes and effective interventions, will perhaps eventually enable society to reduce abuse. This chapter provides the reader with the most recent knowledge regarding these important psychosocial precursors of substance abuse and the potential processes which link these precursors to substance abuse. The chapter ends with a thorough exposition of many avenues to prevention, both primary and secondary, for those seen to be at high risk.

Chapter 15, by Gatz, Pearson, and Fuentes, focuses on the mental health problems of older women. As the authors suggest, the 1980s may well be remembered as the decade of the older woman. Older women, especially those 75 and older, are the fastest growing portion of the U.S. population. Furthermore, more than 2.7 million older women live below the poverty line, with older women living alone overrepresented among this group. This large, growing, and economically disadvantaged segment of our population is currently emerging from the invisibility it had been accorded in past decades.

Until recently, older women have been neglected in academic literature, since most aging research has paid little systematic attention to sex differences, while research on sex differences has rarely extended through the latter part of the lifespan. Hence, programs and policies designed to meet the needs of this growing population may well be based on belief rather than data.

Gatz, Pearson, and Fuentes in Chapter 15 use a lifespan developmental perspective as a framework for organizing ideas considered to be helpful in conceptualizing older women's psychosocial worlds. Myths (emphasizing disadvantage and deterioration) and countermyths are presented, followed by a summary of the current factual data on the topic. Some of the myths are: "older women are plagued with sickness," "older women are sexless," and "older women are poor, dumb, and ugly." Finally, the relationship of the myths and countermyths to mental health is discussed. The authors point out the necessity of designing appropriate interventions for older women, since many past traditional treatment models have been of limited usefulness. What is needed are several diverse approaches to a diverse group which is just now beginning to be both acknowledged and understood. The final portion of Chapter 15 is replete with a multitude of such intervention strategies.

We conclude this volume with Chapter 16, which presents new directions for women beyond the 1980s.

11

Depression in Women

The Postpartum Experience

A. Kathleen Atkinson and Annette U. Rickel
Wayne State University

INTRODUCTION

Both the popular and professional literature acknowledge that postpartum depression is the most common emotional problem following childbirth. The popular literature cautions new mothers that they may experience the "baby blues," a mild depression, following the birth of their infant. While this literature may suggest ways to relieve the depression (get a babysitter, talk to other new mothers, take walks), the standard advice is that the new mother should accept these "blue" feelings as a common, natural occurrence after childbirth and that this depression will pass in time, once the woman has adapted to her new role as a mother.

The professional literature on postpartum depression is more complex. In the professional literature, there is disagreement over every aspect of postpartum depression—its incidence, symptoms, course, severity, and even its existence as specifically "postpartum." Questions about postpartum depression persist due to lack of good experimental, controlled studies of women during pregnancy and postpartum. Perhaps research focusing specifically on postpartum depression is lacking due to an attitude among professionals that parallels what is found in the popular literature, i.e., that postpartum depression is a natural companion of childbirth that treated with benign neglect will remit with time.

HISTORICAL BACKGROUND

The first clinical description of postpartum mental illness was written by Hippocrates in the fourth century B.C.; however, little was added to Hippocrates' speculations until the 19th century (Hamilton, 1962). In 1858, Marcé reported on 310 cases of mental illness associated with childbearing in his *Traité de la Folie des Femmes Enceintes*.

The majority of the early literature on postpartum mental illness was concerned with psychotic reactions, many presumably due to toxic conditions (Seager, 1960). With improved medical techniques, the number of postpartum disturbances obviously attributable to physiological variables decreased and investigators became interested in other possible etiologies—heredity, personality, environmental—and in a wider range of postpartum disturbance (Eastman & Hellman, 1966).

In 1945, Helene Deutsch's *Psychology of Women* was published. In this work, Deutsch presented an analysis of the impact of childbearing on women in a psychoanalytic framework. Following her work, psychoanalysts began addressing themselves to the dynamics of pregnancy, childbirth and motherhood (Benedek, 1952; Bibring, 1959, 1961). Their writings seemed to stimulate interest in postpartum adjustment and began a trend in the study of postpartum disturbance via case studies and theorizing.

Hamilton (1962) states that prior to 1961, the literature on postpartum problems does not have a single paper in which the conclusions drawn were proven by classic experimental methods. The following literature review finds that since Hamilton's monograph, the literature on postpartum disturbance has been improved only slightly. Many of the articles appearing in medical and social science journals after 1960 continue to be descriptive and impressionistic. While more studies, both experimental and quasi-experimental in design, have been executed, they tend to be unreliable due to inadequate experimental control.

In the late 1960s, more experimental work on postpartum disturbance began appearing. The increased interest in postpartum depression specifically seems to coincide with the renewed interest in the 1960s in depression in general. Much of this research was carried out by medical personnel and emphasized physiological variables, perhaps following the trend set by earlier investigations of the toxic postpartum psychoses. Many of these studies focused on the immediate postpartum period when physiological effects are most likely to be seen. Other work in the 1960s was based on psychoanalytic theory and attempted to investigate personality variables. A notable exception to this trend to examine physiological and personality variables was a large research project directed by R. E. Gordon, which focused on the impact of social stress on postpartum adjustment (Gordon et al., 1965).

Following the lead of Gordon and his associates, a few studies have recently been undertaken to examine social and environmental factors in postpartum adjustment. A large scale, longitudinal project, *Psychological Aspects of a First Pregnancy and Early Postnatal Adaption* (Shereshefsky & Yarrow, 1973), has been published. In addition, recent doctoral theses appearing in Dissertation Abstracts reflect a trend to examine attitudinal, social and environmental variables associated with the pregnancy and postpartum experience (e.g., Tauber, 1974; Gladieux, 1975; Atkinson, 1979).

Still, systematic, controlled research on postpartum problems remains limited. Most of the current studies are exploratory, and investigate a large number of variables in a small sample of subjects, enabling only tentative conclusions to be drawn.

DEFINING POSTPARTUM DEPRESSION

A major reason for the tentative and vague nature of the research on postpartum problems is researchers' lack of consensus on how postpartum depression is to be defined. The range of disturbance labeled postpartum depression is as great as the range of disturbance considered depression in the clinical literature on depressive illness, from psychotic depression and depressive reaction to the "blues." The controversy over whether postpartum depression is continuous in degree parallels the clinical literature's argument on depressive illness.

Depending on their research interests, authors settle individually on how severe the depression must be in order to be included as "postpartum depression" in their study. Some authors do not address themselves to the problem of delineating their criteria at all. Rather than look at specific postpartum adjustment problems, they use gross measures of "emotional adjustment" or "disturbance" (e.g., Kaij & Nilsson, 1972). Thus, postpartum depression is lumped, along with other emotional problems of greater or lesser degree, under the general heading "postpartum emotional disturbance." The validity of studying all forms of postpartum disturbance as a single group has not been demonstrated experimentally and is questionable. One would expect significant differences between subjects manifesting different forms of postpartum disturbance and different degrees of disturbance within those forms. Use of gross categories of disturbance may produce misleading results due to various interactions between different characteristics of the various types of disturbances.

INCIDENCE

A good deal of the literature on postpartum depression is concerned with incidence rates. Studies of the incidence of postpartum depression have sought to determine whether postpartum depression differs from depression occurring at times other than postpartum and/or the degree of "added risk" of depression following childbirth. While these studies were some of the first to shed light on the problem of postpartum depression, a review of the incidence rate literature illustrates the definitional and methodological problems that permeate the literature on postpartum depression.

Incidence rates reported for postpartum depression range from less than 1 percent to 80 percent (Pitt, 1968) depending upon the population studied, how depression is defined and how depression is determined (e.g., self-report or clinical interview). Hemphill (1952) estimated the incidence of mental illness (severe depressions included) in 81,000 women delivered in Bristol, England, between 1938 and 1948, to be 1.4 per 1000. Pugh et al. (1963) studied the relation of childbearing to mental illness among Massachusetts women and found an added risk of admission to mental hospitals of 3.0 to 3.6 per 1000 women for the first six weeks after delivery. Paffenberger and McCabe (1966) found that the rate of mental illness for the first six months postpartum approximated that for non-childbearing women but was characterized by an "explosive peak" in the first month following delivery.

A more accurate picture of the extent of postpartum depression may be gained by looking at all women after childbirth, and not limiting the study of postpartum depression to that of women hospitalized. The studies that have surveyed women in the general population for postpartum depression report varying incidence rates depending on the severity of symptoms forming the studies' criteria for postpartum depression.

Rees and Lutkins (1971) administered the Beck Depression Inventory (BDI) to 99 women as they were seen routinely by a general practitioner-obstetrician. Using cutting scores on the BDI indicating severe and moderate depression, they found incidence rates of 3 percent and 10 percent, respectively, which is similar to that suggested by Cox et al. (1982), Pitt (1968), Ryle (1961), and Tod (1964) who assessed depression via clinical interview. At a cutting score indicating mild depression, Rees and Lutkins found 30 percent of their subjects to be mildly depressed. Also using the BDI at a cutting score indicating mild depression, Atkinson and Rickel (in press) found postpartum depression in 26 percent of a sample of 78 primiparous women at 8 weeks postpartum. Similarly using the Self-Rating Depression Scale, Hayworth et al. (1980) found mild to moderate depression in 24 percent of their sample at 6 weeks postpartum. Thus, evidence is accumulating to indicate 15 to 30 percent of women score in the depressed range on standardized measures of depression during the first few weeks postpartum (Manley et al., 1982; O'Hara et al., 1982).

Studies using less structured measures of postpartum depression frequently report higher incidence rates. Pitt (1968) reports that a questionnaire circulated by the Association for the Improvement of Maternity Services in Great Britain found 65 percent of mothers describing postpartum depression, and in 25 percent of these, symptoms continued for longer than a few weeks. Atkinson (1979) asked 78 primiparous women to rate the degree of depression they had experienced in the previous 8 weeks. Ninety percent of the women reported experiencing some degree of depression in the 8 weeks since childbirth. Many investigators believe that the higher figures encompass what has been referred to as a "transitory syndrome" (Hamilton, 1962) or the "postpartum blues," i.e., a transient mild depression occuring postpartum (Yalom et al., 1968). However, there is no study on the cause and outcome of depression which begins shortly after childbirth to provide evidence for this assumption.

Although incidence rates vary according to the population studied and the severity of the criteria for postpartum depression, the above studies demonstrate that postpartum depression of varying degrees is a problem for a significant number of women.

A SUMMARY OF THE LITERATURE

Because so few studies of postpartum adaptation focus specifically on postpartum depression, studies of postpartum disturbance *in general*, which may shed light on postpartum depression *per se*, are included in this chapter's review of experimental and quasi-experimental studies investigating postpartum depression.

This review begins with a summary of the literature describing normal pregnancy and postpartum adaptation, and is followed by a description of potential moderators of postpartum adjustment. The section on moderator variables is divided into two areas: (1) Individual variables: physiological, developmental, psychological; and (2) Social-Environmental variables: interpersonal relationships, and environmental supports and stresses.

COURSE OF PREGNANCY AND POSTPARTUM
ADAPTION: THEORY AND FINDINGS

Many researchers have described the pregnancy experience as a crisis period for the woman, defining "crisis" as a "decisive stage in the course of events—a turning point that brings with it the unsettling and dislodging of habitual situations" (Bibring, 1966). The main thesis of Bibring's research (1959, 1961, 1966) is that "every pregnancy includes intrinsically an element of crisis as an indispensable factor of the process that leads from the condition of childlessness to the significantly different state of parenthood" (Bibring, 1966, p. 100).

Cohen (1966) conducted psychological screening and therapy in an antenatal clinic at the University of Nebraska. From his experience, Cohen theorizes that pregnancy involves a maturation process and describes three normal adaptive phases of the pregnancy process: (a) acceptance of pregnancy in the first trimester;

(b) developing an affiliative response to the fetus after quickening (usually in the second trimester); (c) assignment of a reality based identity to the neonate after birth. According to Cohen, successful resolution of the crises of pregnancy depends upon adaptive movement through these three "tasks" of pregnancy. Cohen states that "any stress which is of sufficient intensity so as to interfere with one of the three adaptive tasks is likely to produce some degree of maladaptive behavior in the mother" (p. 563).

In their study of pregnancy adaption in primiparous parents, Shereshefsky et al. (in Shereshefsky & Yarrow, 1973) found statistically significant changes occurring between the first and second trimesters which reflect better adaption to pregnancy in these aspects: (a) less anxiety regarding infant care; (b) clarity and confidence in visualizing oneself as a mother; (c) effect of pregnancy on feeling of well-being; (d) adaptability to the changes of pregnancy; (e) evidence of growth toward new family identity; (f) pregnancy as confirmation of feminine identity; (g) validation of the couple in their identity; (h) husband-wife adaption.

According to these authors, the "psychological movement" in adaption to pregnancy was not clearly defined until between the second and third trimesters. They report that through the pregnancy period, women generally experienced some heightening of emotional sensitivity and more lability than usual, especially in the first trimester. At three months, 51 percent of the women were rated as having "diminished vitality," at seven months, 33 percent. At three months, 23 percent were rated as having "enhancement of feelings of well-being," at seven months, 49 percent. This data reflects the stress of the pregnancy crisis and the general adaption to it.

The arrival of the new family member has been shown to constitute a period of crisis not only for the new mother but also for the new father and other family members. In a retrospective interview study of 46 primiparous couples (primips), LeMasters (1957) reports that 83 percent reported "extensive" or "severe" crisis (4 and 5 on a 5-point scale of coded interview data) with the addition of their first child. Dyer (1963) in a study based on the LeMasters study found in his sample of 32 primip couples that 53 percent experienced "extensive" or "severe" crisis. According to crisis theory, ". . . crisis is self-limiting in a temporal sense . . . the actual period of the crisis tends to last from one to six weeks. Some solution is sought for the state of upset to restore a sense of equilibrium . . ." (Rapoport, 1962). In accord with crisis theory, most studies of postpartum mental illness support Cohen's (1966) finding that the majority of postpartum disturbance occurs in the first postpartum month (White et al., 1957; Seager, 1960).

INDIVIDUAL PHYSIOLOGICAL MODERATOR VARIABLES

Almost every study of postpartum disturbance and depression includes a statement about the probable influence of physiological changes associated with pregnancy and childbirth. There appears to be an interaction between physiological and psychological factors in affective illness following childbirth (Treadway et al., 1969).

Hamilton (1962) found that some women experiencing severe emotional disturbance postpartum had thyroid difficulties and reports dramatic recoveries when these women were treated with thyroid compounds. Several researchers (Jarrahi-

Zadeh et al., 1964; Yalom et al., 1968) suggest that the imbalance in the sex hormones, the dramatic reduction in estrogen and progesterone that occurs at the end of pregnancy, can trigger depression. Blumberg and Billig in 1942 established that progesterone was useful in preventing premenstrual relapse of patients who had recovered from postpartum disturbance, even though these patients were originally treated by other methods (cited in Hamilton, 1962). Nevertheless, Pitt (1968) found no correlation between hormonal changes and postpartum depression and no differences between lactating and non-lactating mothers.

However, Nilsson and Almgren (1968) report that in a prospective investigation of 165 women during pregnancy and postpartum, a comparison of 54 women who were taking oral contraceptives during the postpartum period with 100 women who used other contraceptive methods demonstrated a significantly higher frequency of psychiatric symptoms, especially of a neurasthenic and depressive nature, in the oral contraceptive group. Nilsson and Almgren suggest that the increase of psychiatric symptoms may be causally related to the medication and can presumably be ascribed to hormonal factors. In contrast, Ballinger et al. (1979) find no increased risk of emotional disturbances in women on the oral contraceptive pill. They suggest that the negative publicity regarding oral contraception has influenced the more anxious individuals to discontinue its usage.

Treadway et al. (1969) studied a large number of psychological and biochemical factors in pregnant ($n = 21$) and non-pregnant ($n = 9$) women. They found a significant correlation between decreased norepinephrine in the bloodstream and increased depressive self-reports of pregnant and postpartum women compared to non-pregnant controls. No other significant correlations were found between psychological and biochemical variables. Decreased norepinephrine has also been found in certain kinds of clinical depression (Mendels, 1975). Ballinger et al. (1979) report decreases in the urinary excretion of cyclic AMP was also associated with depression following childbirth. Treadway and his associates suggest that postpartum depression is the result of a combined lack of rebound from the biochemical changes of pregnancy and environmental stress. They hypothesize that hormonal levels affect norepinephrine and produce an increased susceptibility to depression postpartum.

Both Hamilton's (1960) and Treadway et al.'s (1969) physiological measures were taken shortly after childbirth. Nilsson and Almgren's (1968) data cover only the first four months postpartum. No longitudinal studies of physiological changes and postpartum depression have been reported. Thus, there is no information available on the interaction of physiological changes and postpartum depression over time, and no data to shed light on questions of cause and effect in physiological and psychological disturbance.

There is some evidence that physical stress may increase a woman's vulnerability to postpartum depression. Many researchers find significant correlations between physical complications of pregnancy and postpartum disturbance or emotional disturbance (Gordon & Gordon, 1959; Rose, 1961; Cohen, 1966; Nilsson et al., 1967; Yalom et al., 1968; Shereshefsky & Yarrow, 1973). Most researchers note that any solely physiological exploration of postpartum depression is likely to be insufficient. There appears to be an interaction between physiological and psychological factors in postpartum disturbance (Treadway et al., 1969). The women in Shereshefsky and Yarrow's (1973) study reported that the physiological changes of pregnancy made them feel that they lacked control of their situation. Feelings of noncontrol or helplessness have been demonstrated to be associated with depression (Seligman, 1975; Friedman & Katz, 1974). Perhaps then the woman's emotional response to physiological changes is an important moderator of the biological variables associated with postpartum depression.

Another important aspect relative to the physiological framework is the genetic factor. Heredity appears to play a significant role in puerperal depression and schizophrenia. A genetic model tends to identify why some women suffer greater emotional impairment than others. According to Huhn and Drenk (1973), "positive heredity" was cited as high as 32 percent and in Osterman's (1963) study, a 65 percent figure—the highest proportion ever recorded—indicated the genetic role in postpartum disorders. In further support, Thuwe (1974) in a controlled longitudinal study, reported a 47 percent frequency of psychiatric disorders in the children of women who have been under treatment for postpartum psychiatric syndromes and a 58 percent frequency of psychiatric problems when grandchildren were added to the study. These studies serve to provide evidence of dominant hereditary factors contributing to a general category of postpartum disorders.

DEVELOPMENTAL VARIABLES

Age and parity are the most frequently examined variables in the postpartum depression literature. Easily and objectively determined, they are routinely examined in the course of many larger studies on postpartum depression. Studies are generally consistent in reporting primips are mainly at risk (Gordon & Gordon, 1959, 1960; Paffenberger, 1964; Gordon et al., 1965; Cohen, 1966; Pitt, 1968; Yalom et al., 1968; Kaij & Nilsson, 1972).

Kaij and Nilsson (1972) state that the preponderance of primips is most easily explained if social and psychological insecurity of coping with the new situation of parenthood is considered. White et al. (1957), however, theorize that the association of postpartum mental illness with first pregnancies is due to a statistical misunderstanding. White points out that since there are more first-born persons than any other sibling rank, one would expect the incidence of postpartum mental illness to decrease with the birth rank of all children, since the actual number of such pregnancies must also decrease with the rank of the child born.

Pitt (1968) in a study of 305 women, found that in addition to the first pregnancy, there is a greater probability that postpartum depression will follow a third pregnancy. Gordon & Gordon (1959) found this to be true for the fourth or later child. Similarly, Kaij et al. (1967) found that 3/5 of their sample of 861 women reported an increased incidence of emotional symptoms with more pregnancies. They rule out age and social class as explanations for their findings. These findings may reflect the increased pressures of caring for more children.

Any explanation for these findings must consider that parity is not randomly determined. Physical and mental health influence parity. Thus, multiparae as a group may be physically and/or mentally healthier than primiparae and, thus, less apt to experience postpartum depression. Indeed, Kaij et al. (1967) found multips to be physically healthier before delivery. On the other hand, age is naturally correlated to parity and on the whole, it seems higher age implies a slightly increased risk of physical and emotional illness postpartum, which partly explains conflicting data on age and parity (Kaij & Nilsson, 1972). While some studies find no correlation between age and postpartum emotional disturbance (Hemphill,

1952) or postpartum depression (Yalom et al., 1968), most studies do report that older women are more at risk (Gordon & Gordon, 1959; Paffenberger, 1964).

Interval between pregnancies: A longer interval between pregnancies appears to be related to postpartum depression (Paffenberger, 1964; Yalom et al., 1968; Kaij & Nilsson, 1972). Yalom et al. (1968) suggest this longer interval may reflect an endoctrinological aberration resulting in postpartum sterility or that these women may have experienced a previous postpartum depression and have, thus, unconsciously delayed "subjecting themselves to another pregnancy." It may be that a long interval between pregnancies makes the multip more like the primip in re-experiencing the adjustments required by pregnancy and mothering a new-born. Rose (1961) found that women having children at very short intervals (10–12 months apart) are another high risk group for postpartum disturbance. This may reflect the increased demands of caring for more than one infant in addition to the physical stress of pregnancies close together.

Early mothering experience: Parity, age, and interval between pregnancies are individual variables which can be easily and objectively determined. The variable which has received the greatest amount of attention in the postpartum disturbance literature, the new mother's own experience with being mothered, is much more complicated as it must be in some way subjectively and retrospectively assessed. To date, no study has attempted to follow a woman through her life span into pregnancy.

Psychoanalytic theory has always emphasized the importance of a positive mothering experience in a woman's development. According to psychoanalytic theory, the prerequisite of successful functioning as a woman is an identification with her mother and achievement of independent functioning (Anthony & Benedek, 1970; Bieber & Bieber, 1978; Blum, 1978). Bibring (1959) asserts that only neurotic women will be affected adversely by pregnancy. Writing of postpartum adjustment, she states that a "large part of disturbances in the early mothering experience have their roots in the woman's neurotic entanglement with her own mother."

Most studies examining this multidimensional variable, "early mothering experience," report that women experiencing emotional disturbance postpartum have had a deficient or disturbed relationship with their own mothers (Markham, 1961; Pines, 1972; Tauber, 1974; Uddenburg, 1974). All of these researchers point out that one result of an unsatisfactory relationship with one's own mother is a poor or deficient maternal role model. This could retard or inhibit the acquisition of mothering skills and thus upset the woman's adaption to parenthood.

Child care experience: In the one prospective study investigating the mother-daughter relationship, Shereshefsky and Yarrow (1973) found few statistically significant relationships among developmental variables. The one variable with a highly significant correlation to maternal adjustment was the amount of experience the new mother had had with children. Likewise, Tauber (1974) found highly depressed women to have had less babysitting experience and to have stopped babysitting at a younger age. Gordon and Gordon (1959, 1960) also conclude that the women in their studies who became emotionally disturbed postpartum had had inadequate training for motherhood.

In light of these findings, it appears that one critical developmental variable protecting a woman from postpartum depression may be that she have had the opportunity to develop good mothering skills—whether it be through role modeling, experience or instruction.

PSYCHOLOGICAL VARIABLES

Researchers of postpartum emotional disturbance have asked whether postpartum disturbance is merely a continuation or exacerbation of a previous disturbance. Findings on the relationship of mental illness or maladjustment antepartum to postpartum disturbance are contradictory.

White et al. (1957) found evidence of longstanding maladjustment among 100 women hospitalized with postpartum mental illness. Seager (1960) in a comparative study of 84 women after childbirth found a higher incidence of previous psychiatric illness and predisposing personality traits in those patients developing mental illness. These writers argue that childbirth is a precipitating event in a woman predisposed to mental illness.

Within the framework of affective disorders many investigators point to a definite relationship between manic-depressive disorders and the affective reactions associated with childbirth. According to Bratfos and Haug (1966), women already suffering from an affective disorder before the onset of pregnancy risk a 10–40 percent chance of having another episode of affective disorder postpartum. Reich and Winokur (1970) further propose that women with bipolar illness were found to be three and one-half times more likely to experience a depressive or manic postpartum period than at any other time of their lives.

Puerperal schizophrenia also appears to identify with the same pattern. Again, Semenov and Pashutova (1978) report that the hereditary predisposition of mental diseases among the mothers was 43 percent, a high figure in the case of recurrent schizophrenia. Protheroe (1969) further suggests that there is a high risk, as great as 1 in 5, that a schizophrenic woman will develop a second schizophrenic puerperal episode in future pregnancies.

Kaij and Nilsson (1972) and Zajicek and Wolkind (1978) state that a history of neurosis is the most important predictor of postpartum emotional disturbance. They argue that most postpartum emotional disorders are the re-emergence of a prior disturbance. However, they acknowledge the existence of a smaller group of women who become disturbed for the first time in association with childbirth.

Yalom et al. (1968) found no correlation between history of mental illness or maladjustment assessed in a clinical interview prior to childbirth and postpartum depression. However, they did find that previous postpartum depression predicted postpartum depression following subsequent deliveries. Supporting this, Melges (1968) reports a very high recurrence rate among the 100 women suffering postpartum disturbance in his study.

Researchers such as Paffenberger and McCabe (1966) and Stein (1967) studying mental illness occurring antepartum and postpartum argue that postpartum mental illness is a distinct entity, and that the women who become disturbed postpartum share common characteristics, differing from those becoming disturbed antepartum. Pitt (1968) is one author who holds that depression experienced postpartum is "atypical," unique to the postpartum period, with characteristics that distinguish it from depression occurring at other times. Pitt found no correlation between previous mental illness and postpartum depression in his study of 305 women. He reports that the women in his sample experiencing postpartum depression answered "no" when asked if they had ever before experienced anything like their postpartum depression.

Many studies screen out women with previous mental illness and still find a substantial number of women experiencing postpartum depression (Shereshefsky &

Yarrow, 1973; Tauber, 1974). Thus, it appears that pregnancy and childbirth are stresses which may precipitate postpartum depression in both previously disturbed and previously stable women. The relative proportions of these two groups have not been established, nor have their characteristics been delineated. Yalom et al.'s (1968) and Melges' (1968) findings that previous postpartum depression predicts subsequent postpartum depression suggests that there may be a group of women who are made especially vulnerable to depression by the childbearing experience.

Neurotic symptoms during pregnancy: Studies examining whether neurotic symptoms during pregnancy predict postpartum depression are also contradictory. Research on the emotional aspects of the pregnancy experience suggests that all pregnant women experience some degree of anxiety and other emotions which would at another time in life be labeled "neurotic." Tod (1964) found "pathological anxiety" during pregnancy to predict postpartum depression. Kaij and Nilsson (1972) report that the onset of "neurotic" symptoms during pregnancy predicts postpartum disturbance.

Blaker (1974) in a small sample ($n = 30$) found that women depressed antepartum tended to be depressed postpartum. Similarly Atkinson and Rickel (in press) found a measure of prepartum depression to predict postpartum depression in 78 primiparous women. In contrast, Rees and Lutkins (1971) found no tendency for antepartum depression to be followed by postpartum depression, although they did find women equally likely to be depressed antepartum as postpartum.

Personality characteristics and attitudes: Research on depression in women (Weissman & Paykel, 1974) has shown that certain characteristics (e.g., dependency, submissiveness, guilt) present during depression which have often been attributed to the type of person who becomes depressed, do not ncessarily exist prior to or after the depressive episode. Thus, conclusions based on studies of women while they are depressed must be considered carefully.

From his study of 305 maternity patients, pre- and postpartum, Pitt (1968) describes a personality predisposed to postpartum depression which is overcontrolled and tends toward introversion. In the most extensive research on personality variables, Shereshefsky and Yarrow (1973) found two factors emerging from personality characteristics predicting maternal adaption: ego strength and nurturance. Shereshefsky and Yarrow also found that women with a "chronic maladaptive pattern of response to new maturational tasks" were vulnerable to postpartum disturbance. However, the Shereshefsky and Yarrow work, like most studies of personality characteristics, involves mainly indirect measures, e.g., clinical interviews and judgments, factor analyses, and thus is subject to considerable variance in interpretation.

More direct measures may be taken of attitudes. Several studies have investigated the influence of attitudes toward pregnancy, childbirth and mothering on postpartum adjustment. These findings are consistent. Negative or ambivalent attitudes toward pregnancy and motherhood predict postpartum disturbance (Newton, 1955; Gordon & Gordon, 1960; Nilsson et al., 1967; Grimm, 1967; Shereshefsky & Yarrow, 1973). Newton (1955) found intercorrelations between attitudes toward several areas of feminine development and functioning, e.g., menstruation, sex, childbearing, breastfeeding, etc. Newton's work provides evidence for the predictability of reactions to childbirth from knowledge of attitudes toward other aspects of feminine development. Shereshefsky and Yarrow (1973) also found acceptance and adaption to pregnancy to be related to maternal adaption. They indicated that the ability to visualize oneself as a mother and clarity and confidence in maternal functioning were strong predictors of maternal adaption. Shereshefsky and Yarrow feel they are tapping a complex of attitudes related to "feminine identification."

Many investigators of women's attitudes toward pregnancy and motherhood assume that a woman with less than positive attitudes must experience problems assuming the "feminine" role (Pitt, 1968, 1973; Kaij & Nilsson, 1972). In discussing "feminine identification," role conflicts and postpartum depression, much research takes a psychological approach and focuses on early learning experience. Such an approach fails to control for sociocultural factors (Magnus, 1982; Rosengren, 1971, 1962). When woman's role is being socially and culturally redefined as it is today, an examination of attitudes toward pregnancy and motherhood based on the assumption that these reflect underlying personality characteristics originating in childhood in order to determine problems in feminine identification or feminine role conflict is somewhat simplistic. Such examinations neglect important sociocultural variables, such as personal satisfaction derived from other roles—student, work, expectations of family and friends, availability of day care, which influence a woman's comfortableness in and satisfaction with the motherhood role (Rickel et al., 1982).

The research of Gordon and his associates (1965) demonstrates the interaction between attitudes and socioenvironmental variables. They found a factor emerging from the personal and social history of the 435 women they studied which they labeled "Maternal Role-Conflict." This factor demonstrates the stresses facing the new mother's changing role in life today. Maternal Role-Conflict was characterized by items related to preparedness for achievement in the world outside the home, as well as for "getting ahead" socially, educationally and economically. These interests might bring a woman into conflict with the maternal role. However, Maternal Role-Conflict was also associated with items related to lack of assistance and emotional support for the responsibilities associated with motherhood. This factor was related to "abnormal reactions to pregnancy and childbearing" along with a second factor, "Personal Insecurity." Gordon et al. (1965) report that "women whose problems were related primarily to personal insecurity were less likely to have long-lasting postpartum emotional problems than were those whose emotional problems were associated with role-conflict." Thus, while attitudes toward motherhood and pregnancy measured during pregnancy may provide indicia of a woman's adjustment postpartum, attitudes are not sufficient to predict postpartum adjustment.

SOCIAL-ENVIRONMENTAL VARIABLES

Interpersonal Relationships

Studies of social influence, supports and stresses on postpartum emotional adjustment must consider the influence of the woman's husband, immediate family, relatives, friends, other interpersonal contacts outside the home, and the newborn (Martin, 1977).

Marital: Most research on social variables focuses on the marital relationship. A positive relationship has been consistently demonstrated between postpartum adaption and marital satisfaction (White et al., 1957; Gordon et al., 1965; Cohen, 1966; Kaij & Nilsson, 1972; Shereshefsky & Yarrow, 1973; Tauber, 1974; Gladieux,

1975). Variables indicating strains in the familial relationships have also been related to postpartum disturbance (Ketai & Brandwin, 1979). In their series of studies of the effect of social and environmental stress on postpartum adjustment, Gordon and his associates found that when the husband was considerably older or of a different religious background (1959) or was ill or away from home a great deal (1965), there was a greater probability of emotional disturbance. Tauber (1974) also showed women married fewer years (indicating less time to adjust to marriage) experienced a greater degree of postpartum depression. Tauber compiled a "marital stress score" composed of the sum of a subject's affirmative answers to (a) wish husband helped more with baby, (b) husband ill for more than 3 days in the last 10 months, (c) husband recently changed jobs, (d) new job keeps husband away from home more, (e) felt closer to husband before delivery, (f) husband did not help with housework during previous week. In Tauber's study, women with high marital stress scores postpartum experienced a greater degree of depression.

Blaker (1974) investigated postpartum depression in both husband and wife and found that couples with low scores of self-disclosure (indicating problems in communication) tended to be more depressed postpartum. Markham (1961) also found that women who failed to use their husbands as support during pregnancy and postpartum were more likely to be disturbed postpartum. Similarly, Shereshefsky and Yarrow (1973) report that a strong husband-wife relationship "characterized by mutuality" was in itself a deterrent to the development of external stresses. This research suggests that the husband's support may be an important moderator of difficulties the woman may experience in her new role as mother. It is also possible that a positive marital relationship is an indication of the ability to form a warm interpersonal relationship which is important in mothering.

Family and Friends: Research on the role of family and friends is limited. Perhaps this is in part due to the widespread belief that a breakdown has occurred in such institutions as the extended family network, ethnic neighborhoods, church, etc., thus, that today's woman must rely increasingly on the nuclear family, especially on the marital relationship, for support. Work on kinship functions in the United States has shown that (a) the nuclear family may not be as isolated as is commonly believed, often relying on relatives, especially the wife's, for guidance and support, particularly when there are children, and (b) close friends often assume many of the former support functions of the extended family when actual family is not accessible (Adams, 1970).

Gladieux (1975) found that while a woman's satisfaction with the pregnancy experience depended to a large degree on her spouse's flexibility and favorableness of attitudes regarding pregnancy and parenthood, her ultimate satisfaction depended on the interaction between the marital relationship and social network factors. Tauber (1974) further hypothesizes that the primary cause of postpartum depression is the increased isolation often associated with childbearing and motherhood. Her study showed higher isolation scores to correlate significantly with more severe depression. Some studies report that isolation from family or friends (particularly if a move is involved,Gordon & Gordon, 1959; Cohen, 1966; Tauber, 1974) or loss of family or friends through illness or death (White et al., 1957; Cohen, 1966) may predict postpartum disturbance. Gordon et al. (1965) found that greater separation from family in age, economic or social status, was characteristic of women experiencing emotional disturbance postpartum.

Infant: White et al. (1957) found that the infant itself may be a stress precipitant to postpartum depression if the child is unwanted or is seen as an excessive increase in responsibility or a financial burden. Nilsson et al. (1967) confirm that there is a statistically significant correlation between unplanned pregnancies and depression in the puerperium. Blumberg (1980) found significantly more depression during the first five days postpartum in mothers of high risk infants. The high risk variable tended to overwhelm the contribution of other independent variables in the study.

While it has long been accepted that maternal behavior influences infant adaption, recent literature on the family has demonstrated the importance of considering the infant as an important mediator of a mother's behavior. Melges (1968) states that ambiguities of newborn communication led to misinterpretation and confusion on the part of the mothers in his sample of women who developed severe postpartum disturbances. Research has also demonstrated that different infant temperaments (e.g., how much they cry, how soothable they are, how sociable or "cuddly" they are) may be a strong contributing factor to the mother's feeling of effectiveness, depending on the mother's own disposition (Schaffer & Emerson, 1964; Ainsworth & Bell, 1969). Cohen (1966) suggests that the low level of obvious reinforcement for the extensive energy commitment in mothering a newborn leads to depression.

Environmental

In her review of the literature on "psychological and social factors in pregnancy, delivery, and outcome," Grimm (1967) summarizes "... no conclusions can be drawn about the relationship of personality variables assessed early in pregnancy to postpartum adjustment ..." However, she states that *environmental factors* have been shown to be important in determining postpartum adjustment. Grimm bases this conclusion on the work of R. E. Gordon and his associates, which remains the only systematic investigation of social and environmental factors associated with postpartum adjustment.

Gordon and Gordon (1959) report that certain socioenvironmental stresses (e.g., change in residence, little help for the wife in the first weeks home from the hospital, husband unavailable in the weeks after the baby's birth) predicted postpartum emotional disturbance. Based on these findings, they developed an antenatal program aimed at preventing postpartum disturbance. Changes made by parents according to the program's suggestions were associated with positive postpartum adjustment (Gordon & Gordon, 1960). These changes included: increasing husband's availability at home, increasing social contacts with couples with young children; obtaining experienced help for the infant.

Findings which support Gordon's hypothesis that socioenvironmental stresses are related to postpartum disturbance are occasionally reported. Cohen (1966) found residence relocation in the postpartum period and job loss of either spouse to be related to postpartum emotional disturbance. Doty (1967) reports more emotional disturbance postpartum among women of lower socioeconomic statuses. LeMasters (1957) further found that the couples he studied who experienced extensive or severe crisis (83 percent of the sample) with the arrival of their first child, felt they had had very little effective preparation for parental roles. This demonstrates the importance of training for parenthood. Rossi (1968) argues that an important reason the transition to parenthood is extremely difficult in American society is due to the failure of the society to provide institutionalized assistance for the mother. The few screening programs which exist for assessing high-risk pregnancies (Caplan, 1951, 1961; Bibring, 1966; Cohen, 1966; Horsley, 1972) and the antenatal programs aimed at facilitating postpartum adjustment and/or preventing postpartum disturbance (Gordon & Gordon, 1960; Shereshefsky & Yarrow, 1973) emphasize the importance of a stable environment for maternal adjustment and focus their efforts at intervention there. The importance of socioenvironmental conditions has been demonstrated in practice, through antenatal programs facilitating maternal adaption and in research. However, Gordon's research remains one of the few studies to systematically examine the impact of environmental variables on postpartum adjustment.

Perhaps one reason for the limited research on environmental supports is due to the fact that institutional supports for new mothers are so limited—medical follow-up is usually restricted to one six-week checkup; child care is often difficult to obtain and/or expensive; community services geared to young families are rare.

Another reason for the lack of research on social and environmental variables may be the difficulty in assessing the nature of an individual's environment. To adequately assess the stressfulness of an individual's environment, many dimensions must be considered: the number of stresses; the subject's rating of the severity of each stress and the discomfort caused by it; the number of available compensating supports and the subject's ratings of the helpfulness of these supports.

Thus, lack of methods for assessing the parameters of an individual's environment—social, situational, institutional—and lack of knowledge about the impact of these parameters, together with an historic trend to look for physiological and intrapsychic causes of postpartum depression, has resulted in a deficit of studies investigating the relationship between postpartum disturbance and social and environmental factors.

PROBLEMS WITH EXISTING RESEARCH

Since no single variable appears *necessary* to precipitate postpartum depression, and as there are no data available which allows an assessment of the way the variables identified as sufficient to precipitate depression operate singly or in combination, it is difficult to plan person-specific prevention or intervention programs at this time. Most of the research on postpartum disturbance as stated previously is exploratory, conducted without a guiding theory, and suffers from inadequate experimental control. If progress is to be made in preventing, identifying and treating postpartum depression, future studies must attempt to correct the deficiencies of prior research. Thus, some of the problems with the postpartum adjustment research are outlined:

(a) First, the *paucity of research* in this highly significant area must be addressed. Long-term studies involving large numbers of subjects are needed which focus on the course of normal pregnancy and postpartum adaption in addition to postpartum disturbance. Existing research requires replication, extension and follow-up.

(b) The second major problem is the lack of a *theoretical model* for investigating postpartum disturbance. Without a theory to dictate the selection of crucial independent variables and hypotheses to be tested, studies vary according to researchers' preferences as to the choice of variables, measurement procedures and methods, making it difficult to generalize findings across studies.

(c) Perhaps the major stumbling block in interpreting research on postpartum depression is the *lack of a standard, precise definition of postpartum depression.* The criteria for postpartum depression varies between studies and is often vaguely stated within studies.

(d) *Lack of a standard method for measuring postpartum depression* also leads to confusing findings when studies are compared. Use of a standardized measure avoids the problems of interviewer bias or individual subject differences in openness, which may occur in evaluations by professionals or subject self-reports.

(e) Adding to the methodological confusion, *two types of research design* have been used to study postpartum depression which view the problem from different perspectives. The retrospective design is the most common. While this design saves time by eliminating measures during or prior to pregnancy, it is subject to so many problems from subject memory bias alone that its validity is questionable. Prospective designs are superior as incidence can be determined, the role played by predictor variables can be assessed, and of course, the design is free of memory bias.

DIRECTIONS FOR FUTURE RESEARCH

Reviewing the problems in the literature on postpartum adjustment demonstrates the need for an integrated research approach. Researchers from varied backgrounds—medicine, psychology, sociology, social work, public health—have worked independently on the problem of postpartum adjustment without a guiding theory. This has resulted in findings which are often confusing and at times seemingly contradictory. Fortunately, three theoretical viewpoints which have dominated the recent empirically oriented literature on depression appear to have value for the study of postpartum depression: (a) *Beck's (1972) cognitive view of depression hypothesizes that a "negative cognitive set" predisposes the individual to depression.* An individual with a negative cognitive set distorts negatively interpersonal experience, self-evaluations and expectations of the future. The finding that a woman's perception of herself as a competent, loving mother is significantly related to positive postpartum adjustment (Shereshefsky & Yarrow, 1973) is interpretable within Beck's theory. (b) *Seligman's (1975) helplessness model views depression as the behavioral manifestation of "learned helplessness"*: the expectation that responding and reinforcement are independent or the perception of noncontrol. Seligman's theory would predict Gordon's conclusions that a supportive environment and the woman's belief in her ability to handle (control) the new stresses in the postpartum situation are important factors in postpartum adaption. (c) *Lewinsohn (1974) views depression as due to an individual's low rate of response-contingent positive reinforcement.* In accord with his theory, Gladieux (1975) found that satisfaction with the motherhood role was positively related to the degree to which maternal behavior was valued by husbands/friends.

Recently results of research designed within these theoretical frameworks of depression have been reported. Atkinson and Rickel (in press) studied the degree to which postpartum depression is a function of the disruption of parents' prepartum functioning by the demands of infant caretaking. Seventy-eight primiparous, married couples, screened for history of depression, volunteered through private physicians and childbirth preparation classes to complete questionnaires at eight weeks prepartum and again at eight weeks postpartum. The modal subject in the study was white, and in the mid-twenties, middle-class, well educated, and healthy. This was one of the few studies to assess uniformly both parents of the same infant as well as employ a relatively large sample compared to most studies of postpartum adjustment.

The set of measures compiled to assess indicators of stress due to childcare included an Inventory of Caretaking Behavior (ICB) which was developed for this study to assess the amount of time parents expected to and did spend in childcare; Broussard and Hartner's Neonatal Perception Inventory and Degree of Bother Inventory (NPI and DPI), assessments of parents' perceptions of their infant's behavior as problematic or bothersome; an assessment of the amount of positive reinforcement experienced by the parent, MacPhillamy and Lewinsohn's MR Scale of the Pleasant Events Schedule (PES); and a standardized measure of depression, the Beck Depression Inventory (BDI).

For both women and men prepartum depression level was the strongest predictor of depression. However, independent of the prepartum depression score, postpartum depression was significantly related to the variables chosen to assess disruption experienced by the parent due to the infant's caretaking demands. The combination of variables which were most strongly associated with postpartum depression for women and men are consistent with a behavioral theory interpretation of postpartum depression, which hypothesizes depression to be related to a low rate of experienced positive events (Lewinsohn, 1974).

Findings from multiple regression analyses indicated that when the level of prepartum depression was controlled, postpartum depression in women, as measured by the BDI, was most strongly related to a reported low frequency and enjoyability of pleasant events. Other variables in this study which were significantly related to postpartum depression for women included greater amounts of time reported spent in childcare and a greater degree of bother expressed toward their infant's behavior as can be seen in Table 1.

When the level of prepartum depression was controlled, postpartum depression

Table 1 Intercorrelations among prepartum and postpartum variables for women and men

	Women		Men	
	Pre BDI	Post BDI	Pre BDI	Post BDI
Prepartum				
Inventory of caretaking behavior	0.23*	0.22*	−0.02	0.09
Neonatal perception inventory	0.11	0.10	−0.05	0.16
Degree of bother	0.08	0.05	0.25**	0.14
Pleasant events schedule	−0.26**	−0.10	−0.18	0.08
Pre BDI		0.56***		0.59***
Postpartum				
Inventory of caretaking behavior	0.23*	0.24*	0.04	0.19*
Neonatal perception inventory	0.01	−0.05	−0.01	−0.30**
Degree of bother	0.24*	0.20*	0.26**	0.28**
Pleasant events schedule	−0.22*	−0.38***	−0.17	0.23*

*$p < 0.05$.
**$p < 0.01$.
***$p < 0.001$.

for men as assessed by the BDI was most strongly related to viewing the infant's behavior less positively. Furthermore, postpartum depression for men was significantly related to reporting a lower frequency and enjoyability of pleasant events, a greater degree of bother expressed toward the infant's behaviors and reporting more time spent in childcare. These results are also presented in Table 1.

Hayworth et al. (1980) studied the relationship of perceived control, as a personal coping style, and attitudes to postpartum depression at 6 weeks postpartum in 127 women. Women who perceived themselves as less in control of their lives were likely to rate high on the postpartum depression measure. The authors feel this provides support for Seligman's theory of depression. There was a relationship between intrapunitiveness and perceived control which suggested individuals who feel controlled by events yet project blame inwardly are particularly vulnerable to postpartum depression.

Basing their research on two different theoretical views of depression, these two studies were successful in producing integrated findings on depression with implications for future research and application in the prevention and treatment of depression.

In a summary and comparison of the research on depression generated by the theories of Beck et al. (1977) concludes that three variables are important in depression: *perception* of events (Beck, Seligman); *control* of experience (Seligman, Lewinsohn); and *rate* of reinforcement (Lewinsohn). Blaney suggests that each element may be sufficient to lead to depression while none is necessary, and he suggests a research approach that encompasses all three variables. These three precipitations of depression could be encompassed by a socioenvironmental stress theory of postpartum depression. This theory elaborates on hypotheses presented by Gordon and others who contend that the overall stressfulness of the environment in which childbirth occurs must be considered when predicting postpartum depression. Thus, social and environmental strains or stresses assessed in terms of (a) the actual number of existing stresses (rate of reinforcement; loss of control), (b) the valence attributed to these stresses by the individual (perception), (c) the availability of practical assistance or supports, and (d) the opportunity and ability to utilize those supports and to eliminate present-day strain (control of experience) should predict postpartum adjustment. Research designed within the framework of the three theories of depression and the socioenvironmental hypothesis should produce findings valuable for postpartum depression specifically and for depression in general.

Blaney points out the need for longitudinal studies in which variables posited as important in depression would be monitored over time with the focus on the sequencing among them. The pregnancy experience defines a population at risk for, depression with the potentially depression-inducing event focalized and predictable, making longitudinal studies in this area more efficient. Questions Blaney would like to see answered about depression, such as "Is an increase in perception that one lacks control over important outcomes in one's life a usual antecedent to a depressive condition?" and "Does a drop in activity level predict an increase in depression?", are especially applicable to the postpartum situation with its numerous new stresses which require the parents to rearrange former behavior patterns in order to meet the infant's needs.

POSTPARTUM DEPRESSION—PREVENTION
AND INTERVENTION

Social scientists, practitioners, and policy makers in the mental health field agree that early detection of emotional disturbance, crisis intervention, and primary prevention must be priorities if the incidence of mental health problems is to be reduced. Crisis intervention emphasizes helping the ordinarily adequately functioning individual, who is responding with disabling emotions to environmental stress, to modify the stressfulness of the environment, in order to find a positive resolution to the crisis. Help at crisis points is designed to prevent the development of long-standing problems which may result from inadequate crisis solutions. Primary prevention sets the goal of maximizing coping ability and minimizing emotional distress in periods of life which are potentially disruptive to the individual, hence reducing the need for crisis intervention. For example, parents do not receive any formal training to be parents, although they receive training for most jobs they undertake in life. A primary preventive approach would involve teaching parents effective ways to deal with child rearing and child management issues before they experience any difficulties in these areas (Rickel et al., 1980; Rickel & Dudley, 1983). Thus the primary preventive strategy addresses a more basic issue, that is, the creation of psychologically healthy environments.

The postpartum period is a life crisis which affects the development of all the members of a family. Ensuring an emotionally stable prenatal and postpartum environment is the first step in producing emotionally healthy individuals. There is a great practical need for the development of prevention and intervention programs to help individuals deal with the postpartum situation. While the state of our knowledge of the antecedents, course, and outcome of postpartum depression is limited, prevention and intervention programs can still be instituted, building on the available findings of factors that seem to mitigate the debilitating effects of postpartum stress, for instance, instilling confidence in ability to control the new situation. In turn, evaluations of these programs should be reported as leads for future research. As an example, research on crisis intervention with surgical patients demonstrates the necessity for developing person-specific intervention techniques since individuals differ in their typical mode of dealing with stress (Auerbach & Kilmann, 1977). It is likely that research on postpartum depression needs to be designed not only to identify the stresses precipitant to depression, but to identify different reactions to stress and different ways of coping. To aid efforts in prevention, research needs to identify the protective and causative factors in postpartum depression, determing optimal conditions for parenthood and identifying high risk conditions.

For developers and investigators of prevention and crisis intervention programs, the postpartum situation provides a unique opportunity for practice and research, as few life crises have such a predictable onset or defined period available for preparation as childbirth and pregnancy. There are opportunities to intervene during the preimpact and postimpact stages and there is time to institute programmed treatment packages at the critical stress impact periods. The crisis of pregnancy and childbirth is complex in its "piggyback" nature. Pregnancy, childbirth and parenthood, and the fast-moving stages of the infant's development create ever-changing patterns of stresses. Just as one level of adjustment is reached, a new one is required. Thus, longitudinal studies of the way individuals adapt to pregnancy and the postpartum situation should provide valuable information about the ways in which individuals cope with and adapt to major life change.

If postpartum adjustment programs in research, prevention, and crisis intervention are to be implemented, the prejudice of the layman and the professional against recognizing and/or acknowledging the problem of postpartum depression must be addressed. In the past, researchers have focused on the more severe forms of postpartum disturbance, neglecting milder disturbances which they dismissed as the "postpartum blues," which they assumed to be "natural" and self-correcting. The professional community and the general public need to be educated with regard to the gravity of even mild postpartum disturbance, its impact and prevalence.

Perhaps our cultural myths of "blissful motherhood" and parenthood as "doing what comes naturally" keep us from acknowledging how difficult and potentially painful the adjustment to parenthood can be. Such a blind spot drains energy from efforts to ease the transition to parenthood. Thus, we are a society which provides increasingly little opportunity to learn parenting skills and roles before parenthood, and few available supports once parenthood is reached. The literature on postpartum disturbance and depression demonstrates that research and programs designed to facilitate postpartum adjustment for the entire family are essential to our national mental health.

REFERENCES

Adams, B. N. *The American Family: A Sociological Interpretation.* Chicago: Markham Publishing Company, 1970.

Ainsworth, M. D. & Bell, S. M. Some Contemporary patterns of mother-infant interaction in the feeding situation. In A. Ambrose (ed.), *Stimulation in Early Infancy.* London: Academic Press, 1969, 133–170.

Anthony, E. J. & Benedek, T. *Parenthood: Its Psychology and Psychopathology.* Boston: Little, Brown & Co., 1970.

Atkinson, A. K. Postpartum depression in primiparous parents: Caretaking demands and prepartum expectations. Unpublished Doctoral Dissertation, Wayne State University, Detroit, Michigan, 1979.

Atkinson, A. K. & Rickel, A. U. Postpartum depression in primiparous parents. *Journal of Abnormal Psychology* (in press).

Auerbach, S. M. & Kilmann, P. R. Crisis intervention: A review of outcome research. *Psychological Bulletin,* 1977, *84,* 1189–1217.

Ballinger, C. B., Buckley, D. E., Naylor, G. J., & Stansfield, D. A. Emotional disturbance following childbirth: Clinical findings and urinary excretion of cyclic AMP. *Psychological Medicine,* 1979, *9,* 293–300.

Beck, A. T. *Depression: Causes and Treatment.* Philadelphia: University of Pennsylvania Press, 1972.

Benedek, T. *Psychosexual Functions in Women.* New York: Ronald Press, 1952.

Bibring, G. L. Some considerations of the psychological processes in pregnancy. *Psychoanalytic Study of the Child,* 1959, *14,* 113–121.

Bibring, G. L. Reconition of psychological stresses often neglected in obstetrical care. *Hospital Topics,* 1966, *44,* 100–103.

Bibring, G. L., Dwyer, T. F., Huntington, D. S., & Valenstein, A. F. A study of the psychological processes in pregnancy and of the earliest mother-child relationship: Some propositions and comments. *Psychoanalytic Study of the Child,* 1961, *16,* 9–24.

Bieber, I. & Bieber, T. B. Postpartum reactions in men and women. *Journal of the American Academy of Psychoanalysis,* 1978, *6,* 511–519.

Blaker, K. L. Self-disclosure and depression during the antepartum and postpartum periods among primiparous spouses. *Dissertation Abstracts,* 1974, *34,* 12-B part 1, 6190.

Blaney, P. H. Contemporary theories of depression: Critique and comparison. *Journal of Abnormal Psychology*, 1977, *86*, 203–223.

Blum, H. P. Reconstruction in a case of postpartum depression. *Psychoanalytic Study of the Child*, 1978, *33*, 335–362.

Blumberg, N. L. Effects of neonatal risk, maternal attitude, and cognitive style on early postpartum adjustment. *Journal of Abnormal Psychology*, 1980, *89*, 139–150.

Bratfos, O. & Haug, J. O. Puerperal mental disorders in manic-depressive females. *Acta. Psychiatrica Scandinavica*, 1966, *42*, 285–294.

Caplan, G. Mental hygiene work with expectant mothers—A group psychotherapeutic approach. *Mental Hygiene*, 1951, *35*, 41–50.

Caplan, G. *Prevention of Mental Disorders in Children*. New York: Ed Basic, 1961.

Cohen, R. L. Some maladaptive syndromes of pregnancy and the puerperium. *Obstetrics and Gynecology*, 1966, *27*, 562–570.

Cox, J. L., Connor, Y., & Kendall, R. E. Prospective study of the psychiatric disorders of childbirth. *British Journal of Psychiatry*, 1982, *140*, 111–117.

Deutsch, H. *The Psychology of Women: A Psychoanalytic Interpretation. Volume II Motherhood*. New York: Grune & Stratton, Inc., 1945.

Doty, B. Relationships among attitudes in pregnancy and other maternal characteristics. *Journal of Genetic Psychology*, 1967, *111*, 203–217.

Dyer, E. D. Parenthood as crisis: A restudy. *Marriage and Family Living*, 1963.

Friedman, R. J. & Katz, M. M. (eds.), *The Psychology of Depression: Contemporary Theory and Research*. New York: John Wiley & Sons, 1974.

Gladieux, J. D. Pregnancy—the transition to parenthood: Satisfaction with the pregnancy experience as a function of the marital relationship and the social network. *Dissertation Abstracts*, 1975, *36*, 2468-B.

Gordon, R. E. & Gordon, K. Prediction and treatment of emotional disorders of pregnancy and childbearing. *American Journal of Obstetrics and Gynecology*, 1959, *77*, 1074–1083.

Gordon, R. E. & Gordon, K. Social factors in the prevention of postpartum emotional difficulties. *Obstetrics and Gynecology*, 1960, *15*, 433–434.

Gordon, R. E., Kapostins, E. E., & Gordon, K. Factors in postpartum emotional difficulties. *Obstetrics and Gynecology*, 1965, *25*, 158–166.

Grimm, E. R. Psychological and social factors in pregnancy, delivery, and outcome. In S. A. Richardson and A. F. Guttmacher (eds.), *Childbearing—Its Social and Psychological Aspects*, 1967.

Hamilton, J. A. *Postpartum Psychiatric Problems*. St. Louis: C. V. Mosby Co., 1962.

Hayworth, J., Little, B. C., Carter, S. B., Raptopaulos, P., Priest, R. H., & Sandler, M. A predictive study of postpartum depression: Some predisposing characteristics. *British Journal of Medical Psychology*, 1980, *53*, 161–167.

Hemphill, R. E. Incidence and nature of puerperal psychiatric illness. *British Medical Journal*, 1952, *2*, 1252–1235.

Horsley, J. Psychological management of the prenatal period. In J. G. Howells (ed.), *Modern Perspectives in Psychoobstetrics*. Edinburgh: Oliver & Boyd, 1972.

Huhn, A. & Drenk, K. Clinical classication and prognosis of postpartum psychoses. *Fortschritte Der Neurologie Psychiatrie*, 1973, *41*, 363–377.

Jarrahi-Zadeh, A., Kane, F. J., Van De Castle, R. L., Lachenbruch, P. A., & Ewing, J. A. Emotional and cognitive changes in pregnancy and early puerperium. *British Journal of Psychiatry*, 1964, *115*, 797–805.

Kaij, L., Jacobson, L., & Nilsson, A. Postpartum mental disorder in an unselected sample: The influence of parity. *Journal of Psychosomatic Research*, 1967, *10*, 317.

Kaij, L. & Nilsson, A. Emotional and psychotic illness following childbirth. In J. G. Howells (ed.), *Modern Perspectives in Psychoobstetrics*. Edinburgh: Oliver and Boyd, 1972.

Ketai, R. M. & Brandwin, M. A. Childbirth-related psychosis and familial symbiotic conflict. *American Journal of Psychiatry*, 1979, *136*, 190–193.

LeMasters, E. E. Parenthood as crisis. *Marriage and Family Living*, 1957, *19*, 352–355.

Lewinsohn, T. M. A behavioral approach to depression. In R. J. Freidman and M. M. Katz (eds.), *The Psychology of Depression: Contemporary Theory and Research*. New York: John Wiley & Sons, 1974.

Magnus, E. M. Sources of maternal stress in the postpartum period: A review of the literature and an alternative view. In J. E. Parsons (ed.), *The Psychobiology of Sex Differences and Sex Roles*. New York: Hemisphere, McGraw-Hill, 1980.

Manly, P. C., McMahon, R. J., Bradley, C. F., & Davidson, P. O. Depressive attributional style and depression following childbirth. *Journal of Abnormal Psychology*, 1982, *91*, 245–254.

Marcé, L. V. *Traité de la folie des femmes enceintes, des nouvelles accouchees, et des nourrices.* Paris: J. B. Balliére et Fils, 1858.

Markham, S. A. A comparative evaluation of psychotic and nonpsychotic reactions to childbirth. *American Journal of Orthopsychiatry*, 1961, *31*, 565-578.

Martin, M. E. A maternity hospital study of psychiatric illness associated with childbirth. *Irish Journal of Medical Science*, 1977, *146*, 239-244.

Melges, F. T. Postpartum psychiatric syndromes. *Psychosomatic Medicine*, 1968, *30*, 95-108.

Mendels, J. (ed.), *The Psychobiology of Depression.* New York: John Wiley & Sons, 1975.

Newton, N. *Maternal Emotions.* New York, Hoeber, 1955.

Nilsson, A., Kaij, L., & Jacobson, L. Postpartum mental disorder in an unselected sample: The psychiatric history. *Journal of Psychosomatic Research*, 1967, *10*, 327-329.

Nilsson, A. & Almgren, P. E. Psychiatric symptoms during the postpartum period as related to use of oral contraceptives. *British Medical Journal*, 1968, *5*, 453.

Osterman, E. Les etats psychopathologiques du postpartum. *L'Encephale*, 1963, *5*, 385-420.

O'Hara, M. W., Rehm, L. P., & Campbell, S. B. Predicting depressive symptomatology: Cognitive-behavioral models and postpartum depression. *Journal of Abnormal Psychology*, 1982, *91*, 457-461.

Paffenberger, R. S. Epidemiological aspects of parapartum mental illness. *British Journal of Prevention and Social Medicine*, 1964, *18*, 189-195.

Paffenberger, R. S. & McCabe, L. J. The effect of obstetrical and perinatal events on risk of mental illness. *American Journal of Public Health*, 1966, *56*, 400.

Pines, D. Pregnancy and motherood: Interaction between fantasy and reality. *British Journal of Medical Psychology*, 1972, *45*, 333-343.

Pitt, B. "Atypical" depression following childbirth. *British Journal of Psychiatry*, 1968, *114*, 1325-1335.

Protheroe, C. Puerperal psychoses. A long term study, 1927-1961. *British Journal of Psychiatry*, 1969, *115*, 9-30.

Pugh, T. F., Jerath, B. K., Schmidt, W. M., & Reed, R. B. Rates of mental disease related to childbearing. *New England Journal of Medicine*, 1963, *268*, 1224.

Rapoport, L. The state of crisis: Some theoretical considerations. *The Social Service Review*, 1962, *36*, 77-94.

Rees, W. D. & Lutkins, S. G. Parental depression before and after childbirth. *Journal of the Royal College of General Practitioners*, 1971, *21*, 20-31.

Reich, T. & Winokur, G. Postpartum psychoses in patients with manic depressive disease. *Journal of Nervous Mental Disorders*, 1970, *151*, 60-68.

Rickel, A. U., Dudley, G., & Berman, S. An evaluation of parent training. *Evaluation Review*, 1980, *4*, 329-403.

Rickel, A. U. & Dudley, G. A parent training program in a preschool mental health project. In M. Rosenbaum (ed.), *Handbook of Short-Term Therapy Groups.* New York: McGraw-Hill, 1983.

Rickel, A. U., Williams, D. L., & Loigman, G. L. Personal and situational predictors of child-rearing: Implications for intervention. Paper presented at American Psychological Association Convention, Washington, D.C., 1982.

Rose, J. The prevention of mothering breakdown associated with physical abnormalities of the infant. In G. Caplan (ed.), *Prevention of Mental Disorders in Children.* New York: Ed Basic, 1961.

Rosengren, W. R. Social sources of pregnancy as illness or normality. *Social Forces*, 1961, *35*, 260-267.

Rosengren, W. R. Social status, attitudes toward pregnancy and childrearing attitudes. *Social Forces*, 1962, *41*, 127-134.

Rossi, A. S. Transition to parenthoood. *Journal of Marriage and the Family*, 1968, *30*, 26-39.

Ryle, A. The psychological disturbances associated with 345 pregnancies in 137 women. *Journal of Mental Science*, 1961, *107*, 279.

Schaffer, H. R. & Emerson, P. E. Patterns of response to physical contact in early human development. *Journal of Child Psychology and Psychiatry*, 1964, *5*, 1-13.

Seager, C. P. A controlled study of postpartum mental illness. *Journal of Mental Science*, 1960, *106*, 214-230.

Seligman, M. *Helplessness.* San Francisco: W. H. Freeman, 1975.

Semenov, S. F. & Pashutova, E. K. Clinical features and differential diagnosis of puerperal schizophrenic psychoses. *Neuroscience and Behavioral Psychology*, 1978, *9*, 39-44.

Shereshefsky, P. M. & Yarrow, L. J. *Psychological Aspects of a First Pregnancy and Postnatal Adaption.* New York: Raven Press, 1973.

Stein, R. F. Social orientation to mental illness in pregnancy and childbirth. *International Journal of Social Research*, 1967-1968, *14*, 56-64.

Tauber, M. A. Postpartum depression, environmental stress and educational aspiration. Doctoral Thesis, University of California, Berkeley, 1974.

Thuwe, I. Genetic factors in puerperal psychosis. *British Journal of Psychiatry*, 1974, *125*, 378–385.

Tod, E. D. Puerperal depression: A prospective epidemiological study. *Lancet*, 1964, *2*, 1264–1266.

Treadway, C., Kane, F., Jarrahi-Zadek, A., & Lipton, M. A psychoendocrine study of pregnancy and the puerperium. *American Journal of Psychiatry*, 1969, *125*, 1380–1386.

Uddenberg, N. Reproductive adaption in mother and daughter: A study of personality development and adaption to motherhood. *Acta Psychiatrica Scandinavica*, 1975, Supplement No. 254.

Weissman, M. M. & Paykel, E. S. *The Depressed Women*. Chicago: University of Chicago Press, 1974.

White, M. A., Prout, C. T., Fixsen, B. A., & Foundeur, M. The obstetrician's role in postpartum mental illness. *Journal of the American Medical Association*, 1957, *165*, 138–143.

Yalom, I. D., Lunde, D. T., Moos, R. H., & Hamburg, D. A. "Postpartum Blues Syndrome": A description and related variables. *Archives of General Psychiatry*, 1968, *18*, 16.

Zajicek, E. & Wolkind, S. Emotional difficulties in married women during and after the first pregnancy. *British Journal of Medical Psychology*, 1978, *51*, 379–385.

12

The Relation of Stressful Life Events to Gender

Anne Mulvey
University of Lowell

Barbara Snell Dohrenwend
Columbia University School of Public Health

The contemporary Women's Movement and other social, economic, and historical trends have encouraged interest in examining and understanding the lives of women. There has been a tremendous increase in popular and scholarly writing and research which investigates and documents the richness and variety of women's experiences as well as the many barriers to their equality. This literature raises substantive questions and provides new frameworks for understanding and possibly changing the lives of women as well as men. However, much of this work either focuses on specific roles which distinguish women from men, or studies women and men separately, even as it acknowledges the relationship between the two groups or among multiple roles. Little research exists which investigates the variety of roles and experiences in the lives of both women and men without subsuming one group into a framework based on the life conditions or values of the other. It is important to encourage research and theory that explores the multiple life experiences of women and of men using a broad range of categories that will allow for the possibility not only of differences but also of similarities in these groups and their experiences.

A stressful life events paradigm could provide a comprehensive framework for assessing whether life experiences are different for women and men or are seen differently by them. By stressful life events we mean occurrences which disrupt the usual routine or day to day pattern of activity of an individual as, for example, returning to school, taking a trip, or having a new person move into the household (Dohrenwend & Dohrenwend, 1974). By evaluating whether patterns of life events are related to gender, we can begin to answer the following questions: Are the lives of women and men similar or different; if they are different, what is the content of this difference on a descriptive level; is the difference consistent across situations or over the life cycle, or might the differences vary from context to context, or from time to time?

Although differences between women's and men's lives have existed as far back as we can go in recorded and prerecorded history, women's lives have not been of interest in their own right and have usually been investigated as abnormal or aberrant variations from a standard based on male norms and masculine values. What-

ever differences did exist were considered proof of woman's nature or female falli-
bility in a "man's world"; and it was that male world and reality which captured
public interest and scholarly inquiry (Rosenberg, 1974; Shields, 1975; Smith-
Rosenberg & Rosenberg, 1973; Weistein, 1970). Recently, however, attention has
been focused not only on the life experiences of women but also on the importance
of non-psychological factors such as education, economics and the legal system in
understanding these experiences (Baxandall et al., 1976; Bernard, 1974; 1981;
Lerner, 1977; Millman & Kanter, 1975; Tavris & Offir, 1977). Issues that have
been hotly debated include the origin and institutionalization of sex differences,
the social, psychological, and political consequences of gender, and the possibility,
feasibility, and desirability of changing women's and men's roles and options. Most
of these controversial topics involve possible or actual changes in women's lives as,
for example, issues related to abortion and reproductive rights, dual career families
which in reality means a career for the woman as well as the man, women in nontraditional occupations, the Equal Rights Amendment, and the existence and right
to existence of displaced homemakers.

These issues clearly have implications for the lives of men, and reflect not only
personal issues but also structural realities. The experience of gender occurs, then,
in a general social-historical context and numerous particular situations involving
not only individuals of one sex or the other, but also social relationships, social
roles, and institutional structures. A fundamental tenet of the contemporary
Women's Movement which illustrates this perspective is that the personal is political (Morgan, 1970). These dimensions are related to each other in a dialectical
manner. However, the social sciences do not usually investigate gender-related issues
in ways that allow us to capture this complex reality.

A stressful life events approach offers the possibility of descriptively and qualitatively analyzing life experiences in a real world context. The number and contents
of women's and men's life events provide a summary description of their life experience. The amount of disruption or change involved in the events, and the social
value of events whether positive, negative, or neutral provide a measure of the
quality of that experience. In addition to secondary measures like these which refer
to characteristics of the events, there are also secondary measures based on the
perceptions of the person experiencing an event which constitute a subjective
measure of life experience. An example of this sort of measure would be the degree
of anticipation or the amount of control a person perceives she/he has over the
occurrence of her/his stressful life events. Looking at the perceptions individuals
have of their own stressful life events could shed light on whether women and men
have different styles of approaching life experiences regardless of whether the
events are similar or different in content and quality.

We begin this chapter by discussing the ways that the social sciences usually
investigate sex differences or gender roles in order to illustrate that a stressful life
events approach provides a heuristic alternative for exploring the content of
women's and men's lives across situations and life phases, the qualitative dimensions
of their life experiences, and the responses of women and men to these experiences.
We then describe a study of stressful life events from our own work. The results of
this research are presented together with a discussion of methodological issues the
study raises for future stressful life events research and for other research aimed
at understanding the complex role gender plays in structuring the life experiences
of ordinary women and men. Finally, we suggest practical applications and social
interventions which are consistent with this research and perspective.

LIMITS OF TRADITIONAL RESEARCH

Discussion of gender roles is often conducted in terms of traits and persistent personality attributes associated with women or men, as evidenced in the following traditional and all too familiar assumptions: "Men are strong, women are weak; men are instrumental, women are nurturant and expressive." Psychology has done its part in perpetuating, or even encouraging, this perspective by conceptualizing gender-related variables as bipolar, dichotomous dimensions which separate all people neatly into two groups, with women's characteristics, roles and experiences associated with less value and given less recognition than men's (Broverman et al., 1970, Shields, 1975; Weistein, 1970). However, in the past several years, this approach has been criticized. New research techniques have been used to identify sub-groups, or multiple groups, on the basis of combinations of these sets of stereotypic feminine and masculine characteristics (Bem, 1972; 1974; 1975; Spence et al., 1974; 1975). Attempts have been made to acknowledge the positive aspects of traits typically found in women, to illustrate that traits stereotypically associated with one sex may be found in individuals of either gender group, and to highlight the positive mental health implications and adaptive quality of non-stereotypic combinations of these traits. But even this more recent and progressive analysis of sex differences or styles rests on the assumption of relatively consistent internal traits or personality as the basis for understanding women and men as individuals and as groups (Block, 1973; Constantinople, 1973; Grady, 1977; 1979).

We assume that life conditions and situations are essential for understanding the meaning and influence of gender in people's lives; gender is not a static or exclusively internal phenomenon. Rather, a person experiences her/himself not as "a woman" or "a man" in an abstract or static manner but as a "65-year-old, widowed woman" or "a middle-aged man visiting relatives in New Hampshire" or by any number of other descriptors in which sex may or may not be particularly salient. Gender is experienced, then, in relation to other people, situations, and events and in co-occurrence with other personal characteristics and status variables.

The psychological literature which investigates sex differences in mental health and illness also reflects a tendency toward internal and static explanations of health and illness. We note first that psychologists have largely accepted the general position that behavior is determined by both personal dispositions and situational demands. Scientists and practitioners concerned with understanding and treating mental illness have, however, given more attention to the former than the latter. They have tended to focus on early childhood experiences and the vulnerabilities and handicaps that certain types of experiences may generate in the developing person (Albee, 1968; Bloom, 1973; Rappaport, 1977; Rieff, 1968). Although this perspective may contribute to understanding the causes of mental illness in general and gender differences in particular, we suggest that it is inadequate as a framework for thinking about prevention. For this purpose we propose to focus on life situations normally encountered by women, with the idea that changes in these situations might promote greater mental health in women. This approach is based on the assumption that the girl who, as a function of positive early-life experiences, grows to womanhood in good mental health may nevertheless be psychologically impaired by exposure to situational difficulties in adulthood.

Sociology, in contrast to the psychological tradition, tends to focus on global sex roles or social roles associated with gender, as, for example, the mother role or the married role, or even roles like the "macho male" or the "liberated woman."

Such roles are abstract concepts rather than specific or tangible phenomena and may include a number of kinds of experience and multiple levels of influence. The role concept has been criticized for its vagueness and for the often unspecified relationships contained within it (McIntosh, 1971). The role concept serves as a summary term or convenient abbreviation for the diverse influences which are associated with a particular gender group. However, the summary descriptive nature of the term "gender role" limits its utility. Hence, we suggest that the investigation of specific stressful life events associated with the various roles women and men play offers a more comprehensive and meaningful index of the life experience of women and men.

In reviewing the sociology of gender research, Millman (1971) concluded that another weakness of the role approach lies in its tendency to focus "heavily on women" implying that sex roles have only to do with women. Bart (1971, p. 58) noted: "In fact, the term sex role almost always refers to women in the same way that 'urban problems' or 'inner city problems' is a euphemism for 'what are we going to do about blacks'." Following de Beauvoir's (1949) analysis, this differential treatment of the female and male gender roles may be seen as a manifestation of the pervasive assumption that man is "subject" while woman is "object" or "other." It appears that the choice of the roles studied, the interpretation of what is appropriate in the enactment of roles, and the value attached to them, is generally a reflection of current social norms and serves to maintain the status quo even when other arrangements might be feasible and preferable as far as individual well-being is concerned. It is important, therefore, to use a framework which is broad enough and varied enough to allow comparable analysis of the life situations and roles of women and men in order to understand the experiences of women in this sex-typed culture.

There has, of course, been much research concerned with the way in which women's adult life experiences may contribute to poor mental health (Bart, 1971; Bernard, 1972; 1973; Chesler, 1972; Clay, 1977; Gove, 1972; Gove & Tudor, 1972; LeShan, 1974; Neugarten, 1968; Radloff, 1975; Riley, 1969; Rossi, 1968; Scarf, 1980; Sommers, 1974). In general, however, analyses of these experiences have been more concerned with the generic experiences of women as a social status than with the heterogeneous life experiences of women as individuals. This tradition has emphasized female roles prescribed by societies, and the limitations and conflicts implicit in these role prescriptions. Contemporary studies have focused on roles such as mother, wife, worker, and widow, often looking at one apart from the others. Although these analyses have heuristic value, they need to be tested, and perhaps modified, by examination of the concrete life events that women actually experience. Further, as noted above, this investigation must be carried out in relation to the actual, diverse lives of women in order to understand the social meaning, value and psychological impact which may flow from various interrelated roles, situations and demands.

STRESSFUL LIFE EVENTS APPROACH

If we assume, then, that gender is a dynamic social variable which stratifies experience in combination with other systematic and random influences, it becomes essential to use research techniques and theory which will allow both similarities and differences to be discerned, and which will facilitate the investigation of diverse areas of situational experience in a time-limited way. Assessing stressful life events offers this possibility by providing a concrete way to look at the day to day experiences of individuals in these groups. As mentioned earlier, stressful life events refer to occurrences which disrupt the normal routine or day to day activity of an individual as, for example, changing jobs, getting married or divorced, moving, or experiencing an illness. These events may be positive or negative in content; they may involve a great deal of change and disruption or relatively little; they may be socially desirable or undesirable; they may be anticipated or unanticipated; they may or may not be under the person's control.

Research on stressful life events has generally focused retrospectively on the consequences of life events in terms of mental and physical health (Dohrenwend & Dohrenwend, 1974). The major concern in this research has been the nature of a stressful life event or combinations of events and the impact the experience of stressful life events has on subsequent well-being regardless of the particular person or group of persons who may be experiencing the events, and regardless of the particular content of the events. Thus, this area has primarily explored the symptomatic consequences of disruption or change for the individual. Although research on stressful life events has not been particularly concerned with the pattern of life events in healthy groups or with using life events as an indicator of general life experience, patterns of stressful life events could serve as a meaningful indicator of the everyday experiences of people.

An analysis of the overall pattern of stressful life events that women and men experience offers an empirical way to assess the effects of socially defined gender roles and of the structural dimensions involved with them in daily life. Stressful life events may also provide a measure of people's experience which falls outside of whatever systematic influence sex roles exert. The occurrence of a flood, fire or other natural disaster, for example, or the taking of trips, are probably not regulated by gender; thus we would expect these events to be independent of it. Stressful life events may be conceptualized as variables which intervene between the influence of the expectations and demands associated with an individual's sex role and the subsequent consequences of these status-related expectations and demands. They provide a way to look not only at the overall content but also at the general quality of women's lives as compared with men's lives.

Research and theory investigating sex differences and gender roles as well as everyday beliefs about sex differences suggest ideas about how women's and men's life events might differ. The literature on gender roles suggests that women are either understimulated relative to men, since men lead more varied and meaningful lives outside the home, or that women are overburdened by the roles of primary parent, wife, and paid worker.

The former hypothesis is supported to some extent by the findings of a community study in Canberra, Australia reported by Henderson et al. (1981). In comparing the content of women's and men's stressful life events, they found that men reported significantly more work, financial, and legal events, while women reported significantly more events only in the category of pregnancy and childbirth, which are of course limited to women. It should be pointed out that there are very few events in the category of pregnancy and childbirth. No gender differences were found for illnesses and injuries, bereavements, changes in relationships, separations, changes in living conditions, or school-related events.

The literature on gender roles also suggests that greater opportunities and higher status are available to men (Bernard, 1972; Bird, 1968; Broverman et al., 1970; Kanter, 1975). This status difference implies that men have more positively valued experiences; that they are more likely, for example, to be promoted, or elected to a position of leadership in a social or community organization (Clifford & Walster, 1972; Deaux & Taylor, 1973; Touhey, 1974). We should emphasize that we are concerned with the consensual value of an event rather than the value placed on it by a particular individual who has experienced it. For example, divorce is consensually valued as negative even though persons who have recently been divorced sometimes say they are glad that it happened. Further, statistics on sex stratification in employment categories and income indicate that men enjoy higher status and income than women (Ehrlich et al., 1975; Etkowitz, 1971; Sommers, 1974; U.S. Department of Commerce, 1976).

Another implication of the lower or subordinate status of women relative to men is that they would have less control over their lives. This is particularly interesting in relation to mental health because, placed in the context of the theory propounded by Seligman and colleagues (1975) that helplessness and depression result from situationally determined lack of control, it implies that women more often suffer from depression than men. This implication is consistent with observed gender differences in rates of depression (Dohrenwend & Dohrenwend, 1976).

Along with hypotheses about overall differences between women and men, the literature on roles suggests that gender differences vary with other statuses, particularly age and marital status. A hypothesis suggested by lifespan and aging literature is that as women and men grow older their roles become more alike and may even reverse (Cumming & Henry, 1961; Hochschild, 1975; Jung, 1971; Neugarten, 1968). Late middle-age finds women more involved than previously in work activities which is related to the lessened commitment necessary to carry out the post-parental family roles. Women at this time are often experiencing the crest of their involvement and status in paid employment or in social and community activities. There is evidence that there is a loosening of the role constraints of femininity which allows older women to be more independent, active, and in control of various areas of their lives. Men, on the other hand, are less involved than previously with work activities. Many are retired or are looking ahead to it. A contraction of instrumental activities and fewer promotions are characteristic of this time (Brim, 1976; Kimmel, 1974). While women are evidencing more traits associated with the male role, men are taking on more "feminine" traits: a shift of focus from the public world of work to the home and community, coupled with less activity and instrumentality and more emphasis on socio-emotional relationships.

Some empirical support for the latter, crossover hypothesis is provided in gross quantitative terms by Markush's and Favero's findings from two community studies (1974). Among adults under 35 a greater proportion of men than women had high life change scores representing greater activity or change for the young men. Among those over 55 the proportion was greater for women suggesting that levels of activity or involvement are reversing for women and men in late middle age with women becoming more active or instrumental. This gender difference held only in their urban study, however, not in their rural study.

Research on the relationship of marital roles to mental health suggests the general hypothesis that married women are at a disadvantage relative to married men. The marital roles of women and men are qualitatively different: married women occupy a subservient position relative to married men and carry out numerous social and physical support services for their husbands. Married women report more psychological symptoms and stress reactions than married men, single men, and single women (Bernard, 1973; Chesler, 1972; Gove & Tudor, 1972; Laws, 1971). Further, as Gove and Tudor (1972) suggested, this pattern of symptoms may be less extreme but similar for single women as compared with single men.

AN ILLUSTRATIVE STUDY OF STRESSFUL
LIFE EVENTS AND GENDER

Some of our own recent research was designed to investigate the relationship between stressful life events and gender (Mulvey, 1979). A summary of the design and implications of our study is presented here as an example of how a stressful life events paradigm can be used to explore and compare the everyday life experiences of women and men. The themes discussed earlier suggest ways in which the stressful life event patterns of women and men might differ.

In terms of overall number of stressful life events, it was predicted that men would report a greater number of events than women. This was expected as a consequence of men's greater participation in instrumental roles as well as their greater involvement in decision-making and positions of authority both at home and at work. Further, in terms of content of stressful life events, it was expected that women would report more life events than men centering on the family and family-related activities, and that men would report more stressful life events than women centering on work-related activities.

The nature of women's family roles, particularly the housewife role, suggested that women would experience less anticipation of and control over the occurrence of their stressful life events than men. This hypothesis was also based on the nature of women's and men's work outside the home. Another hypothesis suggested by the position of women and men in the home and work spheres concerns the magnitude of events or the amount of change or disruption they entail. It was predicted that the stressful life events of men would involve more change or be of greater magnitude than those of women. This was expected due to the more varied and responsible nature of men's jobs involving decisions and higher risks than women's work as well as the boring and repetitive nature of housework in which most women are involved.

The fact that women are often dependent upon men for economic support and for their sense of personal worth suggested an additional hypothesis. It was predicted that the life events of men would be more desirable than those of women. Also, the higher status of men might serve to give men an advantage or easier access to opportunities and preferred situations which would be associated with desirable stressful life events.

Age and marital status were also expected to influence the stressful life event patterns of women and men. For example, it was predicted that women's and men's life events would be more similar in the middle years than in young adulthood and that their stressful life event patterns might reverse still later in life. This was expected in terms of number of stressful life events, in terms of desirability, and in terms of women's and men's ability to anticipate and control the occurrence of their stressful life events. In terms of the influence of marital status, it was predicted that married women would experience fewer and less desirable stressful life events than married men, and that married women would report less anticipation and control of their events than married men. Further, single women were expected to experience fewer and less desirable stressful life events than single men and were expected to report less anticipation and control of their life events than single men.

The study we report here is based on interviews with a probability sample of New York City residents between the ages of 21 and 64. An interview was conducted in which data on life events were collected as part of a more extensive methodological study of measurement of psychological disorders in heterogeneous community populations. The instrument employed here is the PERI Life Events List. This list consists of a series of 102 life events including events from previous life event lists as well as events drawn from the experience of the local population in two earlier methodological studies carried out in the Washington Heights section of New York City. This procedure was used in order to compile a representative pool of the potential life events of the particular subsample to be studied. As Table 1 illustrates, the PERI Life Event List taps a number of areas of daily living including family, work, legal and community activities. The events involve various degrees of importance ranging, for example, from "getting married," "changing jobs for one that was no better and no worse than the last one," to "change in the frequency of family get-togethers." Different kinds of experiences are sampled as, for example, "graduated from school or training program," and "pet died." For a detailed description of the sampling procedures and the rationale used in the construction of the PERI Life Event List, see B. S. Dohrenwend, 1973; and B. P. Dohrenwend, 1974.

The sample of respondents was a stratified subsample of a probability sample of the population. The larger sample had been interviewed approximately four years earlier. Ths subsample as drawn was 30 percent Black, 30 percent Puerto Rican, and 40 percent non-Puerto Rican White. Within each of these ethnic groupings social class was controlled by sampling similar proportions of each of four levels of years of formal education of the head of the household.

Interviews were originally completed with 169 respondents. Four years later a subsample of 104 respondents completed the stressful life events portion of the interview discussed here. Fifty-two percent of the one hundred four respondents, or 61 percent of the sample, were women; 65 respondents, or 39 percent of the sample, were men. This large sample loss resulted primarily from the general increase in the proportion of urban respondents who refused to be interviewed, and from the fact that the interview was administered in two sittings, one week apart, with questions concerning stressful life events administered in the second sitting. Twenty-one percent of the sample loss was due to refusal to participate in the second part of the interview.

Although they were systematically drawn from a representative sample, clearly the 160 respondents do not constitute a sample from which generalizations could be made, after appropriate weighting of strata, to the population of New York City. Our main purpose in using this sample is, however, not to generalize to a particular geographically defined population but to guard against sociocultural parochialism. For this purpose we believe that this sample is useful.

For investigating the relationship between gender and age, respondents were divided into by gender into three age groups. The young group aged 23 to 39

Table 1 PERI stressful life event list

Content area and event

School
1. Started school or a training program after not going to school for a long time
2. Changed schools or training programs
3. Graduated from school or training program
4. Had problems in school or in training program
5. Failed school, training program
6. Did not gráduate from school or training program

Work
7. Started work for the first time
8. Returned to work after not working for a long time
9. Changed jobs for a better one
10. Changed jobs for a worse one
11. Changed jobs for one that was no better and no worse than the last one
12. Had trouble with a boss
13. Demoted at work
14. Found out that was not going to be promoted at work
15. Conditions at work got worse, other than demotion or trouble with the boss
16. Promoted
17. Had significant success at work
18. Conditions at work improved, not counting promotion or other personal successes
19. Laid off
20. Fired
21. Started a business or profession
22. Expanded business or professional practice
23. Took on a greatly increased work load
24. Suffered a business loss or failure
25. Sharply reduced work load
26. Retired
27. Stopped working, not retirement, for an extended period

Love and marriage
28. Became engaged
29. Engagement was broken
30. Married
31. Started a love affair
32. Relations with spouse changed for the worse, without separation or divorce
33. Married couple separated
34. Divorce

Love and Marriage
35. Relations with spouse changed for the better
36. Married couple got together again after separation
37. Marital infidelity
38. Trouble with in-laws
39. Spouse died

Having children
40. Became pregnant
41. Birth of a first child
42. Birth of a second or later child
43. Abortion
44. Miscarriage or stillbirth
45. Found out that cannot have children
46. Child died
47. Adopted a child
48. Started menopause

Family
49. New person moved into the household
50. Person moved out of the household
51. Someone stayed on in the household after he was expected to leave
52. Serious family argument other than with spouse
53. A change in the frequency of family get-togethers
54. Family member other than spouse or child dies

Residence
55. Moved to a better residence or neighborhood
56. Moved to a worse residence or neighborhood
57. Moved to a residence or neighborhood no better or no worse than the last one
58. Unable to move after expecting to be able to move
59. Built a home or had one built
60. Remodeled a home
61. Lost a home through fire, flood or other disaster

Crime and legal matters
62. Assaulted
63. Robbed
64. Accident in which there were no injuries
65. Involved in a law suit
66. Accused of something for which a person could be sent to jail
67. Lost drivers license
68. Arrested
69. Went to jail

Table 1   PERI stressful life event list (*Continued*)

Content area and event

Crime and legal matters
   70. Got involved in a court case
   71. Convicted of a crime
   72. Acquitted of a crime
   73. Released from jail
   74. Did not get out of jail when expected
Finances
   75. Took out a mortgage
   76. Started buying a car, furniture or other large purchase on the installment plan
   77. Foreclosure of a mortgage or loan
   78. Repossession of a car, furniture or other items bought on the installment plan
   79. Took a cut in wage or salary without a demotion
   80. Suffered a financial loss or loss of property not related to work
   81. Went on welfare
   82. Went off welfare
   83. Got a substantial increase in wage or salary without a promotion
   84. Did not get an expected wage or salary increase
   85. Had financial improvement not related to work

Social activities
   86. Increased church or synagogue, club, neighborhood, or other organizational activities
   87. Took a vacation
   88. Was not able to take a planned vacation
   89. Took up a new hobby, sport, craft or recreational activity
   90. Dropped a hobby, sport, craft or recreational activity
   91. Acquired a pet
   92. Pet died
   93. Made new friends
   94. Broke up with a friend
   95. Close friend died
Miscellaneous
   96. Entered the Armed Services
   97. Left the Armed Services
   98. Took a trip other than a vacation
Health
   99. Physical health improved
  100. Physical illness
  101. Injury
  102. Unable to get treatment for an illness or injury

constituted 37 percent of the sample; early middle age group from 40 to 54 constituted 40 percent of the sample; and the later middle age group, 55 through 64, constituted 24 percent of the sample.

In order to investigate the influence of marital status, each gender age group was divided into two categories, married and unmarried. This yielded a total of 12 groups: young, early middle age, and late middle-age, married and unmarried women and men. It should be noted that some of these groups were quite small, ranging from 2 to 26 respondents in the twelve cells. Due to the small number in some cells, the unmarried category includes single, separated, divorced, and widowed people.

Near the end of the interview the respondent was asked, "What was the last major event that, for better or worse, changed or interrupted your usual activities?" This question was followed by probes concerning the participants in the event and its date. After these questions, respondents were told, "Now I'll ask you about a number of other experiences that people have. Some of these things happen to most people at one time or another, while some of these things happen to only a few people." Following this question, respondents were presented with ten lists of stressful life events in various areas of activity, such as school, work, and family, and asked, for each list, "During the last 12 months, did any of these things happen to you, or to a member of your family or to another person who is important to you?"

After each event was reported, probes were asked to determine the extent to which the respondent had anticipated the occurrence of the event, the extent to which she or he had control over its occurrence, and the date of the event. We should emphasize that the probes concerning control were focused on the occurrence of the event rather than the equally important but separate issue of control over sequelae of the event. The questions concerning anticipation and control were designed to measure these variables on a five point scale, with one representing complete absence of anticipation or of control and five representing complete certainty or total control. Three on the control scale represents a balance or sharing whereby the individual was neither subordinated to outside circumstances or other persons nor dominant over circumstances or other persons (Dohrenwend, 1977).

In order to respond with some sensitivity to the meaning of the stressful life events reported by respondents it was necessary in some instances to omit probes about anticipation or control of the occurrence of events, or both. This omission occurred either when the answer seemed too obvious or the question too threatening. For example, when respondents reported a death, we inquired about their anticipation but not about their control over the occurrence of the event; if a person reported being robbed, we asked about neither. Events that were not probed are included in the analysis when anticipation or control could be scored in common sense terms.

Each event was classified as a gain or desirable, as a loss or undesirable, or as ambiguous either because there appeared not to be a social consensus, for example, about the desirability of the birth of a later child, or because the description of the event was inherently ambiguous as for example, "changed school or training program." These classifications were based on consensus among four judges. Thirty of the 102 stressful life events were classified as gains, 53 events as losses, and 19 events as ambiguous. Stressful life events classified as gains or desirable events were scored 2, ambiguous events 1, and losses or undesirable events 0. See B. S. Dohrenwend et al. (1978) for a complete description of the rating procedure.

The first question we asked was whether women and men differed in the number of stressful life events they had experienced in the previous year. We found no significant difference in the number of life events experienced, with women reporting an average of 3.5 events and a range of one to 10 events, and men reporting an average of 3.6 events and a range of one to 13 events. Nor did we find any differences in number of events when we compared young, early middle-aged, and later middle-aged women and men. When we introduced marital status, however, there was a significant gender by marital status interaction effect ($F = 9.72$, $df = 1,142$, $p < 0.005$). The most striking finding is that single men reported significantly more life events on the average, 6.33, than married men, who reported 3.30, and than both married and single women who reported an average of 3.75 and 3.19, respectively.

We turn next to the question of whether there are differences in the social desirability of stressful life events between women and men in general or as a function of age or marital status. Again, as with number of events we found no overall gender difference in desirability and no difference when we compared young, early middle-aged, and later middle-aged women and men. Similarly, there was no difference when we compared married and unmarried women and men although there was a main effect for marital status such that married people's stressful life events were significantly more positive across gender groups.

The next question concerns the extent to which women and men in general, in three age groups, or married versus unmarried, are able to anticipate their stressful life events. There are no significant gender, gender by age or gender by marital status differences in anticipation scores.

When we made the same comparison of scores describing reported ability to control the occurrence of stressful life events we likewise did not find a significant main effect for gender. However, we did find a significant gender by age interaction ($F = 6.75$, $df = 2,138$, $p < 0.0005$). Post hoc analysis of the gender by age means shown in Table 2, using the relatively conservative Sheffé test, revealed one significant difference among the six cells. The mean stressful life event control level reported by young men, 3.8, is significantly higher than the mean control level of the five other groups, which range from 2.2 to 2.7. Note, in addition, among these five groups who do not differ significantly from one another the two older male groups have lower levels of control than any of the groups of women. The level of control experienced by women over their stressful life events does not differ noticeably across age categories.

These results can be interpreted in absolute as well as relative terms. Recall that the midpoint, 3, on the control scale represents balance or sharing of control over the occurrence of stressful life events. The mean scores in Table 2 indicate, therefore, that only young men are, on the average, dominant over circumstances and other persons in their lives. The average scores of older men and of women of all ages are below the midpoint in the range indicating that circumstances or other persons hold the balance of control over their stressful life events.

We also found a significant three way interaction effect of gender, age, and marital status on level of control of the occurrence of stressful life events ($F = 3.01$, $df = 4,132$, $p < 0.02$). While most of the means cluster between two and three, young married men deviate in the high direction, with a mean control level of 3.97, and late middle-aged nonmarried women deviate in the low direction, with a mean score of 1.73. Given the small numbers involved in some cells in this analysis, however, these differences may not be reliable.

IMPLICATIONS OF THIS SAMPLE STUDY

The finding that control over the occurrence of stressful life events varies with gender and age and, in a complex interaction, with marital status as well, is based on responses that are open to two interpretations. People's reports of their levels of control over their stressful life events may primarily express feelings about life

Table 2 Person mean control ratings broken down by gender and age

	Age							
Gender	Young adult		Early middle-age		Late middle-age		Total	
	$\bar{X}$	n	$\bar{X}$	n	$\bar{X}$	n	$\bar{X}$	n
Women	2.71	36	2.75	38	2.48	13	2.70	87
Men	3.84	19	2.46	21	2.24	17	2.84	58
Total	2.10	55	2.65	59	2.34	30	2.76	145

experiences that reflect their underlying self concept, which would constitute an expressive interpretation, or, alternately, may primarily be realistic responses reflecting the objective qualities of these experiences. Several considerations favor the latter interpretation. First, a previous analysis specifically designed to deal with this issue indicated, on balance, more evidence of realistic appraisal than of projection of personal feelings or consistent styles in responses concerning control of occurrence of events. In this study, intraclass correlations at two points in time for person means and for event means on control scores provided evidence for consistency in levels of control based on particular events, but not based on particular persons (Dohrenwend & Martin, 1979). Furthermore, the expressive interpretation of these responses implies that they were determined by an internal characteristic deeply embedded in the personality. Such a deeply embedded personality characteristic would presumably arise from early socialization and be likely to persist in adulthood especially if defended from the impact of reality. This interpretation would fit gender differences observed consistently through adulthood. It is, however, not a parsimonious interpretation of the reports of control of occurrence of stressful life events, since we found them to differ between younger and older men. Thus, evidence previously developed (Dohrenwend & Martin, 1979) together with parsimonious interpretation of our present results argue that the reported level of control over the occurrence of life events is better interpreted as primarily indicating actual experience than as primarily revealing a stable characteristic of the respondents' self concepts.

Of interest, then, is what these results tell us about the concrete experiences of gender age groups. Young men stand out from the other five groups with significantly higher levels of control. They appear to be dominant or in control of their lives relative to women and older men.

The groups that we had expected to be in control of their daily lives in our society characterized by some as male-dominated or sexist (Grady, 1979; Morgan, 1970; Sommers, 1974) reported that they are not. Middle-aged and late middle-aged men reported least control on the average over the occurrence of their life events. Note, however, that this study investigated ordinary events in the lives of ordinary people, not management of the affairs of state or of the world economy.

Nonetheless, the pattern for men is quite different from that which we would expect from stereotypic assumptions about gender roles. Although the differences did not reach significance, two of the three groups of men reported lower levels of control than any of the groups of women. This contradicts the expectation that men would have greater control over their stressful life events than women due to the more positive opportunities open to men in the work and public spheres and to their higher social status. It also contradicts the stereotype based on sex roles that women are helpless and men are "in control" due to pre-disposition whether constitutional or learned at an early age as part of the sex role.

The negative status of increasing age appears to interact with the positive gender status men enjoy resulting in unexpectedly low levels of control for older men. We suspect that a relative deprivation phenomenon may be occurring with the older men. Perhaps they exaggerate, reflecting greater childhood expectations for adulthood or are affected by a fall from their earlier position of dominance. In contrast, women of all ages experience concrete obstacles and pervasive, though often ambiguous, effects of lower status. For women, then, the negative status of aging may not be as obviously problematic as it is for men who experience unrealized expectations or a more drastic and unilateral reduction of status and opportunity.

This pattern relates to another conflicting theme discussed in the lifespan and gender role literature concerning the advantages and disadvantages associated with women's social roles. While society does not value middle-aged or older women, there is a growing awareness of a positive experience some women have in middle-age as a consequence of "losing" their culturally defined and ambivalently valued "femininity." Some women are relieved that they are no longer perceived of or treated as sex objects and, the cultural value of motherhood notwithstanding, that they no longer have to worry about birth control, unwanted pregnancy, or full-time parenting. There may be greater opportunity for some women to engage in, and be accepted in, culturally valued male roles and styles since these do not conflict as much with the image of the older woman as with that of the younger woman (Clay, 1977; Hochschild, 1975; LeShan, 1974; Rollins, 1971; Rossi, 1968). Men, on the other hand, have little to gain and much to lose as they move into middle-age and later years since freedom from the male role which comes with age offers fewer secondary benefits. Rather, the aging process for men may be a stripping away of male privileges, or of the expectations of power and control associated with them.

The gender by age control pattern, then, does not present a picture of simple convergence or direct reversal as expected. Rather, the interaction is due solely to the high perception of control that young men report. Moreover, the indication that the least control is experienced on the average by older non-married women suggests a more complex pattern of age-related changes in women's and men's control over their life events. As with gender and age, the interaction of age and marital status appears to be different for women and men but lends itself to no obvious interpretation.

These results do suggest, however, that what we are observing is not an intra-psychic developmental process of personality change associated with natural gender differences as the bulk of the literature on sex-role reversal or convergence would suggest. Rather, we speculate that the phenomenon we are tapping is related in some way to particular social status categories and to the qualitatively different life circumstances associated with them. The high levels of control reported by all young men, in combination with the larger number of stressful life events reported by young men who are not married, contrasts most sharply with the lowest level of control reported by late middle-aged women who are not married. These differences are consistent with the qualitatively different social status positions and structural realities of these groups. Older women who are not married—whether widowed, divorced, or single—constitute a marginal group in our society both socially and economically. Young men, on the other hand, occupy a more favored economic position and hold a position of social privilege relative to all women, especially older unmarried women. This points to the complexity of gender stratification both in terms of its co-occurrence with other status factors and in terms of its consequences on a personal level as evidenced by differential levels of control over associated stressful life events.

FUTURE DIRECTIONS: RESEARCH, PRACTICE, AND THEORY

In order to explore these complex relationships further, studies of stressful life events similar to the one discussed above should be repeated with larger samples to substantiate the validity of the results and to introduce further interactional analyses. Meanwhile, we suggest that the meaning and influence of gender should be studied in the context of the complex social structure in which women and men go through various life stages. We should assume until proven otherwise that differences between women and men are not static and may vary not only with age but also with other status and structural variables.

We can only speculate at this point about the effects on mental health of the patterns of control that we have seen. Is it worse to always have relatively low control over events in one's life, as seems to be the case for women, or to lose control, as seems to be the case for men? Or is it not a question of which is worse, but what qualitatively different effects these experiences may have? Whatever the answer, we suggest that our analysis points to the need for thinking about individual well-being and prevention of psychological disorder in terms of improving the quality of concrete life events for both women and men by eliminating stratification based on gender and age and reducing other inequitable social arrangements.

We have argued that the investigation of stressful life events using currently available instruments and rating methods provides a meaningful index of the experience of women and men in normative life situations, and we have conducted and encouraged such research on this basis. At the same time, however, we suggest that stressful life event instruments and methods might be modified to make them more sensitive to possible differences in experience between gender groups and across the life cycle. Stressful life events might be categorized on the basis of dimensions associated with specific gender roles. For example, the female role has traditionally been characterized as passive while the male role has been defined as active. The traditional female role is associated with sensitivity to and involvement with others, and value is placed on the socio-emotional skills and caretaking behaviors which are expected. The traditional male role is associated with instrumental or task-oriented values and behaviors. Coding of stressful life events along these dimensions would allow investigation of these assumed sex-typed traits in real situations and across various spheres including the areas of family and work.

Another dimension of stressful life events that may be important to the investigation of differences concerns the identification of who actually experiences the life event. Some stressful life event instruments ask about life events in which the respondent is the central figure and about life events which happened to others who are important to the respondent. The analysis of these stressful life events is sometimes conducted using summary scores which combine self and other events. Such summary scores could well be misleading since there is a great deal of difference between experiencing an event directly and indirectly experiencing something that happened to someone else, even someone important. This combination of self and other life events is particularly inappropriate in the investigation of gender differences since a fundamental aspect of women's gender role is involvement with others. Much literature regarding women's roles characterizes them as requiring over-involvement with others, or living through others, at the expense of independent activity. It is reasonable to expect, therefore, that women will report more stressful life events that happened to others than men will report. This would mean that women's summary score would be more heavily weighted to the life events of others than to their own life events than men's would. We have found this to be the case in a related study which we conducted (Mulvey, 1979).

Combining these different types of stressful life events misrepresents the index of life events in which the respondent is actually involved. It also obscures the qualitative experience associated with the stressful life events of the respondents. The qualitative dimensions are lost; the more life events the respondent reports that happened to others, the more lost or obscured their own life events become. Thus, secondary measures of desirability, amount of change, or perceived anticipation and control would not be meaningful measures of possible gender-stratified experience. For example, the summary measure of a married woman's stressful life events would probably include some life events that happened to her children or husband, obscuring the distinctiveness of her own experience. This sort of analysis may be responsible for the low levels of control sometimes reported for women over their stressful life events (Dohrenwend, 1977). It may well be that women's perception of control over their own stressful life events is similar to men's perception of control over their life events, especially if their life events are comparable as found here. If so, the summary score is actually a reflection of women's greater involvement in the lives of others whose stressful life events quite understandably allow less control than do their own.

While discussion of the results of our research was focused on the meaning of the differences found between gender groups, the study also points to the need for the investigation of similarities. Criticisms have been raised regarding the limits of the psychological research method which allows the reporting and exploration of differences but not of similarities particularly in the study of women. Psychological research also emphasizes internal variables or person variables rather than investigating situational conditions or social system factors which may account for group differences. This methodology coupled with pervasive social belief in sex differences may encourage inappropriate conclusions about women as a group and may be used to justify or encourage the inferior social position of women. This may perpetuate the assumption of differences in a sex-typed, sex-stratified world in which women's characteristics are usually interpreted as deficits relative to norms which are based on male culture and values. For example, personality research labels women as being "field dependent," and as having an "external locus of control" which is described in the literature as being less desirable and effective than being "field independent" and than having "internal locus of control." Thus, women may be subtly blamed for whatever inequities exist in their treatment or in the general social structure (Grady, 1981; Shields, 1975; Wallston, 1981; Weistein, 1970). The investigation of overlap and similarity among groups and of variety within groups is as relevant and appropriate to social science research as the traditional strategy which isolated only differences, thereby fostering global generalizations and unnecessary divisions based on a limited, possibly misleading piece of the picture.

Probably the most striking finding in this study is that the stressful life events of women and men as discrete groups do not differ in any clear or consistent manner. Men and women reported very similar numbers of stressful life events and these events were of comparable desirability and magnitude. Paralleling this, there was no difference in the amount of anticipation or control the women and men themselves perceived having over the occurrence of their life events. Thus, no significant differences were found in relation to gender either in the consensually judged aspects of magnitude and desirability representing the social value of the events, or in the respondents' own ratings of anticipation and control representing their subjective experience of the events.

A study such as this one also points to even more complexity and the need for a broader, interdisciplinary framework. Attention should be focused on other co-occurring status variables lest we attribute to gender, age, or marital status that which might be the result of other factors. Ethnic differences may also shape gender role experience, though the particular form this takes may be hard to define. We know, for example, that life expectancy varies across ethnic groups as do the stereotypic gender roles (Mulvey, 1979). Some cultures are noted for their "macho man" or their "super mothers." To investigate these sorts of relationships it is necessary to go beyond the psychological level and to incorporate the influence of social structural factors and macro variables within their historical context.

It is important, also, to consider other more immediate influences that are relatively independent of gender stratification. For example, there are factors such as social and economic crises, as with the current recession or increased public awareness of the reality of nuclear threat, that come on the scene rapidly and interact with gender and other status variables in complex ways to inform life experience.

The task of developing an interdisciplinary and historical framework is a difficult one, but the appropriateness of such a conceptual perspective warrants the effort. Stressful life events research offers this possibility and we hope the perspective presented here will encourage more work in this direction. Gender is not a static or homogeneous variable and research should be encouraged that has the potential to document the variety and heterogeneity of life experiences associated with it as well as the possibly minimal role it plays in relation to other powerful influences.

REFERENCES

Albee, G. W. Conceptual models and manpower requirements in psychology. *American Psychologist*, 1968, *23*, 317–320.

Bart, B. Depression in middle-aged women. In V. Gornick (ed.), *Woman in sexist society*. New York: Basic Books, 1971.

Baxandall, R., Gordon, L., & Reverby, S. *America's Working Women*. New York: Vintage Books, 1976.

Bem, S. Psychology looks at sex roles: Where have all the androgynous people gone? Paper presented at UCLA Symposium on Women, May 1972.

Bem, S. A measurement of psychological androgyny. *Journal of Consulting and Clinical Psychology*, 1974, *42*, 155–162.

Bem, S. Sex role adaptability: One consequence of psychological androgyny. *Journal of Personality and Social Psychology*, 1975, *31*(4), 634–643.

Bernard, J. *The Future of Marriage*. New York: Bantam Book, 1972.

Bernard, J. *The Future of Motherhood*. New York: Penguin Books, 1974.

Bernard, J. *The Female World*. New York: The Free Press, 1981.

Bird, C. *Born Female*. New York: David McKay and Company, 1968.

Block, J. Conceptions of sex-role: Some cross-cultural comparisons and longitudinal perspectives. *American Psychologist*, 1973, *28*, 512–527.

Bloom, B. L. The domain of community psychology. *American Journal of Community Psychology*, 1973, *1*, 8–11.

Broverman, I. K., Broverman, D. M., Clarkson, F. E., Roencrantz, P. S., & Vogel, S. R. Sex-role stereotypes and clinical judgments of mental health. *Journal of Consulting and Clinical Psychology*, 1970, *34*, 1–7.

Chesler, P. *Women and Madness*. New York: Avon Books, 1972.

Clay, V. S. *Women and menopause and middle-age*. Pittsburgh, PA: Know, Inc., 1977.

Clifford, M. M. & Walster, E. The effect of sex on college admission, work evaluation, and job interviews. *Journal of Experimental Education*, 1972, *41*, 1–5.

Constantinople, A. Masculinity-femininity: An exception to a famous dictum. *Psychological Bulletin*, 1973, *80*, 389–407.

Cumming, E. & Henry, W. *Growing old: The process of disengagement*. New York: Basic Books, 1961.

De Beauvoir, S. (1949). *The second sex*. New York: Bantam Books, 1970.

Deaux, K. & Taylor, J. Evaluation of male and female ability: Bias works both ways. *Psychological Reports*, 1973, *32*, 261–262.

Dohrenwend, B. P. Problems in defining and sampling the relevant population of stressful life events. In B. S. Dohrenwend & B. P. Dohrenwend (eds.), *Stressful life events: Their nature and effects*. New York: Wiley, 1974.

Dohrenwend, B. P. & Dohrenwend, B. S. Sex differences in psychiatric disorder. *American Journal of Sociology*, 1976, *81*, 1447–1454.

Dohrenwend, B. S. Life events as stressors: A methodological inquiry. *Journal of Health and Social Behavior*, 1973, 167–175.

Dohrenwend, B. S. Anticipation and control of stressful life events: An exploratory analysis. In J. S. Strauss, H. N. Babigian, & M. Roff (eds.), *Origin and course of psychopathology*. New York: Plenum Press, 1977.

Dohrenwend, B. S. & Dohrenwend, B. P. (eds.), *Stressful life events: Their nature and effects*. New York: Wiley, 1974.

Dohrenwend, B. S., Krasnoff, L., Askenasy, A. R., & Dohrenwend, B. P. Exemplification of a method for scaling life events: The PERI life events scale. *Journal of Health and Social Behavior*, 1978, *19*, 205–229.

Dohrenwend, B. S. & Martin, J. L. Personal versus situational determination of anticipation and control of the occurrence of stressful life events. *American Journal of Community Psychology*, 1979, 7(4), 453–468.

Gove, W. The relationship between sex roles, marital status, and mental illness. *Social Forces*, 1972, *51*, 34–44.

Gove, W. & Tudor, J. Adult sex roles and mental illness. *American Journal of Sociology*, 1972, *78*, 812–835.

Grady, K. Sex as a social label: The illusion of sex differences. (Doctoral Dissertation, City University of New York, 1977). Dissertation Abstracts International, 1977, *38*, 416B. (University Microfilms, No. 77-13,658).

Grady, K. Androgyny reconsidered. In J. H. Williams (ed.), *Psychology of women: Selected readings*, New York: Norton, 1979.

Grady, K. E. Sex bias in research design. *Psychology of Women Quarterly*, 1981, *5*(4), 628–636.

Henderson, S., Burne, D. G., & Duncan-Jones, P. *Neurosis and the Social Environment*. New York: Academic Press, 1981.

Hochschild, A. Disengagement theory: A critique and a proposal. *American Sociological Review*, 1975, *40*, 553–569.

Jung, C. G. (1930). The stages of life. In J. Campbell (ed.), *The portable Jung*. New York: The Viking Press, 1972.

Kanter, R. M. Women and the structure of organizations: Explorations in theory and behavior. In M. Millman & R. M. Kanter (eds.), *Another voice: Social life and social science*. New York: Anchor Books, 1975.

Laws, J. A feminist review of marital adjustment literature: The rape of the Locke. *Journal of Marriage and the Family*, 1971, 483–516.

Lerner, G. *The female experience: An American documentary*. Indianapolis, IN: Bobbs-Merrill Company, 1977.

LeShan, E. J. *The wonderful crisis of middle age*. New York: Warner Paperbacks, 1974.

Markush, R. E. & Favero, R. V. Epidemiologic assessment of stressful life events, depressed mood, and psychophysiological symptoms—A preliminary report. In B. S. Dohrenwend & B. P. Dohrenwend (eds.), *Stressful life events: Their nature and effects*. New York: John Wiley & Sons, 1974.

McIntosh, M. The homosexual role. In A. S. Skolnick & J. H. Skolnick (eds.), *Family in Transition*. Boston, MA: Little Brown and Company, 1971.

Millman, M. Observations on sex-role research. *Journal of Marriage and the Family*, 1971, 772–776.

Millman, M. & Kanter, R. M. *Another voice: Social life and social science*. New York: Anchor Books, 1975.

Morgan, R. (ed.) *Sisterhood is powerful*. New York: Random House, 1970.

Mulvey, A. The relationship of life events, gender and age: A community study of adulthood (Doctoral Dissertation, City University of New York, 1979). Dissertation Abstracts International, *40*, (University Microfilms, No. 52123).

Neugarten, B. L. (ed.), *Middle-age and aging*. Chicago: The University of Chicago Press, 1968.

Radloff, L. Sex differences in depression: The effects on occupational and marital status. *Epidemiological Studies*, NIMH, 1975, *1*(3), 249 ff.

Rappaport, J. *Community psychology: Values, research, and action*. New York: Holt Rinehart and Winston, 1977.

Rieff, R. Social intervention and the problem of psychological anslysis. *American Psychologist*, 1968, *23*, 524-531.

Riley, M. W., Foner, A., Hess, B., & Toby, M. L. Socialization for the middle and later years. In D. A. Goslin (ed.), *Handbook of Socialization Theory and Research*. Chicago: Rand McNally, 1969.

Rollins, B. Motherhood: Who needs it? In A. S. Skolnick and J. S. Skolnick (eds.), *Family in transition*. Boston: Little Brown & Co., 1971.

Rosenberg, R. The dissent from Darwin, 1890-1930: The new view of woman among American social scientists. Unpublished Doctoral Dissertation, Stanford University, 1974.

Rossi. A. Transition to parenthood. *Journal of Marriage and the Family*, 1968, *30*, 26-39.

Scarf, M. *Unfinished business: Pressure points in the lives of women*. Garden City, NY: Doubleday and Company, 1980.

Seligman, M. E. P. *Helplessness*. San Francisco: W. H. Freeman and Company, 1975.

Shields, S. Functionalism, Darwinism, and the psychology of women: A study of social myth. *American Psychologist*, 1975, *30*, 739-754.

Smith-Rosenberg, C. & Rosenberg, C. The female animal: Medical and biological views of woman and her role in nineteenth century America. *The Journal of American History*, 1973, *9*, 58-80.

Sommers, T. The compounding impact of age and sex. *Civil Rights Digest*, Fall 1974.

Spence, J., Helmreich, R., & Stapp, J. The personal attributes questionnaire: A measure of sex-role stereotypes and masculinity-femininity. *Journal Supplement Abstract Service Catalogue of Selected Documents in Psychology*, 1974, *4*, 43 (MS. no. 617).

Spence, J., Helmreich, R., and Stapp, J. Rating self and peers on sex-role attributes and their relation to self-esteem and conception of masculinity and femininity. *Journal of Personality and Social Psychology*, 1975, *32*, 29-39.

Tavris, C. & Offir, C. *The longest war: Sex differences in perspective*. New York: Harcourt Brace Jovanovich, Inc., 1977.

Touhey, J. C. Effects of additional women professionals on ratings of occupational prestige and desirability. *Journal of Personality and Social Psychology*, 1974, *29*, 86-89.

Wallston, B. S. What are the questions in psychology of women? A feminist approach to research. *Psychology of Women Quarterly*, *5*(4), 597-617.

Weistein, N. Kinde, Kuche, Kirche as scientific law: Psychology constructs the female. In R. Morgan (ed.), *Sisterhood is powerful*. New York: Random House, 1970.

13

Differential Needs and Treatment Approaches for Women in Psychotherapy

Raymond P. Lorion
University of Tennessee, Knoxville

Kathleen G. Broughan
Child and Adult Clinical Associates, Knoxville

INTRODUCTION

"Can a male therapist *really* understand the needs of a woman client?" That question was asked of the senior author nearly ten years ago as he was interviewed for a faculty position at a large northeastern university. The woman student who asked the question quickly followed it up with "and what must *he know before he* attempts to treat her?" Albeit that these questions were asked during an "informal" opportunity for the clinical psychology graduate students to meet the faculty candidate, neither the setting nor the question felt "informal" at that moment. Had he not known better, he would have sworn that his chair was equipped with a heating element because it certainly felt quite warm! In fact to ease the tension in the room (it seemed that you could cut it with a knife) and to gain at least a moment to formulate a coherent answer, he responded facetiously to the second question with: "at the very least, the therapist must recognize that his client is a woman."

Needless to say, that attempt at levity hardly accomplished its goal. The men in the room interpreted it as a "put-down" of the questioner; the women in the room felt that it was insensitive, at best, and insulting, at worst. Although unspoken, the label "sexist" seemed to hang in the air.

What followed was a reasonably useful discussion of the problems of providing psychotherapeutic services to women, specifically, and disenfranchised and/or minority groups in general. At issue was whether the majority of psychotherapists (i.e., white, middle and upper-income males) could appreciate and empathize with the experiences of members of those segments of the population. Equally important, however, was whether a therapist, of whatever gender, race, or cultural background, could make assumptions about the sociopolitical views of a client merely on the basis of that client's demographic characteristics.

It became obvious that the two questions highlighted an important *potential*

The authors wish to express their sincere appreciation to the many colleagues and friends with whom they have discussed these issues during the past year. Equal appreciation is expressed to the many clients, male and female, who have taught us so much.

Note: All case material represents a composite of patients seen by authors over the last ten years.

239

confound in the development of the client-therapist relationship and in the accuracy of assumptions about the etiology of the client's presenting concerns. For some clients, the development and continuation of reported symptoms was heavily related to the pressures which accompanied their commitment to the ongoing social struggle. Desired occupational and life style roles were perceived as denied, limited, or unnecessarily and unfairly costly. For others, the seeming devaluation of their lives and themselves as wives, mothers, and home-makers contributed to feelings of worthlessness, depression, and helplessness as they perceived alternative roles as undesired and/or unreachable. For yet others, the struggle was irrevelant to their longstanding psychological needs and inabilities to cope effectively with past and current stressors. For all, however, gender had suddenly become an unavoidable issue and men and women became more uncertain than ever about expected interactional and interpersonal responses. Within the therapeutic relationship, client and therapist alike engaged in the initial stages of treatment with concerns about where the other stood on the "Issue." Consequently, for some therapists a heretofore practiced art of assisting an individual became instead awkward and uncomfortable. For others, therapy became a soapbox for the expression of political views; clients who did not initially share such views were "treated" in order to facilitate the acquisition of such "insights."

Without really answering either question, a general consensus appeared to emerge that to respond to *any* client as a member of a class of individuals with presumed homogeneous characteristics and attitudes rather than as an individual with unique needs, views, experiences, and goals was antitherapeutic regardless of who did it. In addition, the self-defeating and illogical nature of rigid exclusionary positions (e.g., only women should treat women) became apparent. Realistically, the majority of service providers available at that time were men and the majority of consumers of those services were women. To exclude the former would result in significantly limiting access to treatment for the latter. Moreover, if carried to its logical extreme the requirement of similarity between client and therapist could not be limited to gender. Should one not also add such factors as race, sexual orientation, age, marital status, and economic background? As each criterion was added to the list, the number of potential service providers appropriate for any given client would dwindle geometrically. More important, it seemed to all in the room that attention should be paid to resolving the second question (i.e., "what must *he* know before *he* attempts to treat her?") in its most global form. Hence, the real issue appeared to be what must we know about someone, regardless of their demographic characteristics, to be able to help them? As the very least it appeared that the therapist, male or female, recognize his/her political/cultural attitudes toward women's changing roles and monitor his/her need to have the client adopt that same view. It appeared equally important to explore, at some point in the treatment, the client's perception of the relevance of the ongoing social change processes to presenting issues. Finally, given the intensity with which such attitudes were held, it seemed reasonable that each therapist attempt to develop some means, be it through professional supervision, cotherapy, or whatever, to monitor his/her objectivity and openness in the treatment process.

Given the quality of its initial moments, the end-product of that afternoon's meeting was both unexpected and much appreciated. Reflection even now reveals the inappropriateness of the initial hostility as well as the absurdity of the facetious

(?) response. Although both sets of comments clearly reflected the awkwardness of the time, neither contributed to the search for productive solutions to what was and remains a very significant issue for the providers and consumers of mental health services—how to respond most sensitively to the needs of women.

In spite of extensive interest in the initial questions during the past decade by numerous clinicians, researchers, and lay persons, satisfactory answers remain elusive. As one reads that literature and learns this or that "fact" about "women," their relevance to specific individuals seems minimal. "Women" don't seek treatment! A person, who happens to be a woman, contacts someone in order to gain assistance in resolving a source of pain, distress, and personal discomfort. That person wants to find someone who can understand her experience, empathize with her pain, and, most importantly, help her to do something effective to resolve it. The nature of the pain will differ for each individual. For some it is chronic, a dull ache long endured whose removal, however much desired, seems unlikely. For others, it is sharp, like a toothache, needing immediate and decisive attention/ intervention. Most, if not all women, however, seek consultation for personal not political reasons.

Consistent with that fact, this chapter represents an attempt to discuss the individuals who seek treatment. As reflected in the title, our focus is on women and we hope to share with the readers our experience as individual and conjoint therapists in responding to their needs. Our presentation is based on clinical rather than empirical data and, ideally, will serve both informational and heuristic purposes. As we worked together we learned what should have always been obvious—each of us, as a function of idiosyncratic, personal and professional experiences, theoretical orientation and therapeutic style and, yes, gender, has something unique and, in many instances complementary to offer to the women who seek our help. The success of this chapter depends on our ability to communicate the complementarity of those differences and their differential application to individual client needs. Toward that goal, our discussion considers the following questions: 1) in a very general sense what is psychotherapy?; 2) using composite case histories, what are the presenting problems of contemporary women who seek treatment?; and 3) how does one match presenting issues and therapeutic strategies?

PSYCHOTHERAPY—OUR PERSPECTIVE

Apart from its conceptual basis, consideration of the pragmatics of psychotherapy provides interesting insights into its processes. An individual (labelled "client" or "patient") experiencing some form of emotional distress approaches a second individual (labelled "therapist" of whatever discipline) in order to obtain relief for that distress. Typically neither has had prior contact with the other, nor are they likely to continue interacting once the distress is relieved. The client's selection of the therapist is often unsystematic if not, in fact, happenstance. In many cases, the potential client learns of the therapist through word-of-mouth from former clients, attorneys, clergy, and/or physicians. Since, typically, little explanation is provided as to the "what" of the distress and little understanding exists as to the "why" of the distress, the appropriateness of the referral is often based at best on a hunch, i.e., a sense that "you'll be able to work together." In other cases, the client simply consults the yellow pages and relies on the assumption that professional credentials assure the likelihood of competence and relief.

However the contact is made, the client's task slowly becomes evident. The client speaks; the therapist listens. In most instances what comments are made by the latter are intended to encourage, facilitate, perhaps even guide the former to gain perspectives on the feelings of distress; its antecedents; its victims; its costs; and its rewards. Regardless of theoretical orientation, the competent therapist is likely to convey interest, understanding, empathy, acceptance, and to encourage the client to translate a growing understanding into action. The latter step occurs, in our view, because the essence of the therapeutic relationship is trust. The client comes to trust the therapist with secrets unknown to anyone (including at times the client); to trust that the therapist will be supportive and available if attempts at resolution become difficult and painful; and to trust the therapist's assurances that the client can reach and resolve the problems. In essence, the strangers engage in a very intense unidirectional exchange of highly personal and intimate information and one (i.e., the therapist) conveys through word and attitude, the other's (i.e., the client) capacity to consider what seemed unacceptable to consider and to attempt what heretofore appeared impossible to do. Thus, the therapeutic process, however conceptualized, involves one person facilitating another to step out, look at, and change that which nurtured and maintained the distress.

As therapists we share the view that our role is to assist the client to look at, assess, accept, and gain control over herself. We view our goal as facilitating the client's knowledge of how she gets in her own way and stops herself from obtaining what she wants. We attempt to aid her in seeing where she is going, what she is doing, and whether or not those activities reflect adequate potential for attaining what she wants. Our bias is that the process requires a therapeutic understanding of the dynamics of behavior from multiple theoretical perspectives including dynamic, social-learning, and behavioral theories but that the client need not necessarily acquire a similar theoretical perspective. We believe that much distress in people's lives results from faulty assumptions about unavailable options, ignored alternatives, and choices and thereby enable the client to weigh desired outcomes and assume responsibility for seeking or not seeking those outcomes. The exercise of choice is central to our view for we accept the possibility that a client may choose not to opt, not to change, or not to actualize her potential because of considerations about (un)acceptable costs relative to potential benefits. That is not intended to suggest that we would prefer or encourage that choice but we respect and accept it as a client's prerogative.

A final bias which should be mentioned is our firm commitment to a prescriptive orientation toward the therapeutic process. In other words, we endorse the idea that individuals, being unique, require different therapeutic approaches and techniques and, attempt insofar as possible, to match both what we do and who does it with what the client needs. This process reflects our rejection of *uniformity perspectives*, however expressed. Consequently, we disagree with the view that any therapeutic orientation (e.g., psychoanalysis or behavior modification) or strategy (e.g., group psychotherapy or family therapy) is applicable to all clients. We also recognize the fact that each of us as therapists may be differentially appropriate for and effective with different clients. This may at times be due to gender, our respective personalities, or some interactional effect of these variables. Finally, as emphasized repeatedly, we believe that the most serious uniformity error that one can make relates to the identification of the client with a group rather than as an individual and contingent erroneous generalizations about attitudes, feelings, goals, expectations, and conflict areas. As will be evident in the section which follows, the heterogeneity which exists among a population subgroup, in this instance among women, is highly significant and must be appreciated if the treatment process is to be responsive to individual needs.

WOMEN SEEKING TREATMENT—WHO ARE THEY?

A decade ago, when the senior author initially encountered the questions discussed at the beginning of this chapter, the song, "I Am Woman" served as a vivid expression of the newly emerging view of women as autonomous, competent, assertive, and self-confident individuals committed to assuming an equal place in the world with men. During that decade, significant albeit incomplete advances have been made relative to women's increased involvement particularly in the professions, business and government. For some individuals, those gains were made without significant disruptions of long-standing roles vis-a-vis themselves in relation to men, home, family, etc. In essence, these women established a comfortable balance between the old and the new which provided both a positive sense of self as effective, competent people and as women with needs, desires, and capabilities which differ from those of men. For others, however, gains were won on a battlefield in which the "enemy" was perceived as all men as well as those women who, for whatever reason, chose not to be "liberated." Those fighters experienced the past decade as a period of intense struggle and, in many cases, felt it necessary to sacrifice and/or deny many aspects of themselves as women on the altar of equality. This latter group represents a significant component of the current population of women who seek treatment as a means of resolving intense underlying feelings of anger, deception, loneliness, and despair. Their plight is reflected in the words of a recent popular ballad, "I've Never Been to Me":

Sometimes I've been to crying for unborn children that might have made me complete. But I, I took the sweet life and never knew I'd be bitter from the sweet. I've spent my life exploring the subtle whoring that costs too much to be free. Hey lady, I've been to paradise, but I've never been to me.

The intensity of that continuing struggle has abated somewhat and the present time appears to represent a period during which many women are appraising where they have come, what it has cost them, and, most importantly what their priorities in terms of self, relationships, and career will be. The decade's events have redefined, forever perhaps, the role-expectations of and for women. Many are currently attempting to integrate these changes into a meaningful sense of self. As reflected in numerous personality theories, cognitive, emotional, and interpersonal developments occur in a relatively orderly sequential fashion. If significant difficulty is experienced in managing the issues in any phase of development, the individual is likely to suffer from some degree of developmental arrest in that area. Although the individual may proceed to activities associated with higher levels of development, these unresolved areas remain "weak spots" in the personality that interefere with the total functioning of the individual. Our clinical experience suggests to us that these "weak spots" assume different forms at various stages of development as does the task of establishing a viable, well-integrated identity. In the following composite case descriptions, we have attempted to illustrate several examples of the problematic resolutions which exemplify those whom we have seen in psychotherapy in the past few years.

The Adolescent Crisis

The contemporary female adolescent who enters treatment appears to be affected directly and/or indirectly by the as yet undefined resolution of traditional and contemporary roles for women. Pressured singly or in combination by parents, teachers, peers, and other significant persons in their lives to be assertive, competent, successful, etc.—to actualize their potential as individuals—the adolescent female also experiences considerable pressure to accept and integrate her feminity. In some instances, she is pressured to emphasize one and deny the other, perhaps in reflection of a parent's earlier choice among the two. In other instances, she chooses to deny one in response to a highly competitive, liberated, and dominant parent who serves as a model either to emulate or to avoid. Among the manifestations of these conflicts which we have observed are three major subtypes: the "Lolitas," the "Missy Anns," and the "Baby Dumplings."

The "Lolitas" are typically quite attractive, physically precocious young women whose parents openly fought the "battle of the sexes" throughout the adolescent's early childhood. In many cases, by the time adolescence occurs for the client, the marriage is dissolved legally and/or emotionally. Yet the battle continues to rage on, at times using the needs, rights, ambitions, etc. of the adolescent (as perceived and defined by each parent) as a vehicle for waging war against each other. For the adolescent, each of her moves is evaluated in terms of its possible interpretation of loyalty or betrayal by one or the other parent. Thus, each positive step taken by the adolescent becomes, in essence, evidence for or against one or the other parent rather than testimony to the benefit of their combined efforts. The solution to this conflict adapted by the "Lolitas" is to engage in behaviors which neither parent takes credit for and which, simultaneously, at an unconscious level express both the anger felt by the adolescent toward both of them and the need for some evidence of love and caring. Symptomatic manifestations include marked opposition, sexual acting out, substance-abuse, and academic failure. Ironically, the more desperately that "Lolita" cries out for someone to confirm their caring for her by imposing and enforcing appropriate limits on her behavior, the more intensely both parents struggle to fix blame for her misconduct on the other. The absence of a clear and consistent expression of concern about the child's welfare, via establishing a firm structure of behavioral rules, consistent limits, and appropriate punishment of transgressions, is interpreted by the adolescent as justification for continued acting-out. A case in point is D.R., an attractive, well-built 17-year-old girl who was a merit scholar prior to the onset of her parents' marital difficulties. During her junior year, D.'s father became involved with another woman, for whom he eventually left his wife of 20 years and daughter. D. initially engaged in minor 'tactics' to win back her father, i.e., lowered grades, truancy from school, and violations of curfew. As the extent of her father's desertion became an increasingly undeniable reality, D.'s frantic attempts to force him into some active role in her life became evident as did her ambivalence toward him. Her grades plummeted, she became sexually promiscuous, abused alcohol and drugs in dangerous proportion, and virtually defied anyone in authority to do anything about her behavior. Blaming her ex-husband's abandonment for D.'s difficulties, D.'s mother assumed an understanding, patient stance in response to her daughter's behavior and welcomed her ex-husband's occasional gestures of concern and long distance help.

Although D.'s mother was in therapy herself, her therapist initially found it impossible to move her out of her hostile dependency upon her ex-husband into a more effective, competent mode of dealing with her daughter. It was only after the mother was able to disengage herself from her ambivalence regarding her husband's abandonment and resolve her own fantasies of his "rescue" that she was able to begin setting and enforcing appropriate limits on her daughter's behavior and demonstrating her care and concern for her limiting her self-destructive acting-out.

The "Missy Anns" manifest an almost total lack of autonomy in interactions with others. They have typically been overprotected throughout life, pampered to the point of never having had to engage in effective activities in response to their own needs, and denied until adolescence the opportunity to make any independent substantive decisions. The "Missy Anns" tend to be "perfect ladies" in the most stereotypically traditional sense of the term. The rigidity of their highly structured early years left little room for misbehavior. Emotionally, the onset of adolescence finds "Missy Ann" poorly equipped to cope with increased peer contact and influence, sexual maturation, and multiple demands for independent decision-making. Demands for continued parental protection are, in many cases, received negatively. Recognizing their mistake, the parents compound the error by deciding to force the adolescent to grow up and "learn to take responsibility." "Missy Ann" is suddenly deserted and overwhelmed by the combination of parental betrayal and multiple options at every point. Uncertain of how to decide and the consequences of the "wrong decision," "Missy Ann" chooses what appears to be the safest option—she does nothing. In other words, she "freezes" emotionally perhaps even to the point of approaching a psychotic-like regression reflecting gross denial of the need to choose. "Missy Ann's" immobility is often the presenting problem when she is hurriedly entered into treatment by a concerned family member. J. was brought to her first therapy session by her mother, a large, domineering woman who immediately entered into a disagreement with the secretary about how she would handle the insurance billing. During her initial sessions J. sat as if in a trance, mechanically answering the therapist's questions in her affectless monotone and repeating a litany of symptoms including an inability to think clearly, lack of desire to see friends or involve herself in social activities, fears of failing in school, and episodes of binge eating. For all of her reported social apathy, her appearance was flawless. Her make-up was always perfectly and tastefully applied, her dress in the finest traditional styles. She slowly revealed the constriction and oppressiveness of her early history. Following her father's death at age seven, her mother made every attempt to protect her daughter and rear her 'properly'. Prohibited from exploring the world in any manner, (to the extent that she was not allowed outside the yard until age twelve except in the presence of her mother) J. became increasingly dependent upon the "always right' dictates of her mother and increasingly questioned her own judgment. As her therapist encouraged her to explore her feelings, it became apparent that J. was terrified by the onset of adulthood and the concomitant responsibility that was imminent. She had little sense of who she was as a separate being, and no sense of herself as functioning independently in adulthood. Flowery as it may sound, contributing to and observing the increasing recognition of her own strengths, emerging competencies and potential was like participating in a spring thaw.* J. decided to take up studies in medical science, and enthusiastically made straight A's in her first semester's work. At the time of her termination from therapy she was looking forward to finding her own apartment, having made plans to live with a female classmate that she had met and had developed a relationship with a young man to whom she was quite attracted and was seeing on a regular basis.

The "Baby Dumplings" represent a variation of the "Missy Anns." Materially spoiled although emotionally deprived by highly competitive and ambitious parents, "Baby Dumplings" have also failed to develop the foundation necessary for auto-nomous functioning. When confronted by the demands for independence charac-teristic of adolescence, however, "Baby Dumpling's" refusal to give up the de-pendent child role (often expressed by means of some variant of a temper tantrum) is responded to by the parent with reassurance rather than desertion. "Baby Dumpling's" parents confirm her Peter Pan fantasy that "little girls don't have to grow up" and continue to provide for all of her needs, except the emotional sup-port necessary for developing an independent sense of self. As one "Baby Dump-ling," daughter of judge/lawyer parents, so aptly put it, "I feel like I'm on the edge of the nest and afraid that I can't fly. I really wish my mother would nudge me out or something, but instead she just keeps feeding me worms."

The Young Adult Crisis

This period in a woman's life represents that point at which an initial decision about goals and life styles has been made and strategies for their attainment are undertaken. The women in this age group whom we see are typically living alone or are married to ambitious and promising young professionals or businessmen. Beyond those generalities, this group presents highly diverse needs and conflicts. Categorically, we can identify four primary subgroups: the "Lonely Lottas," the "Piranhas," the "Alice in Wonderlands," and the "Wonder Womans."

The "Lonely Lottas" are in many ways the older version of the "Lolitas." Their serious conduct disorders and substance abuse have been brought under control as a result of external factors (such as probation, school expulsion, etc.) which made evident to them the need to work toward independence and control over themselves. Numerous disappointing interactions with men have made "Lonely Lotta" very reluctant to trust them. In many cases, she defines men as the oppres-sor and, unwilling to let them use her again (only later does she begin to recognize her contribution to the process), she adopts an isolated existence with very limited contacts with others. "Lonely Lotta" works very hard at being independent but, in the absence of feedback from others, she makes numerous mistakes. Early on, she attempts to use each mistake as justification for returning to the prior state of over protection from parents who reject her approaches and continue to insist that she grow up but refuse to assist her in the process.

The "Piranha" represents a variant of the "Lonely Lotta." This group of women also perceive men as the source of their problems. Rather than avoid them, how-ever, the "Piranhas" have identified with the 'aggressor'. They adopt what they

*The range of alternatives which define therapeutic goals and outcomes is so much more extensive that the likelihood of growth is significantly increased as is the therapist's sense of accomplishment. In essence, this is a very exciting time to be working with women as clients.

perceive as stereotypic masculine characteristics of ambitiousness, ruthlessness, aggression, and selfishness. At times, their behavior represents a reaction to earlier interactive patterns in which they were victimized by exploitative men. If married, these women adopted very passive dependent roles toward their husbands and very overprotective, self-sacrificing roles toward their children. Disappointed by both, the "Piranha" decides to "find herself" through success and to achieve that success by using and abusing the enemy—men. Their targets often resemble male counterparts of their earlier selves—i.e., weak, passive, insecure males. Their anger toward these men is expressed in highly manipulative and emasculating relationships which leave the "Piranha" with a bitter sense of victory since each "success" provides further confirmation of her inability to rely on men for genuine support. The growing sense of depression which accompanies her disappointment and loneliness is often the precipitant for entry into treatment.

The "Alice in Wonderland," an older version of the "Missy Ann," wanders around the big world in which she is expected to be assertive, ambitious, and successful and "pretends" to be what others want of her. She feels, however, that she must forever guard against allowing others to see how insecure and incompetent she really is. In order to do so "Alice" acts out the career expectations of others and relies upon their plaudits to confirm the value of her actions. "Alice" may adopt a very aggressive unfeeling facade as a defense against acknowledgement of her marshmellow core. She feels attracted toward traditional roles yet fears that her choice will disappoint and alienate others. "Alice's" game often continues until she meets her knight who sweeps her off her feet and unknowningly provides her an opportunity to resume prior levels of dependence. "Alice" literally jumps at this chance to terminate her false sense of identity and at the knight's apparent guarantee of security and protection. "Alice's" retreat into passivity and dependence, compounded often by multiple pregnancies to protect her against having to return to wonderland is a very negatively received surprise for the knight. He expects and demands from "Alice" the ambition, assertiveness, and independence which characterize the woman he married. Their conflict around this issue is often "Alice's" presenting concern.

Unlike "Lonely Lotta," the "Piranha," and "Alice," "Wonder Woman" appears to have it all together. Externally, she presents herself as a successful career woman, spouse, devoted and effective parent, and active community volunteer. The only problem is she is not happy. Her anger and resentment reflect her inability to select her own priorities and her need to satisfy everyone except herself. Her pursuits of perfection in all she does, of being the "complete" role model leaves her tired, angry, and guilty about wanting to do anything for herself. Given the unacceptability of psychological problems ("Wonder Woman" perceives them as indulgences and weaknesses), "Wonder Woman" frequently manifests her unhappiness through somatic complaints and physical disorders. After all, physical symptoms represent justifiable reasons for slowing down and "reluctantly" refusing requests for additional responsibilities. Frequently, "Wonder Woman" arrives in therapy expressing anger at the physician who made the referral. In "Wonder Woman's" view, the physician has yet to find the *real* problem. Participation in treatment is viewed by her as an unnecessary interruption in the search for the physical causes of her disorders. Unconsciously, "Wonder Woman" may perceive a serious physical disorder as the only escape from her never ending worldwind existence of pleasing everyone except herself. The central task in therapy is to enable "Wonder Woman" to say "no" to others and "yes" to herself.

Mid-life Crisis

This period of a woman's life represents yet another significant transition point. In many cases, children have grown and begun to lead independent lives. Those children who remain dependent make limited demands for mother's time and, frequently, urge mother, if she has been a homemaker, to "get out" of the house and "do something." Those without children must accept the finality of that fact. In either event, a central issue for this period is the evaluation of where they have come, how they got there, and most importantly, where they are going. For many, relatinships with mates must be redefined and renegotiated. Complicating the woman's re-evaluation process, is the frequent simultaneity of her partner's own mid-life crisis. Thus, many of the women in this group who ultimately seek treatment do so, at least in part, because their spouse who was previously perceived as a major source of real or potential emotional support, is suddenly absent from or wavering in his commitment to the relationship. Representative of the women from this group who seek treatment are the following composite case descriptions: the "Empty-nester," "Terrified Tanya," and "Bitter Bertha."

The "Empty-nester" suddenly finds herself in her early to mid-40's with her twenty or more years' career as a homemaker and mother significantly changed. As each child leaves, the "Empty-nester's" self-concept shrinks a bit more. Unwillingly forced by circumstances outside of her control to retire from a career which she found both satisfying and rewarding, the "Empty-nester" begins to look elsewhere for a meaningful role. Having devoted her life to the service of others, she immediately attempts to shift her attention toward her husband or, if available, grandchildren. The former, himself attempting to resolve his reactions to the mid-life period, struggles with work responsibilities, his own sense of aging, questions about his actual career achievements, and himself as a man. Consequently, he is either unresponsive or hostile toward "Empty-nester's" increased demands for attention, reassurance, and support. Outsiders, for the most part, are equally unresponsive. In many cases, their attempts at reassurance ("now you can finally do what you *really* want to" and "you have a lifetime ahead to something *really* meaningful") are felt by the "Empty-nester" as devaluations of her efforts as a mother and homemaker (e.g., "I really thought *that's* what I wanted to do!"). Children, engaged in their own attempts at independent living and assumption of adult responsibilities, are rarely able or willing to respond to mother's seemingly incessant demands for involvement in their lives.

In response to apparent rejection from all sides, "Empty-nester" experiences a pervasive sense of abandonment, rejection, and fear. Her self-concept, long defined by her effective functioning as a mother and homemaker, is shattered by the apparent devaluation of these roles. Knowing few other ways to fill in the hours, "Empty-nester" suddenly feels a deep sense of incompetence and insecurity. In many instances, she enters treatment at the point that her demands for support threaten to strain the marriage to the breaking point, isolate her from children and friends, and her depressive reaction to her incomplete sense of self approaches immobility.

"Terrified Tanya" represents a variant, and in some instances, a later stage of the "Empty-nester." In addition to "Empty-nester's" problems, "Tanya" is confronted with the loss of her sense of self as wife, typically as a function of divorce, although sometimes due to the death of her spouse, "Tanyas" almost universally deny any awareness of marital conflict prior to their husband's "sudden" announcement that he wants a divorce. "Tanya" responds initially with understanding, patience, and an external calm which belies the turmoil within. "Tanya" offers husband room to find himself, accepts through denial his involvement with one or more women, attempts to anticipate and respond to his every request. "Tanya" assumes that all is *really* well and following a brief period of helping him through his "troubled time," all will return to normal. "Tanya" may even move out of the house in response to his cry for "space" and freedom. Occasionally, "Tanya" will insist that he leave, but is forever willing to give him yet another chance to return. Most of all, "Tanya" responds to the threatened loss of her husband by refusing to confront him, by refusing to compete for him, and by gradually adopting a seemingly apathetic and inactive stance which, self-defeatingly, increases husband's motivation to leave ("she doesn't care anyway!") and justification for his choice.

Once confronted with the undeniable reality to her aloneness, "Tanya" frequently responds with a deep sense of panic, unsure of her ability to perform even the simplest task such as balance a checkbook, change a light bulb, or arrange to have a car repaired. Unconsciously, perhaps, she assumes that her level of helplessness will force husband to give up his foolishness and return home. Subsequently, "Tanya" may begin to somatize her feelings of rage and abandonment and vigorously go from one physician to another in an effort to find the one who is able to diagnose her problem and cure it quickly so that she can get on with her life. The central therapeutic task with "Tanya" is to enable her to acknowledge, express, and resolve her intense feelings of rage toward her (ex-)husband, her children (for allowing their father to do that to her and for continuing to relate to him), and his new wife or companion (who obviously "stole" him). Gradually, "Tanya" also comes to experience her contribution to the dissolution of the marriage and begins to recognize alternative patterns for responding to her own needs as well as those of others. At times, pending divorces are dismissed and the couples reunite to try again, typically supported with some form of marital counseling. In most cases, however, "Tanya's" future depends on accepting the finality of the divorce and developing a new sense of identity and new relationship patterns.

"Bitter Bertha" is the final composite case to be described. In some cases, she represents a negative resolution of the "Empty-nester" and "Tanya" conditions; in other instances, she represents a later instance of the "Piranha." Whatever the case, "Bertha" arrives at mid-life alone, with few, if any, friends, and a long history of negative interpersonal and occupational experiences. "Bertha" typically has a history of multiple unsuccessful marriages. If she has children, they have long ago terminated their involvements with her because of her disruptive influence on their lives. She is the ultimate "nag," complaining about everything and unhappy even when she gets her way. Within minutes of her arrival, her children's homes are tense and uncomfortable. Within minutes of her departure, they are fighting with their spouse about her return. Their ultimate decision to no longer welcome her is never understood by her and serves merely as proof of how unfeeling they are.

If they occur at all, "Bertha's" involvements with men are equally short-lived. As the level of closeness becomes increasingly uncomfortable to her, "Bertha" forces distance through her negative and critical style. "Bertha's" negative and hostile interpersonal style has had equally negative occupational consequences. In spite of high levels of competence and productivity, "Bertha" has been asked to resign from numerous positions. In her view, the request to leave frequently came "just as everything seemed to be going well." She failed, however, to recognize the impact of her constant criticism of others and complaining about all aspects of the position on her acceptability as a co-worker and employee. Rarely does "Bertha" seek treatment on her own. In most instances, she arrives under pressure from an employer who threatens to terminate her unless she can get along with others. Thus, she approaches treatment with little enthusiasm for the process and considerable concern about the outcome. Moreover, she resents the fact that control over her life is in the hands of a therapist about whom she knows very little and who appears unmoved by her hostility.

THERAPEUTIC STRATEGIES

The composite case descriptions presented above represent only a sampling of the diversity of issues which bring women into psychotherapy. It should be apparent to the reader that no single therapeutic strategy, or therapist for that matter, is likely to be appropriate in all cases. The focus of this segment of the chapter is a discussion of the primary variables which should be considered in attempting to match patient needs, therapist gender, and therapeutic modality. Ideally, the matching of patient with the appropriate therapist(s) and modality would be based on a set of systematic criteria derived from rigorous empirical evidence. In its absence, however, clinicians must rely on their professional judgment and their mastery of their art.

In our view, each therapeutic modality offers advantages and disadvantages to each client. Selections among alternatives should therefore be based on the relevance of each to the client's needs, her readiness to handle its unique demands, its expediency, and the personal and financial resources which will be available to her during the treatment process. In each case, it is appropriate to review alternatives with the client, explain their relative advantages and disadvantages, and obtain the client's input into the selection process. The ultimate decision, however, we perceive to be a professional one which is the therapist's responsibility. Prior to considering the relevance and demands of alternative treatment strategies for each client, we would like to discuss brliefly the issue of expediency and patient resources.

An important consideration in the selection of a treatment modality must be reducing the client's distress as quickly as possible. To do so, the therapist may engage in time-limited problem oriented strategies which will reduce anxiety and depression to manageable levels. Utilization of such strategies enables the client to become familiar both with the process of treatment and its potential for effecting change. It also enables the client to decide in a more considered fashion whether or not to engage in treatment strategies which focus on intrapsychic determinants of behavior and require more open-ended time commitments to the treatment process. In our experience, the initial utilization of problem-solving strategies enables us to combine an ongoing diagnostic process with an immediate response to the client's distress. Moreover, by recommending steps which the client may take immediately to reduce her distress, we are able to assess her potential commitment to the treatment process as well as her willingness to give up presenting problem behaviors. Information obtained from this stage of treatment is essential to us in making subsequent treatment decisions. In the first place, it is very possible that a time-limited approach which reduces the client's presenting distress is sufficient to meet the client's needs and enable her to resume with her life without continued therapeutic involvement. Should additional intervention be necessary, its optimal form, likely duration, and prognosis can more readily be determined on the basis of the client's progress, involvement, and resistance to that point. Finally, as noted, the client's participation in the selection among treatment options becomes more viable given her increased understanding of the process, less demanding distress level, and, at that point, familiarity with the therapist's personality and treatment style.

The issue of the client's personal and financial resources which will be available during treatment also merits discussion since both impact the selection among treatment modalities and, consequently, the likelihood of success. That the financial realities of treatment need to be considered very seriously is true both in private practice and public service delivery facilities. For some clients, the financial demand is significantly lessened by the availability of third-party reimbursement and/or above average family income. For other clients, the desire for treatment is so overwhelming that treatment is sought "at any price" during its initial stage only to be abandoned shortly thereafter because of its financial demands. If such an outcome is likely, it should be recognized as early as possible, and incorporated within the overall treatment plan. At the onset of treatment is the point at which the private vs. public alternatives should be reviewed and, if appropriate, a referral made to insure maximum likelihood for continuity of care.

It should also be recognized that a frequent consequence of psychotherapy is the modification of the client's relationship with her family and/or spouse. Hence, the *source* of the funds which will be used to reimburse treatment costs should be discussed and the possibility considered that progress resulting in increased independence and freedom to make choices may be perceived as threatening by the spouse. Consequently, he may attempt to subvert the treatment process by refusing to reimburse its costs. In similar fashion, as an adolescent begins to reconsider maladaptive behaviors which serve parental purposes, the process of treatment may be subverted by the sudden insistence that it has become "too expensive." If possible, the client should be assisted to identify ways in which she can be both responsible for and in control of the monetary aspects of treatment. Given the intermingling of relationship and self-concept factors which are typically observed in psychotherapy clients, it is especially important for clients without independent sources of income, to be aware of and, if at all possible, protect themselves against the disruptive consequences of a spouse's or parent's "blackmail" at significant treatment points.

The therapist should give equal consideration to the interpersonal resources which will be available to the client during the treatment process. As she questions past beliefs and relationships and experiments with new roles and attitudes, she will need external sources of support and stability to enable her to try various changes "for size." Since the changes related to treatment often involve redefinitions of her relationships with parents, spouses, lovers, and/or peers, many women clients experience intense feelings of aloneness and are tempted to retreat to prior unsatisfying forms of interaction in order to protect themselves against the feared total abandonment. Knowledge of important relationships and of significant others to whom the client can turn as she experiments with new forms of self-expression can be a valuable asset to the therapeutic process.

In our work as individual therapists, and particularly as co-therapists for marital counseling and family therapy, we have become increasingly sensitive to what each of us brings into treatment as a function of our gender. We perceive this contribution to be independent of our individual personalities and therapeutic styles. In essence, what our respective genders enable us to give to the client is a perspective against which to compare their personal experiences as well as their assumptions about the attitudes and experiences of members of a particular sex. In those instances in which there is a same sex therapeutic dyad, the therapist can serve as a baseline model and/or projected "ideal self" against which the client can compare his/her attitudes, reactions, assumptions, etc. with those of the therapist and with the therapist's statements about typical gender-related behaviors. Similarly, in cross-sex dyads, the therapist can assist the client to recognize the impact of his/her actions on members of the opposite sex. The therapist can also provide the client with insights into attitudes, assumptions, expectations, etc. held by the opposite sex. Thus, whether it be in same-sexed or cross-sexed dyads, the therapist as a member of one gender group can assist the client to develop insights into gender-related issues.

In our work as a therapeutic team for marital and family counseling, we perceive part of our role to be the provision of a model of at least some aspects of male-female interaction and relationships. It is evident to us that we communicate genuine liking for each other as well as respect for our respective expertise and competence. Yet, as part of our therapeutic approach, we engage in open discussion of the differences in our views of something occurring during a session, disagreement, at times, as to the appropriate course of treatment, and, if indicated, correction of evident errors in memory or procedures. We have intentionally chosen not to omit this aspect of our interaction from clients because we believe that it is therapeutically advantageous for them to observe both the expression and resolution of disagreement. When they occur they are discussed openly with the clients and used as opportunities for modeling effective and ineffective strategies to their resolution. At times, we will suggest that the clients demonstrate their typical strategies for resolving such disagreements. In this way self-defeating and self-fulfilling patterns of interaction can be identified and alternatives modeled and efficiently adapted.

In general, therapist gender can be an effective therapeutic tool if applied cautiously and selectively. The primary risk in its use involves the potential that the client will misinterpret the therapist's input relative to gender-related issues as criticism, competition, or even seductiveness. In each instance, the efficacy of the therapeutic relationship may be jeopardized unless the client's misinterpretation is recognized and interpreted.

14

Substance Abuse in Women

Etiology and Prevention

Brenna H. Bry
Rutgers University

Substance abuse, or the use of alcohol or drugs to the extent that normal functioning is impaired, is often viewed as a unique behavior, not subject to the same laws that govern other behaviors. This assumption has led to a plethora of conflicting theories about its etiology that do not take into account extant knowledge about behavior development. (See Lettieri et al., 1980.) This chapter is based upon the assumption that substance abuse has multiple determinants, both within and across individuals, as do other complex behaviors, such as working long hours, driving very fast, eating a lot of sugar, or talking very much. This viewpoint enables us to integrate findings from diverse studies into a coherent picture of substance abuse, including the variables and processes that increase its probability of occurrence.

The chapter begins with a description of substance abuse among women—its prevalence and unique consequences, such as fetal alcohol syndrome and reproductive difficulties. Then etiological research is presented from two different lines of inquiry: (a) research into psychosocial precursors, such as low religiosity and high sensation seeking, and (b) research into processes that may link those precursors with substance abuse. Finally, significant findings are discussed in terms of possible implications for prevention, both secondary and primary. Unfortunately, very few studies have separated prevalence, etiology, or intervention results for women from results for all subjects, including adolescents and men. Those that specifically mention women will be highlighted, but much of the chapter is based upon studies that aggregated results for males and females.

The concepts of alcohol and drug problems, alcoholism and addictions, excessive substance use, misuse and abuse are used interchangeably in this chapter, but all such problem use is carefully differentiated from non-problem use, such as social drinking or marijuana use that does not interfere with other life tasks. The word substances denotes all consciousness-altering substances, including alcohol; while the term drug refers only to non-alcoholic substances.

SUBSTANCE ABUSE AMONG WOMEN

Alcohol

Alcohol is the most frequently abused substance among women. The best estimate of the proportion of the female adult and adolescent population that is affected is seven percent, but estimates range from two to eleven percent (Ferrence & Whitehead, 1980). Some writers claim that these figures are too low because of hidden alcoholism among suburban housewives (e.g., Curlee, 1969), but Ferrance and Whitehead (1980) have empirically investigated this hypothesis and found little evidence to support it.

Another common misconception is that the rate of women's alcoholism will soon equal the rate for men, which traditionally has been two or three times greater. When they investigated this "convergence hypothesis," Ferrence and Whitehead (1980) found the number of women with alcohol problems is indeed increasing, but the number of men is increasing proportionately. The misconception that the rates are converging is probably based upon the fact that the rates of male and female high school seniors who have ever used alcohol are about equal, 93.7 and 92.5 percent, respectively (Johnston et al., 1980). Girls use smaller amounts less frequently than boys do, however, and that appears to account for the difference in problem rates. This conclusion is consistent with the finding of Robins et al. (1962) that the ratio of heavy drinkers to alcoholics is the same for women and men—four or five to one.

Drugs

The above estimates of rates of female alcohol problems are based upon general population surveys, alcohol sales figures, records of alcohol use in accidents, alcohol-related disease (e.g., cirrhosis of the liver), and deaths. Parallel data about drugs are difficult to obtain because of their illegality, the absence of drug-specific consequences like cirrhosis of the liver, and the absence of simple devices such as the breathalyzer to measure drug levels in the blood. In attempt to learn about women's drug problems, Ferrence and Whitehead (1980) performed secondary analyses upon past drug surveys. Although the data do not differentiate problem from non-problem use, their findings are nevertheless instructive. The percentage of women who use heroin and cocaine is relatively low (1–3 percent), both in comparison to women's use of other drugs and in comparison to men's use (2–5 percent). Women's use of marijuana is greater than their use of other drugs (6–10 percent), but is still less than men's (8–14 percent). By far, the greatest use of drugs among women is in the psychotropic category—tranquilizers, stimulants, and sedatives (10–15 percent), and in this category women's use exceeds men's (8–12 percent). This latter finding is consistent with other studies that show women outnumbering men (60 percent to 40 percent) in sedative abuse treatment programs (Pickens & Heston, 1981) and women outnumbering men (60 percent to 40 percent) among regular nonopiate drug users (Finnegan, 1978).

This difference between women's and men's psychotropic drug use appears to be partly a function of prescription patterns. Parry et al. (1973) found that 8 percent of women and only 1 percent of men had ever received a stimulant prescription. Physicians prescriptions are not the only vehicles for obtaining psychotropic drugs, however, for Finnegan (1978) found that approximately 10 times as many regular nonopiate drug (excluding marijuana) users reported obtaining their drugs without legal prescriptions as those using legal means. Ellinwood (1979) reports that only 25 percent of the amphetamines mentioned in emergency room records of abuse cases come from legal prescriptions; the remaining 75 percent is attributed to street buys, thefts and/or illegal manufacture.

CONSEQUENCES OF SUBSTANCE ABUSE IN WOMEN

Substance abuse lowers the quality of life and life expectancy in both men and women by decreasing productivity and increasing psychological distress, accidents, and disease in the cardiovascular, respiratory, and central nervous systems, the liver and digestive tracts (Kalant, 1980). Women who abuse substances, however, suffer the additional consequences of reproductive disorders, poor pregnancy outcomes, and problems in parenting (Finnegan, 1979). Drug abuse, for instance, is associated with dysmenorrhea and amenorrhea, which make birth control and pregnancy detection difficult. Once pregnancy occurs, the chances of premature birth and low birth weight are increased, along with the associated possibilities of perinatal death, asphyxia and hyaline membrane disorders (Rothstein & Gould, 1974).

All infants of drug-abusing mothers also face the possibility of neonatal abstinence syndrome, or withdrawal symptoms. In the past, withdrawal symptoms, such as tremors, respiratory distress, feeding difficulties, and decreased muscle tone, were associated with only heroin or methadone dependence; but recently they have also been attributed to Darvon, codeine, barbiturates, bromides, diazepam (Valium), and imipramine (Finnegan & Fehr, 1980).

The risk that alcohol use will affect a fetus increases as consumption increases (*Healthy People*, 1979). Congential defects occur in only 8 percent of the infants of non-drinking women; whereas they occur in 14 percent of the infants of moderate drinkers, 29 percent of heavy drinkers (10 drinks a day), and an astounding 71 percent of infants born to very heavy drinkers (more than 10 drinks a day)! These defects can be low birth weight, mental retardation, or behavioral, facial, limb, genital, cardiac, or neurological abnormalities. Although the term fetal alcohol syndrome (FAS) is sometimes used to describe the above occurrences, Rosett (1980), who has investigated the syndrome thoroughly, prefers to reserve its use for the relatively rare instances where all three of the following effects are present: (a) pre- or postnatal growth retardation (below 10th percentile), (b) central nervous system impairment, and (c) characteristic facial dysmorphology (with at least three signs).

Substance abuse also apparently affects the ability to parent (Finnegan, 1979). Although the most common reason for excessive drinking is tension reduction, chronic alcohol use actually increases a mother's irritability, depression, and anxiety (Mello, 1980). Similarly, pentobarbital abuse, which is usually motivated by excessive tension, actually increases tension and irritability (Pickens & Heston, 1981). Combined with the fact that other frequent consequences of intoxication are aggression and decreased ability to gain from experience (Mello, 1980), the above suggests that substance-abusing mothers are at risk for child abuse. In sum, the severity of both the social and personal consequences of substance abuse among women, coupled with the fact that addictive behaviors are so difficult to change once they are established (Schuckit & Winokur, 1972), points to the necessity of improving understanding of etiology so that abuse may be prevented before it develops.

ETIOLOGY

For decades, researchers assumed that substance abuse was caused by an "addictive personality" and sought to discover its characteristics (Pihl & Spiers, 1978).

They compared addict and non-addict groups on a myriad of demographic and personality variables, searching for the variable that differentiated them. Instead of discovering just one reliable characteristic, they discovered at least 11, none of which accounts for the majority of variance between groups but each of which increases the probability of drug abuse to a certain extent.

Consequently, the "addictive personality" quest was replaced by a search for the one *combination* of those established variables that best explained substance abuse (e.g., Jessor & Jessor, 1978; Kandel et al., 1976; Pandina & Schuele, in press; Segal et al., 1980b; Smith & Fogg, 1978). Well-designed, multivariate, longitudinal studies have been conducted using path analyses, multiple regression analyses, and discriminant analyses. Again, almost every study has produced a different set of explanatory variables, all of which are related to substance abuse in a statistically significant manner but none of which explain more than a moderate amount of variance. Although some commonalities exist among the findings (see Kandel, 1978), there are also puzzling discrepancies. For instance, some researchers found relationships to parents among the important variables (Pandina & Schuele, in press); while others measured that variable but did not find it important (Kandel et al., 1976; Jessor & Jessor, 1978).

Bry et al. (1982) responded to these discrepancies by offering the multiple risk factors hypothesis—the notion that the disparate findings are due to the fact that substance abuse is a function of the *number* of etiological factors instead of a particular set of them. When this hypothesis was tested on a data set containing six of the eleven most commonly supported etiological characteristics, the results revealed a highly significant relationship between number of these characteristics and the probability of current abuse. (See Fig. 1.)

A magnitude of risk of 1.00 in Fig. 1 represents the base rate of substance abuse in the population studied, which was 11 percent in this case. Subjects exhibiting none of the risk factors reported a lower percentage of substance abuse than the population at large, with the presence of each additional risk factor being associated with a higher percentage of abuse until the presence of four risk factors was associated with a four and a half times increase in magnitude of risk.

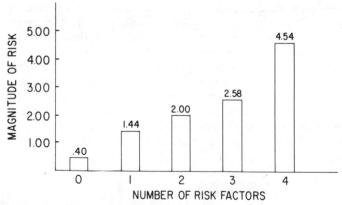

Figure 1 Drug abuse risk as a function of number of risk factors
(Magnitude of risk of 1.00 = Base rate for population).

It is important to note that the relationship in Fig. 1 is not accounted for by one predominant combinations of risk factors. Twenty-four different combinations occurred among the 156 subjects who exhibited two, three, or four risk factors, and none of the combinations accounted for more than 20 percent of the cases. These results must be replicated, extended to include other common etiological characteristics, and tested longitudinally; but they suggest, as others have hypothesized that there may be almost as many salient combinations of etiological variables as there are substance abusers (e.g., Nathan & Harris, 1980).

This notion that causal factors combine non-linearly and uniquely in each individual is not surprising if one views substance abuse as a complex behavior governed by the same laws that govern other behaviors, but this conceptualization certainly increases the challenge of substance abuse prevention. It suggests that no "most effective" prevention program will be found. Multiple causation calls for multiple prevention programs, perhaps one for each psychosocial precursor. As will become evident when the etiology research is described in the next sections, only a few of the known precursors are currently amenable to direct preventive intervention and gaps still exist in our knowledge of salient determinants. Nevertheless, several conditions are known to increase the probability of substance abuse, and this knowledge, combined with knowledge of linking processes and effective interventions, will eventually enable society to reduce abuse.

ESTABLISHED PSYCHOSOCIAL PRECURSORS

Behavior can be thought of as a function of past history, current need state or deprivation, available reinforcers, other current contingencies, and genetic predisposition (Skinner, 1938). Although few psychosocial researchers use such a framework when designing their studies, it is useful to organize their findings accordingly to discover gaps in our understanding of substance abuse.

Past History

Childhood experiences with medications, age of first substance use, and previous experiences with other deviant behaviors, have all been shown to affect the probability of substance abuse (Blum & Associates, 1970; Gossett et al., 1972; Tennant & Detels, 1976).

Family Misuse of Substances

In a survey of twelve hundred college students, Blum and Associates (1970) uncovered interesting relatinships between the use of medicines and substances in family of origin and subsequent substance abuse. For some time, it had been known that family alcohol problems increase the probability of substance abuse (Templer et al., 1974), but their research suggested that family use of *legitimate drugs* also increases substance abuse. College students were more likely to report illicit drug use if, as children, they (a) had received strong pain killers such as Percodan or codeine, (b) had received a prescription of psychotropic drugs, or (c) had made "considerable" use of non-prescription preparations (aspirin, Nodoz, Compoz). In addition, students whose parents were "quick to give medicine" and who pampered them when they were sick were more likely to report illicit substance use. The magnitude of this relationship can be seen by the fact that 56

percent of those who used aspirin or Compoz heavily as a child were using illicit
sedatives in college; whereas only 18 percent of those who had used aspirin spar-
ingly reported current illicit use.

Early Use of Substances

Early independent alcohol use, i.e., before thirteen was initially associated with
substance abuse in retrospective studies (Tennant & Detels, 1976), but in 1978,
Jessor and Jessor investigated this prospectively, asking junior and high school
students to report their drug use every year for four years. They found that indeed
those who were already using substances at the beginning of the study were using
much more at the end of the four years than those who initiated their use during
the study. This finding is so consistent across populations, settings, and substances
(except inhalants) that some researchers have used age of first substance use instead
of substance abuse as a dependent variable in etiological research (e.g., O'Donnell &
Clayton, 1979; Smith & Fogg, 1978).

Other Early Problem Behavior

Gossett et al. (1972) found the most striking difference between high school
substance-users and non-substance users was the number of past non-drug related
problems, such as failing a grade in school, being expelled, being questioned by
the police, being in trouble in their neighborhood, or being arrested and convicted. As a result. O'Donnell and Clayton (1979), used path analysis to compare
the importance of early deviant behavior with eleven other established psychosocial
precursors in predicting early marijuana use. Early problem behavior was located
temporally between family influence and peer influence and proved to be one of
the five most important causative variables. As with early substance use, the
mechanisms linking early problem behavior with substance abuse are yet unclear,
but other lines of research may eventually explain the linkage.

Current State of Need

Substance ingestion can increase positive affect (Vuchinich et al., 1979), reduce
fear (Rimm et al., 1981), reduce anxiety, both subjective and behavioral (Bradlyn
et al., 1981), increase feelings of well being, relaxation, and self esteem (Jasinski,
1981), increase verbal and social behaviors (Stitzer et al., 1981), reduce aggression
(Wallace, 1979), and reduce awareness of behavioral consequences (Parker et al.,
1981). Consequently, Crowley (1972) proposed that increased need in any of these
areas could increase substance use, just as hunger increases food ingestion. Animal
and human studies have shown that the need does not have to be in the same area
as the reinforcement in order to increase the frequency of a behavior. Rats use
more opium when deprived of food (Meisch & Kliner, 1979), and humans drink
more coffee when deprived of food (Keys et al., 1950). Findings concerning the
next five psychosocial precursors are consistent with this notion, for each represents a need state.

Low Self Esteem

Segal (1977) asked regular marijuana users why they used marijuana, and was
told "to help you forget you're not the kind of person you would like to be." In
a prospective study to investigate the role of self rejection in the initiation of

substance abuse, Kaplan (1978b) assessed deviant behavior and self derogation ("I wish I had more respect for myself," "I'm inclined to feel I'm a failure," "I certainly feel useless at times") annually in 3148 junior high students. He found that self derogation is associated with membership in devalued groups such as females, blacks, and learning disabled (Kaplan, 1978a) and can lead to gender-linked deviant behavior (Kaplan, 1978b)—alcohol abuse and aggression in boys, and narcotics and marijuana abuse in girls. He found that increases in self derogation increase the probability of deviant behavior, including substance use; and the initiation of deviant behavior results in decreases in self derogation. These findings strongly suggest that low self esteem leads to substance abuse because substance abuse raises self esteem. While the explanation for this relationship is not at all clear, Kaplan (1978a) speculates that abusing substances makes one feel like a member of a valued social group, and that perceived membership raises self esteem.

Psychological Distress

Emotional problems have long been seen as a predisposing factor in substance abuse (Ausubel, 1952). Pandina and Schuele (in press) confirmed this relationship in a 1976 school survey ($n = 1960$) where psychological distress scores on the John Hopkins Symptom Checklist (Derogatis et al., 1976) correlated significantly with reported substance use.

In a hospital research study, Pickens and Heston (1981) found that the Hypomania scale scores on the Minnesota Multiphasic Personality Inventory of 22 sedative abusers (mean 43.2 years old) who had *ad lib* access to pentobarbital correlated positively with amount of substance ingested, especially for women and the clinically depressed. The causal direction of this relationship must be determined in future research, but if indeed amount of irritability, for example, determines substance intake, reducing irritability by other means could be one component of a multifaceted substance abuse prevention program.

Stressful Life Events

Stressful life events have been associated with many other human problems (Dohrenwend & Dohrenwend, 1974), but only recently have they been empirically linked to substance abuse. Newcomb et al. (1981) grouped 39 life events into seven interpretable clusters and canonically correlated them with five alcohol and drug use indices. Several significant correlations were found, including one between family problems and alcohol use. This potential precursor to substance abuse warrants further research, particularly among women.

Poor Relationship with Parents

Blum and Associates (1970) came across evidence of this precursor when they unexpectedly found that young people with the highest proportion of drug use reported that their parents showed little interest in their general health. Streit (1973) followed this up by exploring what dimensions of child-parent relationships best differentiated abusers from non-abusers. He found that extremes along a hostility-love dimension and an autonomy-control dimension were most important. Too much parental permissiveness and too much parental control both increased the likelihood that subjects would report "my family is not very close" and also very high drug use. Hendin et al. (1981) confirmed these results in representative case studies of 17 marijuana abusing adolescents and 11 of their non-abusing siblings. The results indicated that either due to too high expectations or with-drawal of love on the parents part, the abusers felt more alienated and unhappy in their families than their non-abusing siblings did. The researchers were also able to show that this sense of ostracism had preceded the substance abuse.

Sensation Seeking

Through the use of his Sensation Seeking Scale, Zuckerman (1979) has de-veloped extensive empirical evidence that people who report a need for varied, intense sensations, e.g., "I like the tumult of sounds of a busy city" vs. "I prefer my meals at regular times" tend to report more substance use. In one study, he found that 74 percent of undergraduates who scored highly on sensation-seeking have used at least one drug; whereas only 23 percent of the low sensation seekers have used a drug. Similarly, 53 percent of the high sensation seekers drink more than 6 alcoholic drinks a week; whereas only 13 percent of the low sensation seekers drink these amounts (Zuckerman et al., 1970). In another series of studies, Segal et al. (1980b) found that two subscales of the Sensation Seeking Scale (Ex-perience Seeking and Disinhibition) predict substance abuse more accurately than did 46 other variables. Theoretically, high sensation seekers are always seeking stimulation in order to keep themselves in a homeostatic state, and drugs and alcohol are just two of many different sources of stimulation available to them.

Current Availability of Reinforcers

Past history and current need cannot affect substance use unless the substances are available. Perhaps this is why substance availability and peer substance use are often shown to be the best single predictors of individual substance use (see Kandel et al., 1976; O'Donnell & Clayton, 1979). Initially, these results were given a "deviant drug sub-culture" interpretation, i.e., that people are initiated into deviant reference groups and thus engage in a lot of common deviant behavior. In a cross-validated study, users of various classes of drugs were indeed found to associate with others who used the same drugs, but no evidence of deviant subcultures was found (Huba et al., 1979). Substance use was the only deviant behavior that asso-ciates had in common. It is particularly interesting that male rather than female companions seem to determine female substance use (Ferrence & Whitehead, 1980).

Competing Schedules of Reinforcement

Most behavior is determined not only by its own consequences but also by the consequences of other competing behaviors such as studying, going to church, watching TV. Thus, for young people at least, their involvement in studying or extracurricular activities such as religious ones, plays a role in determining sub-stance abuse.

Low Religiosity

Exploratory studies have consistently linked low religiosity with substance abuse (e.g., Blum & Associates, 1970; Tennant et al., 1975). Young people with fewer religious beliefs, whose parents do not consider religion important (Blum & Associates, 1970), who do not attend church or synagogue with their family, and who show little interest in religious activities (Gossett et al., 1972) are more likely to abuse drugs. Given the consistency of these findings, it is interesting that there has been no further research into this relationship. Is the precursor a general dearth of competing community or family activities, or a third unidentified variable?

Low Achievement Motivation

In an exploratory study, Streit and Oliver (1972) found that the following statements to differentiate heavy drug users from other students: "Life is boring," "I don't care about grades in school," "I don't expect to go to college." Smith and Fogg (1978) demonstrated that this lack of interest in achievement is a precursor rather than a consequence of drug abuse in a longitudinal study in which high school students who started using drugs before others had been previously characterized as not working hard, not ambitious, not striving for achievement, being absent a lot, and having poor grades despite adequate intelligence. The researchers suggest that the findings mean students with a low sense of involvement in competing activities are more likely to initiate early drug use.

Genetic Constitution

Alcoholism in men is one of the few complex behavior patterns for which clear evidence of genetic determinants has been found. Goodwin et al. (1977) describe a study of male twins who were reared apart that shows that alcoholic biological parents contribute considerably more to the observed risk for alcoholism in the children (even if the biological parents were physically absent) than do alcoholics in the environment. Vaillant and Milofsky (1982) also found compelling evidence, in a longitudinal study, for a strong genetic component in male alcoholism. Goodwin et al. (1977) speculate that three alcoholism-producing processes could be genetically determined: (a) alcoholics must be able to drink large amounts without experiencing physiological adverse reactions, (b) alcoholics must be able to experience an intense euphoria when they drink, (c) alcoholics probably experience the dysphoria that comes after the initial euphoria particularly intensely, also, thus being more likely to drink large quantities repeatedly.

As is true in most lines of inquiry, far less research has been done into the genetic determinants of female alcoholism or drug abuse. When Goodwin et al. (1977) turned their attention to female twins who were reared apart, they failed to find the same conclusive evidence that they found for men. Indeed, alcoholism occurred four times as frequently as expected in adopted daughters of alcoholic biological parents, but since similar findings occurred in the controls, the question of determinants remains open.

POTENTIAL PROCESSES

Several of the above precursors such as stressful life events and high sensation seeking are inaccessible to preventive intervention. Consequently the processes linking these precursors to substance abuse must be studied as possible targets of intervention. What exactly links parental medication use with children's substance abuse? What governs the relationship between low achievement motivation and substance abuse? What processes link early use with later abuse? I shall devote the next section of this chapter to research from outside the prevention field that has implications for these questions.

Operant Conditioning

Animal research has confirmed what clinicians already knew—that drug and alcohol effects can serve as powerful primary positive reinforcers. When given access to a mechanism such as a chain pull that results in intravenous or oral delivery of a substance, animals will perform complicated series of behaviors in order to receive most of the same substances that humans abuse (Thompson, 1981), indicating that the substances themselves are primary reinforcers.

Substances can also produce negative reinforcement effects, i.e., increasing behavior that leads to the termination of an aversive situation. Meisch and Kliner (1979), for instance, found that food deprivation led to an increase in behavior that resulted in opioid intake in rats. Studies with humans have also found evidence of both positive and negative reinforcement processes. Reasons subjects give for substance use consistently fall into two distinct clusters: (a) to increase positive affect or (b) to decrease negative circumstances such as pain, anxiety, fear, or guilt about being a substance abuser (Mello, 1968; Pervin, 1981; Segal et al., 1980a).

Substances can further be secondary reinforcers—becoming reinforcers through their association with the obtaining of other primary reinforcers. Drugs may be used to maintain the company of desirable companions or to elicit responses from otherwise unresponsive parents (Crowley, 1972). More research into conditioning processes that produce low and high levels of substance use could contribute to abuse prevention efforts. Promising areas are the schedule of substance availability (variable interval reinforcement schedules reduce response rates), competing reinforcement schedules, extinction, punishment, and response cost, i.e., the amount of effort that is required to obtain a substance. The ratio of animal substance intake to cost decreases as the behavioral requirement for it increases (Griffiths et al., 1980), and the same holds for humans (Nurco, 1979). Research on the effects of punishment or response cost found that alcoholics drink less when access to social situations is made contingent upon an intake decrease (Stitzer et al., 1981).

Adjunctive Behavior

Falk (1961) discovered a conditioning phenomenon which can indirectly increase substance abuse and other excessive behaviors. Food-deprived rats placed upon a thin, intermittent, reinforcement schedule (small bits of food available only once a minute) drank three times their usual intake of water even though they were not water deprived. This schedule-induced increase in adjunctive behaviors has also been produced in rats, pigeons, squirrels, monkeys, mice, rhesus monkeys, and chimpanzees by restricting access to a valued commodity and concomitantly making an alternative behavior available (Falk, 1981). Food deprived rats, that otherwise will not drink enough *ad lib* alcohol to become physiologically dependent, have become physiologically dependent when placed on a restricted feeding schedule (Samson & Falk, 1974). Polydipsia has also been produced in humans by restricting access to earned pennies and making a drinking fountain available (Kachanoff et al., 1973).

There are many every-day situations that are characterized by intermittent valued reinforcers, such as poverty, police work, housework, night guard work, gambling, and medical work. Research could investigate whether increasing the

rate of reinforcement in these spaced reinforcement situations or providing opportunities for alternative adjunctive behaviors would decrease substance abuse associated with them. For instance, Samson and Falk (1974) found that when saccharin
water was available along with alcohol in a spaced reinforcement situation, rats
drank less alcohol. Falk (1981) suggests that exercise or creativity opportunities in
commodity constraint situations may reduce non-constructive adjunctive behaviors
in humans.

Drug-Compensatory Conditioned Responses

Siegel (1975) has isolated a classical conditioning process that could partially
explain the clinical phenomena of craving and tolerance. He found that the repeated pairing of a substance (the unconditioned stimulus—UCS) administration
(the conditioned stimulus—CS) with the unconditioned physiological and subjective
responses (UCRs) that result from its ingestion leads to the development of a conditioned response (CR) that is the converse of the unconditioned response. For
example, the CR that becomes associated with morphine administration procedures
(CS) is heightened pain sensitivity (Siegel, 1975). Animals that repeatedly experience the unconditioned response of hypothermia after alcohol ingestion develop a conditioned hyperthermia following the presentation of the alcohol administration stimulus (Lê et al., 1979).

These drug compensatory CRs, as Siegel calls them, could explain the craving
sensations that habitual substance users report when they are in situations where
they usually use substances. In the absence of the substance, their only response
is the drug compensatory response or a "felt need" for the substance. Thus, classical conditioning may play a role in the genesis of withdrawal symptoms, which up
until recently were assumed to be totally physiological. If withdrawal symptoms
are partially the result of a classical conditioning process, then it is possible that
they could be reduced through the application of extinction procedures.

Furthermore, if drug compensatory CRs indeed develop in recreational drug
use, then substance use designed to increase positive affect at the time of use could
actually increase negative affect when the user returns to the same situation. The
conditioned negative affect could increase the probability of substance use again
and recreational use could lead to excessive use if the person spends extended
periods of time in the situation where the original use occurs. In fact, studies
have shown that craving is more likely to occur in situations where previous ingestion has occurred (e.g., Teasdale, 1973). This process could partially explain why
early drug use is associated with excessive drug use.

Poulos et al. (1981) suggest that if substances tend to be used when non-drug-
related negative affect is present, drug compensatory CRs (cravings) can become
associated with that negative affect just as drugs can become associated with environmental variables. Such pairings could explain why alcoholics report experiencing cravings when they are "depressed," "nervous," or "under stress"
(Ludwig & Stark, 1974).

Siegel's work also has implications for the phenomenon of tolerance, i.e., the
decreased response to a substance that occurs after repeated administrations.
Tolerance has traditionally been viewed as biologically based, but it also could
be the result of the interaction between a developing compensatory CR and the
original UCR. As the CR becomes stronger, the net subjective drug effect will

become weaker due to the CR-UCR interaction, and the user will have to ingest more substance to experience the same effect.

As critics O'Brien et al. (1981) point out, while Siegel's phenomenon has been demonstrated to be robust in the laboratory, the extent to which it occurs and its degree of influence in human substance use has yet to be determined. If it indeed represents an important process however, prevention research must investigate the conditions under which it occurs so that those conditions can be minimized.

Modeling

In contrast to the above processes, considerable laboratory and naturalistic setting evidence has accumulated regarding the extent to which modeling can account for human substance use and the conditions that increase and decrease its effects (Collins & Marlatt, 1981). The use patterns of independent models, particularly of warm, active peers, influence amounts of substance ingestion, both in the presence of the model and afterward. There is evidence that this effect occurs even when subjects have been told that an attempt is being made to influence their drinking behavior (DeRicco & Garlington, 1977).

Of particular relevance to women are the findings that, for both men and women, the consumatory behavior of the male rather than female partner is likely to be modeled (Hendricks et al., 1978). These results are consistent with the evidence from a clinical study that 77.8 percent of the female addicts obtained their drugs through their husbands and 72 percent of those females first used heroin in company of males (Chambers & Moffett, 1970). It is also noteworthy that, given both moderate and heavy drinking models, males and female heavy drinkers are more likely to be influenced by the male heavy drinking models (Cooper et al., 1979; Lied & Marlatt, 1979).

PREVENTION

Secondary Prevention

Once excessive substance use is established, the prevention of birth defects, reduced productivity, and increased accidents and disease requires that abusing women either terminate abuse themselves, as do about 1/3 of female problem drinkers according to Fillmore (1974, 1975), or enter an intervention program. For those who enter them, traditional substance abuse treatment programs are apparently as effective (33 percent improved) for women as for men (Annis & Liban, 1980). Studies show however that substance abusing women are less likely to enter treatment programs than men. In addition, women tend to wait longer to enter programs after their substance use has become a problem, than do men (Robins & Smith, 1980). Alcoholics Anonymous (AA) has a reputed better success rate (50 percent) than tradition treatment for those who stay in the program, but their dropout rate is high. About four out of five who enter drop out (Sarason, 1972).

New secondary prevention approaches hold promise for women because they do not require that one assume the identity of a patient with a disease. Employee Assistance Programs for substance abuse are appearing in many work-settings; Health Maintenance Organizations (HMOs) are offering brief substance use-reduction workshops along with regular medical care, and communities are offering controlled drinking training for apprehended drunk drivers. Preliminary data regarding the effectiveness of the latter show greater success rates for teaching moderate use after a drunk-driving arrest than treatment programs show after the problem has become more severe (Alden, 1982).

Drunk driving intervention programs have the advantage of natural aversive consequences—the loss of a license—if substance use is not reduced. In fact, the best results in any type of substance-use intervention effort, whether treatment of a severe problem or prevention of the initiation of use, apparently occur when there are clear contingencies attached to the target behavior. For instance, Boudin (1972) reports that a black woman was able to reduce an extremely high rate of amphetamine abuse by contracting that her personal money would be sent to the Klu Klux Klan if her use exceeded a criterion amount. Pickens et al. (1973) showed long-term reduction in alcohol abuse through making valued social activities contingent upon moderate use. Bigelow et al. (1972), Miller (1975), Hunt and Azrin (1973), and Azrin (1976) all reduced substance use by either providing time out or restricting admittance to a valued community agency when too many substances had been used.

Successful interventions tend to not only teach abusers to reduce use but also to add positive experiences to their lives (alternative "highs") and cope with needs in new ways, such as through assertiveness (Gomberg, 1974). Since the etiology of abuse may be different for each woman, each intervention will be somewhat different. In an outcome study however, Pemberton (1967) found one common theme differentiating successful from unsuccessful female alcoholics. The successful clients were still living with their families and had succeeded in modifying the structure of their family group so that they could play a more satisfying role within it. To attain these outcomes, the women probably needed not only contingency contracting around their substance use but also assertiveness training, conjoint marital therapy, and child management skills training.

Not all abusers can be helped and, as was stated earlier, a relatively low percentage of female abusers avail themselves of help; so primary prevention efforts, both during adolescence and adulthood, are probably the most viable routes to reducing female abuse.

Primary Prevention

Given that adult substance abuse patterns tend to develop in adolescence (Tyler & Thompson, 1980; Wechsler & McFadden, 1976), primary prevention must occur in adolescence or in childhood. The multiple independent precursors of substance abuse call for multiple prevention programs to reduce those precursors and thus the incidence of substance abuse in a community.

Maccoby et al. (1977) have shown that such a multiple prevention program approach, coupled with a media campaign, can indeed reduce the risk of another public health problem in a whole community by reducing the number of precursors exhibited by the population. Over a two-year period, they provided 50 television spots, three hours of television programming, over 100 radio spots, several hours of radio programming, weekly newspaper columns, newspaper advertisements and stories, billboards, posters, and printed material through the mail about specific behavioral measures members of two California communities could take to reduce heart attack risk. In one of the communities, they also offered workshops on how to reduce specific precursors, such as cigarette smoking and obesity. Knowledge about the precursors increased and objective precursors decreased in both communities, but the greatest impact occurred in the community with both the educational campaign and the workshops.

Consequently, the remainder of this chapter will be devoted to reviewing interventions that have been shown to reduce one or more of the various precursors of substance abuse. It is assumed that, as Maccoby et al. (1977) found, the simultaneous provision of a media campaign and these interventions to the members of a community who exhibit the targeted precursors would reduce a whole community's incidence of abuse, but that assumption has yet to be tested.

Other early problem behavior was reduced as a precursor in DeKalb County, Georgia, when some concerned parents met with other parents and school officials to agree upon guidelines that were eventually presented to their teenagers in an open discussion ("Parent Power," 1978). Parents agreed to establish curfews, chaperone parties, help the school implement its regulations, accept liability for any possession of illegal substances in the family car, and to ground their teenagers or remove privileges if regulations regarding substance abuse or other school rules were broken. Results showed a dramatic decrease of teenagers in the school halls or on the streets during school classes or after evening curfews.

Low self esteem has been reduced in several different ways. Hughes (1977) found that Alateen meetings raised the self esteem of children of alcoholics. Penfield and Whitely (1977) observed that weekly lunch hour rap groups with a specially trained teacher improved low self esteem in junior high school students.

Psychological distress, particularly depression, can be reduced as a precursor through psychotherapy (Woody et al., 1981). Beck et al. (1979) describe in detail Beck's Cognitive Theory, and Ricks (1974) reports what characteristics differentiate a therapist that is successful with high risk young people from others. In light of the above findings that approaches with clear contingencies are particularly successful in treating adult substance abuse, it is noteworthy that Ricks observed that the successful adolescent therapist was firmer and more directive than the less successful ones.

Stressful life events, such as death, divorce, children leaving home, and moving, are difficult to remove from women's lives, but adolescents can already be introduced to effective ways to deal with their consequences. Brown et al. (1975) found that women in full and part-time employment are less likely than others to become depressed following acute stresses. Apparently, having multiple roles such as mother, aunt, and wage earner gives women a sense of achievement in the face of uncontrollable stressful events (Baruch & Barnett, 1980).

In addition to multiple roles, social support seems to prevent problems that could be caused by stressful life events (Wilcox, 1981). Some hypothesize that the employment situation is helpful simply because it provides social support. If employment is not available however as a source of social support, self-help groups are an option. Danish and D'Augelli (1980) have reviewed the self help movement and found ample evidence of positive effects of self help groups. All of this suggests that adolescent girls will be less likely to abuse substances in the face of stress if they are prepared for satisfying employment and introduced to the rewards of self help group membership.

Poor relationship with parents has been reduced in two very different family interventions. Klein et al. (1977) has shown improvement in parent-child relationships in a short term family therapy that relies heavily on contingency contracting. Streit (1977) observed improved "perceived family closeness" scores in high risk adolescents who attended multiple family discussion groups with their parents and practiced communication skills.

Availability of substances to abuse covaries with substance use among peers. Well-designed, long-term, school education programs have been shown to reduce the amount of heavy use in a school. Blum et al. (1976) compared the effects of two years of didactic information about substances and two years of affective education and found them both to be effective in reducing heavy use. Kleber et al. (1975) found several approaches, including comprehensive teacher training and integrating drug education into the whole curriculum, to be effective in reducing level of problematic use in a school.

Low achievement motivation has been reduced among high risk adolescents in both urban and suburban settings by Bry and her associates (Bry & George, 1979, 1980; Bry & Witte, 1982). Students who demonstrate low achievement motivation through poor attendance, poor grades, and discipline referrals are seen at least once a week in school for two or three years in small group meetings where positive school behaviors are discussed and rewarded. (See Stanley et al., 1976 for more details.) By the end of two years in the program, students achieve better grades and attend school more than do similar students who did not receive the intervention (Bry & George, 1979, 1980). There is also evidence that the behavior change is accompanied by increased self esteem and increased sense of internal causality (Bry & Witte, 1982). In addition, in the next five years, young people who experienced this preventive intervention are less likely than all other high risk youth to be arrested, which is another precursor of substance abuse (Bry, 1982).

Thus, long-term, behavioral programs in the schools for high risk young people can reduce several of the substance abuse precursors. We are nevertheless far from accounting for all of the variance and thus being able to establish the environmental conditions that will truly prevent substance abuse in women. More research must be done to uncover more controlling variables and better understand the determining parameters of the already established etiological variables.

REFERENCES

Alden, L. *Behavioral self-management techniques in the treatment of drinkers in the early stages of abuse.* Paper presented at the Fourteenth Banff International Conference in Behavioral Sciences, Alberta, Canada, March 1982.

Annis, H. M. & Liban, C. B. Alcoholism in women: Treatment modalities and outcomes. In O. J. Kalant (ed.), *Alcohol and drug problems in women.* New York: Plenum, 1980.

Ausubel, D. P. An evaluation of recent adolescent drug addiction. *Mental Hygiene*, 1952, *36*, 373–382.

Azrin, N. H. Improvements in community-reinforcement approach to alcoholism. *Behaviour Research and Therapy*, 1976, *14*, 339–348.

Baruch, E. K. & Barnett, R. C. On the well-being of adult women. In L. A. Bond & J. C. Rosen (eds.), *Competence and coping during adulthood.* Hanover, NH: University Press of New England, 1980.

Beck, A. T., Rush, A. J., Shaw, B. F., & Emery, G. *Cognitive therapy of depression.* New York: Guilford Press, 1979.

Bigelow, G. E., Cohen, M., Liebson, I., & Faillace, L. A. Abstinence or moderation? Choice by alcoholics. *Behaviour Research and Therapy*, 1972, *10*, 209–214.

Blum, R. H. & Associates. *Students and drugs.* San Francisco: Jossey-Bass, 1970.

Blum, R. H., Blum, E., & Garfield, E. *Drug education: Results and recommendations.* Lexington, MA: D. C. Heath & Co., 1976.

Boudin, H. M. Contingency contracting as a therapeutic tool in the deceleration of amphetamine use. *Behavior Therapy*, 1972, *3*, 604–605.

Bradlyn, A. S., Strickler, D. P., & Maxwell, W. A. Alcohol, expectancy and stress: Methodological concerns with the expectancy design. *Addictive Behaviors*, 1981, *6*, 1–8.

Brown, G. W., Bhrolchain, M. N., & Harris, T. Social class and psychiatric disturbance among women in an urban population. *Sociology*, 1975, *9*, 225–254.

Bry, B. H. Reducing the incidence of adolescent problems through preventive intervention: One and five year follow-up. *American Journal of Community Psychology*, 1982, *10*, 265–276.

Bry, B. H. & George, F. E. Evaluating and improving prevention programs: A strategy from drug abuse. *Evaluation and Program Planning*, 1979, *2*, 127–136.

Bry, B. H. & George, F. E. The preventive effects of early intervention upon the attendance and grades of urban adolescents. *Professional Psychology*, 1980, *11*, 252–260.

Bry, B. H., McKeon, P., & Pandina, R. J. Extent of drug use as a function of number of risk factors. *Journal of Abnormal Psychology*, 1982, *91*, 273–279.

Bry, B. H. & Witte, G. *Impact of a behaviorally-oriented, school-based, group intervention program upon alienation and self esteem.* Paper presented at the Eastern Evaluation Research Society meeting in New York City, May 1982.

Chambers, C. D. & Moffett, A. Negro opiate addiction. In J. C. Ball & C. D. Chambers (eds.), *The epidemiology of opiate addiction in the United States.* Springfield, IL: Charles C Thomas, 1970.

Collins, R. L. & Marlatt, G. A. Social modeling as a determinant of drinking behavior: Implications for prevention and treatment. *Addictive Behaviors*, 1981, *6*, 233–239.

Cooper, A. M., Waterhouse, G. J., & Sobell, M. B. Influence of gender on drinking in a modeling situation. *Journal of Studies on Alcohol*, 1979, *40*, 562–570.

Crowley, T. J. The reinforcers for drug abuse: Why people take drugs. *Comprehensive Psychiatry*, 1972, *13*, 51–62.

Curlee, J. Alcoholism and the empty nest syndrome. *Bulletin of the Menninger Clinic*, 1969, *33*, 165–171.

Danish, S. J. & D'Augelli, A. R. Promoting competence and enhancing development through life development intervention. In L. A. Bond & J. C. Rosen (eds.), *Competence and coping during adulthood.* Hanover, NH: University Press of New England, 1980.

DeRicco, D. A. & Garlington, W. K. The effects of modeling and disclosure of experimenter's intent on drinking rate in college students. *Addictive Behaviors*, 1977, *2*, 135–139.

Derogatis, L. R., Rickels, L., & Rock, A. F. The SCL-90 and the MMPI: A step in the validation of a new self-report scale. *British Journal of Psychiatry*, 1976, *108*, 280–289.

Dohrenwend, B. S. & Dohrenwend, B. P. *Stressful life events: Their nature and effects.* New York: John Wiley, 1974.

Ellinwood, E. H., Jr. Amphetamines/anorectics. In R. I. Dupont, A. Goldstein, & J. O'Donnell (eds.), *Handbook on drug abuse.* Rockville, MD: National Institute on Drug Abuse, 1979.

Falk, J. L. Production of polydipsia in normal rats by an intermittent food schedule. *Science*, 1961, *133*, 195–196.

Falk, J. L. The place of adjunctive behavior in drug abuse research. In T. Thompson & C. E. Johanson (eds.), *Behavioral pharmacology of human drug dependence*, Research Monograph 37. Rockville, MD: National Institute on Drug Abuse, 1981.

Ferrence, R. G. & Whitehead, P. C. Six differences in psychoactive drug use: Recent epidemiology. In O. J. Kalant (ed.), *Alcohol and drug problems in women.* New York: Plenum, 1980.

Fillmore, K. Drinking and problem drinking in early adulthood and middle age. *Quarterly Journal of Studies on Alcohol*, 1974, *35*, 819–840.

Fillmore, K. Relationships between specific drinking problems in early adulthood and middle age. *Journal of Studies on Alcohol*, 1975, *36*, 882–907.

Finnegan, L. P. (ed.) *Drug dependency in pregnancy: Clinical management of mother and child.* Services Research Monograph Series. Rockville, MD: National Institute on Drug Abuse, 1978.

Finnegan, L. P. Women in treatment. In R. L. DuPont, A. Goldstein, & A. J. O'Donnell (eds.), *Handbook on drug abuse.* Rockville, MD: National Institute on Drug Abuse, 1979.

Finnegan, L. P. & Fehr, K. O. The effects of opiates, sedative-hypnotics, amphetamines, cannabis, and other psychoactive drugs on the fetus and newborn. In O. J. Kalant (ed.), *Alcohol and drug problems in women*. New York: Plenum, 1980.

Gomberg, E. S. Women and alcoholism. In V. Franks & V. Burtle (eds.), *Women in therapy: New psychotherapies for a changing society*. New York: Brunner/Mazel, 1974.

Goodwin, D. W., Schulsinger, F., Knop, J., Mednick, S., & Guze, S. B. Psychopathology in adopted and nonadopted daughters of alcoholics. *Archives of General Psychiatry*, 1977, *34*, 1005-1009.

Gossett, J. T., Lewis, J. M., & Phillips, V. A. Psychological characteristics of adolescent drug users and abstainers: Some implications for preventive education. *Bulletin of the Menninger Clinic*, 1972, *36*, 425-435.

Griffiths, R. R., Bigelow, G. E., & Henningfield, J. E. Similarities in animal and human drug-taking behavior. In N. K. Mello (ed.), *Advances in substance abuse*. Greenwich, CN: JAI Press, 1980.

Healthy People: The Surgeon General's Report on Health Promotion and Disease Prevention, 1979. Washington, DC: Department of Health, Education, and Welfare, 1979.

Hendin, H., Pollinger, A., Ulman, R., & Carr, A. C. *Adolescent marijuana abusers and their families*. Research Monograph 40. Rockville, MD: National Institute on Drug Abuse, 1981.

Hendricks, R. D., Sobell, M. B., & Cooper, A. M. Social influences on human ethanol consumption in an analogue situation. *Addictive Behaviors*, 1978, *3*, 253-259.

Huba, G. J., Wingard, J. A., & Bentler, P. M. Beginning adolescent drug use and peer adult interaction patterns. *Journal of Consulting and Clinical Psychology*, 1979, *47*, 265-279.

Hughes, J. M. Adolescent children of alcoholic parents and the relationship of Alateen to these children. *Journal of Consulting and Clinical Psychology*, 1977, *45*, 946-947.

Hunt, G. & Azrin, N. A. A community-reinforcement approach to alcoholism. *Behaviour Research and Therapy*, 1973, *11*, 91-104.

Jasinski, D. R. Stimulus control and drug dependence. In T. Thompson & C. E. Johanson (eds.), *Behavioral pharmacology of human drug dependence*. Research Monograph 37. Rockville, MD: National Institute on Drug Abuse, 1981.

Jessor, R. & Jessor, S. L. Theory testing in longitudinal research on marijuana use. In D. B. Kandel (ed.), *Longitudinal research on drug use: Empirical findings and methodological issues*. Washington: Hemisphere, 1978.

Johnston, L. D., Bachman, J. D., & O'Malley, P. M. *Monitoring the future: Questionnaire responses from the nation's high school seniors 1979*. Ann Arbor, MI: University of Michigan Institute for Social Research, 1980.

Kachanoff, R., Leveille, R., McCelland, J. P., & Wayner, M. S. Schedule-induced behavior in humans. *Physiology and Behavior*, 1973, *11*, 395-398.

Kalant, O. J. Six differences in alcohol and drug problems—Some highlights. In O. J. Kalant (ed.), *Alcohol and drug problems in women*. New York: Plenum, 1980.

Kandel, D. B. Convergences in prospective longitudinal surveys of drug use in normal populations. In D. B. Kandel (ed.), *Longitudinal research on drug use: Empirical findings and methodological issues*. Washington: Hemisphere, 1978.

Kandel, D. B., Treiman, D., Faust, R., & Single, E. Adolescent involvement in legal and illegal drug use: A multiple classification analysis. *Social Forces*, 1976, *55*, 438-458.

Kaplan, H. B. Social class, self-derogation, and deviant response. *Social Psychiatry*, 1978, *13*, 19-28. (a)

Kaplan, H. B. Deviant behavior and self-enhancement in adolescence. *Journal of Youth and Adolescence*, 1978, *7*, 253-277. (b)

Keys, A., Brozek, J., Henschel, A., Mickelson, O., & Taylor, H. L. *The biology of human starvation*. Minneapolis: University of Minnesota Press, 1950.

Kleber, H. D., Berberian, R. M., Gould, L. C., & Kasl, S. V. *Evaluation of an adolescent drug education program* (Final Report of NIDA Grant No. DA-00055). Rockville, MD: National Institure on Drug Abuse, 1975.

Klein, N. C., Alexander, J. F., & Parsons, B. V. Impact of family systems intervention on recidivism and sibling delinquency: A model of primary prevention and program evaluation. *Journal of Consulting and Clinical Psychology*, 1977, *45*, 469-474.

Lê, A. D., Poulos, C. X., & Chappell, H. Conditioned tolerance to the hypothermic effect of ethyl alcohol. *Science*, 1979, *206*, 1109-1110.

Lettieri, D. J., Sayers, M., & Pearson, H. W. (eds.). *Theories on drug abuse: Selected contem-*

porary perspectives. Research Monograph 30. Rockville, MD: National Institute on Drug Abuse, 1980.

Lied, E. R. & Marlatt, G. A. Modeling as a determinant of alcohol consumption: Effect of subject sex and prior drinking history. *Addictive Behaviors*, 1979, *4*, 47–54.

Ludwig, A. M. & Stark, L. H. Alcohol craving: Subjective and situational aspects. *Quarterly Journal of Studies on Alcohol*, 1974, *35*, 899–905.

Maccoby, N., Farquhar, J. W., Wood, P. D., & Alexander, J. Reducing the risk of cardiovascular disease: Effects of a community-based campaign on knowledge and behavior. *Journal of Community Health*, 1977, *3*, 100–114.

Meisch, R. A. & Kliner, D. J. Etonitazene as a reinforcer for rats: Increased etonitazene reinforced behavior due to food deprivation. *Psychopharmacology*, 1979, *63*, 97–98.

Mello, N. K. Some behavioral and biological aspects of alcohol problems in women. In O. J. Kalant (ed.), *Alcohol and drug problems in women*. New York: Plenum, 1980.

Mello, N. K. Some aspects of the behavioral pharmacology of alcohol. In D. H. Effron, *Psychopharmacology: A review of progress 1957–1967*. Washington, DC: U.S. Government Printing Office, 1968.

Miller, P. M. A behavioral intervention program for chronic public drunkenness offenders. *Archives of General Psychiatry*, 1975, *32*, 915–918.

Nathan, P. E. & Harris, S. L. *Psychopathology and society*, 2nd ed. New York: McGraw-Hill, 1980.

Newcomb, M. D., Huba, G. J., & Bentler, P. M. *Cross-validation of a measure of adolescent stress*. Unpublished manuscript, 1981. (Available from authors at Department of Psychology, University of California, Los Angeles, CA 90024.)

Nurco, D. N. Etiological aspects of drug abuse. In R. I. DuPont, A. Goldstein, & J. O'Donnell (eds.), *Handbook on drug abuse*. Rockville, MD: National Institute on Drug Abuse, 1979.

O'Brien, C. P., Ternes, J. W., Grabowski, J., & Ehrman, R. Classically conditioned phenomena in human opiate addiction. In T. Thompson & C. E. Johanson (eds.), *Behavioral pharmacology of human drug dependence*. Research Monograph 37. Rockville, MD: National Institute on Drug Abuse, 1981.

O'Donnell, J. A. & Clayton, R. R. Determinants of early marijuana use. In G. M. Beschner & A. S. Friedman (eds.), *Youth abuse: Problems, issues, and treatment*. Lexington, MA: Lexington Books, 1979.

Pandina, R. J. & Schuele, J. A. Psychosocial correlates of adolescent alcohol and drug use. *Journal of Studies on Alcohol*, in press.

Parent power in Georgia. Prevention Resources, 1978, *3*(1), 3–8. (DHEW Publication No. (ADM) 79-827).

Parker, J. C., Gilbert, G., & Speltz, M. L. Expectations regarding the effects of alcohol on assertiveness: A comparison of alcoholics and social drinkers. *Addictive Behaviors*, 1981, *6*, 29–33.

Parry, H. J., Balter, M. B., Mellinger, G. D., Cisin, I. H., & Manheimer, D. I. National patterns of psychotherapeutic drug use. *Archives of General Psychiatry*, 1973, *28*, 769–783.

Pemberton, D. A. A comparison of the outcome of treatment in male and female alcoholics. *British Journal of Psychiatry*, 1967, *113*, 367–373.

Penfield, D. A. & Whiteley, R. *Final evaluation of an experimental three-year program in drug abuse prevention involving the school system, the community, and the student population in the Piscataway, New Jersey Schools* (Final Report, NIDA Grant No. R25-DA00832-02). Piscataway, NJ: Piscataway Public Schools, August 1977.

Pervin, L. *Affect and addictions*. Unpublished manuscript, 1981. (Available from author at Psychology Department, Livingston College, Rutgers University, New Brunswick, NJ 08903.)

Pihl, R. O. & Spiers, P. Individual characteristics in the etiology of drug abuse. In B. Maher (ed.), *Progress in experimental personality research* (Vol. 8). New York: Academic Press, 1978.

Pickens, R., Bigelow, G., & Griffiths, R. An experimental approach to treating chronic alcoholism: A case study and one-year follow-up. *Behaviour Research and Therapy*, 1973, *11*, 321–325.

Pickens, R. W. & Heston, L. L. Personality factors in human drug self-administration. In T. Thompson & C. E. Johanson (eds.), *Behavioral pharmacology of human drug dependence*. Research Monograph 37. Rockville, MD: National Institute on Drug Abuse, 1981.

Poulos, C. X., Riley, E. H., & Siegel, S. The role of Pavlovian processes in drug tolerance and dependence: Implications for treatment. *Addictive Behaviors*, 1981, *6*, 205–211.

Ricks, D. F. Supershrink: Methods of a therapist judged successful on the basis of adult outcomes of adolescent patients. In D. Ricks, A. Thomas, & M. Roff (eds.), *Life history research in psychopathology* (Vol. 3). Minneapolis: University of Minnesota Press, 1974.

Rimm, D., Briddell, D., Zimmerman, M., & Caddy, G. The effects of alcohol and the expectancy of alcohol on snake fear. *Addictive Behaviors*, 1981, *6*, 47–51.

Robins, L., Bates, W., & O'Neal, P. Adult drinking patterns of former problem children. In D. J. Pittman & C. R. Snyder (eds.), *Society, culture, and drinking patterns*. New York: Wiley, 1962.

Robins, L. N. & Smith, E. M. Longitudinal studies of alcohol and drug problems: Sex differences. In O. J. Kalant (ed.), *Alcohol and drug problems in women*. New York: Plenum, 1980.

Rosett, H. L. The effects of alcohol on the fetus and offspring. In O. J. Kalant (ed.), *Alcohol and drug problems in women*. New York: Plenum, 1980.

Rothstein, P. & Gould, J. B. Born with a habit: Infants of drug-addicted mothers. *Pediatric Clinics of North America*, 1974, *2*, 307–321.

Samson, H. H. & Falk, J. L. Alteration of fluid preference in ethanol-dependent animals. *Journal of Pharmacology and Experimental Therapeutics*, 1974, *190*, 365–376.

Sarason, I. G. *Abnormal psychology*. New York: Appleton-Century-Crofts, 1972.

Schuckit, M. & Winokur, G. A short term follow-up of women alcoholics. *Diseases of the Nervous System*, 1972, *33*, 672–678.

Segal, B. Reasons for marijuana use and personality. A canonical analysis. *Journal of Alcohol and Drug Education*, 1977, *22*, 64–69.

Segal, B., Huba, G. J., & Singer, J. L. Reasons for drug and alcohol use by college students. *International Journal of the Addictions*, 1980, *15*, 489–498. (a)

Segal, B., Huba, G. J., & Singer, J. L. Prediction of college drug use from personality and inner experience. *International Journal of the Addictions*, 1980, *15*, 849–867. (b)

Siegel, S. Evidence from rats that morphine tolerance is a learned response. *Journal of Comparative Physiological Psychology*, 1975, *89*, 498–506.

Skinner, B. F. *The behavior of organisms*. New York: Appleton-Century-Crofts, 1938.

Smith, G. M. & Fogg, C. P. Psychological predictors of early use, late use, and nonuse of marijuana among teenage students. In D. B. Kandel (ed.), *Longitudinal research on drug use: Empirical findings and methodological issues*. Washington: Hemisphere, 1978.

Stanley, H., Goldstein, A., & Bry, B. H. *Manual for the Early Secondary Intervention Program*. Freehold, NJ: Monmouth County Board of Drug Abuse Services, 1976.

Stitzer, M. L., Griffiths, R. R., Bigelow, G. E., & Liebson, I. A. Social stimulus factors in drug effects in human subjects. In T. Thompson & C. E. Johanson (eds.), *Behavioral pharmacology of human drug dependence*. Research Monograph 37. Rockville, MD: National Institute on Drug Abuse, 1981.

Streit, F. A test procedure to identify secondary school children who have a high probability of drug abuse. (Doctoral dissertation, Rutgers University, 1973). *Dissertation Abstracts International*, 1973, *34*, 5177-B. (University Microfilms No. 74-8875)

Streit, F. *Evaluation of Open Door* (Final Report on NIDA Prevention Grant to Open Door). Highland Park, NJ: Streit Associates, June 1977.

Streit, F. & Oliver, H. C. The child's perception of his family and its relation to drug use. *Drug Forum*, 1972, *1*, 283–289.

Teasdale, J. D. Conditioned abstinence in narcotic addicts. *International Journal of the Addictions*, 1973, *8*, 273–292.

Templer, D. I., Ruff, C. F., & Ayers, J. Essential alcoholism and family history of alcoholism. *Quarterly Journal of Studies on Alcohol*, 1974, *35*, 655–657.

Tennant, F. S., Jr. & Detels, R. Relationship of alcohol, cigarette, and drug abuse in adulthood with consumption in childhood. *Preventive Medicine*, 1976, *5*, 70–77.

Tennant, F. S., Jr., Detels, R., & Clark, V. Some childhood antecedents of drug and alcohol abuse. *American Journal of Epidemiology*, 1975, *102*, 377–384.

Thompson, T. Behavioral mechanisms and loci of drug dependence: An overview. In T. Thompson & C. E. Johanson (eds.), *Behavioral pharmacology of human drug dependence*. Research Monograph 37. Rockville, MD: National Institute on Drug Abuse, 1981.

Tyler, J. & Thompson, M. Patterns of drug abuse among women. *International Journal of the Addictions*, 1980, *15*, 309–321.

Vaillant, G. E. & Milofsky, E. S. The etiology of alcoholism: A prospective viewpoint. *American Psychologist*, 1982, *37*, 494–503.

Vuchinich, R. E., Tucker, J. A., & Sobell, M. B. Alcohol expectancy, cognitive labeling, and mirth. *Journal of Abnormal Psychology*, 1979, *88*, 641–651.

Wallace, C. J. The effects of delayed rewards, social pressure, and frustration on the responses of opiate addicts. In N. A. Krasnegor (ed.), *Behavioral analysis and treatment of substance abuse*. Research Monograph 25. Rockville, MD: National Institute on Drug Abuse, 1979.

Wilcox, B. L. Social support, life stress, and psychological adjustment: A test of the buffering hypothesis. *American Journal of Community Psychology*, 1981, *9*, 371–386.

Wechsler, H. & McFadden, M. Sex differences in adolescent alcohol and drug use: A disappearing phenomenon. *Journal of Studies on Alcohol*, 1976, *37*, 1291–1301.

Woody, G. E., McLellan, A. T., O'Brien, C. P., & Luborsky, L. Personality factors in methadone self-administration by heroin addicts. In T. Thompson & C. E. Johanson (eds.), *Behavioral pharmacology of human drug dependence*. Research Monograph 37. Rockville, MD: National Institute on Drug Abuse, 1981.

Zuckerman, M. *Sensation-seeking: Beyond the optimal level of arousal*. Hillsdale, NJ: Lawrence Erlbaum Associates, 1979.

Zuckerman, M., Neary, R. S., & Brustman, B. A. Sensation-Seeking Scale correlates in experience (smoking, drugs, alcohol, hallucinations and sex) and preference for complexity (designs). Proceedings of the 78th Annual Convention of the American Psychological Association, Vol. 5. Washington, DC: American Psychological Association, 1970.

15

Older Women and Mental Health

Margaret Gatz, Cynthia Pearson, and Max Fuentes
University of Southern California

SETTING THE STAGE

The 1980s may well be remembered as the decade of the older woman. Older women, especially those aged 75 and older, are the fastest growing portion of the U.S. population. According to the 1980 census, 11.3 percent of the population are 65 or older and, within this group, there are half again as many women as there are men. Furthermore, over 40 percent of women aged 65 and older are living alone (U.S. Department of Commerce, 1978). The median yearly income for women 65 and older, as of 1980, was $4,226. More than 2.7 million older women live below the poverty line, with older women living alone overrepresented among this group (USDC, 1981). This large, growing and economically disadvantaged population is currently emerging from the invisibility it had been accorded in past decades.

The emergence of older women as a matter of social and public policy concern has been influenced by the convergence of two forces. First, the field of aging has enjoyed increased attention in response to demographic shifts. Medical advances in this century have successfully prolonged life expectancy such that individuals living into their eighth and ninth decades are no longer exceptions but constitute, instead, a new social force. Moreover, elderly persons are assuming advocacy roles on behalf of their own quality of life.

Second, the women's movement has heightened public awareness of the concerns of women of all ages. The movement originally arose from younger women acting to achieve social change on behalf of their own generation. Initially, the movement questioned the value of traditional women's roles, and most women now old have led just such lives. By the mid 1970s, however, older women had been identified as the group that had been "left out" of the liberation (Datan, 1977; Lewis & Butler, 1973), and efforts were underway to remedy this omission. For instance, organizations such as the National Action Forum for Older Women and the Older Women's League are emerging as strong advocates for older women's issues.

Actually, it is not clear whether we are seeing a convergence of interest or the emergence of a new constituency. As Abu-Laban wrote in 1981, "ageism and

Part of this chapter was previously presented in a symposium at Western Psychological Association, "Psychology's responsibilities for research and practice in the '80s: Focus on women," in Sacramento, California on 9 April 1982. We gratefully acknowledge the astute reading of earlier drafts by our friends and colleagues Pat Baltazar, Vern Bengtson, Joan Gildemeister, Kennon Kashima, Virginia Mullin, Sid Roth, Michael Smyer, and Ruth Weg. We also appreciate the bibliographic assistance of Farah Ghadiri and Desiree Mitrovich.

sexism, while often joint concerns of socially conscious women, offend and arouse different segments of the population" (p. 95). Older women are not yet strongly represented in the membership of feminist organizations. Instead, the report of the White House Mini-Conference on Older Women (1981) urges that political power will come with recognition as a specific constituency.

Older women have been invisible in academic literature also, since most aging research has paid little systematic attention to sex differences, while research in sex differences has rarely extended through the latter part of the lifespan. Hence, programs and policies designed to meet the needs of this growing population of older women may well be based on belief rather than data. It is no surprise that the historical myths about older women have a distinctively deleterious quality about them. Picking up on the negative tone of common stereotypes—for example, "poor, dumb, and ugly" (Troll, 1977)—a number of writers have presented evidence to contradict the myths. Palmore (1977, 1981) developed a Facts on Aging quiz to correct frequent misconceptions about older adults, and Payne and Whittington (1976) reviewed and analyzed stereotypes of older women. Interestingly, we have found that what have arisen as antidotes to the negative stereotypes may be no more factual than the myths being combatted. We refer to these more current assertions as countermyths. In brief, while the myths emphasize disadvantage and deterioration, the countermyths focus on successful aging and the absence of problems. Alternatively, the myths could be seen as the fears, the countermyths as the ideals, of a culture confronting an expanded life expectancy.

If the applied behavioral sciences are to exert a constructive force towards the optimization of mental health of older women, it seems essential that we move beyond the rhetoric of myth and countermyth to look at the available data and become aware of the limits of our current knowledge base. Therefore, following a brief section on theory, a major portion of this chapter is devoted to a number of common myths about older women, along with their companion countermyths. For each of these topics we then summarize what is known. Finally, the relationship of the myths and countermyths to mental health is discussed, and implications for intervention are explored.

Lifespan Developmental Perspective

Lifespan developmental theory (Baltes & Schaie, 1973; Riegel, 1976, 1978) provides a framework for organizing the notions that need to be considered in conceptualizing both the dialectic of myth and countermyth as well as older women and their psychosocial worlds. Dialectical psychology requires the incorporation of both of two viewpoints: myth and countermyth; person and environment. A dialectical model of human development then recognizes that one is dealing simultaneously with a changing individual and a changing world, each instrumental in the development of the other. The elements of the model can be encompassed in seven interrelated notions:

1. Identity. Each individual is a whole person, and it is that same whole person who passes through the course of life. Interindividual differences tend to maintain over time (Costa & McCrae, 1980).

2. Age. Although each individual may change over time, there is no single marker for those changes. We tend to use chronological age for that purpose, while also recognizing that age itself is not causative of change (Birren & Renner, 1977).

3. Cohort. An individual person's life history reflects both his or her own individual life experiences and maturation as well as the aggregate of sociocultural influences shared by only their generation. In this chapter it will be noted that we use the expression "women now old" as an occasional reminder that what we observe in today's 70-year-olds, for example, may not be true for the next cohort of 70-year-olds.

4. Variability. Not only are older people different from one another, but also they are more different from one another than are younger people (Krauss, 1980), with the increase in diversity reflecting how, over time, each individual acquires a unique set of life experiences (Schaie, 1981). This large interindividual variability means that performance distributions for old and young groups overlap considerably.

5. Situational variables. The diversity of older adults in part reflects the differential impact of biological and social factors, for example, chronic illness and socioeconomic status.

6. Time. It is, of course, impossible to think about change and aging without thinking about the temporal context. Neugarten and Hagestad (1976) have observed that older adults are aware of there being a social clock of age-related expectations and of their being on-time or off-time. Furthermore, older persons have less time to live than younger persons, and an awareness of time left is part of their reality (Kastenbaum, 1978).

7. Individual as active. Basic to lifespan developmental theory is a model of the person as an actor, a chooser, a creator of meaning. A person is not simply the passive recipient of influences.

This lifespan developmental perspective serves as our implicit model throughout the chapter. Even as we focus first on one aspect and then on another—on myth and countermyth, person and environment—the dialectic process requires the dynamic of both.

MYTHS, COUNTERMYTHS, AND KERNELS OF TRUTH

Women now old have faced the challenge of carving satisfaction for themselves out of a sociocultural milieu that has traditionally defined their major social role as reproduction, nurturance, and transmission of values to the next generation. Once that work is done, they may be perceived, and believe themselves to be, socially redundant, with few hopeful options. The ways women have shaped and adapted to their milieu form the reality of their current lives.

Poverty

Palmore's (1977) Facts on Aging quiz includes the following item: "The majority of older people have incomes below the poverty level (as defined by the federal government)" (p. 316). The item states the myth of poverty. The countermyth, conveyed insofar as the item is scored "false," is that older people are well enough off, if not more affluent than they have ever been (Neugarten, 1978). The data suggest that the message in the statement of the myth should not be totally overlooked.

Currently in the U.S. there are over 15 million women aged 65 and older. Their median personal income is only 57 percent of the median income of elderly men

(Harris Poll, 1981). There was a significant decrease in the poverty rate for women 65 and older from 28 percent in 1970 to 19 percent in 1980, largely attributable to changes in social security benefits (USDC, 1981). Nonetheless, among older women living alone or with non-relatives, 26 percent of white, 48 percent of Spanish-origin, and 60 percent of black women 65 and older live below the poverty line (USDC, 1979a). The financial state of older women reflects years of non-payment for household work, intermittent employment that has led to limited (if any) eligibility for retirement income, and access to lower paying employment while working. While many older men are also faced with severe decreases in financial resources when they retire, elderly women are the largest single group with poverty-level incomes—a fact that tends to disappear when differences by sex are not noted or when "mean income," which includes the very rich, is cited. In addition, apparent sex differences are further mitigated by the fact that the poverty line is lower for women than for men: In 1980, the Bureau of the Census Poverty Guidelines for those 65 and over (non-farm) was $3990 for a single male and $3938 for a single female (USDC, 1981). In sum, poverty may be the single most salient fact in the lives of too many women now old.

Intellectual Incompetence

Actually, the myth of intellectual incompetence has two aspects, sometimes confused with each other, dumb and senile. The countermyth is that there is little if any decline in intelligence in normal aging, at least until the 70s (Schaie & Labouvie-Vief, 1974). Volumes of data speak to cognitive changes with aging. We can only briefly address each of the two aspects introduced by this myth.

"Senility" is not the normal course of aging for any older adult. Senile dementia, which is an inclusive term for several diseases, occurs in 5–7 percent of those aged 65 and older and, by age 80, prevalence increases fourfold (Kay & Bergmann, 1980). Because of their greater life expectancy, women are more likely to experience a dementing condition. Dementia is characterized by diffuse structural changes in many areas of the brain and is associated with progressive impairment of memory and generalized intellectual functioning, which increasingly interferes with normal ability to interact. Alzheimer's-type dementia is the most prevalent type. It is not known what causes the disease and at present there is no known way to reverse its course. Many older adults, and those around them, misinterpret normal forgetting as being the first signs of "senility" and worry excessively about the possibility of progressive, severe decline (Kahn et al., 1975).

Many reversible conditions can cause behavioral changes that are easily confused with dementia. Among the organic factors associated with severe loss of intellectual functioning are malnutrition, hormone imbalance, acute illness, and pharmacological toxicity. If left untreated, irreversible damage may result. In addition, grief reactions and severe depression can mimic the symptoms of organic brain syndromes. The myth of mental incapacity may blind us to remediable circumstances. (See Zarit, 1980, for a review of these issues.)

For the normal older adult, there is much debate about the extent of decline in intelligence with age, a great deal of which centers around methodological issues. Although both sides concur that persons now old perform less well than persons now young, longitudinal studies following the same individuals across a number of years tend to show a high level of stability, while cross-sectional studies measuring people of various ages at the same time show marked declines. As a major proponent of the "decline" position, Botwinick (1977) criticized longitudinal studies because they can only report on the most vital members of a cohort, since the least able are the ones who will drop out of long-term research. Schaie (1980), on the other hand, pointed out that the declines found in cross-sectional research are largely the product of lower levels of education and the intellectual obsolescence that accrue to older cohorts in rapidly advancing technological societies. In other words, persons now old may be performing as well as they ever did.

In truth, both sides of the debate have drawn rather close, with the decliners seeing change as beginning somewhat earlier and being more global, while those supporting stability see more differential shifts. Schaie (1980) summarized the latest research as follows: ". . . from the early sixties to the mid-seventies there is normal decline on some but not all abilities, for some but not all individuals, but beyond eighty decrement is the rule for most individuals" (p. 279). Abilities that show decline during the 50s are those that involve speed of response (Birren et al., 1980). In addition, poor health, especially cardiovascular disease (Eisdorfer & Wilkie, 1977), and lack of environmental stimulation can contribute to decline.

Both sides emphasize the limitations of intelligence tests as predicting useful performance for older people. The declines noted often are more statistically than practically significant (Schaie, 1980). Moreover, they certainly do not measure important cognitive phenomena such as wisdom (Clayton & Birren, 1980). The implications of the two positions are somewhat different, however. If the generational explanation is correct and much of the performance deficit observed in an individual is due to intellectual obsolescence or, what Abu-Laban (1981) called "learned incompetencies" typical of older women, then educational intervention with older adults could be highly effective (Baltes & Labouvie, 1973). The decline position would suggest interventions that make the environment less complex so that it can be managed effectively by older adults.

Finally, it must be remembered that interindividual differences within older cohorts are far greater than between-cohort differences. Since interindividual differences can be expected to maintain, women who were sharp when young are likely to be "sharp as a tack" when old.

Illness

Palmore provides facts that must be reconciled: On the one hand, it is scored "true" that "more older persons have chronic diseases that limit their activities than younger persons" (the alternate form of the quiz, 1981, p. 431). On the other hand, the side of the countermyth, it is also scored "true" that "about 80 percent of the aged are healthy enough to carry out their normal activities" (1977, p. 315). The latter item, referred to by Miller and Dodder (1980) as a "subjective fact," reflects the important perspective of what older people say about themselves in opinion polls.

In support of the myth of the old woman as sick, health problems, especially chronic degenerative conditions, become increasingly prevalent in the later years. In addition, they are often said to be more prevalent among older women than men (e.g., Soldo, 1980). For persons 65 and over, men predominate in heart conditions (21.8 percent versus 19.3 percent for women), while women experience more arthritis (27.1 percent versus 14.9 percent for men) and noncardiac-involved hypertension (8.5 percent versus 4.0 percent for men) (Rockstein & Sussman, 1979). We think these sex differences may be overrated, especially when one takes into consideration the fact that grouping all women aged 65 and over includes a great many more women than men in the upper, more vulnerable, age ranges. In short, because women have a 7.7-year advantage in life expectancy, they are more apt to experience chronic illness than men.

Throughout adulthood, women tend to have higher rates of lesser illnesses, while men have higher rates of diseases that are leading causes of death (Verbrugge, 1976; Gove & Hughes, 1979). This observation provides a commentary on the difference in mortality, rather than explaining it. The variety of explanations that have been offered include that women are inherently biologically superior, lead less stressful lives, are permitted social acceptance for sick behavior, and seek medical attention and engage in preventive measures more appropriately than men. However, of greater importance to older women than either health statistics or explanations is the confusion about what constitutes normal aging. Many pathological processes, especially those that are not strongly associated with high mortality rates, are often discounted as "just getting old" and are left untreated by physicians and unreported by the older individual.

A final datum in support of the myth is the amount of money spent by older adults on health care. In 1977 30 percent of personal health care dollars were accounted for by 11 percent of the population aged 65 and older (*Gray Panthers Network*, 1982).

Turning to the countermyth, although only 14 percent of community-residing elderly report that they are free of chronic illness, for the most part they do not see themselves as grossly impaired, and 70 percent rate their health as good or excellent (Soldo, 1980). These global ratings of health status have been shown to compare well with physicians' ratings, with the elderly tending towards overrating their wellness (Siegler et al., 1980). Differences between men and women in self-rated health are negligible.

Another way of defining health rests more on level of functioning. In 1977 nearly 27 percent of the men aged 65–74 and 36 percent of those 75 and over reported themselves restricted in functioning and unable to carry out a major activity, e.g., household maintenance. Here we see a remarkable contrast: For women in these same age ranges, the figures were 6 percent and 14 percent (Soldo, 1980).

So far we have been talking about older people who live in the community. There is also a health-related myth concerning institutionalization. By way of countermyth, Palmore has scored as "false" the item "at least one-tenth of the aged are living in long-stay institutions (i.e., nursing homes, mental hospitals, homes for the aged, etc.)" (1977, p. 315). Indeed, it is an often cited statistic that only 5 percent of older adults reside in nursing homes at any given time. Following this line of reasoning, 95 percent of older adults are living in the community. These cross-sectional figures, however, may be misleading.

Three studies have looked at death records in order to determine the likelihood of dying in a nursing home or long-term care facility. Kastenbaum and Candy (1973) obtained 23 percent; and Lesnoff-Caravaglia (1978), 30 percent, with more women than men dying in nursing homes and extended care facilities. National Center for Health Statistics data indicated that 21 percent of persons aged 55 and older died in nursing homes (Ingram & Barry, 1977). The figures obtained in these studies still underestimate the proportion of older adults who spend some period of time in a nursing home, because they do not include terminally ill residents who were transferred to acute care hospitals. To correct for this, Vincente et al. (1979) reported 10-year longitudinal data from deceased persons aged 55 and older at the start of the study. Of 455 cases, 38.9 percent had resided in a convalescent or nursing home at least once before death. Again, women and persons living alone were more at risk for institutionalization.

So the truth appears to be that, while poor health is a major concern of older women, the majority of older adults consider themselves to be in good health in spite of increases in chronic diseases. Furthermore, the so-called paradoxical longevity of women increases the likelihood that they will experience health problems and be at risk for institutionalization. Yet older men report more limitations of activity than women. The myth and countermyth taken together describe women who are self-sustaining in the face of increased risk.

Tranquility

What can be said about the personality of older women? We begin with two pictures in tandem: first, the old woman as the blue-haired model of kindly tranquility, serenely crocheting in her rocking chair while waiting to hand out cookies to neighborhood youngsters; and second, the old woman as aggressive, cantankerous, dominating, irascible, and destructive. The intimate relationship of these personae is demonstrated by the witch in Hansel and Gretel, who sweetly seduces the children into her gingerbread house for the explicit purpose of doing them in. The tranquil picture is the myth. The warning of the fairy tale suggests a countermyth: There may be aggressive powers lurking behind that serene smile.

Intriguingly, many outcome measures such as life satisfaction (Neugarten et al., 1961) commonly used in social gerontological research implicitly reflect the tranquility myth. On the other hand, some research has shown a strong relationship between irascibility and longevity (Aldrich, 1964; Tobin & Lieberman, 1976). Historically, the tranquil and the irascible pictures represent the feminine and the masculine in development, and a number of theorists (beginning with Jung, 1933) have suggested that there is a dedifferentiation, or reversal, or convergence of sex roles in the second half of life. Supported by projective data from the TAT, Gutmann (Neugarten & Gutmann, 1968; Gutmann, 1975, 1977) has seen men as becoming more passive and accommodative, attuned to their nurturant and affiliative desires. Women are described as powerful, displaying more active mastery and competitiveness. The middle-aged women studied by Lowenthal et al. (1975) were reaching out for more autonomy but were frustrated by limitations in doing so. Both sexes seemed to be strengthening commitments in areas other than where normative sex roles had bound them, women in mastery, men in interpersonal areas.

Longitudinal data from the Oakland Growth Study showed changes for some but not all people. Livson (1976) identified two groups of women who were psychologically healthy at age 50: the "Traditionals" had remained stable in familiar family patterns and showed little shift toward increased agentic behavior; the "Independents," on the other hand, had been distressed at age 40, but had made major changes towards more independent and ambitious attitudes and behaviors by age 50. Similarly for men: there was one group who reclaimed more nurturant and sensitive attributes.

Do these shifts constitute basic changes in personality, or is it necessary to distinguish between personality and sex roles? Intraindividual consistency of personality traits throughout adult life has been shown to be the rule for most persons (Costa & McCrae, 1980; Maas & Kuypers, 1974). Moreover, the idea of decreasing differentiation of sex roles is not generally interpreted to mean that either sex loses sex-typed capacities. Rather, the individual's behavior repertoire expands to encompass aspects not expressed during the first part of the lifespan, such that individuals become more fully themselves.

This interpretation has led to entertaining the notion of androgyny as optimally descriptive of older adults. It is difficult to tell whether androgyny is a more accurate restatement of the countermyth or whether it is the kernel of truth. According to Bem (1974), there are two orthogonal dimensions for masculinity and femininity, and androgyny is simultaneously scoring high both. Using Bem's scale, Sinnott et al. (1980) found that 54 percent of their 364 older adults scored androgynous (while 27 percent were feminine; 10 percent masculine; and 9 percent undifferentiated), and 71 percent of the androgynous group was female. The highest rates of mental health symptoms were not related to any one sex type; rather, they were concentrated in those persons whose expectations did not match their self-concepts (for example, their self-description might be androgynous while their perceived social expectation was feminine). As an alternative to androgyny, Hefner et al. (1975) proposed a three-stage dialectical model of sex-role development through the lifespan: undifferentiated, wherein the global qualities characteristic of a child's global thinking predominate; polarized, wherein dichotomy is temporarily used as a means of organizing an inherently continuous world; and transcendence, wherein the range of human behavior is no longer sex-typed as masculine or feminine. Transcendence involves both individual and situational flexibility such that personal decisions are made without reference to sex-role norms, and the theory envisions a pluralistic, rather than a unisex, conception of sex roles. The results of Sinnott et al. and the theoretical work of Hefner et al. underscore once again the importance of taking full account of individual differences and respecting them.

One final description of personality change in later life, which is echoed in the work on transcendence (Hefner et al., 1975; Giele, 1980), is Neugarten's (1970) concept of interiority. With age, both women and men become more attuned to the inner dimensions of their experience. This is not unlike the ego integrity Erikson (1950) describes in his eighth stage of development, which involves accepting one's emergent qualities and one's uniqueness as an individual. With increased interiority may come increased self-awareness, frankness, and a lessened sensitivity to the expectations and sanctions of others, such that the older woman becomes a "truth-teller." There are those who might regard truth-telling as irascible and cantankerous. As Agatha Christie wrote in her *Autobiography* (1978):

We are all the same people as we were at three, six, ten, or twenty years old. More noticeably so, perhaps, at six or seven, because we were not pretending so much then, whereas at twenty we put on a show of being someone else, of being in the mode of the moment. If there is an intellectual fashion, you become an intellectual; if girls are fluffy and frivolous, you are fluffy and frivolous. As life goes on, however, it becomes tiring to keep up the character you invented for yourself, and so you relapse into individuality and become more like yourself everyday. This is sometimes disconcerting for those around you, but a great relief to the person concerned. (p. 421)

Bereft through Loss

Papers about aging often begin with a paragraph about the multiple losses sustained by older adults and, as the myth goes for women, the losses that begin in mid-life render her bereft in old age. Various key turning points have waxed and waned in public and professional popularity. Historically speaking, there was menopause and the risk to emotional stability supposedly posed by raging hormonal imbalance and the loss of reproductive capacity. Then there was the empty nest syndrome and its concomitant loss of familial purposefulness. Then there was widowhood, representing loss of spouse-mediated social identity. A fourth frequently-cited loss is of youthful beauty.

Evidence concerning the impact of the losses serves to question the myth. First, if there is a midlife crisis for women, then menopause is not the cause. Not only has the hypothesized relationship between "involutional melancholia" and physiological changes associated with menopause failed to materialize (Butler & Lewis, 1982), but also middle-aged women interviewed by Neugarten et al. (1968) generally found menopause not very distressing.

Recent evidence indicates that the empty nest syndrome also may be a vastly overrated phenomenon. Women interviewed in several studies reported looking forward to their children's departure with relief (Neugarten, 1970; Neugarten & Datan, 1974; Rubin, 1979; Lowenthal et al., 1975). It would seem that most women anticipate this loss, prepare for it, even rehearse it during the later years of parenthood.

Widowhood is another predictable life event for a woman's later years. In 1979, 41 percent of women aged 65-74 were widowed, and for those 75 and over the figure was a staggering 70 percent (USDC, 1979b). Widowhood may involve severe financial losses, and there may be further changes in friendships. Again, the research findings are surprising. Older women adjust to the death of a spouse with less apparent difficulty than either younger women or men at any age (Ball, 1977; Berardo, 1970).

Sontag (1972) eloquently describes how the traditional power of femininity and youthful beauty consigns women to a pattern of premature aging. In short, men mature while women get old. A study by Nowak (1977) hints at the centrality of this issue for middle-aged but not for older women. She asked young, middle-aged, and older men and women to rate pictures of women for attractiveness and for youthfulness. Of the six groups, middle-aged women were most likely to regard attractive faces as younger than their actual age and to describe pictures of middle-aged women as particularly unattractive.

These, then, are normative losses for aging women that research has found to be less problematical than expected. What is less frequently entertained is the notion that these life events are transitions, rather than simply losses, and they involve both a future as well as a past. The future encompasses new possibilities available for the rest of one's life and, for a fifty-year-old woman, that could well be thirty years or more. Thus, if "empty nest" is the myth, "launching" is the countermyth. In this regard, Rubin (1979) asks us to consider the language we use:

> *Not* the awakening, *not* the emergence, *not the words that might suggest that inside that house all those years there lived someone besides a mother; no, we say* the empty nest ... Indeed, the very words empty nest *conjure up a vision of a lonely, depressed woman clinging pathetically and inappropriately to a lost past ... (p. 14)*

The countermyth, however, may be "it's not a crisis; it's a growth-opportunity." In our reformulation (cf. Gutmann et al., 1980), we must keep clear that real losses are incurred, and we must not minimize the impact of these events on any individual. The notion of transition must encompass struggling to create a meaningful life. Women may well feel anxiety about the risks involved in pursuing new life patterns, particularly with respect to disrupting marital relationships. Bart (1971) suggested that distress may be a consequence, not of the event, but of the lack of alternative roles.

An intriguing sidenote reflects how losses are defined in a historical context. Until recently (e.g. Prentis, 1980), women's retirement was not studied and it was simply assumed that a woman would not experience retirement as stressful. As Beeson (1975) explained, since her social identity was not presumed to be invested in her job, it was not important to study her retirement. (When an employed woman was included in studies about male retirement, what was measured was her reaction to her spouse's retirement!) Women's purported lack of investment in occupational roles is a belief that has shaped the research and may also have shaped the women themselves into a lack of preparation for a major transition in their lives; recently it has been shown that women may experience more distress after retirement than men (Atchley, 1976; Fox, 1977). Similarly, Levy (1980–81) reported that women who did not want to retire expressed discontent and depression to an extent not true for men.

In sum, on one hand we see the picture of a woman bereft from losses that begin in midlife and accelerate across later life. Juxtaposed, we have a picture of a woman struggling, usually successfully, to define herself in the face of social proscription of alternative roles when familial roles are increasingly inadequate for her personal resources and desires. The important kernel of truth may be that pursuing the theme of losses had blinded us to what women have really been doing. As Sinnott (1977) and Kline (1975) suggest, the synthesis of conflicting role demands may account for the remarkable resiliency we see in women now old.

Loneliness

Palmore (1977) provides us with a statement of the myth in his item, "The majority of old people are socially isolated and lonely," (p. 315) as well as of the countermyth, insofar as the item is scored for "false."

While the majority of aged do not live alone, more old women live alone than any other subgroup of the population, and the proportion of those maintaining their own households is increasing. In 1978, 36 percent of the women between 65 and 74 lived alone and, of those 75 and over, 48 percent lived alone (USDC, 1978). Widowhood is, of course the principal explanatory factor, although not all old widows live alone.

Living alone does not necessarily mean living in isolation, despite the fact that this equation had often been taken for granted. Kinship networks have been shown to be much stronger than popularly assumed, and most older women have regular contact with siblings, children, and grandchildren (Shanas, 1979). The greater mobility of adult children does not seem to have ruptured the bonds of the nuclear family and led to the abandonment of old mothers. The meaning of contact with family members is not at all clear, however. While older women may turn to children for help in meeting daily necessities, especially when ill health is involved, this contact may be a mixed blessing (Arling, 1976; Beckman & Houser, 1982; Glenn & McLanahan, 1981). Fear of dependence and role reversal may place great pressure on the relationship and color the satisfaction derived, even while the support atten- uates the impact of disabling conditions. Furthermore, the child caregiver may be middle-aged or older, female, and employed, with pressures from her own children (Brody, 1981). Thus the middle-aged woman is balancing caring for her mother, tending her own nearly adult children, and developing her career. This is, of course, only the most often cited circumstance. At the risk of creating another counter- myth, we must not forget the older mothers who continue to contribute to their adult daughters by helping with their multiplicity of responsibilities; help is not all one-way.

Very little is known about the friendships of older women or, for that matter, of older men. Women appear more likely than men to replace lost friendships (Powers & Bultena, 1976). Lopata (1979) found that friendships provided a social support system but they were not mentioned in the exchange of services. Lowen- thal and Haven (1968) have focused on having a confidante (either family member or friend) as an indicator both of an individual's capacity for interpersonal commit- ment and of her resources in times of severe distress.

Much has been written about the unavailability of marriage partners for old women (e.g., Treas & Van Hilst, 1976), and less than 1 percent of the women 65 and over remarry (Cleveland & Gianturco, 1976). Although fully 81 percent of Lopata's (1973) widows expressed no desire to remarry, that still would leave a sizeable number of older women desiring a life companion without much possibility of finding one.

The significance of social interaction has been extensively studied largely as an outgrowth of Cumming and Henry's (1961) suggestion that disengagement from social roles is a natural consequence of the aging process. Countering this view are the activity theorists, who assert that maintaining a high level of social interaction is one of the hallmarks of successful aging. A third view is expressed by continuity theorists who propose that the optimum amount of social participation in old age is and should be a reflection of lifelong patterns and preferences. (See Neugarten & Datan, 1973, and Lowenthal & Robinson, 1976, for a summary of these positions.)

The preceding discussion pertains to social isolation; what about loneliness? Miller and Dodder (1980) highlight the need to separate these issues in pointing out that Palmore's item is "double-barrelled." Many have made a distinction between isolation and loneliness (e.g., Birren & Renner, 1980; Shanas, 1979). Gubrium (1976) differentiates isolation and desolation, emphasizing that desolation often involves a sharp decrease in companionship across time. It is desolation that is associated with loneliness, rather than the simple fact of being isolated. The extent of loneliness is suggested by the results of the 1981 Harris Poll, on which 10 per- cent of those 65 and older endorsed loneliness as a very serious problem for them, the majority of them women.

We can think of many examples to support these distinctions among alone, isolated, and lonely: the older woman caring for a demented spouse who no longer calls her by name; the nursing home resident who sees many persons but no one who cares; the older woman who prefers to live alone at home.

Our kernel of truth, then, is that while loneliness and isolation are not proble- matic to the majority of older women, significant numbers do experience one or the other, but not necessarily both; and the potential for isolation and desolation increases with age. The problems of loneliness and isolation are quite different, and the isolate is in maximum jeopardy when a natural support network is not available to sustain her through periods of ill health when help may be required (Butler & Lewis, 1982).

Sexlessness

What about the myth of the sexless old woman? More often currently we hear the opposite point of view, what we are calling the countermyth, namely, that sexual activity is normal and desirable throughout the lifespan. While the countermyth may portray a welcome state of affairs, our point is to examine data describing the lives of women now old in order to look at aspects of truth in both the myth and the countermyth. In this instance, the two points of view are even battled out in "Dear Abby" (Van Buren, 1981):

> *Dear Abby: My husband has been reading up on the subject of sex, and he is of the opinion that if a woman doesn't enjoy sex right up to the grave, there must be something wrong with her. At age 50, and after 30 years of marriage, I would like to forget about sex altogether. Believe me, I've paid my dues . . . I suspect that many (if not most) women get very little physical satisfaction out of sex; they just go through the motions . . . I can't believe that I'm the only woman who feels this way. Please poll your readers . . . (signed) Tired in Lincoln, Nebraska. (p. 88)*

Many letters arrived supporting the myth:

> *Thanks for asking for this survey. I thought I was the only 50-year-old woman who was tired of sex. I'm also tired of cooking. (signed) Winnipeg, Canada. (p. 92)*

But many letters arrived supporting the countermyth as well:

> *This is the best time of my life! (signed) Happy in Denver. (p. 90)*

And letters arrived that pointed to circumstances mediating sexual behavior:

> *I've been a widow for twelve years. My husband and I both enjoyed sex until he died. He was ninety. I could still enjoy it, but who would have me? (signed) June, Age 81. (p. 90)*

The total responses to "Tired's" letter numbered over a quarter of a million cards and letters, and Abby reported that they divided almost equally between the affirmatives and the negatives.

The more scholarly view is based on smaller numbers of older individuals who, especially during the 1960s, were willing to participate in research on sexuality. Landmark investigations by Masters and Johnson (1970) challenged the notion of a natural transition to sexlessness by finding no evidence that women age in their sexual capacity. Some of the major points regarding age-related changes in the sexual response include: (1) There are no major changes in sexual reponse with age—only a slowing and lessening in intensity for both women and men. (2) In some cases, both illness and medications can interfere with sexual functioning. (3) In general, the best predictor of continued sexual enjoyment in later years is a lifetime of pleasurable sexual activity (Corby & Solnik, 1980; Weg, 1977).

This research supports the countermyth, but some data favor the myth. Part of the problem is captured in Palmore's (1977) item "Most old people have no interest in, or capacity for, sexual relations" (p. 315), which he scores "false." As Miller and Dodder (1980) note, this is another double-barrelled item.

In terms of sexual activity, data from the Duke University longitudinal studies reported by Pfeiffer et al. (1969) indicated that only 16 percent of women aged 65 to 75 remained active, although within that group there was almost no decline of interest and activity 10 years later. Several other studies by Verwoerdt and colleagues (Verwoerdt et al., 1969a, 1969b) and Christenson and colleagues (Christenson & Gagnon, 1965; Christenson & Johnson, 1973) do suggest decline. Christenson and Gagnon's (1965) results indicated that 87 percent of married women were active at age 50 and 50 percent at age 65. Among previously married, 37 percent were active at age 50 and none at age 65. Women who had never been married were similar to those previously married (Christenson & Johnson, 1973). Most women cited death, disability, or disinterest of their partner as the reason for ceasing sexual activity (Pfeiffer et al., 1969). Interestingly, however, Christenson and colleagues found a similar drop off in frequency for masturbation. Among married women, 31 percent at age 50 and none at age 70 reported masturbating. Among previously married the figures were 59 percent at age 50 and 25 percent at age 70 (Christenson & Gagnon, 1965). Again, women who had never been married were similar to those previously married (Christenson & Johnson, 1973).

Many writers intimate that older women have unnecessarily bought into the myth of sexlessness because of inhibitory socialization and narrow definitions of human sexuality. As Weg (1977) and Ludeman (1981) have observed, the emphasis in the literature is on physiological performance, which is probably even more of a distortion for the old than for the young. They have urged more complete definitions emphasizing the importance of sensual intimacy, warmth, and touching. Huyck (1977) and Cavan (1976) cite alternatives to the small pool of traditional older male sexual partners—affairs, self-pleasuring, younger males, polygyny, other women—and suggest that sexuality may be less problematic for future generations of older women. Following Abu-Laban (1981), however, and reflecting individual continuity of preferences, we would speculate that even future generations may find some of these solutions improbable.

What about the many respondents to "Dear Abby" who sided with "Tired"? The countermyth of lifelong sexual capacity, as currently popularized, may be more reflective of the younger generations' desires for old age than of recognition of the preferences of women now old. Clearly there are some older women whose desires for sensual and sexual intimacy are unnecessarily thwarted because of lack of privacy and sensitive and informed care, and some who are necessarily thwarted because of lack of companionship acceptable to them. But there are others who express satisfaction with their asexual lifestyle, and demeaning their sexual disinterest is no better than prejudicing any other sexual preference.

MENTAL HEALTH: MENTAL ILLNESS AND STRATEGIES FOR INTERVENTION

We have now described seven myths and countermyths, presenting them as alternative stereotypes and urging examination of the data. It is relevant at this point to consider directly how these myths may affect mental health. Kuypers and

Bengtson (1973) have proposed a model in which myths should tend to become self-fulfilling prophecies, at least for some especially vulnerable women, through a cycle of societal stereotyping, self-stereotyping, and erosion of skills. Thomas (1981), however, suggests that older people may use negative images adaptively. We have consistently noted that, although many of the myths have an unrealistically negative tone, they do contain some objectively factual aspects; yet we also found indications of greater satisfaction and more optimistic self-assessments than the facts seemingly warrant. Thomas's interpretation is that older individuals have adjusted their standards according to popular images of aging. To the extent that their expectations closely approximate the facts of their lives, their sense of well-being is maintained. Following Thomas's logic, countermyths could prove to be singularly deleterious to the older person by creating impossibly high expectancies. The opposite consequence could be extrapolated from Kuypers and Bengtson's model, insofar as countermyths would seemingly function as constructive self-fulfilling prophecies. From a dialectical perspective (Riegel, 1976), both explanations have merit. The individual woman now old is inescapably confronted with integrating the myths and countermyths with the facts of her own life, and the same challenge that strengthens the coping skills of one may exceed the capacities of another. This perspective on the possible effects of stereotypes on the older woman, taken together with the injunction to build interventions on data rather than myth, provides the context for the following discussion of mental illness and, subsequently, implications for intervention.

Mental Illness

Here we have a curious contrast. As just noted, the myths presented earlier have emphasized the negative and hopeless aspects, while the countermyths have tended towards optimistic assertions that there are few, if any, problems. With respect to mental illness, the situation seems reversed. The myth, if there is one, is that there is not a problem, just eccentricities of old age. The countermyth, on the other hand, is well stated by Butler and Lewis: "The incidence of mental illness increases as people age . . ." (1982, p. 65); furthermore, "The incidence of depression increases gradually with age in both men and women, with a higher incidence in women throughout the lifecycle" (1982, p. 74). Our impression is that these remarks overshoot the mark in a well-intentioned effort to get a valid problem recognized by the mental health establishment. The result is that all elderly, and especially old women, are thought to face increased risk of mental illness. On the basis of sparse existing data, there seems to be little reason to accept this bleak picture, and there are even some indications that the converse may be true (Zarit, 1980; Hagnell, 1970).

To our knowledge, there has been no comprehensive review of the incidence and prevalence studies of mental disorder from the perspective of older women. Summaries either present sex differences or age breakdowns, but not both. For example, Dohrenwend and Dohrenwend (1976) report on sex differences, finding none in the prevalence rates of functional psychoses in general; however there were differences in rates for particular disorders, with men having consistently higher rates for personality disorder and women having higher rates for neurosis and manic depressive psychosis. Then, looking at rates of pathology across the lifespan, Dohrenwend and Dohrenwend (1969) reported inconclusive results: five studies showed the highest rates in adolescence, twelve in middle adulthood, and seven in old age. Prevalence figures cited for older adults range from 10-15 percent (Kay & Bergmann, 1980) to 20-40 percent (Eisdorfer & Cohen, 1978).

There are a host of difficulties in trying to make any inferences about age differences in psychopathology. First, incidence (number of new cases) and prevalence (total number of cases) are not always clearly distinguished. Second, many of the studies were done in the 1950s and 1960s in Europe and in the U.S., hence using outdated nomenclature, as well as reflecting different diagnostic practices in different countries. Third, organic brain syndromes are often included in an omnibus category of mental impairment.

Starting with the third, it was previously noted that organic brain syndromes increase markedly in late life, with Alzheimer's-type dementia being most prevalent. Statements that mental disorder rises steadily with age (e.g. Blazer, 1980; Kay & Bergmann, 1980; Pfeiffer, 1977) generally include organic brain syndromes along with functional disorders (as admittedly arbitrary as this distinction sometimes is). If, however, organic brain syndromes are excluded, the increase in old age disappears. This is true, for example, in the Stirling County study (Leighton et al., 1963) which measured impairment in terms of reported symptoms. Also, it is noteworthy that Leighton et al. found the highest rate of psychiatric symptomatology in persons aged 60-69, with these older adults reporting more psychophysiological symptoms. While these problems may have been caused by emotional factors, they may also have been due to poorer physical health (Zarit, 1980). Thus, physical conditions, especially organic brain syndromes, may inflate the levels of what we usually take to be mental disorder. While including brain diseases may provide an important indication of overall need for services, it obscures both the relationship between younger and older cohorts with respect to mental disorders and also the need for differential treatment considerations.

Returning to the first difficulty, prevalence rates introduce a number of further sources of bias, especially with respect to older women. As Kay and Bergmann (1980) point out, prevalence figures are suggestive of an accumulation of cases throughout life. This reporting practice can affect the data reported for women now old in two ways. First, because of their longevity, the last age category reported (often "65 and over") tends to be inflated for women simply because the category includes proportionally greater numbers of very old persons. Second, the effects of certain disorders that are more common in one sex in younger years (such as depression for women) may continue to be expressed in later life, while the incidence of new cases declines. Although incidence data are scarce, Kay and Bergmann (1980) cite two surveys in which the rates of all new functional disorders are *lowest* after age 65—a remarkably different picture than that suggested by global prevalence rates. In addition, Hagnell (1966, 1970) found that the average annual incidence rate of neuroses for men and women 60 and over was one-half to one-third of the peak incidence rates for all ages.

When the different diagnostic categories of functional disorder are considered, depression emerges as the biggest problem of older adults. This is not to say that depressive disorders increase with age; in fact, the converse appears to be true. Epidemiological data are complicated, however, because what we call depression in current nomenclature was split between affective psychoses and neuroses in earlier nosologies. A further complication arises in interpreting prevalence rates obtained through community surveys that use symptom lists as the means of asesssment because, as will be discussed subsequently, the relationship of depressive symptoms to clinically diagnosed depression is unclear.

Pulling together what is known about affective psychoses and about neurotic depression, on the whole, clinically diagnosed depression increases in young adulthood and peaks in the middle years, with the diagnosis most frequently being made in the 25–64 year age range. It appears to decline thereafter (Kay & Bergmann, 1980). Yet depression is the most common disorder in old age because of the sharp declines in the incidence of most other conditions. Rates for severe (or psychotic) depression are highest in late midlife, while the rates for milder (or neurotic) depression peak before about age 40 (Gurland, 1976). The rates for women far exceed those for men until age 45 and then tend to converge, perhaps even meeting or crossing after age 65. It also appears that men may predominate in more severe depression; for example, Kay et al. (1964) showed that prevalence rates for community-residing older women were 8.8 percent for moderate and severe depression, compared to 12.2 percent for men. (Their rates are somewhat higher than those cited in other studies, presumably because of broader criteria.) Depression is more prevalent in persons with chronic health problems (Zarit, 1980), but appears to present no greater likelihood of developing in those with dementia (Eisdorfer & Cohen, 1978). Depression in older adults is treatable (e.g., Gallagher & Thompson, 1982), and Zarit (1980) suggests that prognosis may be especially favorable if the first occurrence is in late life, underscoring once again the importance of distinguishing nonreversible brain disease or other physical illness from depression.

Depressive symptoms present quite a different epidemiological picture from diagnosed depression. Symptom rates for women and men are quite comparable (Blazer, 1980). While there is general agreement that the rates of symptom reporting are higher in the age ranges over 65 (Gurland, 1976), Kay and Bergmann (1980) conclude that, at least with respect to depressive symptoms, the correlation of age with these indices of depression may be an artifact reflecting social changes that accompany aging rather than intrinsic aging processes. The clinical significance of these symptoms is not at all clear, since transient episodes of sadness, loss of interest and lack of energy are not uncommon among older adults. Blazer (1980) makes the point that symptomatology must be carefully distinguished from actual mental illness: "A rate of 15 percent for dysphoric symptoms does *not* imply that 15 percent of the population should be treated for depressive illness" (p. 257). The danger in confusing mental disorder with an appropriate reaction to an unhappy situation is perhaps nowhere greater than here.

The topography and adaptational aspects of what is being called depression may bear examination. In interviewing middle-aged women, Rubin (1979) identified themes suggesting that, for some women, betrayed by lack of opportunity, depression was a form of rebellion. Freedom from past roles had been favorably anticipated; yet there was anxiety and disappointment about the risks involved in pursuing new life patterns. Others have suggested that anxiety may in fact be the best description of much mental distress in older women (Oberleder, 1966). Additionally, for late life adults, Karpf (1977) has argued that there is an existential component in what is called depression and that it is part of an adaptational process. Following Erikson's (1950) notion that the last task of life is the achievement of ego integrity, for an individual to engage in life review and to come to an appreciation of her life as meaningful must also involve experiencing sadness at the anticipated loss of one's self through death. Since the alternative to ego integrity is despair, then the distinction between sadness and despair may be crucial to interpreting the developmental function of emotional distress. In discussing qualitative differences in the symptomatology of clinically depressed patients of different ages, Zarit (1980) noted that feelings of dysphoria and sadness are expressed less frequently by older than by younger depressives. In older adults, depression is more often characterized by apathy, listlessness, memory loss, and somatic complaints such as insomnia and appetite disturbance—symptoms that bespeak despair. These observations suggest that the relationship between depressive symptoms and clinically diagnosed depression may well be understandable only in terms of developmental theory and social context.

Further evidence of different patterns of mental distress are seen in suicide rates, which are correctly said to increase across the lifespan. McIntosh et al. (1981) reported that those 65 and older accounted for 17 percent of suicides in the U.S. in 1976. What is less often observed is that the rates for women peak in the 45- to 50-year-old range and then steadily decline, while men show a direct linear increase to age 75 (Stenback, 1980). Suicide rates are dramatically lower for women at all ages, but some see trends for increases among older women (Butler & Lewis, 1982), and for attenuation of the midlife peak (Atchley, 1980). The majority of the elderly who commit suicide have been depressed, and alcohol use is the second most common indicator (Pfeiffer, 1977).

In addition to depression, the other diagnositic categories of some importance to older women are paranoia and hypochondriasis. Paranoia is an increasing problem in the elderly and appears to be second only to depression. Paranoid reactions in old age tend to be less bizarre and more reality-based than in younger persons and may sometimes be explainable in terms of the older person filling in sensory or cognitive gaps with accusative ideation (Pfeiffer, 1977). Not unsurprisingly, clinical lore attributes higher rates to old women (Butler & Lewis, 1982). Hypochondriasis also seems to increase with age, and again the higher frequency is typically attributed to old women (Pfeiffer, 1977). However, Zarit (1980) reported equal numbers of studies supporting and refuting higher rates for women.

Taken as a whole, we would summarize this brief survey of mental disorders to be unsupportive of the notions of increased mental distress in old age and of the preponderance of cases being older women. Rather, we see indications that women now old may be less vulnerable to severe functional disorders than their male age-peers, and they are certainly less at risk than their daughters and granddaughters. We do not mean to imply that mental health services are less important for older persons, because prevalence rates clearly indicate that the need is as great in old age as at younger ages. Nor do we intend to imply that organic brain syndromes are not important, especially with respect to the crucial differential diagnosis of treatable conditions. Dementias are different, however, both in their discontinuity with other disorders experienced across the lifespan, and in having distinct implications for interventions.

Strategies for Intervention

The kernels of truth repeatedly point to a population that psychologists would expect to be at risk with respect to mental illness; yet both epidemiological and service utilization data suggest some apparently contradictory considerations. Elderly women bear the brunt of the aging process: They experience more of it, by virtue of their longevity, and they are the most constrained, by virtue of economic insufficiency. What we have noted, however, is a decline in incidence of serious mental dysfunction, with the exception of increased organic brain disease in the very old age ranges. It also seems apparent that needs other than traditional mental health services are more pressing: Older women most often express survival-level concerns such as having enough money, physical problems, fear of crime, insufficient transportation, and difficulty negotiating bureaucratic complexities to obtain needed services (Harris Poll, 1981). In terms of mental health, an often-cited statistic is that older adults, who comprise 11.3 percent of the population, account for only 4 percent of the clients of community mental health centers (National Institute of Mental Health, 1978). Additionally, it has been reported that only 2.7 percent of services rendered by psychologists are to older adult recipients (Vanden-Bos et al., 1981). These data support a pattern not only of underservice by mental health professionals but perhaps also of choices by older adult clients not to use services.

Thus, although it seems reasonable to assume that the mental health needs of some older women are not being met, it seems equally clear that persistently offering the same solutions will continue to be of the same limited usefulness. The problem might be described as an error of logical types (Watzlawick et al., 1974) whereby individual-level solutions, repeatedly applied to system-level problems, consistently lead to no change. For the older person, traditional mental health models of intervention place the burden of change on the older individual while simultaneously implying that she lacks the power for constructive change. The myths we have discussed fit well with this model; the picture of the incompetent, unhealthy, and useless older woman, the passive recipient of the ravages of time, often leads to such comments as, "Well, who wouldn't be depressed under those circumstances." Although the intent is benign, the result is to "blame the victim" (Ryan, 1976) for her circumstances, predict her pathology, and then castigate her for not being "psychologically minded" when she is hesitant to avail herself of traditional mental health services. Even the more enlightened view that suggests mental health professionals may have their own reluctance in dealing with elderly clients (Group for the Advancement of Psychiatry, 1971) stops short of calling for nontraditional professional roles, services and settings.

Designing appropriate interventions, traditional or nontraditional, is not without its hazards. First of all, any intervention runs the risk of creating excess dependency (Kahn, 1975) by undermining the ways in which women now old have negotiated places for themselves in precarious circumstances. Certain choices that seem advantageous to the professional may be incompatible with their commitments. Helping too much can lead to unintended negative consequences such as decrements in coping skills and even increased mortality (Blenkner et al., 1971). Hence, there is a natural tension between respecting an older woman's life choices and writing her off as unable to change. It seems clear that the waiting mode (Rappaport, 1977) has not been effective; in reorienting to a seeking mode, it needs to be remembered that the purpose is to facilitate rather than to provide, and only for as long as necessary.

Second, programs with the goal of life enhancement may maximize benefits to those employed in providing service and to the more socially active, healthy, and economically secure elderly, while discomfitting those elderly who are poor or who have limited mobility (Baltes & Danish, 1980). The countermyths we have discussed embody a sociocultural ideal for old age. Orienting programs to such a future may well blind providers to the current needs of the elderly as well as create standards and expectations that are vastly discrepant from their personal resources (or, for that matter, from society's willingness to subsidize older adults). These standards constitute one more burden for the least powerful.

Third, planning and evaluating interventions is made difficult because there is no single satisfactory measure of outcome. Studies currently alternate between reduced mortality and improved morale. (Ryff, 1972, discusses conceptual difficulties in defining successful aging.) At the level of social policy, cost-effectiveness often becomes a salient criterion. It is easy to see how, in designing intervention programs, these particular goals of quantity, quality, and practicality may collide. Furthermore, it is not always clear which criteria might be most important to individual older women.

In suggesting some of the types of services that have demonstrated effectiveness for older adults, as well as others that might be developed, we encompass direct and indirect services; primary, secondary and tertiary prevention; and different levels of intervention (individual, group, community, institution). At the same time, it is difficult to categorize specific interventions according to any single schema. The approach we have chosen is to use the following five headings, admitting that any given example may incorporate aspects from more than one: traditional mental health, interventions reflecting a holistic perspective of dealing with both physical and mental health, interventions derived from a feminist perspective, community mental health, and community psychology. This rubric posits that, whereas the burden of change in improving the well-being of older women must be sociocultural, it is also necessary and right for a whole range of services to be available when they are needed and wanted.

1. Traditional mental health. Analytic, behavioral, and cognitive therapies have all been used with older clients. Usually more active, goal-directed, and brief approaches are advocated (e.g., Zarit, 1980), and various writers have identified themes particularly characteristic of the elderly (e.g., Steuer, 1982). In general, although most writers devote space to decrying the lack of outcome research, what minimal evidence there is suggests that therapy may be as effective with older adults who have sought it out as with younger individuals (Storandt, 1978).

The family constellation that supports most impaired elderly merits special consideration. Possibly one of the most frequent requests to psychologists is to figure out "what's the matter with Momma." Responding requires traditional psychological and neuropsychological assessment, multidisciplinary collaboration to evaluate medical/pharmacological influences, and consultation with the family (Herr & Weakland, 1979). Facilitating the family's ability to provide continued, long-term support may well determine whether or not an elderly parent will be institutionalized (Smyer, 1980). As noted previously, it is frequently the "woman in the middle" who bears the burden of caring for parents in times of ill health—the same woman who is launching her family and is likely to be employed as well (Brody, 1981; Treas, 1981a). Redistribution of her responsibilities throughout the family and provision of respite services designed to support, rather than supplant familial caregiving is both primary prevention for the midlife daughter and secondary prevention for the elderly parent.

2. Holistic. Programs such as SAGE—Senior Actualization and Growth Exploration—(Lieberman & Gourash, 1979) and the Adults Health and Development Pro-

gram (Leviton & Santa Maria, 1979) reflect the influence of the human potential movement. They feature physical exercise, preventive education, and interpersonal activities. Hospital programs for multiply-impaired older adults (e.g., Kastenbaum et al., 1981) also incorporate attention to the interaction and integration of physical and mental health through such means as fostering hope and positive expectations in both patients and staff and providing each patient with a supportive relationship with an individual therapist.

3. Feminist. Predominantly addressing themselves to younger women, Brodsky and Hare-Mustin (1980) have urged examination of needs specific to women and evaluation of services developed to meet them. Little has been written about strategies distinctively for older women. In one of the few exceptions, Levy (1981) argued that older women have a special need to be helped in creating social networks. Self-help, while not developed exclusively by the women's movement, is an approach particularly compatible with a feminist perspective. Some older persons have found meaningful roles and increased social support in self-help and intergenerational programs such as Widow-to-Widow (Silverman, 1976) and Foster Grandparents (Hirschowitz, 1973). Banding together for mutual support and sharing services is often a determining factor in the mental health of those caring for disabled spouses (Crossman et al., 1981).

4. Community mental health. Physical and psychological accessibility is a major barrier to older women who are seeking involvement or assistance. The coordination of information and professional services is essential to providing a continuum of care, especially when temporary or chronic disabling illness threatens a major disruption of lifestyle. Having service sites located throughout the community; assuring adequate transportation to and from community resources; disseminating effectively targeted information about available programs, services and opportunities—all these contribute to building what Iscoe (1974) has defined as the competent community which empowers individuals by increasing their knowledge and range of choice and control. Older adult community workers, who are usually women, can be effective information-givers and resource persons in linking underserved elderly into existing informal and formal helping networks (Toseland et al., 1979; Wright et al., 1977-78).

A variety of community and institutional settings are appropriate for consultative psychological intervention. We imagine such things as infiltrating medical schools, for example, so that physicians in training would learn facts about aging and develop sensitivity to older adults' special concerns; simultaneously we could be offering classes to help older adults formulate strategies for talking with their doctors. Similar approaches could be used in many educational settings where people are being trained for professions that involve a high level of interpersonal contact, from clergy to hairdressers (Cowen, 1982). In industry, the development and evaluation of preretirement planning programs, flexible employment for older workers who prefer not to retire, and sponsorship of educational programs for the elderly stand to make substantial contributions to the well-being of older adults (Treas, 1981b). Furthermore, the psychological states of aging people are closely linked to their physical environment (Howell, 1980), which includes both their ability to maintain the residence of their choice as well as getting what they need at that location. Issues of insufficient, substandard, and unimaginative housing call for creative solutions that could evolve from collaboration between planners and occupants. Another example is nursing homes and other extended care facilities. As noted, large percentages of older adults (particularly older women) spend some time in such settings. Estimates of need for mental health services within this group are high (Pfeiffer, 1977, suggests a figure of up to 80 percent). Yet very few nursing homes employ psychologists as staff or consultants. Both direct and indirect intervention with the physical environment, staff, families and patients are called for (e.g., Brody et al., 1971; Kastenbaum, 1972).

5. Community psychology. Finally, interventions targeted to elderly populations do little to ameliorate the conditions that brought them about. In discussing the dire financial circumstances of elderly black women, Jackson (1982) warns us that giving more money to the elderly may be a necessary palliative measure, but the disadvantaged status of older black women will be satisfactorily addressed only through rectifying the occupational segregation and sex differentials in earnings that accrue to all women throughout their lives. In a similar vein, Baltes and Danish (1980) stress that providing more education for the aged is no solution for the intellectual obsolescence created by rapid social change; rather, education must be redistributed throughout the lifespan. It quickly becomes apparent that preventive intervention for old-age problems will require major sociocultural changes involving all age, sex, and social groups.

As an example taking into account the entire lifespan, consider indicators that covary with the crossover effect in mental distress observed between the sexes. Psychological distress is maximum for women in their middle years, and the problems older women report often pertain to insufficient economic resources from a history earlier in their lives. Men, on the other hand, have a more continuous, presumably advantageous psychosocial course throughout early and middle adulthood, but for them mortality risk factors escalate in late life, from both illness and suicide. Because of the important social consequences of differential life expectancy, Siegel (1980) was prompted to propose an Equal Health Opportunity program for men. Extending his thinking, we suggest the first components of a program for both sexes: greater opportunity for women to exercise power through the achievement of economic security earlier in life; and for men, greater role flexibility and role discontinuity. (The rub, as women well know, is that role flexibility and discontinuity simply do not pay very well and are downright disastrous when it comes to retirement benefits; hence systems of reimbursement and vestment would have to undergo drastic change.) These are not new suggestions—in fact, they constitute a major thrust of the women's movement. What we are pointing out is that these changes, which might well constitute primary prevention with respect to old age, involve profound institutional and attitudinal changes.

CONCLUSION

One basic message of this chapter is that mental health in older women is, paradoxically, neither an issue of aging nor of women. It is a lifespan developmental and a sociocultural issue that implies the definition of distinctive life courses for both men and women that are both shared within a cohort and yet unique to each individual within it. Intervention is premised on such an understanding. A second basic message is that the advantage to be gained through the new visibility of older women is a greater accumulation of data on which to base change strategies. If our suggestions for strategies of intervention reads like a shopping list, so much the better: That is exactly what we would like older women to have. Mirroring the diversity found in older women on virtually every dimension, a diversity of modest-sized, well-integrated programs will most adequately allow for a continuance of optimal choice and control. Our third and final message is the hope that these perspectives will be incorporated in constructive designs for the futures of new cohorts of older women. At least some of their problems need not be the same as those of women now old, and their preferences most likely will not be.

REFERENCES

Abu-Laban, S. M. Women and aging: A futurist perspective. *Psychology of Women Quarterly*, 1981, *6*, 85–98, Human Sciences Press.

Aldrich, C. Personality factors and mortality in the reaction of the aged. *Gerontologist*, 1964, *4*, 92–93.

Arling, G. The elderly widow and her family, neighbors and friends. *Journal of Marriage and the Family*, 1976, *38*, 757–768.

Atchley, R. C. Aging and suicide: Reflection of the quality of life? In S. G. Haynes & M. Feinlieb (eds.), *Second Conference on the Epidemiology of Aging.* (NIH Publication No. 80-969). Washington, D.C.: U.S. Government Printing Office, 1980.

Atchley, R. C. Selected social and psychological differences between men and women in later life. *Journal of Gerontology*, 1976, *31*, 204–211.

Ball, J. F. Widows' grief: The impact of age and mode of death. *Omega*, 1977, 7, 307–333.

Baltes, P. B. & Danish, S. J. Intervention in life-span development and aging: Issues and concepts. In R. R. Turner & H. W. Reese (eds.), *Lifespan Developmental Psychology: Intervention.* New York: Academic Press, 1980.

Baltes, P. B. & Labouvie, G. V. Adult development of intellectual performance: Description, explanation and modification. In C. Eisdorfer & M. P. Lawton (eds.), *The Psychology of Adult Development and Aging.* Washington, D.C.: American Psychological Association, 1973.

Baltes, P. B. & Schaie, K. W. On lifespan developmental research paradigms: Retrospects and prospects. In P. Baltes & K. W. Schaie (eds.), *Lifespan Developmental Psychology: Personality and Socialization.* New York: Academic Press, 1973.

Bart, P. B. Depression in middle-aged women. In V. Gornick & B. K. Moran (eds.), *Woman in Sexist Society.* New York: Basic Books, 1971.

Beckman, L. J. & Hauser, B. B. The consequences of childlessness on the social-psychological well-being of older women. *Journal of Gerontology*, 1982, *37*, 243–250.

Beeson, D. Women in studies of aging: A critique and suggestion. *Social Problems*, 1975, *23*, 52–59.

Bem, S. L. The measurement of psychological androgyny. *Journal of Consulting and Clinical Psychology*, 1974, *42*, 155–162.

Berardo, F. M. Survivorship and social isolation: The case of the aged widower. *The Family Coordinator*, 1970, *19*, 11–25.

Birren, J. E. & Renner, V. J. Research on the psychology of aging: Principles and experimentation. In J. E. Birren & K. W. Schaie (eds.), *Handbook of the Psychology of Aging.* New York: Van Nostrand Reinhold, 1977.

Birren, J. E. & Renner, V. J. Concepts and issues of mental health and aging. In J. E. Birren & R. B. Sloane (eds.), *Handbook of Mental Health and Aging.* Englewood Cliffs, N.J.: Prentice-Hall, 1980.

Birren, J. E., Woods, A. M., & Williams, M. V. Behavioral slowing with age: Causes, organizations, and consequences. In L. W. Poon (ed.), *Aging in the 1980s.* Washington, D.C.: American Psychological Association, 1980.

Blazer, D. The epidemiology of mental illness on late life. In E. W. Busse & D. G. Blazer (eds.), *Handbook of Geriatric Psychiatry.* New York: Van Nostrand Reinhold, 1980.

Blenkner, M., Bloom, M., Wasser, E., & Nielsen, M. A research and demonstration project of protective services. *Social Casework*, 1971, *52*, 483–499.

Botwinick, J. Intellectual abilities. In J. E. Birren & K. W. Schaie (eds.), *Handbook of the Psychology of Aging.* New York: Van Nostrand Reinhold, 1977.

Brodsky, A. M. & Hare-Mustin, R. T. Psychotherapy and women: Priorities for research. In A. M. Brodsky & R. T. Mustin (eds.), *Women and Psychotherapy: An Assessment of Research and Practice.* New York: Guilford Press, 1980.

Brody, E. Women in the middle and family help to older people. *Gerontologist,* 1981, *21,* 471–480.

Brody, E. M., Kleban, M. H., Lawton, M. P., & Silverman, H. A. Excess disabilities of mentally impaired aged: Impact of individualized treatment. *Gerontologist,* 1971, *11,* 124–133.

Butler, R. N. & Lewis, M. I. *Aging & Mental Health, Positive Psychosocial and Biomedical Approaches* (3rd ed.). St. Louis, MO: C. V. Mosby, 1982.

Cavan, R. S. Speculation on innovations to conventional marriage in old age. *Gerontologist,* 1976, *13,* 409–411.

Christenson, C. V. & Gagnon, J. H. Sexual behavior in a group of older women. *Journal of Gerontology,* 1965, *20,* 351–356.

Christenson, C. V. & Johnson, A. B. Sexual patterns in a group of older never-married women. *Journal of Geriatric Psychiatry,* 1973, *6,* 80–98.

Christie, A. *Agatha Christie, An Autobiography.* New York: Dodd, Mead, 1978.

Clayton, V. & Birren, J. E. The development of wisdom across the lifespan: A reexamination of an ancient topic. In P. B. Baltes & O. G. Brim, Jr. (eds.), *Lifespan Development and Behavior* (Vol. 3). New York: Academic Press, 1980.

Cleveland, W. P. & Gianturco, D. T. Remarriage probability after widowhood: A retrospective method. *Journal of Gerontology,* 1976, *31,* 99–103.

Corby, M. & Solnik, R. L. Psychosocial and physiological influences on sexuality in the older adult. In J. E. Birren & R. B. Sloane (eds.), *Handbook of Mental Health and Aging.* Englewood Cliffs, NJ: Prentice-Hall, 1980.

Costa, P. T., Jr., & McCrae, R. R. Still stable after all these years: Personality as a key to some issues in adulthood and old age. In P. B. Baltes & O. G. Brim, Jr. (eds.), *Lifespan Development and Behavior* (Vol. 3). New York: Academic Press, 1980.

Cowen, E. L. Help is where you find it: Four informal helping groups. *American Psychologist,* 1982, *37,* 385–395.

Crossman, L., London, C., & Barry, C. Older women caring for disabled spouses: A model for supportive services. *Gerontologist,* 1981, *21,* 464–470.

Cumming, E. & Henry, W. E. *Growing Old.* New York: Basic Books, 1961.

Datan, N. *The Lost Cause: The Aging Woman in American Feminism.* Paper presented at invited address at Indiana University, Bloomington, Indiana, October 1977.

Dohrenwend, B. P. & Dohrenwend, B. S. Sex differences and psychiatric disorders. *American Journal of Sociology,* 1976, *81,* 1447–1457.

Dohrenwend, B. P. & Dohrenwend, B. S. *Social Status and Psychological Disorder.* New York: Wiley, 1969.

Eisdorfer, C. & Cohen, D. The cognitively impaired elderly: Differential diagnosis. In M. Storandt, I. C. Siegler, & M. F. Elias (eds.), *The Clinical Psychology of Aging.* New York: Plenum Press, 1978.

Eisdorfer, C. & Wilkie, F. Stress, disease, aging and behavior. In J. E. Birren & K. W. Schaie (eds.), *Handbook of the Psychology of Aging.* New York: Van Nostrand Reinhold, 1977.

Erikson, E. H. *Childhood and Society.* New York: W. W. Norton & Co., 1950.

Fox, J. H. Effects of retirement and former work life on women's adaptation in old age. *Journal of Gerontology,* 1977, *32,* 196–202.

Gallagher, D. & Thompson, L. W. Cognitive therapy for depression in the elderly: A promising model for treatment and research. In L. Breslaw & M. Haug (eds.), *Depression in the Elderly.* New York: Springer, in press.

Giele, J. Z. Adulthood as transcendence of age and sex. In N. J. Smelser & E. H. Erikson (eds.), *Themes of Work and Love in Adulthood.* Cambridge, MA: Harvard University Press, 1980.

Glenn, N. D. & McLanahan, S. The effects of offspring on the psychological well-being of older adults. *Journal of Marriage and the Family,* 1981, *43,* 409–421.

Gove, W. R. & Hughes, M. Possible causes of the apparent sex differences in physical health: An empirical investigation. *American Sociological Review,* 1979, *44,* 126–146.

Gray Panthers Network, March/April 1982, 6.

Group for the Advancement of Psychiatry. Committee on Aging: The aged and community mental health: A guide to program development (Vol. 8, Series No. 81), 1971.

Gubrium, J. F. Being single in old age. In J. F. Gubrium (ed.), *Time, Roles, and Self in Old Age.* New York: Human Sciences Press, 1976.

Gurland, B. J. The comparative frequency of depression in various adult age groups. *Journal of Gerontology*, 1976, *31*, 283–292.

Gutmann, D. The cross cultural perspective: Notes toward a comparative psychology of aging. In J. E. Birren & K. W. Schaie (eds.), *Handbook of the Psychology of Aging*. New York: Van Nostrand Reinhold, 1977.

Gutmann, D. Parenthood: A key to the comparative study of life cycle. In N. Datan & L. H. Ginsberg (eds.), *Lifespan Developmental Psychology: Normative Life Crisis*. New York: Academic Press, 1975.

Gutmann, D., Griffin, B., & Grunes, J. Developmental contributions to the late-onset affective disorders. In P. B. Baltes & O. G. Brim, Jr. (eds.), *Lifespan Development and Behavior* (Vol. 3). New York: Academic Press, 1980.

Hagnell, O. The incidence and duration of episodes of mental illness in a general population. In E. H. Hare & J. K. Wing (eds.), *Proceedings of the Aberdeen Symposium on Psychiatric Epidemiology*. London: Oxford University Press, 1970.

Hagnell, O. *A Prospective Study of the Incidence of Mental Disorder*. New York: Humanities Press, 1966.

Harris Poll: Aging in the Eighties: America in Transition. A national poll conducted by Louis Harris and Associates. Washington, D.C.: National Council on Aging, 1981.

Hefner, R., Rebecca, M., & Oleshansky, B. Development of sex-role transcendence. *Human Development*, 1975, *18*, 143–158.

Herr, J. J. & Weakland, J. H. *Counseling Elders and Their Families*. New York: Springer, 1979.

Hirschowitz, R. G. Foster grandparents program: Preventive intervention with the elderly poor. *Hospital and Community Psychiatry*, 1973, *24*, 558–559.

Howell, S. C. Environments and hypotheses in human aging research. In L. W. Poon (ed.), *Aging in the 1980s*. Washington, D.C.: American Psychological Association, 1980.

Huyck, M. H. Sex and the older woman. In L. E. Troll, J. Israel, & K. Israel (eds.), *Looking Ahead: A Woman's Guide to the Problems and Joys of Growing Older*. Englewood Cliffs, NJ: Prentice-Hall, 1977.

Ingram, D. K. & Barry, J. R. National statistics on death in nursing homes. *Gerontologist*, 1977, *17*, 303–308.

Iscoe, I. Community psychology and the competent community. *American Psychologist*, 1974, *29*, 607–613.

Jackson, J. J. The black elderly. Reassessing the plight of older black women. *The Black Scholar*, 1982, *13*, 2–4.

Jung, C. G. *Modern Man in Search of a Soul*. New York: Harcourt Brace Jovanovich, 1933.

Kahn, R. L. The mental health system and the future aged. *Gerontologist*, 1975, *15*, 24–31.

Kahn, R. L., Zarit, S. H., Hilbert, N. M., & Niederehe, G. Memory complaint and impairment in the aged. *Archives of General Psychiatry*, 1975, *32*, 1569–1573.

Karpf, R. J. The psychotherapy of depression. *Psychotherapy: Theory, Research and Practice*, 1977, *14*, 349–353.

Kastenbaum, R. Personality theory, therapeutic approaches, and the elderly client. In M. Storandt, I. Siegler, & M. Elias (eds.), *The Clinical Psychology of Aging*. New York: Plenum Press, 1978.

Kastenbaum, R. Beer, wine, and mutual gratification in the gerontopolis. In D. P. Kent, R. Kastenbaum, & S. Sherwood (eds.), *Research, Planning and Action for the Elderly*. New York: Behavioral Publications, 1972.

Kastenbaum, R. J., Barber, T. X., Wilson, S. C., Ryder, B. L., & Hathaway, L. B. *Old, Sick and Helpless*. Cambridge, MA: Ballinger Publishing Company, 1981.

Kastenbaum, R. S. & Candy, S. The 4% fallacy: A methodological and empirical critique of extended care facility program statistics. *Journal of Aging and Human Development*, 1973, *4*, 15–21.

Kay, D. W. K., Beamish, P., & Roth, M. Old age mental disorders in Newcastle-upon-Tyne, II. A study of possible social and medical causes. *British Journal of Psychiatry*, 1964, *110*, 668–682.

Kay, D. W. K. & Bergmann, K. Epidemiology of mental disorders among the aged in the community. In J. E. Birren & R. B. Sloane (eds.), *Handbook of Mental Health and Aging*. Englewood Cliffs, NJ: Prentice-Hall, 1980.

Kline, C. The socialization process of women. *Gerontologist*, 1975, *15*, 486–492.

Krauss, I. K. Between and within group comparisons in aging research. In L. W. Poon (ed.), *Aging in the 1980s*. Washington, D.C.: American Psychological Association, 1980.

Kuypers, J. A. & Bengtson, V. L. Social breakdown and competence. *Human Development*, 1973, *16*, 181–201.

Leighton, D. C., Harding, J. S., Macklin, D. B., MacMillian, A. M., & Leighton, A. H. *The Character of Danger: Psychiatric Symptoms in Selected Communities*. New York: Basic Books, 1963.

Lesnoff-Caravaglia, G. The five percent fallacy. *Journal of Aging and Human Development*, 1978, *9*, 187–192.

Leviton, D. & Santa Maria, L. The adults health & development program: Descriptive and evaluative data. *Gerontologist*, 1979, *19*, 534–543.

Levy, S. M. The adjustment of the older woman: Effects of chronic ill health and attitudes toward retirement. *International Journal of Aging and Human Development*, 1980–81, *12*, 93–110.

Levy, S. M. The aging woman: Developmental issues and mental health needs. *Professional Psychology*, 1981, *12*, 92–103.

Lewis, M. I. & Butler, R. N. Why is women's lib ignoring old women? *Aging and Human Development*, 1972, *3*, 223–231.

Lieberman, M. A. & Gourash, N. Evaluating the effects of change groups on the elderly. *International Journal of Group Psychotherapy*, 1979, *29*, 283–304.

Livson, F. B. Patterns of personality development in middle-aged women: A longitudinal study. *International Journal of Aging and Human Development*, 1976, *7*, 107–115.

Lopata, H. Z. *Widowhood in an American City*. Cambridge, MA: Scherkman Publishing, 1973.

Lopata, H. Z. *Women as Widows: Support Systems*. New York: Elsevier, 1979.

Lowenthal, M. F. & Haven, C. Interaction and adaptation: Intimacy as a critical variable. *American Sociological Review*, 1968, *33*, 20–30.

Lowenthal, M. F. & Robinson, B. Social networks and isolation. In R. H. Binstock & E. Shanas (eds.), *Handbook of Aging and the Social Sciences*. New York: D. Van Nostrand, 1976.

Lowenthal, M. F., Thurnher, M., Chiriboga, D., & Associates. *Four Stages of Life*. San Francisco, CA: Jossey-Bass, 1975.

Ludeman, K. The sexuality of the older person: Review of the literature. *Gerontologist*, 1981, *21*, 203–208.

Maas, H. S. & Kuypers, J. *From Thirty to Seventy*. San Francisco, CA: Jossey-Bass, 1974.

Masters, W. H. & Johnson, V. E. *Human Sexual Inadequacy*. Boston: Little, Brown, 1970.

McIntosh, J. L., Hubbard, R. W., & Santos, J. F. Suicide among the elderly: A review of issues with case studies. *Journal of Gerontological Social Work*, 1981, *4*, 63–74.

Miller, R. B. & Dodder, R. A. A revision of Palmore's facts on aging quiz. *Gerontologist*, 1980, *20*, 673–679.

National Institute of Mental Health. *Provisional Data on Federally Funded Community Mental Health Centers, 1976–77*. Rockville, MD: Author, 1978.

Neugarten, B. L. Dynamics of transition of middle age to old age: Adaptation and the life cycle. *Journal of Geriatric Psychiatry*, 1970, *4*, 71–87.

Neugarten, B. L. The future and the young-old. In L. F. Jarvik (ed.), *Aging into the 21st Century*. New York: Gardner Press, 1978.

Neugarten, B. L. & Datan, N. Sociological perspectives on the life cycle. In P. B. Baltes & K. W. Schaie (eds.), *Lifespan Developmental Psychology: Personality and Socialization*. New York: Academic Press, 1973.

Neugarten, B. L. & Datan, N. The middle years. In S. Arieti (ed.), *American Handbook of Psychiatry* (2nd ed.). New York: Basic Books, 1974.

Neugarten, B. L. & Gutmann, D. L. Age-sex roles and personality in middle age: A thematic apperception study. In B. Neugarten (ed.), *Middle Age and Aging*. Chicago: University of Chicago Press, 1968.

Neugarten, B. L. & Hagestad, G. Age and the life course. In R. H. Binstock & E. Shanas (eds.), *Handbook of Aging and the Social Sciences*. New York: D. Van Nostrand, 1976.

Neugarten, B. L., Havighurst, R. J., & Tobin, S. S. The measurement of life satisfaction. *Journal of Gerontology*, 1961, *16*, 134–143.

Neugarten, B. L., Wood, V., Kraines, R. J., & Loomis, B. Women's attitudes toward the menopause. In B. L. Neugarten (ed.), *Middle Age and Aging*. Chicago: University of Chicago Press, 1968.

Nowak, C. A. Does youthfulness equal attractiveness? In L. E. Troll, J. Israel, & K. Israel (eds.), *Looking Ahead: A Woman's Guide to the Problems and Joys of Growing Older*. Englewood Cliffs, NJ: Prentice-Hall, 1977.

Oberleder, M. Psychotherapy with the aging: An art of the possible? *Psychotherapy: Theory, Research and Practice*, 1966, *3*, 139–142.

Palmore, E. The facts of aging quiz: Part II. *Gerontologist*, 1981, *21*, 431–437.

Palmore, E. Facts on aging: A short quiz. *Gerontologist*, 1977, *17*, 315–320.

Payne, B. & Whittington, F. Older women: An examination of popular stereotypes and research evidence. *Social Problems*, 1976, *23*, 488–504.

Pfeiffer, E. Psychopathology and Social Pathology. In J. E. Birren & K. W. Schaie (eds.), *Handbook of the Psychology of Aging*. New York: Van Nostrand Reinhold, 1977.

Pfeiffer, E., Verwoerdt, A., & Wang, H. S. The natural history of sexual behavior in a biologically advantaged group of aged individuals. *Journal of Gerontology*, 1969, *24*, 193–198.

Powers, E. A. & Bultena, G. L. Sex differences in intimate friendships of old age. *Journal of Marriage and the Family*, 1976, *38*, 739–747.

Prentis, R. S. White-collar working women's perception of retirement. *Gerontologist*, 1980, *20*, 90–95.

Rappaport, J. *Community Psychology. Values, Research, and Action*. New York: Holt, Rinehart and Winston, 1977.

Reigel, K. F. The dialectics of human development. *American Psychologist*, 1976, *31*, 688–700.

Riegel, K. F. *Psychology Mon Amour*. Boston: Houghton Mifflin, 1978.

Rockstein, M. & Sussman, M. *Biology of Aging*. Belmont, CA: Wadsworth Publishing, 1979.

Rubin, L. B. *Women of a Certain Age. The Midlife Search for Self*. New York: Harper & Row, 1979.

Ryan, W. *Blaming the Victim* (rev. ed.). New York: Vintage Books, 1976.

Ryff, C. D. Successful aging: A developmental approach. *Gerontologist*, 1982, *22*, 209–214.

Schaie, K. W. Psychological changes from midlife to early old age: Implications for the maintenance of mental health. *American Journal of Orthopsychiatry*, 1981, *51*, 199–218.

Schaie, K. W. Intelligence and problem solving. In J. E. Birren & R. B. Sloane (eds.), *Handbook of Mental Health and Aging*. Englewood Cliffs, NJ: Prentice-Hall, 1980.

Schaie, K. W. & Labouvie-Vief, G. Generational versus orthogenetic components of change in adult cognitive behavior: A fourteen-year cross-sequential study. *Developmental Psychology*, 1974, *10*, 305–320.

Shanas, E. Social myth as hypothesis: The case of the family relations of old people. *Gerontologist*, 1979, *19*, 3–9.

Siegel, J. S. Recent and prospective demographic trends for the elderly population and some implications for health care. In S. G. Haynes & J. A. Ross (eds.), *Second Conference on the Epidemiology of Aging* (NIH Publications No. 80-969). Washington, D.C.: U.S. Government Printing Office, 1980.

Siegler, I. C., Nowlin, J. B., & Blumenthal, J. A. Health and behavior: Methodological considerations for adult development and aging. In L. W. Poon (ed.), *Aging in the 1980s*. Washington, D.C.: American Psychological Association, 1980.

Silverman, P. R. *If You Will Lift the Load I Will Lift It Too. A Guide to Developing Widow-To-Widow Programs*. New York: Jewish Funeral Directors of America, 1976.

Sinnott, J. D. Sex-role inconstancy, biology, and successful aging. A dialectical model. *Gerontologist*, 1977, *17*, 459–463.

Sinnott, J. D., Block, M. R., Grambs, J. D., Gaddy, C. D., & Davidson, J. L. *Sex roles in mature adults: Antecedents and correlates* (Tech. Rept. NIA-80-1). College Park, MD: University of Maryland Center on Aging, 1980.

Smyer, M. The differential usage of services by the impaired elderly. *Journal of Gerontology*, 1980, *35*, 249–255.

Soldo, B. J. America's elderly in the 1980s. *Population Bulletin* (Population Reference Bureau). Washington, D.C.: U.S. Government Printing Office, 1980.

Sontag, S. The double standard of aging. *The Saturday Review*, 1972, *55*, 29–38.

Stenback, A. Depression and suicidal behavior in old age. In J. E. Birren & R. B. Sloane (eds.), *Handbook of Mental Health and Aging*. Englewood Cliffs, NJ: Prentice-Hall, 1980.

Steuer, J. Psychotherapy for depressed elders. In D. G. Blazer (ed.), *Depression in Late Life*. St. Louis, MO: Mosby, 1982.

Storandt, M. Therapy with the aged. In M. Storandt, I. C. Siegler, & M. F. Elias (eds.), *The Clinical Psychology of Aging*. New York: Plenum Press, 1978.

Thomas, W. C. The expectation gap and the stereotype of the stereotype: Images of old people. *Gerontologist*, 1981, *21*, 402–407.

Tobin, S. & Lieberman, M. *Last Home for the Aged: Critical Implications of Institutionalization*. San Francisco, CA: Jossey-Bass, 1976.

Toseland, R. W., Decker, J., & Bliesner, J. A community outreach program for socially isolated older persons. *Journal of Gerontological Social Work*, 1979, *1*, 211-224.

Treas, J. The greatest American fertility debate: Generational balance and support of the aged. *Gerontologist*, 1981, *21*, 98-103. (a)

Treas, J. Women's employment and its implications for the economic status of the elderly of the future. In S. B. Keisler, J. N. Morgan, & V. K. Oppenheimer (eds.), *Aging: Social Change*. New York: Academic Press, 1981. (b)

Treas, J. & Van Hilst, A. Marriage and remarriage rates among Americans. *Gerontologist*, 1976, *16*, 132-136.

Troll, L. E. Poor, dumb, and ugly. In L. E. Troll, J. Israel, & K. Israel (eds.), *Looking Ahead: A Woman's Guide to the Problems and Joys of Growing Older*. Englewood Cliffs, NJ: Prentice-Hall, 1977.

U.S. Department of Commerce, Bureau of the Census. *Demographic aspects of aging and the older population in the United States* (Current Population Reports, Series P-20, No. 338). Washington, D.C.: U.S. Government Printing Office, 1978.

U.S. Department of Commerce, Bureau of the Census. *Money and income in 1977 of families and pensions in the United States* (Current Population Reports, Series P-60, No. 119). Washington, D.C.: U.S. Government Printing Office, 1979. (a)

U.S. Department of Commerce, Bureau of the Census. *Marital status and living arrangements* (Current Population Reports, Series P-20, No. 349). Washington, D.C.: U.S. Government Printing Office, 1979. (b)

U.S. Department of Commerce, Bureau of the Census. *Money, income, and poverty status of families and persons in the United States: 1980* (Current Population Reports, Series P-60, No. 127). Washington, D.C.: U.S. Government Printing Office, 1981.

Van Buren, A. *The Best of Dear Abby*. Kansas City, MO: Andrews and McMeel, 1981.

VandenBos, G. R., Stapp, J., & Kilburg, R. R. Health service providers in psychology. Results of the 1978 APA human resources survey. *American Psychologist*, 1981, *36*, 1395-1418.

Verbrugge, L. M. Sex differentials in morbidity and mortality in the United States. *Social Biology*, 1976, *23*, 275-296.

Verwoerdt, A., Pfeiffer, E., & Wang, H. S. Sexual behavior in senescence. Changes in sexual activity and interest of aging men and women. *Journal of Geriatric Psychiatry*, 1969, *2*, 163-180. (a)

Verwoerdt, A., Pfeiffer, E., & Wang, H. S. Sexual behavior in senescence II. Patterns of sexual activity and interest. *Geriatrics*, 1969, *24*, 137-154. (b)

Vincente, K., Wiley, J. A., & Carrington, R. A. The risk of institutionalization before death. *Gerontologist*, 1979, *19*, 361-367.

Watzlawick, P., Weakland, J., & Fisch, R. *Change*. New York: W. W. Norton & Co., 1974.

Weg, R. More than wrinkles. In L. E. Troll, J. Israel, & K. Israel (eds.), *Looking Ahead: A Woman's Guide to the Problems and Joys of Growing Older*. Englewood Cliffs, NJ: Prentice-Hall, 1977.

The White House Mini-Conference on Older Women: Growing Numbers, Growing Force. Oakland, CA: Women's League Educational Fund, 1981.

Wright, H., Bennett, R., Simon, R., & Weinberg, G. Evaluation study of the exploratory visit: An innovative outreach activity of the ILGWU's friendly visiting program. *International Journal of Aging and Human Development*, 1977-78, *8*, 67-82.

Zarit, S. H. *Aging and Mental Disorders. Psychological Approaches to Assessment and Treatment*. New York: The Free Press, 1980.

16

New Directions for Women

Moving Beyond the 1980s

Annette U. Rickel and Linda K. Forsberg
Wayne State University

Meg Gerrard
University of Kansas

Ira Iscoe
University of Texas at Austin

The decade of the 1980s marks the establishment of a "Second Current" of feminism in this country, which began in the 1970s. From this historical vantage point, the relationship of women to society can be reassessed by viewing past progress and future new directions.

The first ripple in the current of feminism, the notion that women ought to be allowed freedom to choose and define themselves without being coerced into a particular role, had its beginnings some 150 years ago. This First Current established women's right to vote, to own property, to speak in public, to sue in court, to go to school, to sign a will, to keep their own salaries instead of turning them over to husbands or fathers, to have custody of their own children, to leave a husband's home without danger of being forcibly returned, and to escape husbands who could legally beat them. In essence, this First Current in the feminist movement succeeded in changing women's status from that of property to that of independent person with a legal and social identity.

The Second Current has had a different goal. As eyes have focused on women independent from men, the problems and inequalities of opportunities have become visible. This Second Current sought legal and social equality for women. Some of the means and ends to this equality have been the now failed Equal Rights Amendment, equal access to work outside the home with pay and advancement comparable to men, equal access to schools, job training, media, political office, unions, religious institutions, and the military. Table 1 represents a summary of the laws that have been enacted which affect women (Cary & Peratis, 1979).

Within 10 years, this Second Current has made dramatic changes in the country's idea of justice. Many of the victories are symbolic and await tangible implementation. Change brought about by such a swiftly moving current will require constant, continual reinforcement until the ground underneath is truly altered.

What are some of the areas where changes have been initiated?

Today, there is approximately 70 percent nation-wide agreement on the actuality

Table 1 A synopsis of legal rights that effect the legal status of women

Legal right	Impact
Married Women's Property Act, 1860	New York Statute permitting married women to own separate property.
Fourteenth Amendment to the Constitution of the U.S. "equal-protection clause," 1868	No state shall deny equal protection of the laws to any person.
Nineteenth Amendment to the Constitution of the U.S., 1920	Grants the right of women to vote
Civil Rights Act anti-discrimination legislation of 1964	Prohibits discrimination in areas such as employment, federally funded programs, in public accommodations, as well as on the basis of sex, race, religion and national origin.
Title IX of the education amendments of 1972	Outlaws all forms of sex discrimination in schools which receive federal financial assistance, e.g., single sex or sex quota schools, athletic programs, vocational training, and life style regulations.
Criminal Law: 1. Prostitution	Defined somewhat differently in each state; New York's sex neutral statute provides that a "person is guilty of prostitution when they engage, agree or offer to engage in sexual conduct for a fee."
2. Rape	Definition varies from state to state; one current definition is "sexual intercourse with a woman not the wife of the perpetrator, forcibly and against her will or in circumstances under which she was incapable of giving her consent."
Family Law: 1. Marriage	Two major terms that a state's "marriage contract" impose are the husband's obligation to support his wife and likewise the wife's obligation to perform services for her husband.
2. Divorce	Many states have "no-fault" divorce laws where the "fault" of either party is irrelevant to the issue of whether a divorce should be granted. Other state laws provide for payment of alimony in order to protect wives from abandonment.
Reproductive Freedom: 1. Contraception—1965	Married as well as unmarried persons were given access to contraceptives
2. Abortion—1971	Upholds the right of a pregnant woman during the first trimester to have an abortion.
3. Sterilization—1973	Women who wish to be sterilized cannot be refused the operation by a public hospital; and further women cannot be coerced into sterilization against their will or without knowledge of its irreversibility.

and injustice of sex discrimination. Ten years ago, most individuals thought there was no discrimination.

Today rape is considered a violent crime punishable by law. Ten years ago, rape was thought of as a sexual act that was often considered the fault of women who "asked for it."

Now, homosexuality is viewed as an alternative lifestyle and lesbian mothers are gaining custody of their children. Four years ago, it was a psychiatric label which warranted treatment like mental illnesses.

In 1975, California passed the Displaced Homemakers Equal Opportunity Act declaring that these women are a part of the work force, though currently unemployed. Before that, these women were seen only in relationship to the men in their earlier life—"widow," "ex-wife," "divorcee."

In 1981, the first woman in history to become a Justice of the U.S. Supreme Court took her place beside the brethren. Just a short time ago, the only woman in the hallowed legal chambers was the blindfolded marble statue of justice.

Now, women control their own bodies and reproductive systems according to their own beliefs. Ten years ago, abortion was a criminal act punishable by law.

The successes of the 1970s, while substantial, are certainly couched amidst failures and untouched problem areas. It is understandable that the magnitude of the problems and the complexity of the issues surrounding women's place in society warrant constant appraisal and reappraisal of solutions. It is to some of these problem areas that this volume is dedicated. The editors choose to present a sampling of areas which still need attention: unresolved issues which have typically not engendered serious empirical research and topics related to social policy/social programming.

The quest for legal and social equality, the Second Current of feminism, is in process now. Some of the effects of this Current can be seen; some of the ramifications are yet to be felt and understood.

FROM PSYCHOTHERAPY TO PREVENTION

Most of the basic concerns raised in the First Current of feminism now have majority support in national public-opinion polls. The changes in attitudes and laws over the past decade have been substantial. And yet, the papers and data-based programs presented in this volume force even the most skeptical reader to recognize that although some progress has been made, women have a long way to travel along the road of equality. There are indeed many problems and issues unique to women which remain unresolved.

Rather than conclude this volume with a rhetorical call to action or an all-inclusive prescription for society's ills, we have chosen to focus on one specific area of problems—the mental health system as it pertains to women. In doing so, we believe we are also identifying that system which holds out the most promise for building and strengthening women's competencies.

As has already been documented in this volume, the roles traditionally set for women have changed. According to the U.S. Department of Labor (1979), in 1965 only 39 percent of women were in the work force. In 1982, 52 percent were; and in 1995, it is expected that 65 percent of all women will be in the work force. This changing work pattern is not just a temporary trend, but is here to stay. Women are no longer working before their children are born or after they graduate from high school, nor are women working just long enough to buy a new car; women today are working throughout their life cycle. Often this working woman is a single parent. Where previously a women's identity had come through marriage and family, now due to the death of her spouse, separation or divorce, she has been cast into the role of head of household, a totally new experience. It can be expected that women thrust into these new roles are experiencing stressful life events and find themselves questioning their identity.

Stressful life events, such as divorce, violence inside and outside the home, and the crisis of childbirth, may be felt more intensely by women or are unique to women. And, women faced with such disruptive events, with new roles, and with more responsibilities often have problems coping with the stress. Because they tend to blame themselves, and do not fit into either the traditional wife-at-home model or into the media-hyped "superwoman," these women often question their psychological stability and self-refer to a mental health facility. The medical community further reinforces this labelling of pathology without examining the broader context of a woman's environmental stressors as possible etiologies of difficulties and, thus, the real place for intervention (Carmen & Driver, 1982). In either case, the woman inappropriately enters the psychiatric system.

In reassessing the mental health establishment and its effective delivery of services, we would suggest the need for a revision of thinking. Historically, mental health professionals have conceptualized service primarily in terms of direct, one-on-one delivery. Moving beyond the past and present, we must consider the greater possibilities of indirect services.

INDIRECT TREATMENT APPROACHES

In the case of women experiencing particular stressful life events, rather than seeking out individual mental health services, such women might be better served by involvement in a support group. Those who enter the mental health establishment may do so to their detriment. First, the economic burden is great; and, second, the social stigma attached to receiving mental health services may add to a woman's already deteriorating self-concept (Department of Mental Health, 1982). In fact, these two costs may keep women away from the mental health system. Eventually, suffering from no support-system, continued stress, and an internal self-labelling of "sick," the prophecy is self-fulfilled. At the point of mental and/or physical breakdown, these women do enter the mental health establishment. A shift in focus from mental health *direct* services to *indirect* services such as self-help/support groups, not only serves more people, but also decreases the economic and social costs which would accrue when serving women individually. Self-help/support groups should be fostered as an alternative. Their economic costs are minimal in comparison to direct service, and the social stigma associated with becoming a patient or client in the mental health system is virtually nonexistent for the participant in a support group.

Self-help/support groups are at least as successful as traditional psychotherapeutic services (Borman, 1982). By way of group involvement, women share personal problems, develop social support structures, and learn to ameliorate some of their stresses. The experience is both educational and supportive. Some such groups that have been thus far successful are widow-to-widow groups, divorce adjustment programs, parents without partners groups, women in transition programs, and groups for mothers of handicapped or chronically ill children.

Another important aspect of this indirect treatment approach is that service is taken into the community in nonthreatening locations: churches and synagogues, industrial settings, community organizations such as the YWCA, senior citizens' groups, service and professional clubs, and educational settings including PTA and student bodies, all non-stigmatized locations for implementation. Certainly a well-functioning referral system between these community programs and the mental health establishment is essential in this model. The mental health professional's role in this environment is altered as well. Instead of being the on-line deliverer of service, the trained professional becomes consultant, educator, and trainer. This outreach approach will, of course, service a great many more people, and by being educational, function as a preventive measure. Obviously, the potential rewards of such an organized system are worth serious consideration.

Because women are no longer dropping in and out of the work force, but are staying in it, careers have become an integral part of a woman's life (experience) throughout a lifetime and therefore require more forethought and planning. Women need help in viewing their lives more continuously as an unfolding process over which they have much control, rather than as a checkerboard on which they are forced to jump from one life event to another, often under stress. The mental health system, in cooperation with community agencies, schools, and corporations, within this paradigm of indirect service delivery, can assume responsibility for life-planning and career-planning programs. Part of this training might include assertiveness training, since, for the most part, women have been socialized to be passive, dependent citizens. Also high-risk groups, such as low-income minority groups and teenagers, might be targeted.

DIRECT SERVICE TREATMENT

While it is true that many women should not be in the mental health system but rather in support groups, there are still those who do require individual psychotherapy. A second tier to the mental health delivery system is *direct service*. On this level, a woman is receiving one-to-one or group care either as an inpatient or an outpatient.

Within the context of direct service treatment, several recommendations for change can be made. It is now established through research that sex differences exist in the diagnosis and treatment of mental illness (e.g., Kaplan, 1983; Kass et al., 1983). Incidence data reveal that more females than males are given the diagnosis of depression, phobia, anxiety, and hysteria. On the other hand, more males than females are given the diagnosis of psychophysiological disorders (ulcers, heart, and respiratory disorders). These differential sex patterns of diagnoses are extensions or intensifications of stereotypic sex role behavior. For example, depression, the most common psychiatric complaint for women, is characterized by passivity, hopelessness, and lack of self-esteem (Weissman & Klerman, 1979). Women in our society have traditionally been socialized into a dependent role. An accentuation of this role is viewed as illness. However, the "right" amount of the depressive symptomatology is also viewed as mental health for women.

Diagnoses based on stereotypic sex roles are unfair to everyone and offer little therapeutic value. Women who show anger may be diagnosed "sick," while the very same behavior is considered healthy when it is expressed by a male. In a field which deals with effecting change, isn't it time to change some of the long-standing ideas regarding sex roles? By encouraging women to remain in a dependent role, founded on a premise of helplessness, mental health professionals are discouraging personal growth, change, and competency, and encouraging "learned helplessness," which often results in depression.

In a therapy relationship some dependency can have a positive influence, but therapists should be cognizant of the possibility of a negative impact on a woman striving to become self-sufficient, especially when the therapist is a male. It must be added that not all women in therapy are desirous of leaving behind a stereotypic sex role, nor are they in therapy to be able to leave their husbands. Encouraging independence for these women may not be appropriate. At the same time, automatically assuming a woman will continue in a traditional feminine role and will return to a current marital situation is *not* an assumption that any therapist ought to make.

Misdiagnoses are academically reprehensible, but when they contribute to mistreatment, they are inexcusable. Realistically, though, treatment and diagnosis go hand in hand. In the case of women, very often the treatment for a woman's "craziness," i.e., anger and aggression, is medication, even over-medication. Disturbing statistics regarding the issue of over-medication, utilizing psychotropic drugs, have recently come to light. These drugs include major tranquilizers, minor tranquilizers, sedatives, stimulants, and antidepressants. Studies in North America and in Europe indicate that the ratio of females to males in the use of prescribed psychotropic drugs is approximately two to one (Cooperstock, 1976; Ferrence & Whitehead, 1980). Fidell (1977) further reports that although women make up 58 percent of all doctor visits, they receive 78 percent of all prescriptions for psychotropic drugs.

The unfortunate actuality is that if a woman is medicated into compliance, society and the mental health system in particular do not have to deal with the more complex, difficult problems of women's inequality. But the cost for women and ultimately for society is great: medication dulls one's abilities to learn and use coping strategies effectively. This approach does not develop competencies in women; rather, it maintains helplessness.

Other options for treatment must be investigated. Nonsexist therapy is one such option which emphasizes the role of sociological and cultural influences in the development of psychopathology. Emphasis is not only on individual change but on restructuring society (APA Task Force, 1978). According to Marecek and Kravetz (1977), there are at least five characteristics of the nonsexist therapist. First, a knowledge of the psychology of women, of sex roles, of sex differences in the socialization of women and men. Second, the therapist should acknowledge the prevalence of sexism in our society and be aware of his/her own biases. Third, nonsexist therapists believe in the entwining of women's problems and their social, economic, and political environment. Fourth, the therapist recognizes the relationship between a female's lack of power and such behaviors as passivity, dependency, and apathy. A nonsexist therapist uses therapeutic techniques such as assertiveness training to teach women to be more active and independent. Finally, a nonsexist therapist views each client individually, not as a woman or a man. The needs and personal goals of the client, not of a traditional sex-role mandate, are the basis for the therapeutic relationship.

Since women use psychotherapy more than men, they are the persons in a family most likely to approach mental health agencies. Yet, treating the woman is not always the most successful solution, because she is only one part of the family system. Therapists need to involve spouses and other family members in therapy. Treating the family as a unit helps to remove much of the traditional blame placed on mothers for their children's emotional difficulties. As in so many other situations, very often the people present are those with the least problems, while the absent parties, denying their culpability, are in fact the significant contributors to a problematic situation. Research on successful outcomes of therapeutic interventions for children suggests that the more the father is involved in treatment, the greater likelihood of success for the child (Al-Issa, 1980).

Because women who require mental health services are often those women with the fewest resources, mental health agencies should be more responsive to some of their immediate needs. For example, these women may not have automobiles and thus are immobilized without transportation services. Also, the burden of child care is generally their responsibility. Creative resolutions of these dilemmas are necessary; some that have already been implemented are foster grandparents for child care and car-pooling among clients. Others need to be considered. Flexibility in hours for treatment will also alleviate some stresses of the overloaded woman.

Another option to traditional psychotherapy is that of group therapy, an important treatment modality. Women in group therapy profit from perceiving their problems in relation to other women's vulnerabilities as well as gaining peer support and appropriate role models (Voss & Gannon, 1978). Groups also tend to be more educational in nature and, thus, carry less of a mental illness stigma. Although group therapy is an individual corrective experience, it is through interpersonal relationships that the change process occurs.

It is time for stereotypic notions about females and their roles to be eliminated from mental health diagnostic procedures and intervention. The decade of the 1980s is witnessing a revolution in attitudes about sex roles. No longer is the rigid dichotomy the majority view. As we move further along this decade and beyond, we foresee the emergence of an androgynous person—a male or female able to respond to circumstances requiring traditionally labelled, feminine-type behavior (warmth and nurturant) and masculine-type behavior (assertive and independent), without being labelled "crazy." The elimination of sex bias and sex-role stereotyping is crucial for the promotion of true mental health. The future promises a new option—a changed lifestyle that surpasses both "femininity" and "masculinity" by encompassing both (Bem, 1976; Spence et al., 1975).

Research evaluating alternatives to traditional treatment is essential. Pilot demonstration projects and innovative models for service delivery must be explored. These might include: day treatment programs for women where a woman can obtain rehabilitation without the label of being institutionalized; measures to address rural women's mental health needs; and interventions for special groups such as black and Hispanic urban women. Another area virtually untouched by state and federal penal systems is how to meet the psychological requirements of women in the Criminal Justice System.

Research investigation into the allegations made about the *direct* delivery of mental health service is warranted. Examples may include (1) discriminatory and improper reasons cited for females' hospital admissions (e.g. no makeup, sexual promiscuity); (2) variations in length of treatment and modes of treatment; (3) male/female discrepancies in prescribed medication; (4) programmatic assessment of women's services to mitigate the effect of myths and stereotypes; and (5) evaluation of discharge practices (Department of Mental Health, 1982).

In this chapter's discussion of direct and indirect delivery of mental health services to women, suggestions have been made regarding why women use mental health services more than men. Women have learned to seek help in order to complete a task, whereas men were generally expected to figure out on their own how to solve a problem (Sherif, 1982). It is not surprising that more women than men seek help from the mental health system and are more compliant with treatment procedures given the traditional feminine role requirements. Another reason that women have a higher incidence of psychological intervention is the changing role requirements and role overload that women today face. External stresses, then, contribute to a growing need for support. Of the increasing number of single-parent households headed by women, one half live in poverty (Russo & VanderBos, 1980), and the highest rate of depression of any socioeconomic group is among low-income mothers with preschool children (Belle, 1980).

WOMEN IN THE WORK FORCE

In attempting to assess the etiology of women's mental health problems, one is struck with external stressors as one set of predictors for high risk. This volume has included chapters which deal with some of these very problems (divorce, crime, stressful life events). One important area of stress is economic/work-related. The growing number of women in the work force has now reached a majority proportion and the trend is not likely to reverse. Though the rising numbers of working women may be just starting to cause significant changes, it has already and will continue to have considerable influence on all aspects of our society, including business, politics, and the family.

Often semiskilled or unskilled women enter a job market already flooded with highly skilled applicants. Many lack transportation and adequate child care. Simultaneously, they are confronted with the reality that the expense of child care itself will exhaust a sizable portion of their already low income. Women, whether single or married, employed or unemployed, still shoulder the major responsibility for their children's care (Nakamura et al., 1981). Women need relief to participate actively in their jobs and the assurance that their children are being well cared for in their absence. The combination of economic, work, and child care responsibilities represents a stress matrix for many women. As a result of this situation women are likely to manifest a high proportion of stress-related disorders. To prevent these disorders, women need opportunities in their work environment which will enable them to meet all of their responsibilities without endangering their economic security and in turn their mental health.

According to the Wall Street Journal (June 29, 1982), by 1990 55 percent of all married women with children under six will hold jobs outside the home, up from 48 percent in 1981. The shortage of day-care facilities must be addressed. The Children's Defense Fund, a nonprofit child-welfare group, says only a little more than six million day-care slots exist in centers and family-based child-care operations for the 13 million children, 13 years and under, with full-time working mothers. One source of assistance is the employer. It is estimated that about 500 employers nationwide (perhaps double the number of two years ago) provide assistance such as day-care subsidies and referrals (Shellenbarger, 1982).

For other parents, community agencies are teaming with schools and using a variety of financing sources to provide day care at low cost, often at fees based on ability to pay. Some communities are experimenting with other options, such as a program offering a hot-line linking the homes of children of working parents with child-care professionals.

A growing minority of employers offer options in scheduling. Job sharing, where two individuals each work half-time equaling one full-time job, and flex-time, where employees work earlier or later hours, leaving them more quality time at home, are two scheduling innovations. The attitude of the employer toward family responsibilities can also alleviate stress. The availability of paternity leaves, along with maternity leaves, is another option which allows parents to fulfill their family responsibilities without jeopardizing their job security. All of these suggestions are aimed at the marketplace, be it government or private industry. Traditional policies of industry which were drawn up by men for men are no longer adequate as the profile of the work force has altered. Hopefully the profile of the policymakers will change as well. Perhaps only when a majority of women are sitting on the boards of corporations and initiating new policies will real change occur (Wirtenberg et al., 1981).

EDUCATION AND TRAINING OF PROFESSIONALS

In this chapter, we have recommended changes within the mental health system which might better respond to women's needs today and in the future. We have suggested new directions for indirect delivery of services, direct delivery of services, and have examined some goals for primary prevention, viz., stress-related economic, work, and child-care issues. An additional area for primary prevention of some of the mental health problems and biases toward women which this book has documented lies in the area of education and training of mental health professionals. Initial educational experiences within a university as a student is first receiving training, and later continuing education of established professionals, are both areas for investigation.

Training of mental health professionals within a university setting represents an arena of great potential for purposes of primary prevention. As a first step, sex biases must be viewed at the level of systems and institutions as well as individuals. Obviously, the underlying goal of changing basic attitudes toward women should be persuasive throughout society and seems crucial for training purposes. University programs should offer their students adequate training in competencies other than traditional therapy, e.g., family therapy, group therapy, stress-management programs, and assertiveness training. Curricula need to reflect women's life experiences, e.g. psychology of women. Since our culture to date is male oriented, most curricula and research show this bias; this must be changed (Carmen & Driver, 1982).

Female mental health professionals, trained by women, are more likely to be responsive to women. Female faculty and clinical supervisors need to be hired. By the same token, graduate schools should encourage increased numbers of women students. As a component of training, therapists need to be cognizant of their role in female dependency and dependency reinforcement. Development of individuals' treatment modalities should receive careful supervision with an emphasis on that person's needs and strengths, rather than a reliance on sex-role stereotypes.

Once mental health professionals are trained, the necessity for continual in-service education is great and changes here can again supplement primary preventive measures. Curriculum and training materials should be developed which assist community mental health caregivers in shifting from traditional one-on-one outpatient therapy interventions to a role of development, utilization, consultation, and training for support groups for women, placed within the community (Albee, 1982). To appropriately serve females, therapists must gain knowledge of the individual client's social/family/economic circumstances and their ensuing stresses, which when accompanied by sex role bias and discrimination, may be legitimate reasons for women's anger. Inservice training should further the therapist's understanding of women's role overload, normal problems of daily living, medication with women, misdiagnosis, and nonsexist therapy. Finally, following the recommendations of the American Psychological Association's Task Force on Sex Bias and Sex-role Stereotyping in Psychotherapeutic Practice (1978), training must deal with the controversial issue of sexual relations between client and therapist. It must be stressed that sexual relations with a client are exploitive and not beneficial to the therapeutic relationship.

PROMOTING SOCIAL CHANGE

How do the changes we have been recommending, changes of such an important magnitude, occur? According to Bardwick (1979), "the visibility of change increases its pace." Visibility brings awareness and a recognition of shared feelings. As Bardwick (1979) continues, "When shared awareness is coupled with organization and there really is widespread discontent, the potential for significant and real social change is great" (p. 2). This volume has been an effort to make visible some of the problems and injustices that define many women's lives today; this volume is an attempt to increase such visibility.

Some of the kinds of social policy changes which might grow out of this awareness are suggested. Alternatives should be considered to provide funding for women's self-help/support services, because standard health insurance does not reimburse these services. Perhaps third-party payers could be encouraged in this regard. Reference material covering such topics as alcohol and drug abuse, pregnancy, marriage, aging, etc., should be published by state and local mental health agencies. This educational material could then be distributed within the community to support groups. Libraries, churches, YWCA, and schools are non-sick settings where this resource material should be available. The media could become involved in the promotion of self-help groups. Short radio and TV spots reach thousands of at-home women and destigmatize mental health resources. The community college system and adult education programs in recognition of their adult students' emotional needs, might provide opportunities for consciousness raising groups.

State and local departments of mental health can help educate the public to the importance of therapists' attitudes in treatment of female clients. The names of non-sexist therapists in the public and private sectors should be made available.

Government and private industry should be encouraged to provide women more flexibility in work arranging, either through job sharing, flexible work hours, or some other arrangement. Child care is also an issue that can be responded to by industry and governmental agencies. The problem is large enough that all aspects of society share the responsibility for developing new options for women.

Men's closer involvement in child care and child growth and development holds great rewards for all—fathers, mothers, and children. Public policy which is supportive of equal rights for fathers should be encouraged. Fathers ought to be included in all aspects of child-rearing, in childbirth preparation classes, in delivery and birth experiences, in child care from birth through later developmental stages. Increased advocacy for a policy of "paternity leave" could be urged. When children are experiencing psychological problems, fathers should be strongly encouraged to participate in all aspects of treatment.

As we have documented earlier, the high incidence of prescribed drug use by women makes policy toward pharmaceutical companies worthy of our attention. Existing sex biases in medical advertisements can contribute to incorrect attitudes about women and their illnesses; sexist advertisements serve to reinforce sexist ideas. Therefore, pharmaceutical houses should be encouraged to eliminate offensive, biased advertisements.

Research can be a powerful tool to assist policy change. By revealing facts about problem areas, some of the shibboleths about women can be laid to rest. More research is needed on both normal and pathological development in females, since at present much of the treatment of women is based on theory and research with men only. As working women have now become a majority and, in this regard, have work patterns more similar to male patterns, research must be done on the psychological, social, and medical consequences to women.

The decade of the 1980s marks the establishment of a Second Current of feminism in this country. Women's equality is at least accepted by all, at least theoretically, to be the promise for our society. Many changes have occurred within this past decade to implement the theory of legal and social equality. Many changes await operational reality.

REFERENCES

Albee, G. W. Preventing psychopathology and promoting human potential. *American Psychologist*, 1982, *37*, 1043–1050.

Al-Issa, I. *The psychopathology of women*. Englewood Cliffs, NJ: Prentice-Hall, Inc., 1980.

A.P.A. Task Force on sex bias and sex-role stereotyping in psychotherapeutic practice. *American Psychologist*, 1978, *33*, 1122–1123.

Bardwick, J. *In transition: How feminism, sexual liberation and the search for self-fulfillment have altered America*. New York: Holt, Rinehart and Winston, 1979.

Bem, S. Beyond androgyny: Some presumptuous prescriptions for a liberated sexual identity. In J. Sherman & F. Denmark (eds.), *The future of women: Issues in psychology*. New York: Psychological Dimensions, 1976.

Belle, D. Mothers and their children: A study of low income families. In C. L. Heckerman (ed.), *The evolving female: Women in psychosocial context*. New York: Human Sciences Press, 1980.

Borman, L. Introduction to the special issue . . . Helping people to help themselves. *Prevention in the human services*, 1982, *1*, 3–15.

Brodsky, A. M. & Hare-Mustin, R. (eds.). *Women and psychotherapy*. New York: Guilford Press, 1980.

Carmen, E. H. & Driver, F. Teaching women's studies: Values in conflict. *Psychology of Women Quarterly*, 1982, *7*, 81–95.

Cary, E. & Peratis, K. W. *Women and the law*. Skokie, IL: National Textbook Company, 1979.

Cooperstock, R. Sex differences in psychotropic drug use. Paper prepared for Symposium on Sex, Culture and Illness. March 25–27, 1976, Montreal, Quebec.

Department of Mental Health: State of Michigan. *For better or for worse? Women and the mental health system*. Women's Task Force Report, 1982.

Ferrence, R. G. & Whitehead, P. C. Sex differences in psychoactive drug use: Recent epidemiology. In O. J. Kalant (ed.), *Alcohol and drug problems in women*. New York: Plenum, 1980.

Fidell, L. S. Psychotropic drug use by women: Health, attitudinal personality and demographic correlates. Paper presented at the American Psychological Association meetings, August 28, 1977, San Francisco, California.

Kaplan, M. A woman's view of DSM-III. *American Psychologist*, 1983, *38*, 786–792.

Kass, F., Spitzer, R. L., & Williams, J. B. W. An empirical study of the issue of sex bias in the diagnostic criteria of DSM-III Axis II personality disorders. *American Psychologist*, 1983, *38*, 799–801.

Marecek, J. & Kravetz, D. Women and mental health: A review of feminist change efforts. *Psychiatry*, 1977, *40*, 323–329.

Nakamura, C. Y., McCarthy, S. J., Rothstein-Fisch, C., & Winges, L. D. Interdependence of child care resources and the progress of women in society. *Psychology of Women Quarterly*, 1981, *6*, 26–40.

Russo, N. F. & VanderBos, G. R. Women in the mental health delivery system. In W. H. Silverman (ed.), *A community mental health sourcebook for board and professional action.* New York: Praeger, 1980.

Shellenbarger, S. Societal shift: As more women take jobs they affect ads, politics, family life. *Wall Street Journal*, June 29, 1982, Vol. LXII, No. 180, p. 1; 18.

Sherif, C. W. Needed concepts in the study of gender identity. *Psychology of Women Quarterly*, 1982, *6*, 375–398.

Spence, J. T., Helmreich, R., & Strapp, J. Ratings of self and peers on sex role attributes and their relation to self-esteem and conceptions of masculinity and femininity. *Journal of Personality and Social Psychology*, 1975, *32*, 29–39.

U.S. Department of Labor. 1979 Employment and training report of the President. Washington, D.C.: U.S. Department of Labor, 1979.

Voss, J. & Gannon, L. Sexism in the theory and practice of clinical psychology. *Professional Psychology*, 1978, *9*, 623–632.

Weissman, M. M. & Klerman, G. L. Sex differences and the epidemiology of depression. In E. S. Gomberg & V. Franks (eds.), *Gender and disordered behavior.* New York: Brunner/Mazel, 1979.

Wirtenberg, J., Strasburg, G., & Alsektor, R. A. Educational trends for expanding women's occupational lives. *Psychology of Women Quarterly*, 1981, *6*, 137–159.

Index